MW01118357

# YOUR PERSONAL
# HOROSCOPE
# 2012

JOSEPH
POLANSKY

# YOUR PERSONAL HOROSCOPE 2012

## Month-by-month forecast for every sign

The only one-volume horoscope you'll ever need

The author is grateful to the people
of STAR ★ DATA, who truly fathered
this book and without whom it
could not have been written.

HarperElement
An Imprint of HarperCollins*Publishers*
77–85 Fulham Palace Road,
Hammersmith, London W6 8JB

www.harpercollins.co.uk

and *HarperElement* are trademarks of
HarperCollins*Publishers* Ltd

Published by HarperElement 2011

1 3 5 7 9 10 8 6 4 2

© Star ★ Data, Inc. 2011

Star ★ Data assert the moral right to
be identified as the authors of this work

A catalogue record for this book is
available from the British Library

ISBN 978-0-00-738973-5

Printed and bound in Great Britain by
Clays Ltd, St Ives plc

**Mixed Sources**
Product group from well-managed
forests and other controlled sources
www.fsc.org  Cert no. SW-COC-001806
© 1996 Forest Stewardship Council

FSC is a non-profit international organisation established to promote the
responsible management of the world's forests. Products carrying the FSC
label are independently certified to assure consumers that they come
from forests that are managed to meet the social, economic and
ecological needs of present or future generations.

Find out more about HarperCollins and the environment at
**www.harpercollins.co.uk/green**

# Contents

# Introduction

Welcome to the fascinating and intricate world of astrology!

For thousands of years the movements of the planets and other heavenly bodies have intrigued the best minds of every generation. Life holds no greater challenge or joy than this: knowledge of ourselves and the universe we live in. Astrology is one of the keys to this knowledge.

*Your Personal Horoscope 2012* gives you the fruits of astrological wisdom. In addition to general guidance on your character and the basic trends of your life, it shows you how to take advantage of planetary influences so you can make the most of the year ahead.

The section on each sign includes a Personality Profile, a look at general trends for 2012, and in-depth month-by-month forecasts. The Glossary (*page 5*) explains some of the astrological terms you may be unfamiliar with.

One of the many helpful features of this book is the 'Best' and 'Most Stressful' days listed at the beginning of each monthly forecast. Read these sections to learn which days in each month will be good overall, good for money, and good for love. Mark them on your calendar – these will be your best days. Similarly, make a note of the days that will be most stressful for you. It is best to avoid booking important meetings or taking major decisions on these days, as well as on those days when important planets in your horoscope are retrograde (moving backwards through the zodiac).

The Major Trends section for your sign lists those days when your vitality is strong or weak, or when relationships with your co-workers or loved ones may need a bit more effort on your part. If you are going through a difficult time, take a look at the colour, metal, gem and scent listed in the 'At a Glance' section of your Personality Profile. Wearing a piece of jewellery that contains your metal and/or gem will strengthen your vitality, just as wearing clothes or decorating your room or office in the colour ruled by your sign, drinking teas made from the herbs ruled by your sign or wearing the scents associated with your sign will sustain you.

Another important virtue of this book is that it will help you to know not only yourself but those around you: your friends, co-workers, partners and/or children. Reading the Personality Profile and forecasts for their signs will provide you with an insight into their behaviour that you won't get anywhere else. You will know when to be more tolerant of them and when they are liable to be difficult or irritable.

In this edition we have included foot reflexology charts as part of the health section. So many health problems could perhaps be avoided or alleviated if we understood which organs were most vulnerable and what we could do to protect them. Though there are many natural and drug-free ways to strengthen vulnerable organs, these charts show a valid way to proceed. The vulnerable organs for the year ahead are clearly marked in the charts. It's very good to massage the whole foot on a regular basis, as the feet contain reflexes to the entire body. Try to pay special attention to the specific areas marked in the charts. If this is done diligently, health problems can be avoided. And even if they can't be completely avoided, their impact can be softened considerably.

I consider you – the reader – my personal client. By studying your Solar Horoscope I gain an awareness of what is going on in your life – what you are feeling and striving for and the challenges you face. I then do my best to address these concerns. Consider this book the next best thing to having your own personal astrologer!

It is my sincere hope that *Your Personal Horoscope 2012* will enhance the quality of your life, make things easier, illuminate the way forward, banish obscurities and make you more aware of your personal connection to the universe. Understood properly and used wisely, astrology is a great guide to knowing yourself, the people around you and the events in your life – but remember that what you do with these insights – the final result – is up to you.

# A Note on the 'New Zodiac'

Recently an article was published that postulated two things – the discovery of a new constellation, Ophiuchus, making a thirteenth constellation in the heavens and thus a thirteenth sign, and the statement that because the Earth has shifted relative to the constellations in the past few thousand years, all the signs have shifted backwards by one sign. This has caused much consternation, and I have been receiving a constant stream of letters, emails and phone calls from people saying things like: 'I don't want to be a Taurus, I'm happy being a Gemini', 'What's my real sign?' or 'Now that I finally understand myself, I'm not who I think I am!'

All of this is 'much ado about nothing'. The article has some partial truth to it. Yes, in two thousand years the planets have shifted relative to the constellations in the heavens. This is old news. We know this and Hindu astrologers take this into account when casting charts. This shift doesn't affect Western astrologers in North America and Europe. We use what is called a 'tropical' zodiac. This zodiac has nothing to do with the constellations in the heavens. They have the same names, but that's about it. The tropical zodiac is based on the Earth's revolution around the Sun. Imagine the circle that this orbit makes, then divide this circle by twelve and you have our zodiac. The Spring Equinox is always 0 degrees (Aries), and the Autumn Equinox is always 0 degrees (Libra). At one time a few thousand years ago, these tropical signs coincided with the actual constellations – they were pretty much interchangeable, and it didn't matter what zodiac you used. But in the course of thousands of years the planets have shifted relative to these constellations. Here in the West it doesn't affect our practice one iota. You are still the sign you always were.

In North America and Europe there is a clear distinction between an astrological sign and a constellation in the heavens. This issue is more of a problem for Hindu astrologers.

Their zodiac is based on the actual constellations – this is called the 'sidereal' zodiac. And Hindu astrologers have been accounting for this shift all the time. They keep close tabs on it. In two thousand years there is a shift of 23 degrees, and they subtract this from the Western calculations. So in their system many a Gemini would be a Taurus and this is true for all the signs. This is nothing new – it is all known and accounted for, so there is no bombshell here.

The so-called thirteenth constellation, Ophiuchus, is also not a problem for the Western astrologer. As we mentioned, our zodiac has nothing to do with the constellations. It would be more of a problem for the Hindus. But my feeling is that it's not a problem for them either. What these astronomers are calling a new constellation was probably considered a part of one of the existing constellations. I don't know this as a fact, but I presume it is so intuitively. I'm sure we will be getting articles by Hindu astrologers explaining this.

# Glossary of Astrological Terms

## Ascendant

We experience day and night because the Earth rotates on its axis once every 24 hours. It is because of this rotation that the Sun, Moon and planets seem to rise and set. The zodiac is a fixed belt (imaginary, but very real in spiritual terms) around the Earth. As the Earth rotates, the different signs of the zodiac seem to the observer to rise on the horizon. During a 24-hour period every sign of the zodiac will pass this horizon point at some time or another. The sign that is at the horizon point at any given time is called the Ascendant, or rising sign. The Ascendant is the sign denoting a person's self-image, body and self-concept – the personal ego, as opposed to the spiritual ego indicated by a person's Sun sign.

## Aspects

Aspects are the angular relationships between planets, the way in which one planet stimulates or influences another. If a planet makes a harmonious aspect (connection) to another, it tends to stimulate that planet in a positive and helpful way. If it makes a stressful aspect to another planet, this disrupts the planet's normal influence.

# Astrological Qualities

There are three astrological qualities: *cardinal*, *fixed* and *mutable*. Each of the 12 signs of the zodiac falls into one of these three categories.

Cardinal Signs        Aries, Cancer, Libra and Capricorn
                      The cardinal quality is the active,
                      initiating principle. Those born under
                      these four signs are good at starting
                      new projects.

Fixed Signs           Taurus, Leo, Scorpio and Aquarius
                      Fixed qualities include stability,
                      persistence, endurance and
                      perfectionism. People born under these
                      four signs are good at seeing things
                      through.

Mutable Signs         Gemini, Virgo, Sagittarius and Pisces
                      Mutable qualities are adaptability,
                      changeability and balance. Those born
                      under these four signs are creative, if
                      not always practical.

# Direct Motion

When the planets move forward through the zodiac – as they normally do – they are said to be going 'direct'.

# Grand Square

A Grand Square differs from a normal Square (usually two planets separated by 90 degrees) in that four or more planets are involved. When you look at the pattern in a chart you will see a whole and complete square. This, though stressful, usually denotes a new manifestation in the life. There is much work and balancing involved in the manifestation.

# Grand Trine

A Grand Trine differs from a normal Trine (where two planets are 120 degrees apart) in that three or more planets are involved. When you look at this pattern in a chart, it takes the form of a complete triangle – a Grand Trine. Usually (but not always) it occurs in one of the four elements: Fire, Earth, Air or Water. Thus the particular element in which it occurs will be highlighted. A Grand Trine in Water is not the same as a Grand Trine in Air or Fire, etc. This is a very fortunate and happy aspect, and quite rare.

# Houses

There are 12 signs of the zodiac and 12 houses of experience. The 12 signs are personality types and ways in which a given planet expresses itself; the 12 houses show 'where' in your life this expression takes place. Each house has a different area of interest. A house can become potent and important – a House of Power – in different ways: if it contains the Sun, the Moon or the 'ruler' of your chart; if it contains more than one planet; or if the ruler of that house is receiving unusual stimulation from other planets.

| | |
|---|---|
| 1st House | Personal Image and Sensual Delights |
| 2nd House | Money/Finance |
| 3rd House | Communication and Intellectual Interests |
| 4th House | Home and Family |
| 5th House | Children, Fun, Games, Creativity, Speculations and Love Affairs |
| 6th House | Health and Work |
| 7th House | Love, Marriage and Social Activities |
| 8th House | Transformation and Regeneration |
| 9th House | Religion, Foreign Travel, Higher Education and Philosophy |
| 10th House | Career |
| 11th House | Friends, Group Activities and Fondest Wishes |
| 12th House | Spirituality |

## Karma

Karma is the law of cause and effect which governs all phenomena. We are all where we find ourselves because of karma – because of actions we have performed in the past. The universe is such a balanced instrument that any act immediately sets corrective forces into motion – karma.

## Long-term Planets

The planets that take a long time to move through a sign show the long-term trends in a given area of life. They are important for forecasting the prolonged view of things. Because these planets stay in one sign for so long, there are periods in the year when the faster-moving (short-term) planets will join them, further activating and enhancing the importance of a given house.

| | |
|---|---|
| Jupiter | stays in a sign for about 1 year |
| Saturn | 2½ years |
| Uranus | 7 years |
| Neptune | 14 years |
| Pluto | 15 to 30 years |

## Lunar

Relating to the Moon. See also 'Phases of the Moon', below.

## Natal

Literally means 'birth'. In astrology this term is used to distinguish between planetary positions that occurred at the time of a person's birth (natal) and those that are current (transiting). For example, Natal Sun refers to where the Sun was when you were born; transiting Sun refers to where the Sun's position is currently at any given moment – which usually doesn't coincide with your birth, or Natal, Sun.

# Out of Bounds

The planets move through the zodiac at various angles relative to the celestial equator (if you were to draw an imaginary extension of the Earth's equator out into the universe, you would have an illustration of this celestial equator). The Sun – being the most dominant and powerful influence in the Solar system – is the measure astrologers use as a standard. The Sun never goes more than approximately 23 degrees north or south of the celestial equator. At the winter solstice the Sun reaches its maximum southern angle of orbit (declination); at the summer solstice it reaches its maximum northern angle. Any time a planet exceeds this Solar boundary – and occasionally planets do – it is said to be 'out of bounds'. This means that the planet exceeds or trespasses into strange territory – beyond the limits allowed by the Sun, the Ruler of the Solar system. The planet in this condition becomes more emphasized and exceeds its authority, becoming an important influence in the forecast.

# Phases of the Moon

After the full Moon, the Moon seems to shrink in size (as perceived from the Earth), gradually growing smaller until it is virtually invisible to the naked eye – at the time of the next new Moon. This is called the waning Moon phase, or the waning Moon.

After the new Moon, the Moon gradually gets bigger in size (as perceived from the Earth) until it reaches its maximum size at the time of the full Moon. This period is called the waxing Moon phase, or waxing Moon.

## Retrogrades

The planets move around the Sun at different speeds. Mercury and Venus move much faster than the Earth, while Mars, Jupiter, Saturn, Uranus, Neptune and Pluto move more slowly. Thus there are times when, relative to the Earth, the planets appear to be going backwards. In reality they are always going forward, but relative to our vantage point on Earth they seem to go backwards through the zodiac for a period of time. This is called 'retrograde' motion and tends to weaken the normal influence of a given planet.

## Short-term Planets

The fast-moving planets move so quickly through a sign that their effects are generally of a short-term nature. They reflect the immediate, day-to-day trends in a horoscope.

| | |
|---|---|
| Moon | stays in a sign for only 2½ days |
| Mercury | 20 to 30 days |
| Sun | 30 days |
| Venus | approximately 1 month |
| Mars | approximately 2 months |

## T-square

A T-square differs from a Grand Square in that it is not a complete square. If you look at the pattern in a chart it appears as 'half a complete square', resembling the T-square tools used by architects and designers. If you cut a complete square in half, diagonally, you have a T-square. Many astrologers consider this more stressful than a Grand Square, as it creates tension that is difficult to resolve. T-squares bring learning experiences.

# Transits

This refers to the movements or motions of the planets at any given time. Astrologers use the word 'transit' to make the distinction between a birth or Natal planet (see 'Natal', above) and the planet's current movement in the heavens. For example, if at your birth Saturn was in the sign of Cancer in your 8th house, but is now moving through your 3rd house, it is said to be 'transiting' your 3rd house. Transits are one of the main tools with which astrologers forecast trends.

# Aries

♈

---

## THE RAM
*Birthdays from
21st March to
20th April*

---

## Personality Profile

### ARIES AT A GLANCE

*Element* – Fire

*Ruling Planet* – Mars
    *Career Planet* – Saturn
    *Love Planet* – Venus
    *Money Planet* – Venus
    *Planet of Fun, Entertainment, Creativity
      and Speculations* – Sun
    *Planet of Health and Work* – Mercury
    *Planet of Home and Family Life* – Moon
    *Planet of Spirituality* – Neptune
    *Planet of Travel, Education, Religion
      and Philosophy* – Jupiter

*Colours* – carmine, red, scarlet

*Colours that promote love, romance and social
    harmony* – green, jade green

*Colour that promotes earning power* – green

*Gem* – amethyst

*Metals* – iron, steel

*Scent* – honeysuckle

*Quality* – cardinal (= activity)

*Quality most needed for balance* – caution

*Strongest virtues* – abundant physical energy, courage, honesty, independence, self-reliance

*Deepest need* – action

*Characteristics to avoid* – haste, impetuousness, over-aggression, rashness

*Signs of greatest overall compatibility* – Leo, Sagittarius

*Signs of greatest overall incompatibility* – Cancer, Libra, Capricorn

*Sign most helpful to career* – Capricorn

*Sign most helpful for emotional support* – Cancer

*Sign most helpful financially* – Taurus

*Sign best for marriage and/or partnerships* – Libra

*Sign most helpful for creative projects* – Leo

*Best Sign to have fun with* – Leo

*Signs most helpful in spiritual matters* – Sagittarius, Pisces

*Best day of the week* – Tuesday

# Understanding an Aries

Aries is the activist *par excellence* of the zodiac. The Aries need for action is almost an addiction, and those who do not really understand the Aries personality would probably use this hard word to describe it. In reality 'action' is the essence of the Aries psychology – the more direct, blunt and to-the-point the action, the better. When you think about it, this is the ideal psychological makeup for the warrior, the pioneer, the athlete or the manager.

Aries likes to get things done, and in their passion and zeal often lose sight of the consequences for themselves and others. Yes, they often try to be diplomatic and tactful, but it is hard for them. When they do so they feel that they are being dishonest and phony. It is hard for them even to understand the mindset of the diplomat, the consensus builder, the front office executive. These people are involved in endless meetings, discussions, talks and negotiations – all of which seem a great waste of time when there is so much work to be done, so many real achievements to be gained. An Aries can understand, once it is explained, that talks and negotiations – the social graces – lead ultimately to better, more effective actions. The interesting thing is that an Aries is rarely malicious or spiteful – even when waging war. Aries people fight without hate for their opponents. To them it is all good-natured fun, a grand adventure, a game.

When confronted with a problem many people will say, 'Well, let's think about it, let's analyse the situation.' But not an Aries. An Aries will think, 'Something must be done. Let's get on with it.' Of course neither response is the total answer. Sometimes action is called for, sometimes cool thought. But an Aries tends to err on the side of action.

Action and thought are radically different principles. Physical activity is the use of brute force. Thinking and deliberating require one not to use force – to be still. It is not good for the athlete to be deliberating the next move; this will only slow down his or her reaction time. The athlete must act instinctively and instantly. This is how Aries people tend to behave in life. They are quick, instinctive decision-makers and their decisions tend to be translated into action almost immediately. When their intuition is sharp and well tuned, their actions are powerful and successful. When their intuition is off, their actions can be disastrous.

Do not think this will scare an Aries. Just as a good warrior knows that in the course of combat he or she might acquire a few wounds, so too does an Aries realize – somewhere deep down – that in the course of being true to yourself you might get embroiled in a disaster or two. It is all part of the game. An Aries feels strong enough to weather any storm.

There are many Aries people who are intellectual. They make powerful and creative thinkers. But even in this realm they tend to be pioneers – outspoken and blunt. These types of Aries tend to elevate (or sublimate) their desire for physical combat in favour of intellectual, mental combat. And they are indeed powerful.

In general, Aries people have a faith in themselves that others could learn from. This basic, rock-solid faith carries them through the most tumultuous situations of life. Their courage and self-confidence make them natural leaders. Their leadership is more by way of example than by actually controlling others.

**Finance**

Aries people often excel as builders or estate agents. Money in and of itself is not as important as are other things – action, adventure, sport, etc. They are motivated by the need to support and be well-thought-of by their partners. Money as a way of attaining pleasure is another important motivation. Aries function best in their own businesses or as managers of their own departments within a large business or corporation. The fewer orders they have to take from higher up, the better. They also function better out in the field rather than behind a desk.

Aries people are hard workers with a lot of endurance; they can earn large sums of money due to the strength of their sheer physical energy.

Venus is their money planet, which means that Aries need to develop more of the social graces in order to realize their full earning potential. Just getting the job done – which is what an Aries excels at – is not enough to create financial success. The co-operation of others needs to be attained. Customers, clients and co-workers need to be made to feel comfortable; many people need to be treated properly in order for success to happen. When Aries people develop these abilities – or hire someone to do this for them – their financial potential is unlimited.

## Career and Public Image

One would think that a pioneering type would want to break with the social and political conventions of society. But this is not so with the Aries-born. They are pioneers within conventional limits, in the sense that they like to start their own businesses within an established industry.

Capricorn is on the 10th house (career) cusp of Aries' Solar horoscope. Saturn is the planet that rules their life's work and professional aspirations. This tells us some interesting things about the Aries character. First off, it shows that, in order for Aries people to reach their full career potential, they need to develop some qualities that are a bit alien to their basic nature: they need to become better administrators and organizers; they need to be able to handle details better and to take a long-range view of their projects and their careers in general. No one can beat an Aries when it comes to achieving short-range objectives, but a career is long term, built over time. You cannot take a 'quickie' approach to it.

Some Aries people find it difficult to stick with a project until the end. Since they get bored quickly and are in constant pursuit of new adventures, they prefer to pass an old project or task on to somebody else in order to start something new. Those Aries who learn how to put off the search for something new until the old is completed will achieve great success in their careers and professional lives.

In general, Aries people like society to judge them on their own merits, on their real and actual achievements. A reputation acquired by 'hype' feels false to them.

## Love and Relationships

In marriage and partnerships Aries like those who are more passive, gentle, tactful and diplomatic – people who have the social grace and skills they sometimes lack. Our partners always represent a hidden part of ourselves – a self that we cannot express personally.

An Aries tends to go after what he or she likes aggressively. The tendency is to jump into relationships and marriages. This is especially true if Venus is in Aries as well as the Sun. If an Aries likes you, he or she will have a hard time taking no for an answer; many attempts will be made to sweep you off your feet.

Though Aries can be exasperating in relationships – especially if they are not understood by their partners – they are never consciously or wilfully cruel or malicious. It is just that they are so independent and sure of themselves that they find it almost impossible to see somebody else's viewpoint or position. This is why an Aries needs as a partner someone with lots of social graces.

On the plus side, an Aries is honest, someone you can lean on, someone with whom you will always know where you stand. What he or she lacks in diplomacy is made up for in integrity.

## Home and Domestic Life

An Aries is of course the ruler at home – the Boss. The male will tend to delegate domestic matters to the female. The female Aries will want to rule the roost. Both tend to be handy round the house. Both like large families and both believe in the sanctity and importance of the family. An Aries is a good family person, although he or she does not especially like being at home a lot, preferring instead to be roaming about.

Considering that they are by nature so combative and wilful, Aries people can be surprisingly soft, gentle and even vulnerable with their children and partners. The sign of Cancer, ruled by the Moon, is on the cusp of their solar 4th house (home and family). When the Moon is well aspected – under favourable influences – in the birth chart, an Aries will be tender towards the family and want a family life that is nurturing and supportive. Aries likes to come home after a hard day on the battlefield of life to the understanding arms of their partner and the unconditional love and support of their family. An Aries feels that there is enough 'war' out in the world – and he or she enjoys participating in that. But when Aries comes home, comfort and nurturing are what's needed.

# Horoscope for 2012

## Major Trends

For those of you born early in the sign of Aries (March 21–31), 2011 was no piece of cake. There were challenges galore, yet you overcame. You worked harder, perhaps longer hours, but you saw the fruits of your labour. In spite of all the challenges, you prospered. Prosperity is still strong in the year ahead as well. Things were not easy but they were good. (The really worthwhile things in life rarely come easily.) When Saturn leaves Libra on October 5, things start to get easier. Health and energy will improve. The love situation will also improve.

Those of you born later in the sign also had prosperity and the good life last year. But you are feeling the challenges more this year – and in future years.

The main theme of 2012 (actually it began in the spring/summer of 2010) is change. Uranus entered your sign in 2011 and will be there for many years to come. Many of you divorced in the past two years or broke up serious relationships and now you are exploring your personal freedom.

Many of you have been praying for change for some time now, and it is happening. Those of you born early in the sign are having it now. Those of you born later in the sign will have it in coming years. These changes are dramatic ones – not like changing your hairstyle or job. Uranus is saying to you, 'Yes I will bring you the change that you are praying for, but in order to do so, you must allow me to shake things up a bit.'

Love, as we mentioned, has been challenging for the past two years, but should get easier later on in the year, after October (more on this later).

Your spiritual planet, Neptune, makes a major move this year. He moves from the sign of Aquarius, where he has been for 14 or 15 years, into his own sign of Pisces. This is showing shifts in your own spiritual life and a deepening of it.

Though the romantic life is challenging, friendships seem good. You have very devoted friends these days – friends who put your interests ahead of their own.

Jupiter will move into your 3rd house on June 11 and spend the rest of 2012 there. Thus this is a year for expanding the mind – for learning or teaching and for pursuing your intellectual interests. Many of you will get new cars and communication equipment as well.

Your most important interests in the year ahead are the body, the image and personal pleasure; finance; communication and intellectual interests; love, romance and social activities; sex, personal transformation and personal reinvention; and your career.

Your paths of greatest fulfillment this year are finance (until June 11); communication and intellectual interests (after June 11); foreign travel, higher education, religion, philosophy and theology (until August 31); sex, personal transformation and personal reinvention (after August 31).

## Health

*(Please note that this is an* astrological *perspective on health and not a medical one. In days of yore there was no difference: these perspectives were identical. But today there could be quite a difference. For a medical perspective, please consult your doctor or health practitioner.)*

Your 6th house of health is a 'house of power' for the first half of the year and this is good news. You are focused on health; it is a major priority – and it should be, as health is more delicate this year than usual. Three powerful long-term planets – Uranus, Pluto and Saturn – are affecting you, so overall energy is not what it should be. More attention to health is called for this year and you are responding.

There is much you can do to enhance your health and prevent problems from developing. Give more attention to the head, face and scalp (regular scalp and face massage will be especially powerful until July 3; craniosacral therapy is powerful too); the heart (avoid worry and anxiety, the spiritual root cause of heart problems); the adrenals (strong emotions such as fear and anger tend to knock out the adrenal glands: do your best to minimize this); and the small intestine.

Aries are lovers of physical exercise and athletics in general. But this year vigorous physical exercise is very good for the health. Good muscle tone is important. If the muscles lose their tone, the skeleton gets out of whack – the spinal vertebrae get misaligned and this can lead to hosts of other problems. A day at the gym is not only fun but will often do as much for you (if you feel under the weather) as a visit to the doctor.

With Mars, the ruler of your Horoscope, in your 6th house for the first half of the year, good health for you is not just 'no symptoms' or physical fitness, it also means 'looking

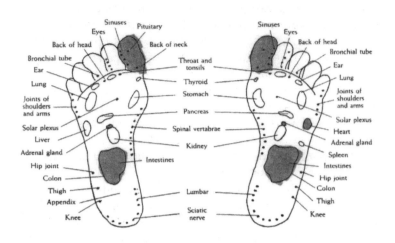

## Reflexology

*Try to massage the whole foot on a regular basis, but pay extra attention to the points highlighted on the chart. When you massage, be aware of 'sore spots', as these need special attention. It's also a good idea to massage the ankles and top side of the feet (see below).*

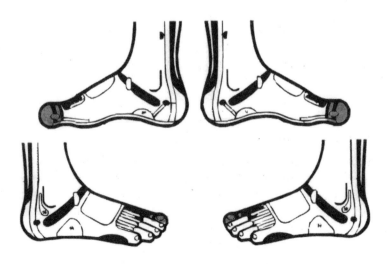

good'. There is a vanity component here. Good health will do more for your personal appearance than a host of beauty treatments. This vanity component can be used for healing as well. If you feel under the weather, buy a new outfit or have your hair or nails done – do something that improves your appearance, and chances are that you will feel 'physically' better as well.

Aries is always the daredevil. The more dangerous or adventurous a project or activity is, the better they like it. But this year, the tendency is even stronger. You are experimenting with the body, testing the limits. This is basically a good thing – the body can do much more than we think – however these experiments need to be done in a 'mindful' way, or injury can result. With Uranus in your 1st house I'd recommend exercises like yoga, tai chi or chi qong – these are safe ways to test the limits of the body.

Your health planet, Mercury, is a fast-moving planet. During the course of the year he will move through all the 12 signs and houses of your Horoscope. Thus there are many short-term health trends that are best discussed in the monthly reports.

As we mentioned, Saturn will move away from his stressful aspect on October 5, improving your health and energy tremendously. However, with Uranus and Pluto still affecting you, you still need to watch your health.

The most important times to rest and relax more this year are from January 1 to January 19; June 21 to July 22; September 22 to October 22; and December 21 to December 31.

## Home and Family

Your 4th house of home and family is not a 'house of power' this year. Normally this would mean a status quo kind of year, with no major changes. But this year, with Uranus in your 1st house (especially for those of you born early in Aries) status quo is not in your lexicon. You are into change, change, change – the more the better!

Usually when Uranus occupies the 1st house (and this will be a trend for many more years) people become nomadic. They are restless. They might not formally move, but will travel around a lot and live in different places for long periods of time. They might have a home, but they behave as if they were 'homeless'.

This also generates a 'passion for personal freedom'. You don't want *any* responsibility, and this can create problems with the family unit. Every family member has responsibilities, whether formal or unspoken, so this could create rifts with the family this year. (Those of you who have Aries people within your family need to give them as much latitude as possible – so long as it isn't destructive. Aries children are more difficult to handle this year; they are more rebellious.)

The Moon is your family planet and she gets eclipsed twice this year – this is pretty normal. This means that twice every year (and sometimes more than twice) you get the opportunity to improve the home and the family relations. The cosmos forces you into it. Thus if there are flaws in the home, or hidden grudges with family members, these are the times when they surface so that they can be corrected. The two lunar eclipses this year are on June 4 and November 28. We will discuss them in more detail in the monthly reports.

We do see dramas with parents or parent figures this year. This began last year, but is more pronounced now. They can be having operations, near-death kinds of experiences and financial changes and shakeups. Like you, parents and parent figures need to watch their health more, especially their overall energy levels.

Siblings and sibling figures are having a very spiritual kind of period until June 11. There is much inner growth happening. After this date they enter a period of prosperity, with increased earnings, luck in speculations, travel and the good life. Siblings of an appropriate age are much more fertile than usual during this period too. There are probably major repairs going on in their homes early in the year.

Children of an appropriate age could have multiple moves this year, but they seem stressful. If they are going to move, it will be better to do it before October 5. Afterwards there are many delays and glitches involved. Grandchildren of appropriate age seem to have a status quo year as far as the home is concerned.

## Finance and Career

In spite of all the challenges you've been facing, last year seems to have been prosperous and the trend continues in the year ahead. Expansive Jupiter – the planet of abundance – is still in your money house until June 11. By then, your financial goals will more or less be attained and your focus will be on other things.

Like last year, assets you already own tend to increase in value. Thus your net worth is increased regardless of your actual earnings. Jupiter is both the generic and actual ruler of your 9th house. Thus there are financial opportunities with foreign companies, or in foreign countries, or with foreigners in your own country.

With Jupiter, the planet of religion and philosophy, associated with wealth this year, it is very important to have a good personal philosophy of wealth: a good metaphysical understanding of what causes it and how to attain it. There is much more to it than just mere 'hard work' (although this is part of it). If there are flaws in your personal philosophy (i.e. if you believe that wealth is just material things), it can hamper your ability to earn.

There are a few complications though. Venus rules both your love life and financial life. Thus, for you, there is a powerful connection between love and money. When love is going well, finances tend to go well. When finances are going well, love tends to go well. Problems in love can cause problems in finance and vice versa. Thus, because the love life has been challenging, this could affect earning power. (In cases where couples are getting divorced or separating, there are often financial conflicts involved.) Love problems tend to be the root causes of financial problems in your Horoscope. If financial problems beset you, do your best to get the love life in order.

Venus is a very fast-moving planet. Like Mercury, sometimes she moves fast, sometimes slow, and sometimes she goes backwards (this year she retrogrades from May 15 to June 27). Thus there are many short-term trends in finance that are best dealt with in the monthly reports.

For the past two years your career planet Saturn has been in the sign of Libra. This is a nice position by the way: Saturn is exalted in Libra and your career energies are at their most 'exalted' status. This situation continues for most of the year ahead, until October 5. The career planet in Libra shows that you advance your career by social means – by attending or hosting the right kind of parties and through your social connections. Your friends (and spouse or current love) seem supportive, career-wise.

Pluto has been in your 10th house of career for some years now and will be there for many more years to come. There are great shakeups and upheavals in your company or industry. This trend accelerates after October 5 when your career planet enters Scorpio, the 8th house of your chart. The rules are changing. A detox is happening in your company and industry, and also within yourself. Your attitudes and approach to your career are getting purified, sometimes by dramatic means such as by 'near-death' kinds of career experiences – situations where you face apparent ruin. However, the career dramas you are facing are really the 'birth pangs' of something new and wonderful.

## Love and Social

As we mentioned, the love and social life has been challenging for some years now. Saturn has been in your 7th house. There are many good things about this, but seldom is this transit pleasant. Singles are better off not marrying this year. We often get into relationships with a honeymoon mentality, but the honeymoon rarely lasts for long. After a while the burdens and responsibilities come in and we have to deal with them. The past two years – and most of the year ahead – is such a time. Many a love relationship has dissolved these past two years and many more will dissolve in the year ahead. Many of you even doubt that love exists, it all seems like a duty and burden. Even good relationships (especially if this is the first marriage) have become dull. The spark of love, the fire of romance, the spontaneity seems lacking. All of you will have to work harder to project love and warmth to others. On some unconscious level, you are projecting a 'coldness', a distance, an aloofness and others are picking up on this. So it is up to you, through your conscious effort, to project love and warmth to counteract these astrological tendencies.

The good part of this transit is that you will learn whether your love is real. We seldom know this when everything is going well. It is only in the tough times that we learn this. The other good thing here is that many of you are learning that duty and responsibility are another form of love. Doing your duty by the beloved, no matter how you feel or how onerous it is, is a form of love. And, in many cultures it is considered the highest form of love.

Aries people tend to jump into relationships much too quickly. They fall in love very quickly and often marry quickly. But now with Saturn in your 7th house the cosmos is cautioning you to go slow in love. Don't rush things, let love develop as it will. There is a need for patience in love this year.

Singles are probably attracted to (and attracting) older lovers this year. Often under this aspect marriage is seen as a career move – a career like any other – and more like a business partnership than a romantic attachment. A person will marry for convenience rather than for romantic love.

Those of you into your first marriage are having the marriages tested right now. Good marriages will survive and get even better. But inherently flawed ones will probably dissolve. Those of you working on your second marriage have opportunities for business partnerships this year. But there are also good marriage opportunities in the first half of the year. Love opportunities happen as you pursue your financial goals and with people who are involved in your finances. Those working on their third marriage have excellent prospects and a third marriage is very likely. There's not much you need to do – this person will find you.

Saturn in your 7th house shows a need to pare down social activities. You need to focus on quality rather than quantity. In general you are mixing with people of high power and prestige, with people who can help you careerwise this year, as has been the case for the past two years. Many of you will be involved in the classic office romance, especially with superiors.

## Self-improvement

There have been many disappointments in love and with friends the past two years, and you are still not finished with this. So there is a need to avoid becoming embittered or vengeful. You can be carrying deep-seated grudges on an unconscious level. This is not constructive and will cause more problems in love and in other areas of life. So, learning and practising the art of forgiveness is very important this year.

Real forgiveness comes not just from the lips. It is an organic forgiveness – the hurt and pain are released from the very cells of the body. With real forgiveness you are able to think of the person who has hurt you without anger, pain, regret, sadness or any other negative emotion. You may not be passionately in love with the person who has wronged you, but at least you will not be emanating more negativity (and thus creating more negative experiences in your life). It might help you to understand that we never forgive the actions – only the people. The actions were wrong and there is no whitewashing these things. But these people's actions were prompted by their own insecurities and errors and they may have had little control over what they did.

As we mentioned, Neptune, your spiritual planet (and

also the generic spiritual planet) makes a major move into your 12th house this year on February 3. Thus spirituality is going to become important for many years to come. Now Aries are activists even in their spiritual life. They serve the Divine through the physical body, through being active in charities or causes. They like to express their spiritual ideals in a physical way. This is all well and good but now, with Neptune's influence upon you, it might be good to also include the more contemplative, meditative paths. Yes, action is good, but stillness is also good. Stillness, silence, will lead to even more powerful actions – and it seems to me that this is the spiritual message for you. Before rushing into a worthy activity automatically, spend some time in the silence communing with the Divine. Then your actions will be more powerful and effective. This is a time in your life where you learn that non-action and action are two sides of the same coin; one gives birth to the other.

Uranus is in your 1st house for many years to come. Thus, as we mentioned, you are more experimental with the body, testing its limits. But along with this many of you will be more rebellious these days. Sometimes rebellion is called for – there are certain situations that we should not submit to. But sometimes people rebel for the sake of rebellion. Change is seen as good for its own sake, and this is not always the case. The positive way to rebel is to create something better than the thing that you are rebelling against. Find a way that really improves things and practise it. This will do more in the long run than a million temper tantrums.

# Month-by-month Forecasts

## January

Best Days Overall: 1, 2, 10, 11, 19, 20, 28, 29
Most Stressful Days Overall: 8, 9, 14, 15, 21, 22
Best Days for Love: 6, 7, 14, 15, 16, 17, 25, 26
Best Days for Money: 3, 4, 6, 7, 12, 16, 17, 21, 25, 26, 30, 31
Best Days for Career: 15, 21, 22

Your year begins with the planetary momentum over-whelmingly moving forward. Until the 24th *all* of the planets are moving forward (highly unusual), and after the 24th 90 per cent are going forward. Not only that, but the universal solar cycle is waxing. So this is a great month to start new projects or launch new products. Try to find days when the Moon is also waxing (from the 1st to the 9th and from the 23rd onwards) and you'll have the best of the best days to start new projects.

Last month the planetary power shifted to the Eastern sector of your Horoscope, and this month the shift is even stronger. By the 8th 70 per cent (and sometimes 80 per cent) of the planets will be in the East. You are always an independent sort, but now even more so. This is a time to create your life circumstances, rather than to adapt to things. Your happiness is up to you. Other people are always important, but they will adapt themselves to you rather than vice versa.

Health needs more watching this month especially until the 20th. Energy and vitality are not up to their usual standards so rest and relax more and try to pace yourself better. Instead of a go-go-go rhythm, try a go-go-rest beat. Happily, you seem more focused on health this month and you will listen to your body. You can enhance your health by giving more attention to the liver and thighs (until the 8th) and to the spine, knees, teeth, bones, skin and overall skeletal alignment, afterwards. Fire therapies – heat-oriented therapies – are powerful until the 8th, after that earth-based therapies (mud bathing, soaking in mineral waters and the like) are strong. Your health planet Mercury travels with Pluto from the 12th to the 14th and thus detox regimes are especially powerful that period. Surgery could be recommended that period and you seem inclined to agree, but get second opinions. (Be careful driving that period too. Cars and communication equipment gets tested then and might need replacement.) Your health planet is in stressful aspect with Uranus from the 8th to the 10th – reinforcing the above, but also suggesting the avoidance of risky, daredevil types of behaviour.

Ever since Jupiter entered your money house in June of last year you have been in a prosperity cycle. This trend continues. Financial intuition seems unusually strong and good this month. Venus travels with Neptune from the 12th to the 15th and then enters mystical Pisces on the 24th. You can't really make financial decisions based on logic alone as there is too much going on behind the scenes now so your premises and assumptions can be faulty. Intuition sees through all these things. Though you are materially minded these days, this is a good month to go deeper into the spiritual realities of wealth. The material thing is only the side effect of a spiritual reality. Spirit is the actual cause of wealth – the activities of the earth are merely effects.

You seem to give more to charity this month. This is good as it opens the doors to the spiritual supply. Involvement with non-profit organizations or altruistic causes brings both love and financial opportunity.

**February**

Best Days Overall: 7, 8, 15, 16, 24, 25
Most Stressful Days Overall: 4, 5, 11, 12, 17, 18
Best Days for Love: 5, 6, 11, 12, 15, 24, 25
Best Days for Money: 1, 5, 6, 9, 15, 17, 24, 25, 27, 28
Best Days for Career: 3, 12, 17, 18, 21

The planetary momentum is still mostly forward this month: until the 6th 90 per cent of the planets are going forward, after that 80 per cent. So this is still a good month for launching new products or starting new projects (and many of you are involved with new projects these days). The planetary power is also still in the East, so keep in mind our discussion of this last month.

The main headline this month is the power in your spiritual 12th house – it is easily the strongest house in the chart right now. Venus entered here last month, Neptune moves in on the 3rd, Mercury on the 14th and the Sun on the 19th. The new Moon of the 21st will also occur here. No question this is a spiritual month. It is normal to feel more reclusive under these transits, to crave solitude to get right with yourself and with the Divine. And, since you are approaching your personal new year (your solar return – your birthday) it is good now (and until your birthday) to review the past year, assess your progress or non-progress, atone for past mistakes, and set your course for the year ahead. These things can only be done in solitude and quiet.

For those of you on the spiritual path, this is a month for spiritual breakthroughs. When these things happen it is most rapturous. It changes the whole outlook on life.

Love has been stressful for some years. Marriages and serious relationships are getting tested. But this month we see some improvement. Venus crosses your Ascendant and enters your 1st house on the 8th. Your spouse, partner or current love seems more devoted to you, more on your side, and you are in a more romantic mood. Singles are not likely to marry this month, but there is love in your life – in fact it pursues you. Still, it is highly unstable and volatile (Venus is conjunct to Uranus from the 8th to the 10th). This means that sudden love can come to you but can also leave you just as quickly. Still it is exciting.

This is a nice aspect for finance too. Financial opportunity, and probably some windfalls, is coming to you. An opportunity for a great business partnership or joint venture occurs. But don't jump into things too quickly. The staying power of this venture is in question. It seems that you are spending more on technology too from the 8th onwards, and it seems like a good investment.

Though health has been stressed for more than a year, this is one of your better health periods in the year. You can enhance your health even further by giving more attention to your ankles and calves (both should be regularly massaged) until the 14th and to the feet after the 14th. Your health planet moves into your spiritual 12th house on that date, so this is a month for going deeper into the spiritual dimensions of healing. Many of you will be involved in spiritual healing for others and this is a good 'entry point' to this vast subject.

**March**

Best Days Overall: 5, 6, 13, 14, 22, 23, 24
Most Stressful Days Overall: 3, 4, 9, 10, 15, 16, 30, 31
Best Days for Love: 7, 9, 10, 15, 16, 25, 26
Best Days for Money: 7, 15, 16, 25, 26
Best Days for Career: 2, 10, 15, 16, 19, 29

The planets are now in their maximum Eastern position of the year. Personal independence is now at its strongest. This is a time for having your way in life and for creating your own happiness according to your personal specifications. You have the power and the support.

This month the planets make an important shift. For the first two months of the year, the upper hemisphere of your chart was the strongest. So ambitions and career were dominant interests. By the 20th, as the Sun crosses your Ascendant, the lower half of the Horoscope becomes dominant. You are in the dusk period of the year; night is falling. Outer career activities are less important for the next six or so months; instead family and emotional issues are more important. Sure you will deal with your career, but perhaps in a different, more 'internal' way. In winter, when everything is bleak and desolate and seemingly dead, nature is 'dreaming and visualizing' her future blossoms and fruits; nature is still alive, but in a more interior way. And when Spring comes, her dreams start to become real. So it is with you. Your outer ambitions are far from dead, but they need to be worked on in a different way. This is a trend for the next six months. Now your emotional harmony is very important. Without emotional harmony you won't be effective in your 'dreaming and visualizing'.

Your 12th house of spirituality is still strong until the 20th, so keep in mind our discussion of this last month. On the 20th the Sun enters your own sign and your 1st house. This is a very happy transit. You enter a yearly personal pleasure peak. You are in a period where the pleasures of the body are easily fulfilled. There is personal optimism and happiness. Health and energy (a problem for more than a year) is much improved now. Whatever your age, you are more the child this month – happy-go-lucky. You look younger too. Aries of appropriate age are more fertile this month. There is luck in speculations now too.

On the 5th, Venus enters your money house where she joins with Jupiter. The two benefactors of the zodiac are now occupying your money house, signalling a month of prosperity. Opportunities for business partnerships and joint ventures are also happening and these seem more stable and serious than last month.

Venus travels with Jupiter from the 11th to the 14th, a great period for both love and money. Singles are perhaps a bit too practical about love – perhaps a bit too materialistic – but they seem to get what they want. They find love opportunities as they pursue their normal financial goals and with people involved in the finances.

## April

Best Days Overall: 1, 2, 10, 19, 20, 29, 30
Most Stressful Days Overall: 6, 12, 13, 26, 27
Best Days for Love: 5, 6, 14, 15, 24, 25
Best Days for Money: 4, 5, 12, 13, 14, 15, 21, 22, 24, 25
Best Days for Career: 6, 7, 12, 13, 15, 25

Your health planet was retrograde most of last month, and is retrograde until the 4th of this month. Health news that you've been receiving – test results and the like – is probably not what you think and perhaps is even amiss. This is a time for doing your homework – reviewing your health regime – rather than for making major changes; not until after the 4th is it safer to make changes. Until the 17th Mercury is still in your spiritual 12th house, so spiritual healing is still very powerful for you, and you respond well to it. Also give more attention to the feet. On the 17th Mercury moves into your own sign, therefore give more attention to the head, face and skull (areas that always need more attention anyway) and to the adrenals. Physical exercise is always good for you but now even more so. It seems that you are making important health changes from the 17th to the 20th. Be a more defensive driver that period as well.

There are job changes happening during that period too. In some cases it is within the same company, in other cases, it is with another company. If you employ others there is instability in the workforce over that period, perhaps employee turnover and dramas in the lives of employees. If you are looking for a job, job opportunities are seeking you out after the 17th. If you employ others, new employees are coming to you.

Last month was a prosperous month and the trend continues even more strongly. The Sun enters your money house on the 20th and you enter a yearly financial peak.

This is one of your best financial months in a great financial year. Enjoy. What I like with this transit is that it shows 'happy money' – money that is earned in pleasurable and enjoyable ways, not through drudgery. Also, it shows that you are enjoying your wealth, spending it on leisure and fun kinds of things. There is luck in speculations from the 20th onwards too. Children in your life are also prospering and seem supportive financially. This works in many kinds of ways. Sometimes the support is in the form of actual money or financial opportunity (if they are of appropriate age), sometimes they have good financial ideas, or they inspire you to earn more. Your personal creativity also seems more marketable now.

Your love planet enters your 3rd house on the 3rd and spends the rest of the month there. Thus love opportunities occur in the neighbourhood and perhaps with neighbours. Love happens in educational-type settings – in school or lectures or seminars. Good communication turns you on. Mental sex is as important as physical sex.

### May

Best Days Overall: 7, 8, 16, 17, 26, 27
Most Stressful Days Overall: 3, 4, 9, 10, 23, 24, 25, 30, 31
Best Days for Love: 3, 4, 11, 12, 21, 22, 30, 31
Best Days for Money: 2, 3, 4, 10, 11, 12, 18, 19, 20, 21, 22, 29, 30, 31
Best Days for Career: 4, 9, 10, 12, 22, 31

Many of the trends of previous months are still in effect. Most of the planets are still in the East (though this is about to change), and most of them are still below the horizon of your Horoscope. Continue to create conditions as you see fit and pursue emotional harmony. With your career planet retrograde for the past few months you can safely downplay the career and focus on the home and family. Many career issues need time to resolve; there is no quick fix right now.

Retrograde activity increases compared with previous months; after the 15th 30 per cent of the planets are in retrograde motion. The pace of life slows down a bit. The most important retrogrades affecting you now are those of Saturn (your career planet) and Venus (your love and financial planet). Three important areas of life are being affected, and so your financial and social judgements are not up to their usual standard; important decisions ought not to be taken. Big purchases, big investments, big changes need serious thought. (Venus is retrograde from the 15th of this month until June 26.)

Love is more complicated now, maybe going backwards instead of forwards. Perhaps your spouse, partner or current love is 'back tracking', or perhaps you are. This is all part of the cosmic agenda to get you to review your love life, your romantic relationship, and see where improvements can be made. Sometimes the way forward is backwards: sometimes the review will lead to greater forward progress in the future. Avoid important love decisions now. Singles should let love develop as it will without trying to force things (this is hard for an Aries).

Your love planet goes retrograde in the sign of Gemini and in your 3rd house. The message here is that you need to be more careful when communicating to your spouse or current love. Don't take things for granted. Make sure you get their message and that they get yours. Many of the problems now come from miscommunication and misunderstanding. A little more care in the beginning can save a lot of heartache later on.

You are still in a very prosperous period – a yearly financial peak. This continues until the 20th. The retrograde of your financial planet will not stop your prosperity, but will perhaps slow it down a little, giving you a bit more breathing room. It is a pause that refreshes, as the saying goes.

There is a solar eclipse this month on the 20th – right on the cusp of your 2nd and 3rd houses. Thus the affairs of both these houses are affected. You will have to make important financial changes in coming months (but take your time and study things carefully). Avoid speculations during the eclipse period. Your spiritual life seems very affected as this eclipse impacts on Neptune. Probably you are changing teachers, practices and the overall regime. Children should avoid risk-taking kinds of activity during the eclipse period. Cars and communication equipment get tested now and it is likely that some of these things will have to be replaced. There are dramas in the lives of siblings, sibling figures and neighbours.

### June

Best Days Overall: 3, 4, 12, 13, 22, 23
Most Stressful Days Overall: 5, 6, 20, 21, 27, 28
Best Days for Love: 8, 9, 17, 18, 27, 28
Best Days for Money: 5, 6, 8, 9, 15, 16, 17, 18, 26, 27, 28
Best Days for Career: 5, 6, 9, 18, 28

Retrograde activity increases further this month. Until the 25th, 40 per cent of the planets are in retrograde motion – a high percentage. The pace of life in the world slows down and this is so on a personal level as well. Patience, patience, patience: this is the watchword. It is a difficult lesson for Aries, but it will do no good to try to circumvent things.

This month the planets are starting to shift to the Western sector of your Horoscope. This is the social sector, the sector of other people. This shift will be more complete next month, but you are starting to feel it now. Over the past five or so months you have created conditions as you wanted them – you have had your way in life. Now, it is time to road test your creation, to enjoy it (if you have built well) or to suffer the discomforts of it (if you have built unwisely). It is more difficult to change things now. You are more dependent on others and their good graces now, and it is best to adapt to things as best you can. Later, towards the end of the year, you will again enter a cycle of independence and will be able to make any changes desired. Now, however, is the time to hone the social skills and gain your way through co-operation with others, rather than on your own. The social side of your nature is being developed this period.

Jupiter is making an important move into your 3rd house on the 11th. For the past year he has been in your money house. By now you have achieved your financial goals and are ready to explore new areas of interest: learning and the expansion of the mind. This is an excellent transit for students, whether pre-college or in college, and there is success in your studies. Learning is easier and more fun. Many of you are taking important tests and exams in coming months and this transit brings good fortune (although you still have to study!). Those of you who are college-bound seem fortunate in this area. (A lunar eclipse on the 4th will create a few bumps on the road, but even the bumps are positive.) Those of you in the workforce will enjoy taking courses, seminars and attending lectures. The mind is hungry and wants to be fed. New and upgraded communication equipment is coming to you, and perhaps a nice car too (looks like an expensive one!).

Siblings and sibling figures in your life are prospering and entering into serious love relationships now.

The lunar eclipse on the 4th will affect you strongly. It not only impacts on the Moon, your family planet, but on your ruling planet Mars as well. So reduce your schedule for a few days before and after the event. Avoid daredevil, risky kinds of activities, and avoid testing the limits of the body – you will have many other opportunities in the next six years to do this in a safer way. This eclipse brings dramas in the lives of family members and perhaps in the physical home as well. If there are hidden flaws there, now is the time you find out about them and take the steps to correct them.

Students can have abrupt changes in school, college or in their choice of studies now. But this will work out in a good way.

**July**

Best Days Overall: 1, 2, 9, 10, 11, 19, 20, 21, 28, 29
Most Stressful Days Overall: 3, 4, 17, 18, 24, 25, 30, 31
Best Days for Love: 5, 6, 15, 24, 25
Best Days for Money: 5, 6, 12, 13, 15, 16, 24, 25
Best Days for Career: 3, 4, 5, 6, 15, 16, 24, 25, 30, 31

Retrograde activity is still strong this month. The players in the drama change, but the overall percentages are still high. Pluto and Neptune are retrograde all month. On the 13th Uranus will start many months retrograde and on the 15th Mercury will also start to move backwards. From the 15th onwards 40 per cent of the planets are in retrograde motion. Like last month, the lesson is patience. Hurry and rush will not achieve anything, and short cuts will actually create more delays. Take your time and be perfect in all that you do – this is the best way to handle these retrogrades.

Mars, the ruler of your Horoscope and a very important planet in your chart, makes dynamic aspects to both Uranus and Pluto from the 15th to the 21st. You will probably feel the effects even earlier and for a few days later, but this is when the aspect is most exact. Don't be afraid, but be more careful and mindful when driving or when handling sharp or dangerous objects or electrical instruments. Avoid confrontations and risky activities. Listen to your body more. If you are working out and you feel a pain, stop. If you are engaged in sports and start to feel a pain, again stop. This is not a time to be testing your body's limits. Your friends should also be more careful then too. Relations with friends seem tense this period: try not to make matters worse. The tension will pass.

In general, health needs more watching this month, especially until the 22nd. Try to rest and relax more. Now is a good time to go on a nice relaxed holiday – and with so many retrogrades, you probably won't be missing much. The heart, which is important all year, is especially important this month and needs more attention. Sunshine and heat-oriented therapies will be powerful. Your health planet goes retrograde on the 15th so avoid making dramatic changes to your diet or health regime then. Study things further.

Health and energy improve dramatically after the 22nd as the Sun moves into Leo. You also enter into one of your yearly personal pleasure peaks. This is a time for enjoying your life. Though your overall energy is not up to its usual standards, there are still nice things happening. Venus is very near to Jupiter this month. The aspect is not exact, but it is still in effect; this brings prosperity and financial opportunity, and love opportunities too.

Like last month, love is close to home. Love happens in educational-type settings – in school, at lectures, seminars, at the library or bookshop.

## August

Best Days Overall: 6, 7, 16, 17, 24, 25
Most Stressful Days Overall: 13, 14, 15, 20, 21, 27, 28
Best Days for Love: 2, 3, 13, 14, 20, 21, 22, 23, 31
Best Days for Money: 1, 2, 3, 8, 9, 10, 11, 12, 13, 14, 20, 21, 22, 23, 29, 30, 31
Best Days for Career: 1, 2, 11, 12, 20, 21, 27, 28, 29, 30

Retrograde activity among the planets is still strong but is less than last month. On the 8th Mercury starts moving forward and the retrograde percentage drops to 30 per cent. With Pluto retrograde, any surgery is better off delayed (unless it is an emergency). Elective surgeries need more research doing now. Friends seem to lack direction this month, they seem 'up in the air' (a trend for the next few months). Purchases of high-tech equipment and software need more homework too; a new and better version could be in the works, or new operating systems could make them obsolete as soon as you buy them. As we mentioned last month, avoid making important changes to the health regime or diet (or job) until after the 8th when Mercury starts moving forward again. Like last month, enhance your health by giving more attention to the heart.

Having said all this, the month ahead seems basically happy – a fun kind of month. (Having fun will tend to improve your health as well.) You are still in a yearly personal pleasure peak until the 23rd. Health and energy are much improved over last month too. Mars is making fabulous aspects to Jupiter from the 8th to the 21st, which is a very happy transit for you. It brings enjoyable travel opportunities. Students hear good news about school or tests. There are religious and philosophical breakthroughs happening and you have good relations with the academics and religious figures in your life. There is luck in speculations and a general feeling of optimism.

Venus, now moving firmly forward since June 27, moves into Cancer on the 8th. This shows many things. There is more socializing with the family and with those who are 'like family' to you. You are probably investing in the home, redecorating it, and spending on objects of beauty for the home. Family and family connections are important financially this period. And family members are playing cupid now. There are a few short-term financial and love upheavals after the 8th but they pass very quickly.

On the 23rd the Sun enters Virgo, your 6th house. This signals a more serious period. You are in the mood for work, and this is a nice transit for job seekers. Job seekers are not just looking for 'a job' – they want work that they will enjoy, and it seems they will be successful. Many of you will sacrifice pay for enjoyable work.

Children seem confused and lacking in direction from the 21st to the 24th – a bit dreamy and other worldly. But this will pass. Avoid speculations that period.

## September

Best Days Overall: 2, 3, 12, 13, 21, 22, 29, 30
Most Stressful Days Overall: 10, 11, 16, 17, 23, 24
Best Days for Love: 1, 12, 16, 17, 21, 22, 29, 30
Best Days for Money: 1, 5, 6, 7, 8, 12, 16, 17, 21, 22, 25, 26, 29, 30
Best Days for Career: 8, 9, 17, 18, 23, 24, 26

Mars entered your 8th house of transformation on the 24th of last month and will be there for the entire month of September. There are many positives to this. It is a great period for detoxing the body and for losing weight (if you need to), and a good period for delving into the deeper things of life – past lives, reincarnation, occult studies, life after death, etc. Whatever your age or stage in life, libido will be stronger than usual, so it is a more sexually active kind of month too.

This celestial position tends to make a person more serious about life; they see beneath the surface of things, beneath all the façades that people put up. There is also more dealing with death, either physically or psychologically. There is a need to come to terms with death, to understand it properly. Mars in the 8th house intensifies the desires of nature. The desires can be good or ill, but they will be more intense than usual. Thus there is a greater likelihood of success. You go after what you want in a very fierce and single-minded way.

Health is good most of the month until the 23rd. After that you need to rest and relax more. Happily you are focused on health this month. You can enhance your health by giving more attention to the heart (all month but especially on the 1st); the small intestine (from the 2nd to the 17th); and the kidneys and hips (from the 17th onwards). Avoid alcohol and other drugs from the 1st to the 3rd. It is always good to keep harmony in your marriage or love relationship, but after the 17th it becomes an actual health issue. If problems arise (God forbid), examine this area and restore harmony as quickly as possible.

The love life has been stressful so far this year, but things are improving this month. Venus moves into Leo on the 7th so there is more joy in the current relationship and in general. You are more fun-loving in love, not as serious and pessimistic as in the past few years. Also, on the 23rd the Sun moves into your 7th house, initiating a yearly love and social peak. Singles have wonderful love opportunities now, but they don't seem like serious ones – more like love affairs. Perhaps they can develop into something in the future, but for now they are just love affairs.

Avoid speculations from the 23rd to the 30th. (You are always a risk taker, but this month even more so than usual.) Children need to be more mindful when driving or handling electrical equipment or dangerous objects. They should avoid risky kinds of activities. If the children are very young, keep dangerous objects away from them. Children are prosperous this month, and there is good financial co-operation between you and them.

## October

Best Days Overall: 1, 9, 10, 11, 18, 19, 27, 28
Most Stressful Days Overall: 7, 8, 14, 15, 20, 21
Best Days for Love: 1, 12, 14, 15, 21
Best Days for Money: 1, 2, 3, 4, 5, 6, 12, 14, 15, 21, 22, 23, 29, 30, 31
Best Days for Career: 7, 16, 20, 21, 24

Retrograde activity increases again this month: Jupiter moves backwards (for the rest of the year) on the 4th, meaning 30 per cent of the planets are retrograde this month from this date onwards. If you are involved in legal issues there are more glitches and complications these days. Take your time with these things. Students should be more cautious about making important educational changes now. Mars in your 9th house from the 7th onwards shows that foreign lands are calling to you; you have the travel itch now, but Jupiter's retrograde motion shows that these trips need carefully planning.

Health still needs watching this month. You probably need more sleep than usual. You can enhance your health by giving more attention to the kidneys and hips (until the 5th); the colon, bladder and sexual organs (from the 5th to the 29th); and the liver and thighs (from the 29th onwards). The good news this month is that after the 23rd, your health and energy will dramatically improve. The short-term planets move away from their stressful aspect and, more importantly, after a two-year stay Saturn leaves his stressful aspect in Libra on the 5th. From that date onwards, for the next two years you will feel like a heavy weight has been lifted off your shoulders. If you have had health problems the past few years you should hear good news about it. Keep in mind though that there are still two long-term planets stressing you. So your health still needs monitoring.

Last month was a sexually active month. Now with Saturn in your 8th house for the next two years, you need to be more 'choosy' about sex. Sexual activity will probably be reduced and there is a need to focus on 'quality' rather than 'quantity'.

Last month was also good for detoxing, slimming down, personal transformation, occult studies and gaining a deeper understanding of death. Likewise this month, especially after the 23rd.

If you are involved in estate, tax or insurance issues, you need more patience. There are many delays here. Things will work out in these affairs, but slowly. Your spouse, partner or current love might feel financially squeezed, but the resources needed are there. He or she just needs to reorganize things a little.

Until the 23rd you are still in a yearly love and social peak. Singles are dating more and have more opportunities for love. For the past two to three years, the social circle was slimmed down, but now it can start to expand again in a healthier way. With Saturn leaving your 7th house this month, a current marriage or love relationship has either healed or broken up. One way or another you are in a new and better social condition.

## November

Best Days Overall: 6, 7, 14, 15, 23, 24
Most Stressful Days Overall: 3, 4, 5, 10, 11, 16, 17
Best Days for Love: 1, 10, 11, 20
Best Days for Money: 1, 2, 11, 19, 20, 26, 27, 28, 29
Best Days for Career: 3, 12, 16, 17, 21

On September 23 the planetary power started to shift from the lower to the upper half of the Horoscope. Last month the shift got stronger, and now 70 per cent (and sometimes 80 per cent) of the planets are now in the upper half – the career half – of your chart. You are in the daytime of your year once again. Enough dreaming and visualizing, now is the time for action towards your career goals, for making your dreams manifest on the physical plane. If you worked properly during your night period, these actions will be very natural and spontaneous. You will expend energy but it won't be stressful: it will just be 'physical follow through' of inner realities. You can safely de-emphasize home and family issues and focus on your career. Mars, the ruler of your Horoscope, enters your 10th house of career on the 17th – reinforcing this message.

Your career planet is now in your 8th house and the ruler of the 8th house is in your house of career (technically these two planets are in 'mutual reception' – they are co-operating with each other – a positive aspect for your career). Your physical body has been detoxing over the past few months (and it's still going on), but your career is also undergoing a detox. You are forced to look at 'near-death' career scenarios and somehow see past them. Many of you are actually changing your career. With the 8th house of transformation so involved in career, activities such as surgery, psychology, money management, insurance, banking and brokerage, and 'intelligence' are favoured. (This is a long-term trend.) There are many shake-ups happening in your company and industry. The old guard is perhaps dying off (not necessarily physically, but perhaps through resignations and reassignments), and the rules of the game are changing.

There are two eclipses this month, which guarantees that the month ahead will be turbulent and full of change. Happily both seem relatively benign to you, but it won't hurt to take things easier at those times.

The solar eclipse of November 13 occurs in your 8th house. Thus your spouse or partner has some financial shake-ups and dramatic changes. Children need to reduce their schedules and avoid risky kinds of activities. They seem emotionally volatile and temperamental that period. Surgery could be recommended to you (or to children) but get a second opinion. There are also encounters with death (generally on a psychological level). Children are redefining their image and personalities now, and for the next six months or so. They might be going through detoxes of the body as well.

The lunar eclipse of the 28th occurs in your 3rd house, and it is the turn of siblings and sibling figures to have financial shake-ups and to make dramatic changes. This eclipse 'sideswipes' Neptune, your spiritual planet, thus you are making important changes in your spiritual regime and practice. There are shake-ups in charitable or spiritual organizations that you are involved with. If there are flaws in the home, now you find out about them and can correct them. Communication equipment will get tested.

## December

Best Days Overall: 3, 4, 12, 13, 20, 21, 22, 30, 31
Most Stressful Days Overall: 1, 2, 8, 9, 14, 15, 28, 29
Best Days for Love: 1, 8, 9, 10, 11, 20, 31
Best Days for Money: 1, 8, 10, 11, 16, 20, 23, 24, 25, 31
Best Days for Career: 1, 10, 14, 15, 18, 28

Between 70 and 80 per cent of the planets are still above the horizon of your chart and the ruler of your Horoscope is still in the 10th house of career until the 26th. On the 21st the Sun also enters your 10th house of career, initiating a yearly career peak. There is a very clear message here: focus on the career and let go of home and family issues. This is a very powerful career month and much progress will be made.

Retrograde activity lessens this month, and the planetary momentum is overwhelmingly forward; by the 13th 90 per cent of the planets are moving forward. Add to this the power of fire in this month's Horoscope and you have a recipe for fast progress and success. The pace of life is quick now – just the way you like it.

Health and energy are even better than last month. Enjoy. With energy all kinds of new opportunities present them- selves to you. Doors that were formerly closed are now open. Things that seemed impossible are now eminently possible. You do need to watch your energy more after the 21st, as the Sun enters Capricorn, but this period will not be nearly as stressful as July or October. Until the 11th you can make your good health even better by giving more attention to the colon, bladder and sexual organs. From the 11th onwards you can enhance health and energy by paying attention to the liver and thighs. Water therapies, soaking in a tub, whirlpool or natural spring, are powerful until the 11th, and detoxes as well. Fire therapies – heat, saunas, steam baths, hot baths and sunshine – are powerful after the 11th.

Your 9th house was powerful last month and is powerful this month too. By the way, the 9th house is considered the most fortunate of houses by the Hindu astrologers. This is a happy-go-lucky kind of period. Students should succeed in their studies. There are religious and philosophical break-throughs for those who are interested in these things (and you will tend to have a greater interest this month). There are happy travel opportunities. But like last month, Jupiter is retrograde, so give these things careful study and analysis. Allow more time for your trips. Plans could change and change again and again.

Finances seem strong this month. Early in the month you have the support of the 'higher ups' in your life – bosses, authority figures, parents, parent figures and elders. Your good professional reputation seems very important. Pay rises and promotions are likely. You seem more cautious in finance until the 16th, which is probably a good thing. After the 16th you spend more freely, but you also earn more. You seem very involved in the earnings of your spouse, partner or current love until that date. Be careful of overspending.

Sexual magnetism seems the most important thing in love until the 16th. Good sex will cover many sins in a relation-ship or marriage. However it is not enough to hold things together. After the 16th there are love opportunities in foreign lands, with foreigners and in religious or educational-type settings. You crave philosophical compatibility in your relationship.

# Taurus

ଧ

---

THE BULL
*Birthdays from*
*21st April to*
*20th May*

---

## Personality Profile

TAURUS AT A GLANCE

*Element* – Earth

*Ruling Planet* – Venus
   *Career Planet* – Uranus
   *Love Planet* – Pluto
   *Money Planet* – Mercury
   *Planet of Health and Work* – Venus
   *Planet of Home and Family Life* – Sun
   *Planet of Spirituality* – Mars
   *Planet of Travel, Education, Religion*
     *and Philosophy* – Saturn

*Colours* – earth tones, green, orange, yellow

*Colours that promote love, romance and social*
   *harmony* – red–violet, violet

*Colours that promote earning power* – yellow,
   yellow–orange

*Gems* – coral, emerald

*Metal* – copper

*Scents* – bitter almond, rose, vanilla, violet

*Quality* – fixed (= stability)

*Quality most needed for balance* – flexibility

*Strongest virtues* – endurance, loyalty, patience, stability, a harmonious disposition

*Deepest needs* – comfort, material ease, wealth

*Characteristics to avoid* – rigidity, stubbornness, tendency to be overly possessive and materialistic

*Signs of greatest overall compatibility* – Virgo, Capricorn

*Signs of greatest overall incompatibility* – Leo, Scorpio, Aquarius

*Sign most helpful to career* – Aquarius

*Sign most helpful for emotional support* – Leo

*Sign most helpful financially* – Gemini

*Sign best for marriage and/or partnerships* – Scorpio

*Sign most helpful for creative projects* – Virgo

*Best Sign to have fun with* – Virgo

*Signs most helpful in spiritual matters* – Aries, Capricorn

*Best day of the week* – Friday

# Understanding a Taurus

Taurus is the most earthy of all the Earth signs. If you under-stand that Earth is more than just a physical element, that it is a psychological attitude as well, you will get a better understanding of the Taurus personality.

A Taurus has all the power of action that an Aries has. But Taurus is not satisfied with action for its own sake. Their actions must be productive, practical and wealth-producing. If Taurus cannot see a practical value in an action they will not bother taking it.

Taurus' forte lies in their power to make real their own or other people's ideas. They are generally not very inventive but they can take another's invention and perfect it, making it more practical and useful. The same is true for all projects. Taurus is not especially keen on starting new projects, but once they get involved they bring things to completion. Taurus carries everything through. They are finishers and will go the distance, so long as no unavoidable calamity intervenes.

Many people find Taurus too stubborn, conservative, fixed and immovable. This is understandable, because Taurus dislikes change – in the environment or in their routine. They even dislike changing their minds! On the other hand, this is their virtue. It is not good for a wheel's axle to waver. The axle must be fixed, stable and unmov-able. Taurus is the axle of society and the heavens. Without their stability and so-called stubbornness, the wheels of the world (and especially the wheels of commerce) would not turn.

Taurus loves routine. A routine, if it is good, has many virtues. It is a fixed – and, ideally, perfect – way of taking care of things. Mistakes can happen when spontaneity comes into the equation, and mistakes cause discomfort and uneasiness – something almost unacceptable to a Taurus. Meddling with Taurus' comfort and security is a sure way to irritate and anger them.

While an Aries loves speed, a Taurus likes things slow. They are slow thinkers – but do not make the mistake of assuming they lack intelligence. On the contrary, Taurus people are very intelligent. It is just that they like to chew on ideas, to deliberate and weigh them up. Only after due deliberation is an idea accepted or a decision taken. Taurus is slow to anger – but once aroused, take care!

## Finance

Taurus is very money-conscious. Wealth is more important to them than to many other signs. Wealth to a Taurus means comfort and security. Wealth means stability. Where some zodiac signs feel that they are spiritually rich if they have ideas, talents or skills, Taurus only feels wealth when they can see and touch it. Taurus' way of thinking is, 'What good is a talent if it has not been translated into a home, furniture, car and holidays?'

These are all reasons why Taurus excels in estate agency and agricultural industries. Usually a Taurus will end up owning land. They love to feel their connection to the Earth. Material wealth began with agriculture, the tilling of the soil. Owning a piece of land was humanity's earliest form of wealth: Taurus still feels that primeval connection.

It is in the pursuit of wealth that Taurus develops intellectual and communication ability. Also, in this pursuit Taurus is forced to develop some flexibility. It is in the quest for wealth that they learn the practical value of the intellect and come to admire it. If it were not for the search for wealth and material things, Taurus people might not try to reach a higher intellect.

Some Taurus people are 'born lucky' – the type who win any gamble or speculation. This luck is due to other factors in their horoscope; it is not part of their essential nature. By nature they are not gamblers. They are hard workers and like to earn what they get. Taurus' innate conservatism makes them abhor unnecessary risks in finance and in other areas of their lives.

## Career and Public Image

Being essentially down-to-earth people, simple and uncom-
plicated, Taurus tends to look up to those who are original,
unconventional and inventive. Taurus people like their
bosses to be creative and original – since they themselves are
content to perfect their superiors' brainwaves. They admire
people who have a wider social or political consciousness
and they feel that someday (when they have all the comfort
and security they need) they too would like to be involved
in these big issues.

In business affairs Taurus can be very shrewd – and that
makes them valuable to their employers. They are never
lazy; they enjoy working and getting good results. Taurus
does not like taking unnecessary risks and they do well in
positions of authority, which makes them good managers
and supervisors. Their managerial skills are reinforced by
their natural talents for organization and handling details,
their patience and thoroughness. As mentioned, through
their connection with the earth, Taurus people also do well
in farming and agriculture.

In general a Taurus will choose money and earning power
over public esteem and prestige. A position that pays more –
though it has less prestige – is preferred to a position with a
lot of prestige but lower earnings. Many other signs do not
feel this way, but a Taurus does, especially if there is nothing
in his or her personal birth chart that modifies this. Taurus
will pursue glory and prestige only if it can be shown that
these things have a direct and immediate impact on their
wallet.

## Love and Relationships

In love, the Taurus-born likes to have and to hold. They are
the marrying kind. They like commitment and they like the
terms of a relationship to be clearly defined. More importantly, Taurus likes to be faithful to one lover, and they expect
that lover to reciprocate this fidelity. When this doesn't

happen, their whole world comes crashing down. When they are in love Taurus people are loyal, but they are also very possessive. They are capable of great fits of jealousy if they are hurt in love.

Taurus is satisfied with the simple things in a relationship. If you are involved romantically with a Taurus there is no need for lavish entertainments and constant courtship. Give them enough love, food and comfortable shelter and they will be quite content to stay home and enjoy your company. They will be loyal to you for life. Make a Taurus feel comfortable and – above all – secure in the relationship, and you will rarely have a problem.

In love, Taurus can sometimes make the mistake of trying to control their partners, which can cause great pain on both sides. The reasoning behind their actions is basically simple: Taurus people feel a sense of ownership over their partners and will want to make changes that will increase their own general comfort and security. This attitude is OK when it comes to inanimate, material things – but is dangerous when applied to people. Taurus needs to be careful and attentive to this possible trait within themselves.

## Home and Domestic Life

Home and family are vitally important to Taurus. They like children. They also like a comfortable and perhaps glamorous home – something they can show off. They tend to buy heavy, ponderous furniture – usually of the best quality. This is because Taurus likes a feeling of substance in their environment. Their house is not only their home but their place of creativity and entertainment. The Taurus' home tends to be truly their castle. If they could choose, Taurus people would prefer living in the countryside to being city-dwellers. If they cannot do so during their working lives, many Taurus individuals like to holiday in or even retire to the country, away from the city and closer to the land.

At home a Taurus is like a country squire – lord (or lady) of the manor. They love to entertain lavishly, to make others feel secure in their home and to encourage others to derive the same sense of satisfaction as they do from it. If you are invited for dinner at the home of a Taurus you can expect the best food and best entertainment. Be prepared for a tour of the house and expect to see your Taurus friend exhibit a lot of pride and satisfaction in his or her possessions.

Taurus people like children but they are usually strict with them. The reason for this is they tend to treat their children – as they do most things in life – as their possessions. The positive side to this is that their children will be well cared for and well supervised. They will get every material thing they need to grow up properly. On the down side, Taurus can get too repressive with their children. If a child dares to upset the daily routine – which Taurus loves to follow – he or she will have a problem with a Taurus parent.

# Horoscope for 2012

## Major Trends

You have been idealistic about your career for many years now, and now that your career planet is in your spiritual 12th house (it entered last year) this trend continues and will go on for many more years. It's not enough for you to just make money and achieve status; you need to do this in a spiritual, socially conscious way. This is the challenge these days.

For the past two years you have been very health conscious. Daily disciplined regimes have been more interesting. Probably you are watching the diet more but it is a struggle. Later in the year it will get easier. The focus on health continues in the year ahead.

Ever since Uranus moved into Aries last year, and into a square aspect with your love planet Pluto, love has been challenging and highly unstable. Instability is perhaps the hardest thing for a Taurus to handle. They need – yearn for – stability, security and an established routine. The love life and marriage has been just the opposite. Love continues getting tested in the year ahead, especially after October 5.

When Jupiter entered your sign in the latter half of 2011, you entered a period of prosperity and this continues in the year ahead. Jupiter will be in your sign until June 11, and then moves into your money house. So, you are living the good life, travelling and enjoying all the pleasures of the body. Also you have the wherewithal to indulge these things.

Neptune makes a move this year (this only happens every 14 or so years) from your 10th house to your 11th house. Thus you are making friends with spiritual types these days. Many of you are joining spiritual organizations and groups or becoming more involved with them than usual. This is a long term trend now.

Your areas of greatest interest this year are the body, image and personal pleasure (until June 11); finance (from June 11 onwards); children and creativity (from January 1 until July 3); health and work (until October 5); love, romance and social activities (after October 5); religion, philosophy, theology, foreign travel and higher education; friends, groups and group activities (from February 3 onwards); and spirituality.

Your paths of greatest fulfilment this year are the body, image and personal pleasure (until June 11); finance (from June 11 onwards); sex, personal transformation, personal reinvention and occult studies (until August 30); and love, romance and social activities (from August 30 onwards).

## Health

*(Please note that this is an astrological perspective on health and not a medical one. In days of yore there was no difference, these perspectives were identical. But these days there could be quite a difference. For a medical perspective, please consult your doctor or health practitioner.)*

Health should be good this year, Taurus. All the major long-term planets are either in a good aspect or leaving you alone. So energy and vitality are basically good. Certainly, over the course of a year there will be periods where your health is less easy than usual, perhaps even stressful, but these things are caused by the planetary transits; they are temporary and not trends for the year ahead. When the stressful transits pass, your natural good health returns. These stressful periods will be from January 20 to February 18; July 22 to August 22; and October 23 to November 21. These are the times to rest and relax more and to pace yourself better.

Your 6th house of health is strong this year, showing a great focus on health. But since health is basically good, I would say that your problem could be an 'over focus' or a tendency to magnify little things into big things – bigger than they actually are.

Good though the health outlook is, you can make it even better. Give more attention to the following areas: the neck and throat (regular neck massage, especially the back of the neck, will be good to release tension there); the kidneys and hips (regular hip massage will be powerful); the gall bladder; and the spine, knees, teeth, bones, skin and overall skeletal alignment (regular visits to a chiropractor or osteopath would be a good idea). Give the skin more protection when you are out in the sun. Therapies such as the Alexander Technique or Feldenkrais would be good to help your posture, and I also like craniosacral therapy, which work with the bones in the neck as well as the head. Give the knees more support when exercising too. All these areas are the most vulnerable ones in the year ahead, and any problems would most likely begin there. So keeping them healthy and fit is sound preventive medicine.

Venus, your health planet, is a very fast-moving planet, and over the course of the year she moves through all the signs and houses of your Horoscope. So there are many short-term health trends that are best covered in the monthly reports.

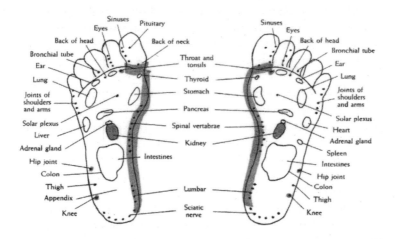

## Reflexology

*Try to massage the whole foot on a regular basis, but pay extra attention to the points highlighted on the chart. When you massage, be aware of 'sore spots', as these need special attention. It's also a good idea to massage the ankles and top side of the feet (see below).*

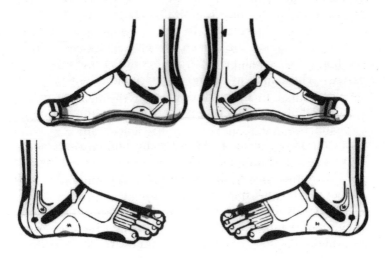

Saturn will move into Scorpio on October 5, which will be a stressful aspect for you, so overall energy will not be up to its usual standards. However, Saturn by itself is not enough to cause major problems. It is when many long-term planets gang up on you that we get concerned. Still, it is an issue. You have to become more selective and choosy as to how you use your energy; you can't do everything and priorities have to be set.

## Home and Family

Your 4th house of home and family is not a 'house of power' this year. This means the trend is to the status quo. You have more latitude and freedom here but no special desire to make changes. You are more or less content with things the way they are.

Your family planet, the Sun, gets eclipsed twice every year and this year is no different. These eclipses tend to bring out problems in the home or with the family (the dirty laundry, the grudges and dissatisfactions) and thus forces correction. This year the eclipses occur on May 20 and November 13 and we will discuss them in the monthly reports.

Your family planet will be travelling with Jupiter from May 6 to May 14, which is basically a happy aspect. You are likely to have opportunities to move (a happy move), reno-vate, enlarge or sell the home or receive expensive items for the home. There will be opportunities in the real estate field as well. The family as a whole (and especially a parent or parent figure) prospers during that period. Your family planet will also make nice aspects to Jupiter from October 3 to October 11.

If you are planning to beautify the home, to repaint or make cosmetic kinds of changes or to buy objects of beauty for the home, July 22 to August 22 and September 6 to October 5 are good times for this.

Siblings or sibling figures in your life may want to move – they seem cramped in their present home. However, this is not advisable this year, although after October 5 is better

than before that date. They need to make better use of the
space that they have: perhaps a renovation would be better
than a move. Children in your life have a status quo kind
of year. Like you they seem more or less content with the
home as it is. Grandchildren (if you have them) are likely to
have multiple moves in the year ahead.

One of your parents or parent figures seems nomadic this
year, moving around a lot. He or she could also be having
surgery or 'near-death' kind of experience.

## Finance and Career

As we mentioned, this is a prosperous year. You catch the
lucky financial breaks. There is luck in speculations (and
speculations not only happen at the casino or bingo hall –
business people make speculations every day). There is
travel, nice clothing and accessories, good foods, good wines,
good restaurants, good personal pleasure. The carnal fantasies get fulfilled in happy ways. Your only concern (and
this is more from a health perspective) is in overdoing it.
Keeping your weight down can be a problem.

Jupiter is the ruler of your 8th house of inheritance. Thus,
there is some sort of inheritance this year. Hopefully no one
need actually die – instead you can be named in someone's
will or be called on to be an executor or trustee. Sometimes
people receive trust funds under this kind of aspect too. If
you have insurance or royalty claims, there is good fortune.

Those of you who are looking for outside investors also
have good fortune. There is much talk about 'tight credit' in
the world these days, but for you this is not so. You personally have good access to outside money.

On June 11 Jupiter will move into your money house and
this more or less reinforces what we have been saying. With
Jupiter in your money house the assets you already own
tend to increase in value. Often people are disappointed
with a Jupiter transit. Though it always brings increase,
sometimes the expectations are unrealistic. If someone is
praying for a million pounds and Jupiter brings an increase

of only £10,000, they might dismiss the transit. The problem isn't with Jupiter but with unrealistic expectations. Regardless of your expectations you should finish the year with greater net worth than when you began.

As we see, finance is not the problem this year: it is career that seems more challenging. Your career planet Uranus is in stressful aspect with Pluto and this signifies career changes – a move to another company, another industry, or even a change of career. Friends, your social circle in general, are not supportive of your career goals this year. It will take more work to get them on board and to get them to co-operate. It is best to rely on your own merits rather than on who you know.

With your career planet in the sign of Aries since last year, you want a more independent kind of career – to be in charge of your own destiny. This entails some risk and most likely your spouse or current love will not be in favour of this. Also, as we mentioned, you want a career that is more meaningful, that helps humanity as a whole and is more socially conscious. Many of you have opted for altruistic careers in recent years and this could still happen now. But even in a worldly type of career, you can enhance and further it by getting involved in charity work or good causes.

### Love and Social Life

As we mentioned, Uranus' move into Aries has been putting stress on the current marriage or love relationship. Last year you felt the beginnings of it, and this year the testing of the marriage or current relationship becomes even stronger. Divorces or breakups this year wouldn't be a surprise. However, these aspects don't mean that you 'must' divorce. Only that this is the tendency. If there is real love between you the relationship can survive, but it will take a lot of effort and dedication to make it work.

Part of the problem seems to be a conflict between your spouse or current love and a parent or parent figure. This seems nasty. Another aspect of the problem could be career issues – the demands of your career pull you away or distract you from your relationship. In the case of those who are not married, you could be transferred to another city, even to another country, far away from your beloved. This too puts stress on the relationship.

Towards the end of the year Saturn will move into your 7th house of love and marriage, which will further strain the marriage. The cosmos is 'road testing' the relationship, subjecting it to extra kinds of stress much in the way that a car is road tested. The underlying sturdiness of the relationship will be revealed through these means, and any flaws will easily be seen and can be corrected. However, if it is a bad relationship the 'road testing' will be too much for it and it will dissolve. (If your relationship survives the next two years, it can probably survive anything.)

With volatile Uranus squaring your love planet all year, the mood changes in love are swift and bewildering. You and your partner can be madly in love one moment and at each other's throats the next. Even in established relationships, you don't know where you stand from moment to moment. It is as if every moment is a new courtship. Taurus people more than most are uncomfortable with this. They like their security, and dealing with instability – sudden change – is one of their biggest challenges.

Those working on the second marriage could reunite with their former spouse or get together with someone who is very much like him or her. It seems to me that there is a spiritual agenda behind this: you get to resolve old issues that couldn't be resolved in any other way. Those working on the third marriage have opportunities with spiritual kinds of people and in spiritual locales and settings.

Singles should probably not marry this year. Things are too unstable, and especially so after October 5. Singles will probably date less after this date too. There is a need to focus more on quality that quantity. Fewer, more meaningful dates, with meaningful people, are preferable to many mediocre dates. Socializing in general is reduced after

October 5 and for the same rationale – to focus on quality, not quantity.

## Self-improvement

As we mentioned, Uranus, your career planet, made a major move last year into your 12th house of spirituality, bringing a need for a career that is meaningful for the world at large and not just for yourself. You want a career that doesn't violate your spiritual principles and ideals, and instead is in harmony with them. No matter how much money and status a company is offering, it is doubtful that you could be happy there (or successful) if there is a violation of these principles.

Different people are at different stages of the spiritual journey. Those just setting out will probably try to incorporate both a worldly career and the pursuit of spiritual goals. Sometimes this is done by being involved in charities or altruistic kinds of causes while the individual pursues their worldly career. Sometimes they choose a more spiritual career, i.e. working for a non-profit organization or being an executive in a charity on a professional level. I know people with these aspects who have opened up profitable yoga and tai chi studios, and some have entered the ministry. But for those of you more advanced on the path, the message here is very clear. Your spiritual practice – your path – is of itself the most important thing and is your mission right now. Yes, these seemingly isolated spiritual disciplines (carried out far from the crowd) do change the world. The world is changed heart by heart, mind by mind, often in quiet and solitude. This is where real change happens. Politicians – people of power and prestige – never create the change; they merely ratify what has already occurred. So, your spiritual practice is of itself a valid career and your mission over the next six or seven years.

Uranus in your 12th house also has other meanings. It is the planet of science and system. Thus the message here is that you need a spiritual path that is scientific and rational.

Yes, the Divine is above all mind and all logic. But the path and the practice have a science to them and this kind of approach seems good for you. The spiritual side of astrology also seems good these days. Neptune, the most spiritual of all the planets, in your 11th house of astrology and science reinforces what we are saying here.

# Month-by-month Forecasts

## January

Best Days Overall: 3, 4, 12, 13, 21, 22, 30, 31
Most Stressful Days Overall: 10, 11, 17, 18, 23, 24
Best Days for Love: 3, 6, 7, 12, 17, 18, 19, 21, 27, 28, 30
Best Days for Money: 1, 2, 3, 4, 5, 6, 7, 12, 21, 22, 30
Best Days for Career: 1, 10, 19, 23, 24, 28

Career is the main headline of the month ahead. You begin the year with 60 per cent (and sometimes 70 per cent) of the planets above the horizon. Your 10th house of career is powerful all month, while your 4th house of home and family is empty (only the Moon will visit there, on the 8th and 9th). Furthermore, on the 20th you enter a yearly career peak. So, career ambitions are strong; you can safely downplay home and family issues in favour of your work. The good news is that the family itself, far from being resentful, seems supportive. Your family as a whole is more ambitious as well, and you and your family achieve much career progress this month. Only your spouse or current love seems non-supportive – perhaps even antagonistic – to career goals. Pursuing your career path seems to involve some social sacrifice this period (and in the year ahead as well).

The new Moon of the 23rd also occurs in your career house. Thus many career dilemmas will get clarified as the month progresses. Relations with bosses, elders and parents (or parent figures) will also become clearer.

Health is good this month, but rest and relax more after the 20th. You can enhance your health and energy through ankle and calf massage until the 24th and through foot massage afterwards. The good news is that health is high on your agenda until that date and you are paying attention to it. It seems that you understand that without good health career progress is not only more difficult but meaningless as well. Success is wonderful, but without health to enjoy it, there is no real satisfaction.

Venus travels with Neptune from the 12th to the 15th. The dream life will be active and you are likely to have spiritual experiences. Avoid dreaminess while driving or when working on the physical plane, however. Stay in your body. Spiritual healing will be powerful this period, and after the 24th as well.

Your finances are good this month, as they will be through until June 11. There is some financial disagreement with your spouse, partner or current love (perhaps business partners as well), but this should straighten itself out after the 24th. Your partner is also doing well, especially until the 24th. Afterwards he or she needs to work harder to achieve financial goals.

Love is being tested all year. It is challenging. However things seem easier after the 24th than before.

### February

Best Days Overall: 1, 9, 10, 17, 18, 27, 28
Most Stressful Days Overall: 7, 8, 13, 14, 19, 20
Best Days for Love: 5, 6, 9, 13, 14, 15, 17, 18, 24, 25, 27
Best Days for Money: 1, 2, 3, 9, 11, 12, 17, 22, 23, 27, 28, 29
Best Days for Career: 7, 15, 19, 20, 24

On January 20 the Sun crossed over from the Western to the Eastern sector of your Horoscope. On January 27 Mercury followed suit, and thus there is a shift in the planetary power. The Eastern sector of the self (self-interest and

personal independence) is now more dominant than the
Western sector (the area of others, social interests and the
needs of others). This represents a psychological shift in you
as well. You are entering a period of greater independence.
You have more control over your destiny for the next six or
so months. If conditions are irksome you have greater power
to change them. You need not put up with them or adapt to
them. Other people are always important, but your happiness doesn't really depend on them now – it's up to you. So
be nice to others, but please yourself. If you are happy
others will be happy.

Most of the planets are still above the horizon of your
chart, and you are still in a yearly career peak. Continue to
focus on the career. Outer achievement is alluring now, and
your drive here tends to produce success.

Continue to rest and relax more until the 19th. After that
your health and energy return to their normal good levels.
You can enhance your health by giving more attention to
the feet (until the 8th) and to the head, face and scalp afterwards. Face and scalp massage will do wonders for you.
From the 8th to the 17th Venus makes some very dynamic
aspects with Uranus and Pluto. Be more mindful when driving. Avoid temper tantrums and confrontations, and avoid
high risk activities. Though this transit brings career success
and opportunity, it can also bring down the wrath of others,
especially the spouse or current love. You seem in a more
rebellious kind of mood during this period, and more willing
to take risks with your body.

Love is stormy from the 8th to the 17th. Weak relationships can break up. You need more patience with your
current love and with friends in general.

Finances are good. Until the 14th, money comes from
your career, thanks to your good reputation or from pay
rises. Parents or parent figures (also bosses) are financially
supportive. After the 14th, friends and social connections
seem important financially. Follow your financial intuition
after the 14th. Remember to keep up to date with the latest
technology, too.

**March**

> Best Days Overall: 7, 8, 15, 16, 25, 26
> Most Stressful Days Overall: 5, 6, 11, 12, 18, 19
> Best Days for Love: 7, 11, 12, 15, 16, 25, 26
> Best Days for Money: 1, 2, 5, 7, 13, 15, 16, 25, 26, 27, 28, 29, 31
> Best Days for Career: 5, 13, 18, 19, 22

The planetary momentum has been overwhelmingly forward for the past few months, so progress has been rapid. Things got done quickly (and we rarely appreciate this until we experience glitches). In January all the planets were in forward motion until the 24th. In February 90 per cent of the planets were forward until the 6th, and 80 per cent of them then after. This month, 80 per cent are moving forward until the 11th, and 70 per cent thereafter. Slowly but surely retrograde activity has been increasing. It is still at tolerable levels, but things are slowing down. Taureans tend to be patient people so this is nothing you can't handle. You just need to be more perfect in all that you do: spend more time in the beginning and get things right, and this will save a lot of heartache and delays later on.

Mars has been retrograde since January 24. He is your spiritual planet. His retrograde motion at this time is very significant as this is a highly spiritual month. Your spiritual 12th house is the strongest in the Horoscope. Thus you are experiencing many spiritual/supernatural phenomena now – prophetic and revelatory dreams, synchronistic kinds of experiences, unexplainable coincidences and enhanced extrasensory perception. But Mars retrograde suggests that you need to verify your intuition and spiritual messages. They might not mean what you think. Also it is not advisable now to make dramatic changes to your spiritual practice. Wait until Mars goes forward next month (April 11).

Mercury goes retrograde on the 12th until the end of the month. So many problems in life – problems with friends, your spouse and the children – are due to miscommunication and misunderstanding. People do not understand you properly and vice versa. Now with your communication planet going retrograde, you need to be even more careful. A little more care in the beginning will save many a hurt feeling and emotional explosion later on. This is especially so when communicating with children or youngsters in your life. Though you are lucky in financial matters this year, with Mercury being your money planet this period is not especially great for speculations.

The retrograde of Saturn (which began on February 7) suggests more caution in foreign travel. It is best to avoid it if possible, but if you must travel allow more time and insure your tickets. Protect yourself. Students need to be more cautious about making important educational changes now. Study things further.

Venus, the ruler of your Horoscope, crosses the Ascendant on the 5th, heralding a happy transit. You look great and attract the opposite sex. You have a great sense of style and this is a good time to purchase clothing, accessories or objects of beauty. Venus travels with Jupiter from the 11th to the 14th and this brings luck in speculations, opportunities to travel, and financial abundance.

## April

Best Days Overall: 4, 12, 13, 21, 22
Most Stressful Days Overall: 1, 2, 8, 14, 15, 29, 30
Best Days for Love: 4, 5, 8, 12, 14, 15, 21, 24, 25
Best Days for Money: 4, 8, 9, 12, 13, 17, 18, 21, 22, 24, 25, 29, 30
Best Days for Career: 1, 9, 10, 14, 15, 18, 19, 29

Love is being tested all year, and Pluto's retrograde (which begins on the 10th and goes on for many months) complicates things further. Avoid making important love decisions one way or another. Neither marriage nor divorce is advisable now (though you could be sorely tempted). You and your current love need more breathing space. You both need time to reflect. In the meantime you can enjoy your life. The same holds true for business partnerships too. On the 20th the Sun crosses your Ascendant and enters your 1st house, initiating a yearly personal pleasure peak. (You will have another one in a few months.)

The body and the spirit are both important this month. Though these interests seem opposite they are very related. Physical well being and harmony are the natural side effects of a healthy spiritual life. So, with your 12th house powerful until the 20th, you are getting the spiritual life in order. (Mars, your spiritual planet, starts to move forward on the 11th helping matters). Spiritual breakthroughs lead to 'physical and material' breakthroughs. The natural consequence of this is a period of personal pleasure that begins on the 20th.

You look great this month. You dress wonderfully. The image shines. In spite of relationship difficulties, you are attracting the opposite sex. Self-esteem and self-confidence are good.

Health is excellent now. You have all the energy you need to achieve any goal you set for yourself. You can (and probably are) having things your way. You are in the maximum period of personal independence from the 20th. Don't wait around for others to make you happy; take matters in your own hands and create it for yourself.

You can enhance your already good health by giving more attention to the neck and throat (until the 3rd – neck massage is wonderful) and to the lungs, respiratory system, arms and shoulders from the 3rd onwards. Breathing exercises are beneficial now. You seem more sensitive to impurities in the air. If you feel under the weather, get out in the fresh air and breathe deeply for an hour or so.

Venus moving into your money house on the 3rd shows a strong personal focus on finance (always a strong interest, but now even more so). It shows earnings through work: job-seekers should have good fortune. Also it shows that your personal appearance, your overall demeanour, is unusually important in earnings. Probably you are spending more on yourself and your image.

**May**

   Best Days Overall: 1, 2, 9, 10, 18, 19, 20, 28, 29
   Most Stressful Days Overall: 5, 6, 11, 12, 26, 27
   Best Days for Love: 1, 2, 3, 4, 5, 6, 9, 10, 11, 12, 19, 20, 21, 22, 28, 29, 30, 31
   Best Days for Money: 2, 8, 10, 18, 19, 20, 21, 22, 28, 29
   Best Days for Career: 7, 11, 12, 16, 26

Retrograde activity increases this month. The major development is Venus turning retrograde on the 5th. The retrograde of Venus is strong on a personal level – Venus is both ruler of your Horoscope and the ruler of the 6th house.

You are very independent these days. You have a lot of personal power and can have things your way. But with Venus retrograde you are not really sure what 'your way' is. This makes it more problematic to implement personal change. However, this is a time to study these things; research them more, review your personal life and conditions and see where improvements can be made. The same holds true for job or health regime changes. This is a time for review, not for action.

The retrograde of Venus, the generic planet of love, complicates your love life even further. Now, both the love planets in your Horoscope are retrograde at the same time. Whatever we said last month is now reinforced.

Last month the Sun entered your 1st house initiating a yearly personal pleasure peak. You've been living the good life for almost a year and this month even more so. All your carnal fantasies are getting fulfilled. The only problem now is overdoing things. Your weight might be a problem.

Family members, especially a parent or parent figure, seem unusually devoted to you this month. They are supportive but perhaps over-controlling. The Sun will travel with Jupiter from the 11th to the 14th forming a happy transit. Family members are prospering. A parent or parent figure has a financial windfall or opportunity; your partner likewise. You have opportunities to move, to buy or sell a home. There is good fortune with insurance claims. This is a good period to pay off or refinance debt.

There is a solar eclipse in your money house on the 20th. This shows important and long-term financial changes happening. It seems to me that these changes are good, although they are disruptive. The changes and disruptions should increase prosperity over the long term. This eclipse happens as the Sun enters your money house, initiating a yearly financial peak – a period of peak earnings. Family, real estate and parent figures seem very involved and supportive of the financial life now.

On the 9th, Mercury moves into your sign and shifts the balance of the entire Horoscope. Now, the bottom half of the chart is stronger than the top. Career goals have more or less been attained in the short term and now it is time to focus more on the home and family. The next five or six months is the time for setting up the conditions – internal and external – for future career success. These conditions include a stable home base, good family relations and the feeling of emotional harmony.

## June

Best Days Overall: 5, 6, 15, 16, 24, 25
Most Stressful Days Overall: 1, 2, 8, 9, 22, 23, 29, 30
Best Days for Love: 1, 2, 5, 8, 9, 15, 17, 18, 24, 27, 28, 29, 30
Best Days for Money: 1, 5, 6, 10, 17, 18, 20, 21, 26, 27
Best Days for Career: 3, 8, 9, 12, 22

The month ahead is full of important changes. Jupiter, the planet of abundance, will move into your money house on the 11th extending the prosperity you've been having even further. A lunar eclipse on the 4th occurs in your 8th house and impacts on the finances of your spouse, partner or current love as well. He or she is forced to make important financial changes and shifts. This eclipse (as well as last month's solar eclipse) affects the family and home. Probably there is some kind of family crisis. Perhaps there are repairs needed in the home. Emotions are more volatile now and there are dramas in the lives of parents or parent figures. Since the Moon, the eclipsed planet, rules your 3rd house, there are likely to be dramas in the lives of siblings and neighbours too. Cars and communication equipment get tested and often need replacement.

The 8th house is the house of death and resurrection – so near-death kinds of experiences, and encounters with death, could happen now too (most likely on the psychological level). Reduce your schedule for this period. This eclipse impacts strongly on Mars, reinforcing what we say here. Do whatever needs to be done, but avoid risk-taking activities that aren't necessary. Mars is your spiritual planet so there are important spiritual changes happening now – changes in the regime, practice and attitudes. Now that Mars is moving forward it is safe to make them. There may be shake-ups in spiritual or charitable organizations that you are involved with too.

Though marriages and serious relationships are still undergoing severe testing, on the financial level there is co-operation and mutual support. One thing has nothing to do with the other. You are involved in your spouse's or partner's finances and vice versa. You have good access to outside money now. If you have ideas and need investors, it seems easy to attract them. They are there. If you need to borrow, this seems easy too. There is good fortune with insurance, estate and tax issues. Perhaps you are paying more tax these days, but this means that you are earning more too. There are financial opportunities through creative kinds of financing.

Your health is still good. You can enhance it further by giving more attention to the lungs, respiratory system, arms and shoulders. Breathing exercises are powerful now.

The Sun makes a dynamic transit from the 28th to the 30th. Family members need to avoid risky, daredevil-type activities. Clear the home of dangerous objects and keep them out of the reach of children. The emotional life is more volatile, and this can lead to accidents, so it's important to stay calm under all provocations – take a few deep breaths when you feel you're about to 'lose it'.

### July

Best Days Overall: 3, 4, 12, 13, 22, 23, 30, 31
Most Stressful Days Overall: 5, 6, 19, 20, 21, 26, 27
Best Days for Love: 5, 6, 15, 24, 25, 26, 27
Best Days for Money: 1, 2, 5, 6, 9, 10, 11, 15, 16, 19, 20, 21, 24, 25, 28, 29
Best Days for Career: 1, 5, 6, 9, 19, 20, 28

Retrograde activity increases this month. Neptune started to move backwards last month. Pluto has been retrograde since April 10. Uranus starts going backwards on the 13th and Mercury on the 15th. From the 15th onwards 40 per cent of the planets are in retrograde motion, the highest percentage so far this year. The pace of life – the pace of events – starts to slow down.

The retrograde of Uranus shows that your career is slowing a bit, which is perhaps a good thing now. Your major focus now is on home and family, and career can be downplayed. Avoid, where possible, making important career decisions at this time.

On June 21, the Sun crossed from the Eastern sector of your Horoscope to the Western sector, and now the Western social sector of your chart is more powerful. You are in a 'paying karma' phase of the year – you have to live with your previous creations, it is not so easy to change them now. If you created well you are enjoying your 'good karma'. If you created amiss, you are paying the price now. You need to adapt to conditions as best you can and make corrections when the next 'independent' cycle begins.

When the Western half of the Horoscope is strong, personal initiative (even personal ability) is not that important. It is the social skills that matter. Attainment happens by the good graces of others. Your 'people skills' are what bring success.

Health is basically good, but after the 22nd you need to rest and relax more. You can enhance your health this month by paying more attention to the heart, the lungs, respiratory systems, arms and shoulders. (Regular shoulder massage will be wonderful.) Good mental health also seems important this month. Avoid thinking or talking too much (big wasters of energy!). Keep your speech positive and constructive and strive for intellectual purity.

Mars enters your 6th house on the 4th and stays there all month. Thus vigorous physical exercise and good muscle tone are important these days. And since Mars is your spiritual planet, spiritual types of exercise seem good too – things like yoga, tai chi or chi qong. You will also get good results from spiritual healing techniques such as prayer, meditation, the laying on of hands and manipulation of subtle energies.

Mars makes a very dynamic transit from the 15th to the 21st: it opposes Uranus and squares Pluto. Everyone needs to be more careful and mindful on the physical plane. Avoid confrontations or risky kinds of activities. Daredevil stunts are to be avoided like the plague. Drive more mindfully, keeping alert and paying full attention.

## August

Best Days Overall: 8, 9, 10, 18, 19, 27, 28
Most Stressful Days Overall: 1, 2, 16, 17, 22, 23, 29, 31
Best Days for Love: 2, 3, 8, 13, 14, 18, 22, 23, 27, 31
Best Days for Money: 1, 2, 6, 7, 11, 12, 16, 17, 20, 21, 24, 25, 29, 30
Best Days for Career: 1, 2, 6, 16, 24, 29, 30

Continue to rest and relax more until the 23rd. Enhance the health in the ways mentioned last month. After the 8th you can also enhance your health by paying more attention to the stomach and breasts. You need to pay more attention to the diet then too.

Last month Mars was making dynamic aspects with Uranus and Pluto. This month, from the 14th to the 17th Venus makes a similar aspect with these planets. Keep in mind our discussion of last month. Take things nice and easy. Slow down and be mindful on the physical plane. This period also seems to test your marriage or current relationship in a very severe way. Emotions are high, so do your best to stay calm and to avoid making things worse. By the 17th the worst of this should be over with. Career changes could also happen under this transit.

When the Sun enters Virgo on the 23rd, you enter another yearly personal pleasure peak. Enjoy. Personal creativity will be a lot stronger than usual. You are more involved with children and health and vitality will also start improving.

Your financial planet, Mercury, retrograde since the 15th of last month, goes forward on the 8th. Avoid major purchases or financial decisions before this date. The financial life – investments and changes – should be being reviewed now. If you do this properly you will be in a good position on the 8th when Mercury starts moving forward. You seem to be spending more on the home and family this period. Family support will tend to be good, and family connections also seem important financially.

The Sun in your 4th house (a powerful position – this is his own sign and house) shows that this is a month for psychological-type breakthroughs. Emotional patterns or moods that have been holding you back are revealed so that you can correct them. You have greater insight into moods and feelings this month, and this helps you in your dealings with family members.

Mars moves into your 7th house on the 24th. This will further test marriages and current relationships. You can make things easier by avoiding power struggles with your partner as much as possible.

### September

Best Days Overall: 5, 6, 14, 15, 23, 24
Most Stressful Days Overall: 12, 13, 19, 25, 26,
Best Days for Love: 1, 5, 12, 14, 18, 19, 21, 22, 23, 29,
    30
Best Days for Money: 4, 5, 7, 8, 15, 16, 17, 25, 26
Best Days for Career: 2, 12, 20, 21, 25, 26, 29

Retrograde activity is reducing this month, and after the 18th only 20 per cent of the planets will be moving backwards. Glitches and complications are slowly but surely resolving themselves and this tendency will get even stronger in coming months. The pace of life quickens.

You are still very much in a yearly personal pleasure peak until the 23rd. This is a time to enjoy your life, to express personal creativity (one of the great joys) and to be more involved with leisure and entertainment. After the 23rd the focus will shift to more serious things such as health and work.

Venus enters your 4th house on the 7th and so home and family remain a major focus. This is a good period to beautify the home, redecorate or buy objects of beauty for the home. It is also good for entertaining. If there has been discord in the family this is a good period to create harmony (you have cosmic support for this).

The health of the family and family members seems a major focus this month, and you seem successful here. It is a good period for making the home itself 'healthier', for example by removing unhealthy kinds of paint or chemicals from the home, and by installing some health or gym equipment. You seem more interested in a healthier diet too, both for yourself and for your family.

Mercury, your financial planet, moves very quickly this month, indicating the achievement of financial goals quickly. Your financial decision-making is probably quicker too (and if you did your homework during Mercury's retrograde period, your decisions will be good). Your spouse's or partner's finances will improve after the 23rd.

Love is still stormy. Like last month the advice is not to make matters worse. Minimize the negativity as much as you can. (The period from the 28th to the 30th seems especially stressful.)

The Sun makes a very dynamic aspect to Uranus and Pluto between the 28th to the 30th. Family members, especially parent figures, need to avoid stressful, risky activities. It wouldn't hurt for your spouse or current love to also avoid taking risks and daredevil-type stunts.

## October

Best Days Overall: 2, 3, 12, 13, 20, 21, 29, 30, 31
Most Stressful Days Overall: 9, 10, 11, 16, 17, 22, 23
Best Days for Love: 1, 2, 12, 16, 17, 20, 21, 29
Best Days for Money: 4, 5, 6, 7, 14, 15, 16, 17, 22, 23, 25, 26
Best Days for Career: 9, 18, 22, 23, 27

Retrograde activity increases on the 4th to 30 per cent of the planets, although this is a temporary state. Jupiter starts to retrograde on the 4th and will be this way to the end of the year. Your spouse, partner or current love needs to be more cautious in financial matters now, and new deals, investments or major purchases need careful homework – especially the ones that seem 'no brainers'. For you it indicates that you need to read the small print very carefully when buying insurance or borrowing money. Any elective surgical operations would be better delayed this month.

On the 23rd you enter a yearly social peak, but it is a social peak in the midst of a difficult love year. Still, it brings some respite. Singles are dating more and attending more parties – in fact all of you are attending more parties and social gatherings now. But marriage is not likely for singles, nor is it advisable. With Saturn moving into your 7th house on the 5th, you begin to reduce the scope of your social life. Love life, marriage, friendships are all going to be reordered and reorganized now and for the next two years. All of you seem more cautious in love matters. Yes, you are going out more, but you are cautious about falling in love. You are looking for relationships that have 'staying power' and this takes time to determine.

This month the planets shift from the lower sector to the upper sector of the Horoscope. By now, you have found your point of emotional harmony and the family situation is more or less in order. Now it is time to focus on the career. Overt moves are not advisable just yet, as Uranus is still retrograde, but you should get ready to make those moves.

It is like waking up from a good night's sleep. Your day is just starting and you are doing the preliminaries, preparing for the day ahead.

Health is still good, but now that Saturn is making a stressful aspect, your energy is not what it was previously. If you organize your day better, delegate and outsource wherever possible, this shouldn't be too much of a problem. After the 23rd though, rest and relax more. Don't be embarrassed to take a nap when you feel tired. Enhance your health by giving more attention to the heart (from the 5th onwards), the small intestine (from the 3rd to the 28th), and the kidneys and hips (from the 28th onwards). Your health planet spends most of the month in your 5th house of fun and creativity (from the 3rd to the 28th), so just being happy will improve your health. If you feel under the weather do some fun kind of activity: have a night out on the town or get involved in something creative and you will feel much better.

### November

Best Days Overall: 8, 9, 16, 17, 26, 27
Most Stressful Days Overall: 6, 7, 12, 13, 18, 19
Best Days for Love: 1, 8, 11, 12, 13, 16, 20, 26
Best Days for Money: 1, 2, 6, 7, 11, 14, 15, 19, 23, 24, 28, 29
Best Days for Career: 6, 14, 18, 19, 23

Many of the trends of the past few months are still in effect. Most of the planets are still in the Western, social sector (and since last month in their maximum Western direction), and most are also above the horizon. Thus you still need to be cultivating your social graces and attaining your goals through co-operation with others. Career is important – more important than home and family matters now. Retrograde activity lessens this month as Neptune starts moving forward on the 11th.

Your health still needs attention, especially until the 22nd. Enhance it in the ways mentioned last month, and also through more attention to the kidneys and hips until the 22nd and to the colon, bladder and sexual organs afterwards. If there are health problems love issues are probably behind them. Do your best to restore harmony here as much as possible (it won't be easy). Detox regimes are powerful from the 22nd onwards too.

There is more socializing with the family and from home these days, ever since your family planet moved into your 7th house on October 23. Old flames could be coming into the picture too.

There are two eclipses this month: a solar eclipse on the 13th and a lunar eclipse on the 28th. The solar eclipse seems to strongly affect you, so reduce your schedule around that time, and avoid risk-taking activities. The solar eclipse occurs in your 7th house of love and marriage, so the testing that we have been seeing all year is intensified even further. Tensions that have been building all year now come to a climax and much pent-up emotion is released. In many cases this indicates a breakup. Relationships that survived the past year and survive this eclipse will probably last forever.

There are dramas in the lives of friends and family members too. If there are problems in the home – hidden flaws – they reveal themselves now so that you can take corrective actions. Family members are more temperamental now, so be more patient.

The lunar eclipse of the 28th occurs in your money house and signals important financial changes and shifts. You need a new strategy and the eclipse will lead you to it. This eclipse – like every lunar eclipse – tests cars and communication equipment. Often they need replacement.

## December

Best Days Overall: 5, 6, 7, 14, 15, 23, 24
Most Stressful Days Overall: 3, 4, 10, 11, 16, 17, 30, 31
Best Days for Love: 1, 6, 10, 11, 14, 20, 23, 31
Best Days for Money: 2, 8, 11, 16, 21, 25, 26, 27, 31
Best Days for Career: 3, 12, 16, 17, 20, 30

Your career planet Uranus starts to move forward on the 13th. Most of the planets are above the horizon (and also moving forward), and in a month you will enter a yearly career peak. Your caution in career matters is paying off now. You have mental clarity, a clear plan, direction, and plenty of gas in the tank to take you where you want to go. From the 16th to the 27th Venus, the ruler of your Horoscope, makes very wonderful aspects to your career planet, so there is success happening – and perhaps even promotion: you are getting on well with bosses and authority figures in this period. Sometimes the planets don't bring an actual, literal promotion, but things happen that promote you in subtle ways on the inner planes. In due course you will see the 'official' side of it.

Mars, your spiritual planet, crosses your Mid-heaven on the 26th and will be there for the rest of the month and well into the next. This shows that you can enhance your career by getting involved in charitable and altruistic activities, which will help you make good connections and 'burnish' your image

Health is good and will get even better after the 21st. You can enhance your health even further through detoxing, giving more attention to the colon, bladder and sexual organs (until the 16th), and to the liver and thighs after that date.

Love is still very complicated, but you seem to be trying very hard. You are going out of your way to please friends and the beloved. Yes, you are more popular, but how lasting is all of this?

Most of the planets are still in the West and your financial planet is in your 7th house until the 11th. This means your fortune comes through others and their good graces and not so much from being such a smart business person. This is especially so in finance. Your affability and social connections open many doors now. There are opportunities for business partnerships or joint ventures until the 11th (these could have come last month too). You are still in a cycle for prospering with other people's money – outside money – through borrowing, creative financing or attracting investors to your ideas. This has been the case for many months, but this month even more. As long as you focus on the financial interests of others ahead of your own, prosperity will happen.

Your 9th house is strong after the 21st. For many of you this is a more religious period, with religious and philosophical breakthroughs. For others this shows the lure of foreign lands; there are happy travel opportunities. Students seem successful in school.

# Gemini

♊

---

---

## Personality Profile

GEMINI AT A GLANCE

*Element* – Air

*Ruling Planet* – Mercury
    *Career Planet* – Neptune
    *Love Planet* – Jupiter
    *Money Planet* – Moon
    *Planet of Health and Work* – Pluto
    *Planet of Home and Family Life* – Mercury

*Colours* – blue, yellow, yellow–orange

*Colour that promotes love, romance and social
    harmony* – sky blue

*Colours that promote earning power* – grey,
    silver

*Gems* – agate, aquamarine

*Metal* – quicksilver

*Scents* – lavender, lilac, lily of the valley, storax

*Quality* – mutable (= flexibility)

*Quality most needed for balance* – thought that is deep rather than superficial

*Strongest virtues* – great communication skills, quickness and agility of thought, ability to learn quickly

*Deepest need* – communication

*Characteristics to avoid* – gossiping, hurting others with harsh speech, superficiality, using words to mislead or misinform

*Signs of greatest overall compatibility* – Libra, Aquarius

*Signs of greatest overall incompatibility* – Virgo, Sagittarius, Pisces

*Sign most helpful to career* – Pisces

*Sign most helpful for emotional support* – Virgo

*Sign most helpful financially* – Cancer

*Sign best for marriage and/or partnerships* – Sagittarius

*Sign most helpful for creative projects* – Libra

*Best Sign to have fun with* – Libra

*Signs most helpful in spiritual matters* – Taurus, Aquarius

*Best day of the week* – Wednesday

# Understanding a Gemini

Gemini is to society what the nervous system is to the body. It does not introduce any new information but is a vital transmitter of impulses from the senses to the brain and vice versa. The nervous system does not judge or weigh these impulses – it only conveys information. And it does so perfectly.

This analogy should give you an indication of a Gemini's role in society. Geminis are the communicators and conveyors of information. To Geminis the truth or falsehood of information is irrelevant, they only transmit what they see, hear or read about. Thus they are capable of spreading the most outrageous rumours as well as conveying truth and light. Geminis sometimes tend to be unscrupulous in their communications and can do both great good or great evil with their power. This is why the sign of Gemini is symbolized by twins: Geminis have a dual nature.

Their ability to convey a message – to communicate with such ease – makes Geminis ideal teachers, writers and media and marketing people. This is helped by the fact that Mercury, the ruling planet of Gemini, also rules these activities.

Geminis have the gift of the gab. And what a gift this is! They can make conversation about anything, anywhere, at any time. There is almost nothing that is more fun to Geminis than a good conversation – especially if they can learn something new as well. They love to learn and they love to teach. To deprive a Gemini of conversation, or of books and magazines, is cruel and unusual punishment.

Geminis are almost always excellent students and take well to education. Their minds are generally stocked with all kinds of information, trivia, anecdotes, stories, news items, rarities, facts and statistics. Thus they can support any intellectual position that they care to take. They are awesome debaters and, if involved in politics, make good orators. Geminis are so verbally smooth that even if they do not know what they are talking about, they can make you think that they do. They will always dazzle you with their brilliance.

## Finance

Geminis tend to be more concerned with the wealth of learning and ideas than with actual material wealth. As mentioned, they excel in professions that involve writing, teaching, sales and journalism – and not all of these professions pay very well. But to sacrifice intellectual needs merely for money is unthinkable to a Gemini. Geminis strive to combine the two. Cancer is on Gemini's solar 2nd house (of money) cusp, which indicates that Geminis can earn extra income (in a harmonious and natural way) from investments in residential property, restaurants and hotels. Given their verbal skills, Geminis love to bargain and negotiate in any situation, and especially when it has to do with money.

The Moon rules Gemini's 2nd solar house. The Moon is not only the fastest-moving planet in the zodiac but actually moves through every sign and house every 28 days. No other heavenly body matches the Moon for swiftness or the ability to change quickly. An analysis of the Moon – and lunar phenomena in general – describes Gemini's financial attitudes very well. Geminis are financially versatile and flexible; they can earn money in many different ways. Their financial attitudes and needs seem to change daily. Their feelings about money change also: sometimes they are very enthusiastic about it, at other times they could not care less.

For a Gemini, financial goals and money are often seen only as means of supporting a family; these things have little meaning otherwise.

The Moon, as Gemini's money planet, has another important message for Gemini financially: in order for Geminis to realize their financial potential they need to develop more of an understanding of the emotional side of life. They need to combine their awesome powers of logic with an understanding of human psychology. Feelings have their own logic; Geminis need to learn this and apply it to financial matters.

## Career and Public Image

Geminis know that they have been given the gift of communication for a reason, that it is a power that can achieve great good or cause unthinkable distress. They long to put this power at the service of the highest and most transcendental truths. This is their primary goal, to communicate the eternal verities and prove them logically. They look up to people who can transcend the intellect – to poets, artists, musicians and mystics. They may be awed by stories of religious saints and martyrs. A Gemini's highest achievement is to teach the truth, whether it is scientific, inspirational or historical. Those who can transcend the intellect are Gemini's natural superiors – and a Gemini realizes this.

The sign of Pisces is in Gemini's solar 10th house of career. Neptune, the planet of spirituality and altruism, is Gemini's career planet. If Geminis are to realize their highest career potential they need to develop their transcendental – their spiritual and altruistic – side. They need to understand the larger cosmic picture, the vast flow of human evolution – where it came from and where it is heading. Only then can a Gemini's intellectual powers take their true position and he or she can become the 'messenger of the gods'. Geminis need to cultivate a facility for 'inspiration', which is something that does not originate in the intellect but which comes through the intellect. This will further enrich and empower a Gemini's mind.

## Love and Relationships

Geminis bring their natural garrulousness and brilliance into their love life and social life as well. A good talk or a verbal joust is an interesting prelude to romance. Their only problem in love is that their intellect is too cool and passionless to incite ardour in others. Emotions sometimes disturb them, and their partners tend to complain about this. If you are in love with a Gemini you must understand why this is so. Geminis avoid deep passions because these would interfere with their ability to think and communicate. If they are cool towards you, understand that this is their nature.

Nevertheless, Geminis must understand that it is one thing to talk about love and another actually to love – to feel it and radiate it. Talking about love glibly will get them nowhere. They need to feel it and act on it. Love is not of the intellect but of the heart. If you want to know how a Gemini feels about love you should not listen to what he or she says, but rather, observe what he or she does. Geminis can be quite generous to those they love.

Geminis like their partners to be refined, well educated and well travelled. If their partners are more wealthy than they, that is all the better. If you are in love with a Gemini you had better be a good listener as well.

The ideal relationship for the Gemini is a relationship of the mind. They enjoy the physical and emotional aspects, of course, but if the intellectual communion is not there they will suffer.

## Home and Domestic Life

At home the Gemini can be uncharacteristically neat and meticulous. They tend to want their children and partner to live up to their idealistic standards. When these standards are not met they moan and criticize. However, Geminis are good family people and like to serve their families in practical and useful ways.

The Gemini home is comfortable and pleasant. They like to invite people over and they make great hosts. Geminis are also good at repairs and improvements around the house – all fuelled by their need to stay active and occupied with something they like to do. Geminis have many hobbies and interests that keep them busy when they are home alone.

Geminis understand and get along well with their children, mainly because they are very youthful people themselves. As great communicators, Geminis know how to explain things to children; in this way they gain their children's love and respect. Geminis also encourage children to be creative and talkative, just like they are.

# Horoscope for 2012

## Major Trends

From 2003 to 2011 your life has been a series of dramatic changes and upheavals. There have been career changes, dramas with the parent figures in your life, and many personal changes. It is safe to say that your personal circumstances are radically different now to what they were in 2003. In hindsight you can see that these upheavals have worked out for the best, and that you were being set free into new and better conditions and circumstances. For most of you the situation is much improved over these past nine years. Happily things are settling down. There is more peace and less drama in your life, and more stability.

Late in 2011 Jupiter entered your 12th house of spirituality, so you have been in a period of internal, spiritual growth. Many of you travelled on pilgrimages of various types, and many of you had amazing spiritual experiences. And this trend continues in the year ahead, until June 11. Neptune, the most spiritual of all the planets, enters your 10th house this year; not only that but he will spend most of the year hovering near the Mid-heaven of the chart (another indication of spirituality). It is perhaps the most important thing in your life right now. This creates a few challenges for you – for spiritual values tend to conflict with worldly values – and following the spiritual path often entails various worldly kinds of sacrifice.

Jupiter will enter your 1st house on June 11 and stay there for the rest of the year. A very happy transit. It ushers in a period of prosperity that will last well into next year.

You are travelling during this period, but this time more for pleasure than for some religious purpose. You will be enjoying the good life – good foods, wines, restaurants and all the pleasures of the physical body. You feel lucky and optimistic, and indeed you are. Love seems very happy this year too (more on this later).

Your areas of greatest interest in the year ahead are spirituality; the body, image and personal pleasure; home and family (until July 3); children and personal creativity (until October 5); health and work (from October 5 onwards); sex, personal transformation and reinvention, occult studies, death and rebirth, life after death; career; and friends, organizations, groups and group activities.

Your paths of greatest fulfilment this year are spirituality (especially until June 11); the body, image and personal pleasure (from June 11 onwards); love, romance and social activities (until August 31); health and work (after August 31).

## Health

*(Please note that this is an* astrological *perspective on health and not a medical one. In days of yore there was no difference: these perspectives were identical. But these days, there could be quite a difference. For a medical perspective, please consult your doctor or health practitioner.)*

Health looks good in the year ahead. Most of the long-term planets are either in harmonious aspect or leaving you alone. Only Neptune begins to make a stressful aspect (on February 3), and only by himself, so this is not a major concern. It is when the long-term planets start to gang up on you that we get concerned.

Good though your health is there will be periods in the year where health and energy are less easy than usual. This is also normal. These things come from the transits and are temporary, not trends for the year. When the stressful transits pass your natural good health and energy will return.

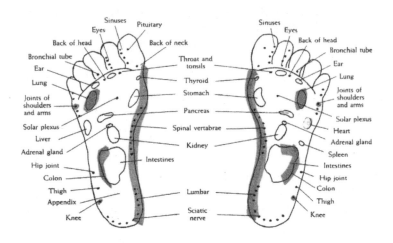

## Reflexology

*Try to massage the whole foot on a regular basis, but pay extra attention to the points highlighted on the chart. When you massage, be aware of 'sore spots', as these need special attention. It's also a good idea to massage the ankles and top side of the feet (see below).*

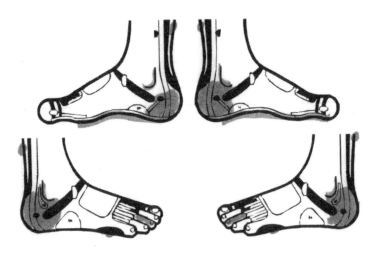

This year the most stressful health periods will tend to be from February 18 to March 20; August 22 to September 22; and November 22 to December 21. These are periods to rest and relax more and pay more attention to health.

Your 6th house of health is not a house of power for most of the year and so you are sort of taking good health for granted. But after October 5, it does become a house of power and you become more focused here.

Good though your health is, you can make it even better. Give more attention to the following organs: the lungs, respiratory system, arms and shoulders (arms and shoulders should be regularly massaged); the colon, bladder, gall bladder and sexual organs (safe sex and sexual moderation is very important); the spine, knees, teeth, bones, skin and overall skeletal alignment (important all year but especially after October 5). Regular visits to a chiropractor or osteopath would be a good idea – the vertebrae need to be kept in the correct alignment. And don't forget regular dental checkups, so you can catch problems before they get too severe. Knees should be given more support when exercising, and regular back and knee massage will be powerful, as will therapies such as Alexander Technique or Feldenkrais.

Pluto is your health planet. In the physical body he rules the colon, bladder and sexual organs – hence their importance in overall health. He rules your health from the sign of Capricorn, which is associated with the spine, knees, teeth, bones, skin and overall skeletal alignment (hence the importance of these organs as well). Saturn, the planetary ruler of these organs, will move into your 6th House of health on October 5, reinforcing what we are saying here.

With your health planet in the conservative sign of Capricorn (and for many years to come) you seem more conservative and traditional when it comes to health. You might be avant-garde in many other areas of life, but not when it comes to your health. You want the tried and true therapies that are accepted and that have stood the test of time. Generally this shows a tendency to orthodox medicine, and even if you indulge in alternative therapies they will tend to be the 'traditional' ones that have been around a long time.

The good part here is that you want long-term cures and not short-term fixes. And this will tend to happen for you. Also you are more able – more inclined – to take on disciplined, rigorous (and even harsh) health regimes.

Geminis of appropriate age are much more fertile this year than usual, especially after June 11. And, these days, with a range of fertility treatments available, even older Geminis will be more fertile.

## Home and Family

Your 4th house of home and family is only temporarily strong this year. Mars spends an unusual amount of time in this house – more than six months from January 1 to July 3. This suggests various things. The most obvious is that there are heavy-duty repairs going on in the home, perhaps even the construction or reconstruction of a home. In all likelihood you are installing high-tech gadgetry in the home and in general being more experimental with your house.

However, there are other meanings here too. Family life can be quite stormy now. Passions run high within the family. Tempers are flaring. There can be conflicts between family members, and if you are not careful even violent behaviour. Your challenge will be to maintain some semblance of calm within the storm, to maintain your emotional equilibrium. This is easy to say but not so easy to do. You should strive not to make matters worse and avoid inflaming an already inflamed situation.

The house should be checked for dangerous items. Matches, knives, weapons or dangerous objects should be kept out of the reach of children. This is always a good policy, but especially so for the first six months of the year.

A friend seems to be staying at your home for a prolonged period. Friends are having many personal dramas this year and this could be the reason for it. A parent or parent figure could be having surgery. Also he or she is more impatient than usual, more in a rush, and this can lead to accidents. This person needs to slow down and watch their temper.

Another parent or parent figure enters a more spiritual kind of year. He or she seems more idealistic, looking for more meaning in life. If he or she is on a spiritual path, this will turn out very well; but if not, this search for meaning could lead to alcohol or drug abuse. This person is likely to move or renovate the home this year, or perhaps buy an additional home.

Children also seem to be doing renovations in the home. Grandchildren could have moved in the past year, but if not it can happen this year as well. Siblings or sibling figures are better off staying where they are, making better use of the space that they have.

## Finance and Career

The year ahead is prosperous and you should see a natural increase in your wealth, in your earnings and in the value of assets that you already own. In the first half of the year you are getting prepared for it – the stage is being set. By June 11 it begins, and it continues well into next year.

When Jupiter moves into your sign at the beginning of June a great feeling of optimism sets in. And this innate optimism, this 'happy go lucky' spirit, helps you financially. Wealth is not really a sum of money, it is a lifestyle. People often confuse the two. It is not so much the money that we want, but what it can buy. Often these are tangible, material things, but quite often they are intangibles – a feeling of freedom, security, comfort, etc. Whether or not you have tangible cash assets, you will be living as if you had them. You will be living above your income level, travelling to exotic places, eating in the finer restaurants, wearing expensive clothing and accessories, and somehow (the cosmos arranges these things very individually) you will have the wherewithal for it.

There is a feeling of luck that comes to you too. And there is luck in speculations in the latter half of the year. No matter how grim a situation seems, you feel inside that you will get through and shine. Overcoming discouragement and setbacks is said to be 90 per cent of the art of success.

Jupiter also happens to be your love planet. So there is love in your life this year. From the financial perspective this would show a happy business partnership. In astrology the aspects for a business partnership and a marriage are the same: the same planets are involved. There is nothing much you need to do to make this happen. It will find you. Just go about your daily business.

Career though is more complicated. You always tend to be idealistic about your career, but now, with Neptune moving into your 10th house on February 3 and staying there for the long term, this idealism is greatly increased. Your career has to be meaningful. It has to be good for the planet. It has to be altruistic and spiritual. Any career path that violates your spiritual principles or ideals will not make you happy or last for too long. And it is not so easy to integrate spiritual values with worldly values – it can be done but it will take work and creativity on your part. Everyone finds their own way of doing things. Sometimes they enter a spiritual career such as the ministry, charity work, working for a non-profit organization, or missionary work (and this could happen). Sometimes people pursue a worldly career while doing much charitable work on the side.

On a more mundane level, with Neptune in your 10th house there is much non-disclosure in career matters, much behind-the-scenes activity and manipulation, and so you need to do your homework before making important decisions. Often there are scandals or unpleasant revelations regarding the authority figures in your life (bosses, parents, parent figures, elders). On a personal level you need to stay 'squeaky clean' in your career. Don't do things that you don't want to see on the evening news or 'twittered' all over the Internet.

## Love and Social Life

Though your 7th house of love and marriage is not strong, other indicators in your Horoscope are showing a very strong love and social year. Love is definitely in the air. And it seems happy.

Two important trends are happening this year. The first, as we mentioned, is that your love planet (Jupiter) is crossing your Ascendant and entering the 1st house on June 11. It will be in your 1st house for the balance of the year. This is a powerful love indicator. Secondly, Venus, the generic love planet of the zodiac, will spend an unusual amount of time in your own sign. Now normally Venus will spend about one month in a sign. Here she is sort of camping out in your sign from April 3 to August 7. This too is a positive love indicator. Indeed, from June 11 to August 7 the two love planets in your Horoscope will be in your own sign.

Love will certainly happen and perhaps even marriage as well. The beauty of these transits is that you don't need to do anything special. Love will find you. Just go about your normal business and it will happen. What I also like here is that you have love on your terms. The lover puts your interests way ahead of his or her own interests. You come first. You have your way.

The same applies to social matters. New friends – and devoted ones – are coming into the picture this year. Existing friends are more devoted than usual as well. You don't need to run around searching for social opportunities; again, they will come to you.

The two love planets in your own sign show that your personal appearance shines; regardless of your age or stage in life, it is better than usual. You exude more grace and charm. You dress more beautifully and stylishly. You have an excellent sense of beauty these days. The opposite sex will certainly take notice.

The above is true for all Geminis but especially those working on the first and second marriages. If you are already married, your spouse is paying more attention and is much more supportive than usual. Those of you working on your third marriage are probably better off not marrying, just dating. Love seems too unstable this year (and for years to come). But those working on the fourth marriage have a wonderful opportunity, and a marriage is likely.

Siblings have a more or less status quo kind of love year. If they are single there is good opportunity after June 11. Children are having their marriages and relationships tested this year, and break-ups are likely. Grandchildren of marriageable age have a status quo kind of year. Singles will tend to stay single; marrieds will tend to stay married.

**Self-improvement**

With Neptune on your Mid-heaven all year and Jupiter in your spiritual 12th house until June 11, you are in a very strong spiritual period, as we mentioned. The invisible world is letting you know that it is around. This is a year (and especially the first part of the year) for all kinds of supernatural kinds of experiences, for an active and prophetic dream life and all kinds of synchronistic experiences. The spiritual world – and the world at large – is waiting for you to step into your real work, your real mission.

Your spiritual life will become the main mission in life for many of you. As you change your own energy field, the energy fields of those you come in contact with will also change. Your individual work will change families, communities and even the country at large.

In June and July you will face one of the classic spiritual conflicts that many people face. Jupiter and Neptune are in stressful aspect with each other. Thus there is a feeling that if you follow your true mission there is some love or social sacrifice involved, and this is always difficult. The so-called sacrifice is only 'apparent' and not real, but it is a good test of your commitment. If you pass the test, love (the equivalent or better) will be restored to you.

Also, your spouse or current love, while very devoted to you personally, is not very supportive of your career,

Perhaps they feel a bit jealous about this, and this will need some effort on your part to work out.

Uranus in your 11th house indicates much instability with friends. It shows many dramas in their personal lives and this could impact on your relationship. While you are socially successful this year, you find it difficult to make long-term social plans as you never know who is available when. Being comfortable with social change is one of the main lessons of the year and for years to come.

# Month-by-month Forecasts

## January

Best Days Overall: 5, 6, 7, 14, 15, 23, 24
Most Stressful Days Overall: 12, 13, 19, 20, 25, 26
Best Days for Love: 3, 4, 6, 7, 12, 18, 19, 20, 21, 27, 28, 30
Best Days for Money: 3, 4, 8, 9, 12, 13, 21, 23, 24, 30
Best Days for Career: 7, 15, 24, 25, 26

You begin your year on a happy note. Your benevolent 9th house is strong from the 20th onwards. Very unusually, all of the planets are moving forwards (until the 24th), bringing rapid progress and achievement. So this is a happy and successful month. You cover a lot of territory and do it well.

Your year begins with 70 per cent of the planets above the horizon. From the 18th onwards the percentage jumps to 80. You are in a very strong career period. Keep the focus on your outer goals. You can downplay home and family issues. You serve your family best, and attain emotional harmony, by being successful in the world. This is the time to attain to career goals through outer, overt, physical actions.

Most of the planets are in the social, Western sector of the Horoscope. This is soon to change but for now you are in a strong social cycle, where you develop your social and diplomatic skills and where you attain objectives through consensus and co-operation rather than through personal initiative. Uncomfortable conditions are more difficult to change right now; you have to adapt to them as best you can.

Your 8th house of transformation is very powerful until the 27th, which means this is a great period for losing weight, detoxing the body and getting rid of old and useless possessions. Clean up the house – not just the physical house but the mind and the emotions as well.

Health and energy are good this month, and will get even better after the 20th. Detox regimes go well as we mentioned, and especially between the 12th and 14th. You can enhance your health in the ways mentioned in the yearly report. This is also a sexually active month.

Mercury, the ruler of your Horoscope, squares Uranus from the 8th to the 10th, bringing a very dynamic aspect. Family members can be more temperamental. You should be more mindful on the physical plane, especially when driving or when handling dangerous objects.

Love is more challenging after the 20th but this is a short-term trend. Overall the love life looks good.

Venus travels with Neptune from the 12th to the 15th. You are getting spiritual messages either directly, through dreams and intuitions, or indirectly from psychics, channels, ministers, astrologers and the like about your career. The dream life is very active at this time too.

## February

Best Days Overall: 2, 3, 11, 12, 19, 20, 29
Most Stressful Days Overall: 9, 10, 15, 16, 22, 23
Best Days for Love: 1, 5, 6, 9, 15, 16, 17, 24, 25, 27, 28
Best Days for Money: 1, 2, 3, 4, 5, 9, 11, 12, 17, 21, 22, 27, 28
Best Days for Career: 4, 13, 21, 22, 23

This month, the planetary power will shift from the Western Sector, where it has been for many months, to the East; 60 per cent (and sometimes 70 per cent) of the planets will be in the East. So you are entering a period of greater independence, greater personal power. You have greater power to create conditions as you like them and no longer have the need to adapt to things. You can have life on your terms. Hopefully you will not abuse this power – many people do. However, when the cycle for 'paying karma' comes – when the planets shift to the Western Sector again (in about six months' time) – you will have to live with your creations, so build well. The main headline this month is your career. Half of the planets are either in or moving through your career house this month. This house is strong quantitatively and also qualitatively: two out of the three most important planets in your chart spend a lot of time there – the Sun and the ruler of your Horoscope. So you are in a period of great outward success. Pay rises, promotions, elevations (perhaps even honours) are happening now. If your career goals are ultra, ultra high you might not attain them this month, but you will see great progress happening there. Career is a life-long project – our life work – one month is not enough to attain these things. So long as we are making progress we can consider ourselves successful.

Family members are also outwardly successful and seem supportive of your career. You seem on very good terms with the authority figures in your life, your bosses, parents and elders. In fact, you yourself are an authority figure these days.

Health and energy are excellent until the 19th, after that you need to rest and relax more. Your career is busy and taxing, but without good health success is an empty shell. You are *very* busy this month, but you can delegate or outsource as much as possible. Focus on essentials and let lesser things go. People at the top – as you are this month (each on their own level) – are often targets for the venom and anger of those less blessed. This is another drain of energy. This is the price paid (one of them) for outward success. There are many ways to deal with this, but it is beyond the scope of this report.

Be more patient with children from the 8th to the 10th. Make sure they avoid dangerous and risky kinds of activities. They seem inclined to daredevil kinds of stunts.

Love seems happy this month and all year.

### March

Best Days Overall: 1, 9, 10, 18, 19, 27, 28, 29
Most Stressful Days Overall: 7, 8, 13, 14, 20, 21
Best Days for Love: 7, 13, 14, 15, 16, 25, 26
Best Days for Money: 3, 4, 7, 11, 12, 15, 16, 22, 23, 25, 26, 30, 31
Best Days for Career: 2, 11, 20, 21, 30

Retrograde activity increases this month. Mars went retrograde on January 24 and will be retrograde all of this month, and so friends seem to lack direction these days. (Make sure you do your homework before buying new high-tech equipment and software, too; some of the claims are not what they seem.) Saturn went retrograde on the 7th of last month and will be retrograde for many more months. (The spouse, partner or current love needs to be doing a financial review now.) Mercury – and this is the most important one for you – goes retrograde on the 12th. You've had a period of great success and now it is time to take stock of where you stand. You seem unsure of what happens next or where you want to go, and so a period of review is in order. You need to gain some mental clarity now. The home and family situation also needs a review.

Retrogrades, when understood and used properly, are the 'pauses that refresh'. They are no more a 'setback' than a good night's sleep. This is when you gather forces for the next leap of forward progress. The glitches and setbacks that seem to happen come because we are not co-operating with the cosmic intent.

Be especially careful in communicating with family members from the 12th onwards. Don't take things for granted. Much of the family drama and hurt feelings that happen come from miscommunication and misunderstanding. A little more care in the beginning will save much heartache later on.

Career is still very strong in your Horoscope until the 20th. You are in the midst of a yearly career peak now. Much of what we wrote of last month still applies.

Finance has not been a big issue so far this year. Your money house is basically empty (only the Moon visits there for a few days a month). Career, status, prestige, promotion seem much more important to you than money. I would read this as a good signal; you are basically content financially and have no need to make major changes. The Moon waxes from the 1st to the 8th and from the 22nd onwards, and these will be the times when your earning power is strongest.

The love life is getting even better than it has been this month. Venus, the planet of love, travels with your love planet Jupiter from the 11th to the 14th. For singles this shows a romantic meeting. For marrieds it shows more romance in the marriage and happy social experiences – invitations, social meetings, happiness from friends.

The Sun opposes Mars from the 1st to the 5th. Then it conjuncts Uranus from the 23rd to the 26th and squares Pluto from the 28th to the 31st. Be more careful driving during those periods, and avoid arguments where possible. Mercury, the ruler of your Horoscope, conjuncts Uranus twice this month (once moving forwards and once backwards); again, be careful driving and be more patient with family members.

## April

Best Days Overall: 6, 14, 15, 24, 25
Most Stressful Days Overall: 4, 10, 16, 17
Best Days for Love: 4, 5, 10, 12, 13, 14, 15, 21, 22, 24, 25
Best Days for Money: 1, 2, 4, 10, 11, 12, 13, 20, 21, 22, 26, 27
Best Days for Career: 7, 16, 17, 26

Your 11th house of friends has been strong since last year. Last month, it got even stronger, and this trend continues until the 20th. This means you are more involved with friends, with groups and group activities and with trade or professional organizations. You are always a good networker, but especially so now. You are probably more involved than usual with online activities. You are personally more inventive and original these days, and perhaps a bit rebellious as well. You want to do unconventional kinds of things, and probably you will. The norm, the routine, seems boring.

On the 4th Mercury starts to move forward and thus you have more personal clarity and a sense of direction. Career goals have more or less been attained (although we never completely attain them, in essence they are infinite) and now your interests are social.

The month ahead is a very powerful social month, both romantically and in terms of friendship. On the 20th the Sun moves into Taurus and starts to have an impact on your love planet. The aspect will be more exact next month, but you will be feeling it after this date. Love is in the air, and this is serious kind of love. Singles might not marry, but they will meet people they would consider marriage material. This seems to be in happening in spiritual settings, such as the yoga studio, the prayer meeting, the meditation seminar or the charity event. It also seems to occur in the neighbourhood rather than far away. Siblings and sibling figures are playing cupid, and they too have romantic opportunity now and next month.

The Moon waxes from the 1st to the 6th and from the 21st to the end of the month. This is when earning power should be greatest and when your enthusiasm for finance is strongest. The job situation seems shaky though.

Your powerful 12th house of spirituality grows even more so on the 20th. You are in a period for inner growth. You might not see it outwardly just yet, but inwardly much growth is happening. You are having spiritual breakthroughs and insights. Many of you are having supernatural kinds of experiences and there is more communication with spiritual types – psychics, gurus, priests and the like. Your taste in reading also seems more spiritual from now on. Your ability to communicate your insights to others is stronger too – and not everyone can communicate well on these subjects.

Mercury once again conjuncts Uranus (this time forward) from the 22nd to the 24th. Like last month be more careful driving and avoid daredevil kinds of stunts. (This applies to family members too.)

## May

Best Days Overall: 3, 4, 11, 12, 23, 24, 25, 30, 31
Most Stressful Days Overall: 1, 2, 7, 8, 13, 14, 15, 28, 29
Best Days for Love: 2, 3, 4, 7, 8, 10, 11, 12, 19, 20, 21, 22, 29, 30, 31
Best Days for Money: 1, 2, 9, 10, 19, 20, 21, 23, 24, 25, 29, 30
Best Days for Career: 5, 13, 14, 15, 23

A solar eclipse on the 20th occurs in your own sign, and so you feel this powerfully, and especially Geminis born early in the sign (May 20–25). All of you should reduce your schedule, particularly those born early in the sign. This eclipse brings a redefinition of your image and personality – your self-concept. It is always good to periodically fine tune this area. Human beings are constantly growing and evolving, and we rarely do this unless forced to – and this is what is happening now. There are all kinds of scenarios as how the redefinition takes place. It might be that people are slandering you and you need to define yourself or allow these people to define you, or may be you fall pregnant or give birth and there is a need to redefine oneself as a parent.

This eclipse also brings financial and career changes. These things needed to happen for some time, but now you are forced into it, and it's a good thing too. (You will probably see this in hindsight.) There are shake-ups in your company and industry. Heads are rolling there. There are dramas in the lives of parents or parent figures, bosses and elders. There will probably be a crisis in the government of your town or city too. Since the Sun rules your 3rd house, cars and communication equipment will get tested; often they need replacement. Your love planet gets sideswiped by this eclipse and thus a current relationship gets a testing. An eclipse on the love planet produces change in the marital status. Singles often marry under this aspect and married couples often divorce (or have relationship troubles). This aspect lasts for the next six months.

Aside from the eclipse period, this is a happy month. Once the dust settles, you find yourself in one of your yearly personal pleasure peaks. Overall health and energy is good too. (This is a blessing, as you want to face an eclipse from a position of strength, not weakness.)

This is a month for getting the body and image in shape. The eclipse is actually helping you in this as it will reveal any hidden flaws and imperfections so that you can correct them. You also have other help. Venus moved into your sign on April 3 and will be there until August 7 – this is a very long transit for her and a very good one for you. And with the Sun moving into your sign on the 20th you look great, you shine, and your self-esteem and self-confidence are high. You are having life on your terms. You are attracting the opposite sex now – you probably have to fight them off! You dress well and have an excellent sense of style. Love seems happy (and this will get even better in the coming months).

The Moon waxes from the 1st to the 6th and from the 20th onwards. These will tend to be your strongest financial periods. You have more enthusiasm and energy to achieve financial goals.

## June

Best Days Overall: 8, 9, 17, 18, 27, 28
Most Stressful Days Overall: 3, 4, 10, 11, 24, 25
Best Days for Love: 3, 4, 5, 6, 8, 9, 17, 18, 26, 27, 28
Best Days for Money: 5, 6, 8, 9, 17, 18, 19, 20, 21, 26, 27, 29, 30
Best Days for Career: 1, 10, 11, 19, 29

Though there are some bumps on the road this month (a lunar eclipse on the 4th has a strong effect on you) this is a happy and successful month. Enjoy.

The planetary power has been in its maximum Eastern position since the 20th of last month, and your 1st house was strong last month and gets even stronger in the month ahead. So you are in your maximum period of personal power and independence. You have the energy to achieve any realistic goal that you set for yourself. You can create conditions as you desire them to be. You need not kowtow to others; in fact the reverse is true – others are bending for you. When Jupiter your love planet moves into your sign on the 11th the two love planets of the Horoscope will be in your own sign and your love life will sizzle. You are romantically and socially in demand. You are being courted. Love finds you rather than vice versa. Wedding bells could be ringing very soon, although with Venus still retrograde until the 27th a wedding might not be advisable just yet.

Fertility is greatly increased now too, and this condition continues for at least another year. Health is also good.

Finances will also be good this month. For the first time this year we see power in your money house. As the Sun enters this house on the 21st, you enter a yearly financial peak.

Jupiter has his ways of announcing his presence in your sign. It is not just some 'mathematical abstraction' that occurs in the heavens. This is a real, tangible energy. People report various kinds of phenomena – a fortunate speculation; a large, unexpected gift; a happy travel opportunity; the manifestation of a long desired 'thing'. When these things start happening, you know that you are under Jupiter's benevolent rays.

The lunar eclipse of the 4th occurs in your 7th house of love. This more or less reinforces last month's solar eclipse. The love life is getting shaken up and changed in dramatic ways. Current relationships get a severe testing. But, as we mentioned, marriages are also likely for singles. The Moon, the eclipsed planet, is your financial planet, and thus there are more financial changes happening. Usually this happens through some sort of disturbance or crisis, but when the changes are made, you are better off than before. Reduce your schedule during this period.

## July

Best Days Overall: 5, 6, 15, 16, 24, 25
Most Stressful Days Overall: 1, 2, 7, 8, 22, 23, 28, 29
Best Days for Love: 1, 2, 5, 6, 15, 24, 25, 28, 29
Best Days for Money: 5, 6, 7, 8, 15, 16, 17, 18, 19, 24, 25, 28
Best Days for Career: 6, 7, 8, 16, 17, 25, 26

By now the dirty laundry in your relationship has been thoroughly aired. You've either made the corrections needed in a good relationship, or ended a bad one. Either way the love life is wonderful now. Astrologically speaking you couldn't ask for better love aspects than what you have now. The two love planets in the Horoscope are in your own sign, and Venus is moving forward again. You radiate love. You are projecting your own best image of love and beauty. You exude amazing grace and charm and the opposite sex is picking up on it. Singles are definitely involved in some serious relationships. And if not, it can still happen in coming months.

You are still in the midst of a yearly financial peak that lasts until the 22nd. By then your financial goals will have been achieved (on a relative level) and you can focus on other things.

Last month the planetary power shifted from the upper half of your chart to the lower half. This indicates a psychological shift in you. Career is less important than before. It is still important, but you will work towards it in different ways – inward, meditative, softer, less aggressive ways. Neptune, your career planet, has been retrograde since June 4 and so there is not much to be done there anyway. Career issues need time to be resolved and should be under review now. This is a time to focus on the home, family and your emotional life. You need to work on the inner conditions that create a successful career – emotional harmony and a stable home base. Sometimes we serve our families by being successful in the outer world, but at other times we serve them by 'being there' for them, by being emotionally and physically available. Now is the time for the latter.

Health is still very good. You can enhance it further in the ways described in the yearly report.

Mars makes a power aspect to both Uranus and Pluto between the 15th and the 21st. Avoid risky, daredevil-type activities and be more mindful on the physical plane and when driving – and especially when handling electrical equipment. The main health danger now is accident or injury. Your friends also need to be more careful.

On the 22nd you enter Gemini heaven. Your 3rd house becomes powerful. The cosmos impels you into areas that you most love – learning, studying, teaching, writing and communicating.

## August

Best Days Overall: 1, 2, 11, 12, 20, 21, 29, 30
Most Stressful Days Overall: 4, 5, 18, 19, 24, 25, 31
Best Days for Love: 1, 2, 3, 11, 12, 13, 14, 20, 21, 22, 23, 24, 25, 29, 30, 31
Best Days for Money: 1, 2, 6, 7, 11, 12, 13, 14, 15, 17, 18, 20, 21, 27, 29, 30
Best Days for Career: 3, 4, 5, 13, 22, 31

Your 3rd house of communication became powerful late last month and is still powerful this month until the 22nd. This pretty much coincides with the retrograde of Mercury, which began on July 15. You have probably been successful in communication projects, but with many glitches. Your avid interest and focus overcame all the various challenges. Mercury is still retrograde until the 8th of this month. Being a Gemini, you are unlikely to cut back on communication, but just exercise more care. Say what you mean, mean what you say, and make sure the other person gets your message correctly.

Mercury retrograde in your Horoscope also affects the family and family issues. Home projects, family decisions – important ones – need more study. A parent lacks direction these days. He or she should be reviewing personal goals now, although the objective is not 'doing' right now, but the attainment of mental clarity. When this happens, 'doing' will happen very naturally.

You are an avid reader and an avid consumer of media. But with Mercury retrograde you need to take all this information with many grains of salt.

The Sun, your communication planet, will oppose Neptune from the 22nd to the 25th. Though Mercury is moving forward by then, you still need to be careful in communications: more careful about signing contracts, completing on a house and making long-term commitments. There is much non-disclosure that you need to know about before signing anything. Be careful driving this period too –

stay alert and don't be daydreaming. This applies to family members too.

The planetary power is starting to shift West this month. The shift begins on the 22nd and will get more pronounced in coming months. Personal independence is coming to an end for a while (it will return again in the next cycle, seven or so months from now). This is the time to start cultivating your 'people skills'. Happily these seem excellent.

Venus, the planet of love, but also your spiritual planet, has been in your own sign since April. We have discussed the love aspects of this transit but there are also spiritual aspects to it. You have been learning to 'beautify' the body via spiritual means; you are learning spirit's absolute control of the body. Yoga, tai chi, chi qong and spiritual-type exercises have been good for you. Now, on the 8th, Venus will move into your money house and you will learn spirit's dominion in the financial realm as well. No matter what your condition or circumstance, spirit can show you or lead you to your abundant supply. The intuition is important financially and is being trained in financial matters now.

Your health is basically good, but it needs more watching after the 23rd. Rest and relax more.

## September

Best Days Overall: 7, 8, 16, 17, 25, 26
Most Stressful Days Overall: 1, 14, 15, 21, 22, 27, 28
Best Days for Love: 1, 7, 8, 12, 16, 17, 21, 22, 25, 26, 29, 30
Best Days for Money: 5, 6, 7, 8, 10, 11, 14, 15, 16, 17, 25, 26
Best Days for Career: 1, 9, 18, 27, 28

Now that Mercury is moving forward, retrograde activity is less than last month. Until the 18th 30 per cent of the planets are retrograde. After the 18th, it is only 20 per cent. The pace of life in general, and especially your own, quickens.

Many of the trends that we have been writing about are still in effect. Your career planet is still retrograde all month, your 4th house of home and family is very strong this month, and most of the planets are below the horizon of your chart. So the focus is on family now. You can safely downplay the career. Your job now is to set up the inner conditions that will produce career success later on.

You seem out of sorts with a boss, parent or authority figure from the 1st to the 3rd. You just don't see eye to eye. You have different, seemingly irreconcilable perspectives on things. But give it time; this is a short-term problem. If you have issues with the authorities around this period, reduce your schedule a bit – it's not such a great time for dealing with these things.

Like last month, avoid drinking, drugs or medication while driving. This applies to family members too. In particular, be more careful driving between the 28th and the 30th. If you can avoid trips (and especially long trips), that would be best. But if you can't, just exercise more caution and drive more defensively. Computer problems – crashes, viruses and the like are also more likely this period.

Venus has been in your money house since August 8 and is there until the 7th. Aside from emphasizing the spiritual dimensions of wealth – the spiritual supply – it indicates that children have been more supportive and vice versa. You are spending on them, but they can also inspire you financially, or give you good ideas. Your personal creativity also seems more marketable (another of the ways that spirit supplies). This has been a period where you enjoy your wealth. You spend on leisure and fun kinds of things.

The job situation still seems highly unstable. There are important changes happening in your health regime too, but wait until Pluto goes into direct motion on the 18th before making them.

Health needs watching until the 23rd. It is nothing too serious, just rest and relax more. Being overtired can make you vulnerable to problems. You can enhance your health in the ways described in the yearly report. Late last month,

Mars entered your 6th house and will be there all of this month. Thus give more attention to the head, face and scalp (massage them regularly) and do more exercise. Good muscle tone is important.

## October

Best Days Overall: 4, 5, 6, 14, 15, 22, 23
Most Stressful Days Overall: 12, 13, 18, 19, 24, 25, 26
Best Days for Love: 1, 12, 18, 19, 21
Best Days for Money: 4, 5, 6, 7, 8, 14, 15, 22, 23, 24
Best Days for Career: 7, 16, 24, 25, 26

On the 23rd of last month, the Sun entered your 5th house initiating another yearly personal pleasure peak. This continues until the 23rd of this month. With Jupiter in your own sign since June 11 you are already in a fun kind of period and personal pleasure and fun kinds of activities increase even more. This is a very happy month. Health is good now. Energy is abundant. It is hard to say whether your 'up' mood and fun times are producing your good health or vice versa. Probably a little bit of both is true. Physical exercise, head and face massage, is still powerful until the 7th. On the 5th Saturn will enter your 6th house of health and stay there for the next two to three years. Thus back and knee massage will also be powerful. Detox regimes are good for the long term. Surgery may have been recommended to you but don't be so quick to jump in – you have this tendency now; get a second opinion.

Though health is good, you seem more involved here this month. Your 6th house becomes very powerful after the 23rd. Most likely you are focused on healthy lifestyles and health regimes – preventive-type measures.

On the 3rd Venus crosses from the Eastern sector to the Western sector of the Horoscope. Up till now, the planets have been more or less balanced in the East and the West and so you have neither been overly dependent on others, or overly independent. But now the Western sector is dominant and so you find yourself more dependent on others than usual. Sometimes this is a good thing. We develop social skills under these aspects. We appreciate others more and their needs. We learn more about ourselves though our interactions with others and through our relationships. Being in control has its charms, but not being in control has other charms.

Most likely there have been job changes recently and the month ahead seems fortunate for job seekers, especially after the 23rd. Job seekers benefit from the 'standard methods' of job hunting now – the media, the wanted ads, letter writing and family connections.

Love has been super all year. On the 4th your love planet starts to retrograde so a breather is in order. This is a time to review your relationship (and general social activity) and see where improvements can be made. Avoid major love decisions, one way or another right now.

### November

Best Days Overall: 1, 2, 10, 11, 18, 19, 23, 24
Most Stressful Days Overall: 8, 9, 14, 15, 21, 22
Best Days for Love: 1, 2, 11, 14, 15, 19, 20, 28, 29
Best Days for Money: 1, 2, 3, 4, 5, 11, 13, 19, 23, 28, 29
Best Days for Career: 3, 12, 21, 22

The job situation has been unstable all year. In the past few months this instability has increased. Job changes have been happening – no question about that. A solar eclipse on the 13th occurs in your 6th house, reinforcing the instability that we see. There are more job changes happening. There is a cosmic agenda here: only the best will do for you and anything less gets 'exploded'. This is especially so if you have been settling for just 'a job' and not something that you really like.

This eclipse can produce health scares, but since your health is good, these will just be scares and nothing more.

Solar eclipses always tend to test your cars and communication equipment, as the Sun rules your 3rd house of communication. And so these things might need replacement or repair. The eclipse can also produce computer crashes, viruses, hard drive failures and the like. Before the eclipse period kicks in (perhaps a week before) it would be good to have all your important data backed up. Take special care here. (Also take more care with these things between the 23rd and the 25th and the 27th to the 30th.)

There is also a lunar eclipse this month on the 28th. This one occurs in your own sign, so you will feel it strongly (especially those of you born early in the sign). Take it nice and easy during that period. Spend more quiet time at home; read a book, watch a movie, pray and meditate more. As with the solar eclipse in May, this eclipse brings about a redefinition of your personality, image and self-concept. You are changing the way that you think of yourself and how you want others to see you. Over the course of the next six months this produces major wardrobe changes – you are projecting a new image. The old you is no more; a new you is being born.

Lunar eclipses always bring financial changes for you – the Moon is your financial planet. With your money house empty for many months, you probably haven't been paying enough attention here and now the eclipse forces you to do so. Next year is going to be very prosperous, so there are changes that need to be made now to prepare you for it.

Mars makes dynamic aspects with both Uranus and Pluto this month. It squares Uranus from the 23rd to the 25th and conjuncts Pluto from the 27th to the 30th. This brings dramas in the lives of friends (and they should be more careful driving and more mindful on the physical plane). Your computer equipment or high-tech gadgetry can be erratic this period. Surgeries could be recommended to you.

The love life has been active since April and now, on the 22nd, you enter a yearly love and social peak; you are in a peak of a peak year. Romance blooms. Singles, if they are still unattached, will meet that special someone now. The only complication is the retrograde of your love planet. The opportunities seem boundless, but go slowly and cautiously. Don't make major love decisions (though you are sorely tempted) just yet.

## December

Best Days Overall: 8, 9, 16, 17, 25, 26
Most Stressful Days Overall: 5, 6, 7, 12, 13, 18, 19
Best Days for Love: 1, 8, 10, 11, 12, 13, 16, 20, 25, 31
Best Days for Money: 1, 2, 3, 8, 13, 16, 22, 25, 28, 29
Best Days for Career: 1, 10, 18, 19, 28

You are still in a yearly love and social peak all month. The Sun will leave your 7th house on the 21st, but Mercury (the ruler of your Horoscope) and Venus (the generic love planet) will be in your house of love from the 16th onwards. So this is an active and happy month for love. Your love planet is still retrograde so keep in mind our discussion of this last month.

On the 16th, when Mercury moves into your house of love, Mercury (you) and Jupiter (the beloved) will be in 'mutual reception'. That is, each will be 'guests in the house of the other'. This is very positive. You are on the beloved's side and he or she is on your side. There is co-operation and mutual support during this period – just the way a good relationship should be. You and your beloved are not clones of each other. You are who you are, you have different ideas and opinions and perhaps see things in radically different ways – yet, you manage to co-operate beautifully. You easily bridge your differences.

In the health department we see a similar phenomenon. Saturn and Pluto are in 'mutual reception', and there is good co-operation between these two forces. In your Horoscope this would show the power of detox in health. Good health is not about adding more things to the body, but about removing material that shouldn't be there. This position indicates surgeries as well. And although you should get a second opinion, surgeries seem successful now.

Last month was a month of important change – two eclipses ensured that. But other things also happened. The planetary power shifted from the lower half of the Horoscope to the upper half. On the 16th of this month, the shift becomes even stronger. Your career planet Neptune started to move forward on November 11 as well. Again the timing is beautiful here. It is now time to focus on the career and your outward goals and ambitions. By now, you should have more mental clarity about your career. You've had many months to review and assess your situation, so your actions should be successful.

The entire year seems a more sexually active kind of year, but this month even more than usual. The main message is not to overdo a good thing. Keep it in moderation. As with food, if you overdo there is a price to be paid later on.

The power in your 8th house all month shows that this is a good time to pay down debt, to gain a deeper understanding of death and life after death, and for all projects involved with personal transformation and personal reinvention. You have been interested in these things all year, but now even more so. You are giving birth to the 'new you'.

# Cancer

♋

---

THE CRAB

*Birthdays from*
*21st June to*
*20th July*

---

## Personality Profile

CANCER AT A GLANCE

*Element* – Water

*Ruling Planet* – Moon
   *Career Planet* – Mars
   *Love Planet* – Saturn
   *Money Planet* – Sun
   *Planet of Fun and Games* – Pluto
   *Planet of Good Fortune* – Neptune
   *Planet of Health and Work* – Jupiter
   *Planet of Home and Family Life* – Venus
   *Planet of Spirituality* – Mercury

*Colours* – blue, puce, silver

*Colours that promote love, romance and social
   harmony* – black, indigo

*Colours that promote earning power* – gold,
   orange

*Gems* – moonstone, pearl

*Metal* – silver

*Scents* – jasmine, sandalwood

*Quality* – cardinal (= activity)

*Quality most needed for balance* – mood control

*Strongest virtues* – emotional sensitivity,
    tenacity, the urge to nurture

*Deepest need* – a harmonious home
    and family life

*Characteristics to avoid* – over-sensitivity,
    negative moods

*Signs of greatest overall compatibility* – Scorpio,
    Pisces

*Signs of greatest overall incompatibility* – Aries,
    Libra, Capricorn

*Sign most helpful to career* – Aries

*Sign most helpful for emotional support* – Libra

*Sign most helpful financially* – Leo

*Sign best for marriage and/or partnerships* –
    Capricorn

*Sign most helpful for creative projects* – Scorpio

*Best Sign to have fun with* – Scorpio

*Signs most helpful in spiritual matters* – Gemini,
    Pisces

*Best day of the week* – Monday

# Understanding a Cancer

In the sign of Cancer the heavens are developing the feeling side of things. This is what a true Cancerian is all about – feelings. Where Aries will tend to err on the side of action, Taurus on the side of inaction and Gemini on the side of thought, Cancer will tend to err on the side of feeling.

Cancerians tend to mistrust logic. Perhaps rightfully so. For them it is not enough for an argument or a project to be logical – it must feel right as well. If it does not feel right a Cancerian will reject it or chafe against it. The phrase 'follow your heart' could have been coined by a Cancerian, because it describes exactly the Cancerian attitude to life.

The power to feel is a more direct – more immediate – method of knowing than thinking is. Thinking is indirect. Thinking about a thing never touches the thing itself. Feeling is a faculty that touches directly the thing or issue in question. We actually experience it. Emotional feeling is almost like another sense which humans possess – a psychic sense. Since the realities that we come in contact with during our lifetime are often painful and even destructive, it is not surprising that the Cancerian chooses to erect barriers – a shell – to protect his or her vulnerable, sensitive nature. To a Cancerian this is only common sense.

If Cancerians are in the presence of people they do not know, or find themselves in a hostile environment, up goes the shell and they feel protected. Other people often complain about this, but one must question these other people's motives. Why does this shell disturb them? Is it perhaps because they would like to sting, and feel frustrated that they cannot? If your intentions are honourable and you are patient, have no fear. The shell will open up and you will be accepted as part of the Cancerian's circle of family and friends.

Thought-processes are generally analytic and dissociating. In order to think clearly we must make distinctions, comparisons and the like. But feeling is unifying and integrative.

To think clearly about something you have to distance yourself from it. To feel something you must get close to it. Once a Cancerian has accepted you as a friend he or she will hang on to you. You have to be really bad to lose the friendship of a Cancerian. If you are related to Cancerians they will never let you go no matter what you do. They will always try to maintain some kind of connection even in the most extreme circumstances.

## Finance

The Cancer-born has a deep sense of what other people feel about things and why they feel as they do. This faculty is a great asset in the workplace and in the business world. Of course it is also indispensable in raising a family and building a home, but it also has its uses in business. Cancerians often attain great wealth in a family business. Even if the business is not a family operation, they will treat it as one. If the Cancerian works for somebody else, then the boss is the parental figure and the co-workers are brothers and sisters. If a Cancerian is the boss, then all the workers are his or her children. Cancerians like the feeling of being providers for others. They enjoy knowing that others derive their sustenance because of what they do. It is another form of nurturing.

With Leo on their solar 2nd house (of money) cusp, Cancerians are often lucky speculators, especially with residential property or hotels and restaurants. Resort hotels and nightclubs are also profitable for the Cancerian. Waterside properties allure them. Though they are basically conventional people, they sometimes like to earn their livelihood in glamorous ways.

The Sun, Cancer's money planet, represents an important financial message: in financial matters Cancerians need to be less moody, more stable and fixed. They cannot allow their moods – which are here today and gone tomorrow – to get in the way of their business lives. They need to develop their self-esteem and feelings of self-worth if they are to realize their greatest financial potential.

**Career and Public Image**

Aries rules the 10th solar house (of career) cusp of Cancer, which indicates that Cancerians long to start their own business, to be more active publicly and politically and to be more independent. Family responsibilities and a fear of hurting other people's feelings – or getting hurt themselves – often inhibit them from attaining these goals. However, this is what they want and long to do.

Cancerians like their bosses and leaders to act freely and to be a bit self-willed. They can deal with that in a superior. They expect their leaders to be fierce on their behalf. When the Cancerian is in the position of boss or superior he or she behaves very much like a 'warlord'. Of course the wars they wage are not egocentric but in defence of those under their care. If they lack some of this fighting instinct – independence and pioneering spirit – Cancerians will have extreme difficulty in attaining their highest career goals. They will be hampered in their attempts to lead others.

Since they are so parental, Cancerians like to work with children and make great educators and teachers.

**Love and Relationships**

Like Taurus, Cancer likes committed relationships. Cancerians function best when the relationship is clearly defined and everyone knows his or her role. When they marry it is usually for life. They are extremely loyal to their beloved. But there is a deep little secret that most Cancerians will never admit to: commitment or partnership is really a chore and a duty to them. They enter into it because they know of no other way to create the family that they desire. Union is just a way – a means to an end – rather than an end in itself. The family is the ultimate end for them.

If you are in love with a Cancerian you must tread lightly on his or her feelings. It will take you a good deal of time to realize how deep and sensitive Cancerians can be. The smallest negativity upsets them. Your tone of voice, your irritation, a look in your eye or an expression on your face can cause great distress for the Cancerian. Your slightest gesture is registered by them and reacted to. This can be hard to get used to, but stick by your love – Cancerians make great partners once you learn how to deal with them. Your Cancerian lover will react not so much to what you say but to the way you are actually feeling at the moment.

## Home and Domestic Life

This is where Cancerians really excel. The home environment and the family are their personal works of art. They strive to make things of beauty that will outlast them. Very often they succeed.

Cancerians feel very close to their family, their relatives and especially their mothers. These bonds last throughout their lives and mature as they grow older. They are very fond of those members of their family who become successful, and they are also quite attached to family heirlooms and mementos. Cancerians also love children and like to provide them with all the things they need and want. With their nurturing, feeling nature, Cancerians make very good parents – especially the Cancerian woman, who is the mother *par excellence* of the zodiac.

As a parent the Cancerian's attitude is 'my children right or wrong'. Unconditional devotion is the order of the day. No matter what a family member does, the Cancerian will eventually forgive him or her, because 'you are, after all, family'. The preservation of the institution – the tradition – of the family is one of the Cancerian's main reasons for living. They have many lessons to teach others about this.

Being so family-orientated, the Cancerian's home is always clean, orderly and comfortable. They like old-fashioned furnishings but they also like to have all the modern comforts. Cancerians love to have family and friends over, to organize parties and to entertain at home – they make great hosts.

# Horoscope for 2012

## Major Trends

Last year was a stressful, difficult year, Cancer. A character-building year. The year ahead is still very stressful, but easier than last year. If you got through 2011 with your health and sanity intact, you will get through the year ahead as well.

Last year four powerful long-term planets were in stressful alignment with you. This year, there are only three – Saturn, Pluto and Uranus. Also by October 5 Saturn will move from a stressful to an easy aspect with you. Thus as the year progresses there is greater and greater improvement. You have gone through the worst of it.

Your overall health and energy is getting better and better, but it still needs watching. More on this later.

Last year Neptune flirted with your 9th House. This year, on February 3, he enters it for the long term. This too is another positive for you, health-wise, for Neptune will be making harmonious aspects to you. If you are involved in legal issues you really need to do a lot of homework now as there is much behind-the-scenes, covert activity happening. Students also need to do more research on the school or college they will attend, as things are not the way they seem.

Last year brought sudden and dramatic career changes, and this trend continues in the year ahead. More on this later on.

Your areas of greatest interest this year are home and family (until October 5); children, creativity and personal pleasure (from October 5 onwards); love, romance and social activities; religion, philosophy, higher education and foreign travel (from February 3 onwards); career; friends, groups, group activities and organizations (until June 11); and spirituality (from April 3 onwards).

Your paths of greatest fulfilment this year are friends, groups, group activities and organizations (until June 11);

spirituality (from June 11 onwards); health and work (until August 31); children, creativity and personal pleasure (from August 31 onwards).

## Health

*(Please note that this is an* astrological *perspective on health and not a medical one. In days of yore these perspectives were identical. But these days there could be quite a difference. For a medical perspective, please consult your doctor or health practitioner.)*

No use beating around the bush here, Cancer. Health is stressful this year and you need to pay more attention than usual. With your 6th house of health pretty much empty, this will be a challenge. You don't really feel like paying too much attention to health matters and you will have to force yourself to do it. (This was the case last year as well.)

The good news is that there is much you can do to improve your health. Give more attention to the following organs: the stomach and breasts (right diet is very important); the liver and thighs (the thighs should be regularly massaged); the neck and throat (important until June 11: regular neck massage would be wonderful, especially the back of the neck where the neck connects to the skull, craniosacral therapy is good for this too); the lungs, respiratory system, arms and shoulders (important from June 11 onwards; arms and shoulders should be regularly massaged to release tension). Regular readers undoubtedly know of the many natural, drugless ways to strengthen these organs, but if they like they can work with the reflexology charts included here.

Just as important as strengthening these organs, is the maintenance of high energy levels. As our regular readers know there is really one primal disease – lack of energy or lack of life force. All the other problems that people face really stem from this. Viruses etc strike when there is not enough innate energy to resist them. Further, when the life energy is low, the sensory mechanisms – the thinking faculties – are not up to par either and thus all kinds of accidents and mishaps can occur.

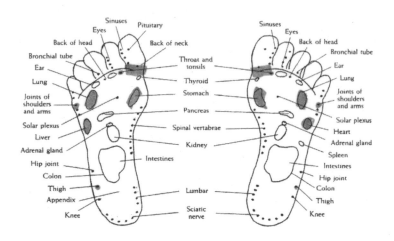

## *Reflexology*

*Try to massage the whole foot on a regular basis, but pay extra attention to the points highlighted on the chart. When you massage, be aware of 'sore spots', as these need special attention. It's also a good idea to massage the ankles and top side of the feet (see below).*

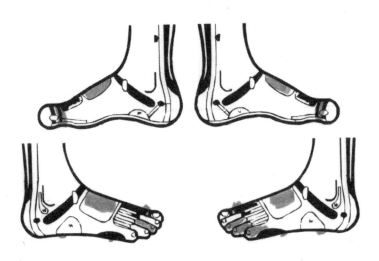

High energy can cover a multitude of sins. But let the energy drop (for example, when the planets are not in right alignment) and risky behaviour can start to take its toll. When her energy is high, a pregnant woman can go to a party where the energy is negative and not be too affected. But let her energy drop, and the same event can affect her health and well-being. A rich person with much money in the bank can afford to be profligate, but if his bank balance drops, the profligacy will take a huge toll on him. It is more or less the same with our life energies.

So, rest and relax more this year (especially from January 1 to January 19; March 20 to April 20; September 22 to October 22; and December 21 to December 31). Keep your focus on the really important things in life and let go of lesser things. Avoid worry and anxiety (these are real energy drains). Do your best and once you have done this, enjoy your life. Learn to enjoy life's challenges as much as the easy things.

The herbs, gems, aromas and metals of Jupiter are natural healing tonics for you. Blue is a healing colour; tin, a healing metal; carnation will work well as an aroma, tea, flower essence or herbal concoction. Even the mere physical presence of this flower will have a healing, uplifting effect. And the large animals such as horses, moose, elephants and whales are healing power animals.

## Home and Family

Your 4th house of home and family has been a 'house of power' for the past few years and this trend continues in the year ahead. In fact it is even more of a major focus than usual.

Saturn has been in this house for some years and thus this area of life has been challenging, to say the least. The family seems like a burden on you rather than a joy. You have been taking on more family responsibilities as well. There is not much you can do about it though; you must pick up the responsibility and handle it as best you can. The character strengthens through this. By willingly taking on the responsibility and not shirking or avoiding it, you will attract spiritual help and it won't be as onerous as you think.

Saturn in your 4th house tends to deny any possibility of a move. It's probably not advisable anyway. You feel cramped at home, the living quarters seem too small for you, but with creativity you can make better use of your space.

Children (and the children figures in your life) have been difficult to handle. They seem more rebellious than usual and seem to be having many dramas in their personal lives. They seem defiant of all authority. Parents and parent figures are also having many personal dramas – perhaps surgery or near-death kinds of experiences. They seem nomadic, restless, wandering around from place to place. They want to explore their personal freedom and have had enough of obligations and responsibilities. Further, your spouse, partner or current love is in conflict with the children and parent figures. Keeping some semblance of harmony in the family is quite a challenge.

Saturn in the solar 4th house is a difficult aspect for most people, but especially for you Cancer. It shows that you feel 'unsafe' in expressing your feelings and the tendency will be to hold them in. Of course, you can't do this for ever, so when you do express them, you tend to go overboard. Like last year, you need a safe way to vent your emotions.

Depression is another symptom of Saturn position, and you must guard against this now (it makes you even more vulnerable to health problems).

Saturn leaves your 4th house on October 5, and thus the family situation should start improving then. The worst of things will have passed, but the issues with children are still challenging.

Siblings and sibling figures are having an easier family period than you; the year ahead seems to be a status quo one for them. Children can move this year, perhaps multiple times. Grandchildren are likely to move as well, but the moves of the grandchildren seem more stable than those of the children. (Probably they are handling it better.)

Saturn is also your planet of love and beauty. Thus you are engaged in beautifying the home this year (this has been going on for a few years). You are redecorating, repainting, landscaping, and buying objects of beauty for the home.

## Finance and Career

Your money house has not been powerful for a number of years. It is more or less empty this year too. This shows that finance is not a major interest in 2012. It tends towards the status quo. If earnings were good last year they will tend to be good this year. If they were difficult last year, they will be difficult this year. Generally though, it indicates that you are more or less satisfied with finances and have no need to make major changes.

Your money house becomes temporarily powerful from July 23 to August 22 (as the Sun, your financial planet, moves through it) and from September 6 to October 3 (when Venus moves through there). These will tend to be your peak earnings periods in the year ahead. The Sun moves through all the signs and houses of your Horoscope every year. Thus there are many short-term trends in finances that are best covered in the monthly reports.

Twice a year the Sun gets eclipsed. Thus twice every year you get a chance to fine tune your finances and make the necessary adjustments and changes that need to be made. This year the eclipses happen on May 20 and November 13.

Earning power tends to be a function of a person's energy levels. Thus, as your overall energy improves over the course of the year I expect finances to improve as well. This year inheritances, insurance claims or royalties are a big source of income.

Career seems more of a focus than money. Money of itself is not that interesting to you, but your status and position in society or in your company or profession *is* very important. Those of you born early in the sign of Cancer have certainly experienced career changes this past year and more are likely to happen as well. The career path seems very unstable. You want change and the freedom to experiment and innovate in your career, and most corporate environments are not conducive for this. You have the kind of chart that a 'freelancer' would have. You take on different assignments at different times. Many of you will opt for the freelance kind of career.

Uranus on the Mid-heaven shows many, many shake-ups in your company, industry and corporate hierarchy. The rules keep changing. The authority figures in your life – bosses, elders, superiors, parents – seem harder to get along with this year, and it is very difficult for you to know where you stand with them. On a personal level many of you are experiencing 'near death' career kinds of experiences. Uranus, the ruler of your 8th house of transformation is in your career house, and thus the message is that a detox is happening in your career; impurities of all kinds are being cleaned out – fears, false attitudes and assumptions, wrong career paths – so that you can give birth to the career of your dreams, the job that you were born to do.

Your career planet, Mars, spends an unusual amount of time in Virgo, your 3rd house. This suggests careers in health (Virgo rules health) or communication – sales, marketing, writing, teaching, advertising and PR. Whatever your business, you further the career through good communication and also through your technological expertise. You need to stay up to date with all the latest technology.

## Love and Social Life

Ever since Pluto moved into your 7th house in 2008 love has been challenging. There is a cosmic detox going on in your love and social life. Impurities in the marriage or current relationship are surfacing so that they can be eliminated and transformed. Detox is seldom a pleasant experience but the end result is good. Love problems always come from internal attitudes that are amiss. When these attitudes are cleansed the love life starts to improve. Many a marriage or love relationship has gone down the tubes in recent years. There may have been an actual death of love (Pluto rules death), but in many cases it was 'near-death' experiences in love. Relationships came close to breaking up (and perhaps did break up for a while) and then were resurrected.

Last year was very challenging in love, for aside from Pluto, your love planet Saturn was receiving very stressful aspects. Marriages and love relationships were severely tested. Many did not make it. If your relationship survived last year, it will most likely survive in the year ahead. Love is still challenging but not as challenging as last year.

Saturn has been in your 4th house of family for some years now. Thus, emotional sharing, emotional intimacy and emotional compatibility are very important in love these days. Good sexual chemistry is not enough. Emotional sex is more interesting than the physical sex. This will change later in the year as your love planet moves into Scorpio and sexual chemistry again becomes important.

In general the social life has been centred in the home these past few years, and this will continue. You are socializing more with the family and with those who are like family to you. Family values are always important to you, but these days more so than ever. Your beloved has to have strong family values.

Singles find love opportunities close to home; there is no need to travel far and wide in the search for love. Parents, parent figures and the family in general are playing cupid. There are love opportunities through family connections as well.

When the Saturn moves into Scorpio on October 5 there will be a dramatic shift in love attitudes. As we mentioned, sex will become more important, although it cannot be the sole basis of a long-term relationship. So this can be a problem, especially for singles. There will also be a focus on fun and singles will be attracted to those who can show them a good time. The problem here is that in a long-term relationship things are not always fun, there are always difficult

periods, and good relationships need more solid underpin-
nings than that.

Singles (those working on their first marriage) will probably not marry this year. Those working on the second
marriage have love opportunities with spiritual and creative
types and in spiritual-type settings. Those working on their
third marriage have wonderful opportunities – love is in the
air now. A serious relationship could have happened last
year and if not, can happen this year too. This seems to
happen with someone you work with or who is involved in
your health.

**Self-improvement**

The Mid-heaven is probably the most important abstract
point in the Horoscope. The Ascendant is important, but the
Mid-heaven is stronger. Right now you have volatile Uranus
on the Mid-heaven (especially those of you born early in the
sign). Thus many of you are dealing with death and death
issues. This seems a long-term trend. It doesn't mean that
you are dying, but that you are very involved with death.
The cosmic object here is to gain a deeper, more spiritual
understanding of this, so that you can live better. We don't
really live properly until we understand death. But this position also has deeper significance. It shows that personal
transformation is a major interest this year and for years
to come. First you will work to transform yourself into the
person you want to be and dream of being (a huge, huge
project). Then as you gain some skill in this you will be helping others to realize their ideal selves.

Neptune has been in your 8th house for many years, but
this year he makes a move into your 9th house. Your
personal beliefs and whole philosophy of life are getting
refined and spiritualized. You are receiving much spiritual
revelation on these issues and are being shown the spiritual
meaning behind these things. Your belief system will cease
being a mere series of do's and don'ts and will come alive
with meaning. This is an important transit for students. It

indicates an interest in spiritual studies – ministry, religion, psychic phenomena.

## Month-by-month Forecasts

### January

Best Days Overall: 8, 9, 17, 18, 25, 26
Most Stressful Days Overall: 1, 2, 14, 15, 21, 22, 28, 29
Best Days for Love: 6, 7, 15, 16, 18, 19, 21, 22, 24, 27, 28
Best Days for Money: 3, 4, 10, 11, 12, 13, 21, 23, 24, 30
Best Days for Career: 1, 2, 3, 4, 12, 13, 21, 22, 28, 29, 30, 31

You begin your year in the midst of a yearly social and love peak. So there is much social activity happening, and for the most part it's happy. Existing relationships are complicated either by children (disagreements about them, or problems with them) or infidelities, potential infidelities and financial disagreements (later in the month). If love is real, everything can be worked out.

Your year begins with most of the planets in the social Western sector. As changing conditions is difficult now, you need to be adaptable and make do within the present situation. You are in a period for cultivating your people and social skills. Later on in the year, you will have the opportunity (and the power) to make dramatic changes to your circumstances, but not just yet. In the meantime, you can learn to enjoy not being in control – there are positive aspects to it. There is less responsibility for what happens; you don't need to berate yourself for what happens or doesn't happen. The main positive is that it is easier to let a Higher Power be in control, and if you do, you will see perfection start to manifest in your affairs.

At least 70 per cent of the planets are above the horizon now. Though home and family are always important to you,

you are in a period for outward – career – achievement. This is the best way to serve your family now. There is much change and ferment happening in the career; many of you are in new careers or on new career paths. But with your career planet retrograde from the 24th, look before you leap or make dramatic changes. If you are making changes make them before that date.

Your social skills are important in most areas of life now, but most especially in finance. You need the good graces of others. A business partnership or joint venture is happening now, or the opportunity for it is there. After the 20th, as your financial planet moves into your 8th house, taxes and debt seem to shape your financial decision making. The good news is that debt is more easily paid off (and it is a good period to focus on this). If you need to borrow, outside money is available, regardless of the state of the economy. You can generate money through creative financing, insurance claims, estates and royalties. Most importantly (and this applies all month) keep the financial interests of others – partners and friends – uppermost in your mind. Be helpful to others financially and your own prosperity will happen naturally. After the 20th it is good to get rid of possessions that you no longer need or use. Clean up the clutter in your financial life: get rid of redundant savings accounts or credit cards. Prosper by cutting back on non-essentials and waste.

Your health needs watching, especially until the 20th. Enhance it in the ways mentioned in the yearly report. Until the 8th give more attention to the lungs, small intestine, arms, shoulders and respiratory system. Most importantly rest and relax more to maintain high energy levels (although energy improves after the 20th).

## February

Best Days Overall: 4, 5, 13, 14, 22, 23
Most Stressful Days Overall: 11, 12, 17, 18, 24, 25
Best Days for Love: 3, 5, 6, 12, 15, 17, 18, 21, 24, 25
Best Days for Money: 1, 2, 3, 7, 8, 9, 11, 12, 17, 21, 22, 27, 28
Best Days for Career: 1, 9, 10, 17, 18, 24, 25, 27, 28

Most of the planets are still above the horizon of your chart and your 10th house of career gets even stronger on the 8th. So you are in a career period, like last month. Your career planet is also retrograde in your 3rd house. As regular readers know, the retrograde of a planet slows things down. There is a need for more study and homework with respect to career decisions and changes. Avoid career short cuts – most likely they will not be short cuts, but will actually delay things further. Slow, steady and methodical progress is called for now. Be especially careful when communicating with bosses and superiors. Be sure they get what you really mean and that you thoroughly understand what they mean. If there are career problems this period they will probably arise from miscommunication and misunderstanding.

Your love planet also starts to retrograde this month, on the 7th. The marriage or current love is now under review, the whole social life as well. Re-thinking, re-evaluating is in order. Go slow and steady in love and avoid rushing things. Let love grow and develop as it will. Your job in the coming months is to attain clarity in your love life. Once this is attained, love decisions will be easy.

Your 8th house of transformation is still very strong until the 19th – review our discussion of this from last month.

Finances are good this month. Your spouse, partner or current love is prospering, and is probably more generous with you too. On the 19th the financial planet enters Pisces, your 9th house, and your financial intuition gets very sharp. (Financial intuition will be especially sharp from the 18th to the 21st as the Sun travels with Neptune. Be alert for financial guidance and messages: they are good.) The 9th house (and its ruler) is considered very lucky, so there are happy financial events going on. Spiritual techniques such as prayer and meditation will have 'bottom line' consequences on earnings. Financial opportunities come from foreign lands, foreign investments, foreigners and foreign companies. Financial opportunity also comes from the religious people in your life – the people at your place of worship.

Power in the 9th house indicates foreign travel. For students it shows success in their studies. There is a greater interest in religion, philosophy, theology and higher education.

Health is much improved this month, especially after the 19th. Enhance your health in the ways described in the yearly report.

### March

Best Days Overall: 3, 4, 11, 12, 20, 21, 30, 31
Most Stressful Days Overall: 9, 10, 15, 16, 22, 23, 24
Best Days for Love: 2, 7, 10, 15, 16, 19, 25, 26, 29
Best Days for Money: 3, 4, 5, 6, 7, 11, 12, 15, 16, 22, 23, 25, 26
Best Days for Career: 7, 8, 15, 16, 22, 23, 24, 25

The main headlines this month are the power in your career house from the 20th onwards – you enter a yearly career peak then. The shift in planetary power from the West to the East also occurs around that time. By the 20th, 60 per cent (sometimes 70 per cent) of the planets will be in the Eastern sector – the sector of personal power and independence. The cycle of 'people pleasing' is over. Sure, other people are important and you treat them with courtesy and respect, but you need not kowtow to them or sacrifice your happiness because of them. It's who you really are that matters now, your abilities and initiative.

In the past six or so months you have probably identified areas in your life that are uncomfortable and need to be changed. Now is the time to do this. You have greater power over your own affairs. You are in more personal control than usual. As the months go by you will find that people, the world at large, will start adapting to you rather than vice versa.

Career is successful now, and especially after the 20th. But your career planet is retrograde so keep in mind our discussion of last month. Make haste slowly and steadily. Aim for perfection in all that you do.

Your health starts to get very delicate after the 20th. Yes, you are busy and active in your career, but try to rest and relax more. With some creativity you can blend work and rest in a good way. Take siestas or massages in the middle of the day. Delegate and outsource more. At least 60 per cent of the planets are in stressful alignment with you at one time or another, so this is not something to take lightly. You will get through it – you got through last year and this year is easier. But you need to do your part. Enhance your health in the ways mentioned in the yearly report.

Finances are good this month, but there are some bumps on the road. The financial planet is still in the 'bullish' 9th house – the luckiest house in the Horoscope (according to the Hindu astrologers). Much of what we wrote of last month still applies until the 20th. After that the financial planet moves into Aries, your 10th house. Basically this is good; it shows that finance is high on your priorities and that you are focused here. This focus tends to bring success. At the Mid-heaven (the top of the chart) the Sun is in his most powerful position. Thus earnings are strong. This kind of transit shows that money comes from the career – from your good professional reputation (which brings referrals and other opportunities), from pay rises, from the support and good graces of authority figures, and perhaps even from the government.

You are a big earner but also a lavish spender. You have an appetite for risk after the 20th.

The Sun opposes Mars from the 1st to the 5th. This shows some financial disagreement with a boss, parent or parent figure. This will pass, but try not to make matters worse. The Sun conjuncts Uranus from the 23rd to the 26th, which is basically a good transit; money, windfalls, expensive items come to you suddenly and out of the blue. From the 28th to the 31st the Sun squares Pluto, and so avoid speculations in that period. Be more cautious about borrowing.

### April

Best Days Overall: 8, 16, 17, 26, 27
Most Stressful Days Overall: 6, 12, 13, 19, 20
Best Days for Love: 5, 6, 7, 12, 13, 14, 15, 24, 25
Best Days for Money: 1, 2, 4, 10, 11, 12, 13, 20, 21, 22, 29, 30
Best Days for Career: 3, 4, 12, 19, 20, 21

Health still needs watching until the 20th. Review our discussion of last month. Although health and energy improve somewhat after that, you should still be careful. You are still in the midst of a yearly career peak until the 20th. Your career planet has been retrograde since January 24 and some of you might feel that you are going backwards in your career instead of forward, but this is only a feeling and not reality. Much progress is being made behind the scenes. You have a lot of help and support career-wise. Your career planet is making fabulous aspects to Pluto all month. Children in your life are supportive of your career goals, and you find it easier to enjoy your career path, to have fun and be creative with it. And this tends to bring success.

Mars will start to move forward on the 17th and this will bring more clarity to the career. Cloudy areas will clear up. Mercury will cross the Mid-heaven and enter your 10th house on the 17th, which will be positive. Communication between you and your superiors will improve. There is better mutual understanding. Since Mercury is both your spiritual and family planet, this shows that you have good family support in your career. The family itself as a whole is very ambitious, and seems successful now. Your family values and dedication actually help your career (often it is considered a distraction, but not now). Career is enhanced through involvement with charities and altruistic causes. Your spiritual practice is ultra important now.

The financial trends are pretty much like last month. Until the 20th the Sun is in Aries and your 10th house. Thus you have the financial favour and grace of your bosses. This indicates rises in salary and income from your good professional reputation. Excessive risk taking is the main financial danger now. Start-ups and new ventures are very appealing at present.

On the 20th the Sun moves into Taurus (also a good financial position). Your financial judgement is astute. You become more cautious in your financial dealings. Earnings and wealth are perhaps less exciting, but much more stable. The financial planet in your 11th house indicates many things: social connections are important in this period; friends are rich and supportive. You are spending more on technology, but you can also earn from this. Perhaps there is new software that gives you more control of your finances or that enhances your earning power. Your financial hopes and wishes are coming to pass this period.

The financial planet opposes Saturn from the 14th to the 18th. Definitely slow down and avoid risk taking in money matters. Often people experience financial delays – payments aren't made on time or promised projects get delayed, things of this nature. However, this is short term and not a trend for the year. This aspect also shows some financial disagreement with the spouse, partner or current love.

The Sun squares Pluto on the 1st. Avoid speculations then.

Love has been problematic this year, but things should improve after the 20th as the Sun moves away from it stressful aspect to your love planet.

**May**

Best Days Overall: 5, 6, 13, 14, 15, 23, 24, 25
Most Stressful Days Overall: 3, 4, 9, 10, 16, 17, 30,
   31
Best Days for Love: 3, 4, 9, 10, 11, 12, 21, 22, 30, 31
Best Days for Money: 1, 2, 9, 10, 19, 20, 21, 26, 27, 29,
   30
Best Days for Career: 1, 2, 9, 10, 16, 17, 19, 20, 28, 29

On April 3 Venus entered your spiritual 12th house (and will be there for four months, until August 7). Your spiritual planet, Mercury, crossed the Mid-heaven and entered the 10th house of career. So spirituality has become an important focus. New, spiritual-type friends are coming into your life. The family seems more spiritual and perhaps you are holding spiritual meetings at your home. Only a spiritual understanding will solve certain family conundrums and this understanding is coming to you. You are learning the importance of 'right mood' for success in your meditative and prayer life. Anger, irritation, discord will block the flow of spiritual energy. The focus on spirituality continues this month and gets even stronger. On the 20th the Sun enters the 12th house and on the 29th Mercury joins him. Many spiritual breakthroughs and supernatural-type experiences are happening now.

Cancerians always have an active dream life, but now even more so. Pay attention here as there are important messages for you.

Health is much improved now, but still needs watching. You are spending more on health (especially from the 11th to the 14th), which is probably a good thing now. The state of your finances affects your health and since finances are good, this is a positive signal.

You are approaching your personal new year, your solar return. For many of you this will happen next month and for some the month after. In our Western culture New Year is party time. But in many cultures New Year is a more solemn occasion. There is celebration, but there is much soul-searching, review and atonement for past mistakes before the celebrations. Astrology seems to support this perspective. Before your new year – your new solar cycle – your 12th house of spirituality is ultra powerful. This is so for all the signs. This house is about atonement, correcting old karmas and mistakes and clearing the psychological debris that obstructs the flow of spiritual power so that the new cycle can start in a positive way. The celebration will come – have no fear – but you want to get there in the proper way. So a review of the past year is in order. What has been achieved, what was left undone, where do you want to go from here? Set your goals for the coming cycle. This is your job for this month and the next.

There is a solar eclipse on the 20th that occurs right on the cusp of the 12th house. This eclipse is basically benign to you but it won't hurt to take reduce your schedule any-way. This eclipse produces dramatic financial and spiritual changes. Flaws in these areas are revealed so that you can make corrections.

### June

Best Days Overall: 1, 2, 10, 11, 20, 21, 29, 30
Most Stressful Days Overall: 5, 6, 12, 13, 27, 28
Best Days for Love: 5, 6, 8, 9, 17, 18, 27, 28
Best Days for Money: 5, 6, 8, 9, 17, 18, 19, 22, 23, 26, 27, 29, 30
Best Days for Career: 5, 6, 7, 12, 13, 15, 16, 25, 26

Your house of spirituality gets even more powerful this month, so keep in mind our discussion of this last month. On June 11, Jupiter enters this house and will stay there for the year ahead. Spirituality is going to be important for the rest of the year – important and happy.

Jupiter also happens to be your health planet. His move into your 12th house has important (and positive) health implications. Health, as we mentioned, has been stressful of late, and you have probably tried all the conventional treatments – most likely with mixed results. Now you are being called to try the inner, spiritual ways to take care of health problems. You will see amazing results, but you will need faith, practice and persistence. Read as much as you can on spiritual healing. What you really need for your health is a spiritual breakthrough, not more pills or potions.

The health planet's change of sign and house shows changes in the health regime and practice. And, to reinforce this, there is a lunar eclipse on the 4th in your 6th house of health. Perhaps there is some health scare that produces the change of heart and change of regime. Often this is how change happens, but not necessarily.

Every lunar eclipse (and there are at least two every year) brings a change to the image and personality – a redefinition of yourself. This is a very healthy practice. Humans are evolving, growing creatures and thus a periodic change of image is natural. You are not the person you were six months ago, and in six months' time you will be different again. So twice a year you get the opportunity to fine-tune this area. Generally this produces important wardrobe changes, changes of hair style, etc. You will be projecting a new look in keeping with the new you. Job changes are likely now too. If you employ others there may be employee turnover or dramas in the lives of employees (or both). Take it easy during this period and avoid risky types of activities.

If you've done your yearly review properly, it's time to celebrate and enjoy life as the Sun enters your 1st house (and your own sign) on the 21st. This is a good period to get the body and image in shape, where you want it to be.

Finances will be good this month too, especially after the 21st. There are windfalls and opportunities seeking you out. You feel rich and project this image. Personal appearance is important in earnings, more so than usual. Until the 21st follow your intuition.

## July

Best Days Overall: 7, 8, 17, 18, 26, 27
Most Stressful Days Overall: 3, 4, 9, 10, 11, 24, 25, 30, 31
Best Days for Love: 3, 4, 5, 6, 15, 16, 24, 25, 30, 31
Best Days for Money: 5, 6, 7, 8, 15, 16, 18, 19, 20, 21, 24, 25, 28
Best Days for Career: 4, 5, 9, 10, 11, 15, 24

On the 21st of last month you entered one of your peak health periods for the year. Though health has been problematic, during this period the problems seem more or less in abeyance. This trend continues in the month ahead.

The planets are starting to shift from the upper to the lower half of the Horoscope. Right now they are more or less equally balanced between the two hemispheres. The upper half of the Horoscope is no longer dominant as it has been since the beginning of the year. Career and ambitions are winding down now, and very soon you get to focus on your real love – the home and the family. This month you are shuttling back and forth between these two interests, now focusing on your career and now focusing on the family.

Since June 21 the planets are in their maximum Eastern position, so make use of this by creating conditions as you like them. Don't be afraid to make changes – design your life according to your personal specifications.

Saturn, your love planet, started to move forward on June 25. So love, although problematic, is getting clarified. Finance seems a challenge in the relationship from the 12th to the 15th – perhaps your spouse, partner or current love's financial thinking and planning is not realistic.

Your personal finances are very good now. The Sun, your financial planet, is in your 1st house until the 22nd – which is a prosperous transit – review our discussion of this last month. On the 22nd, the Sun enters your money house and you enter a yearly financial peak.

Mars makes stressful aspects with both Uranus and Pluto from the 15th to the 24th. Parents and children need to be more careful driving and more mindful on the physical plane. Avoid confrontations and risky kinds of activities. Keep dangerous objects out of the reach of children. There can be some temporary career challenges as well.

Mercury goes retrograde on the 15th so take more care in communicating. Avoid, where possible, signing contracts or making long-term commitments. Information you receive might not be too reliable so withhold judgement; study things more deeply. Mercury is also your spiritual planet, so spiritual messages, dreams and intuition need verification now.

## August

Best Days Overall: 4, 5, 13, 14, 15, 22, 23, 31
Most Stressful Days Overall: 6, 7, 20, 21, 27, 28
Best Days for Love: 1, 2, 3, 11, 12, 13, 14, 20, 21, 22, 23, 27, 28, 29, 30, 31
Best Days for Money: 1, 2, 6, 7, 11, 12, 16, 17, 18, 20, 21, 27, 29, 30
Best Days for Career: 1, 2, 6, 7, 11, 12, 20, 21, 31

Retrograde activity among the planets was at its maximum for the year last month from the 15th onwards. And this situation persists until the 8th of this month. You are personally not too affected by this, but others in your life are, and the world is as a whole. Be patient with all the delays happening. When retrograde activity is high, the cosmos is calling us to slow down, avoid short cuts and be perfect in all that we do. This is the best way to go through this. Seeming short cuts are not really short cuts and will wind up slowing you down even more. (Work not done right has to be redone.)

You are still in the midst of a yearly financial peak until the 23rd. From an investment perspective, gold, utilities and entertainment are interesting until then. After that date the health field seems interesting.

Your financial planet has been in Leo since July 22. Thus you speculate more and take more risks in finance. You earn more and spend more too. You want to enjoy your wealth and are thus spending on leisure and entertainment, on fun kinds of activities. After the 23rd you become more conservative and analytical in finance. Probably you will spend less and want better value for your money. Sales, marketing and good use of the media is very important after the 23rd. People need to know about your product or service. You need to create some 'buzz' about it. You are spending on communication equipment after that date too, and on books, magazines, lectures and courses.

The Sun opposes Neptune from the 22nd to the 25th. Do more homework with regard to financial deals, commitments, large purchases or investments. There is behind the scenes activity that you need to know about.

Health still needs watching, but is reasonable this month, and there is no major crisis on the horizon. Continue to enhance the health in the ways previously discussed.

Venus enters your sign on the 8th – a happy transit. You look more glamorous and stylish. Your outward demeanour is more charming and graceful. Dance would be a wonderful exercise now. Friends seem devoted to you, and your family likewise. Love is still problematic but this has nothing to do with you. You are attracting the opposite sex now but it is the actual relationship, the daily details of relating that seem problematic. Mars is in a transit with your love planet from the 11th to the 17th. This can create conflict within the current relationship. For singles it brings opportunities for an office romance. All of you will be socializing with people of high status during this period.

## September

Best Days Overall: 1, 10, 11, 19, 27, 28
Most Stressful Days Overall: 2, 3, 16, 17, 23, 24, 29, 30
Best Days for Love: 1, 8, 9, 12, 17, 18, 21, 22, 23, 24, 26, 29, 30
Best Days for Money: 5, 6, 7, 8, 12, 13, 14, 15, 16, 17, 25, 26
Best Days for Career: 1, 2, 3, 10, 11, 18, 19, 27, 28, 29, 30

Though the main focus now is on the home and family, as it should be, career seems successful. You seem to be enjoying it now. You advance your career as you are involved in leisure activities – perhaps you make important contacts at a party or at the theatre or on the sports field. Children in your life are also more ambitious this month. You are probably more ambitious for them than for yourself. The children are your spiritual mission this month.

You have been through a strong independent cycle these past few months. You had the power to create conditions and have life on your terms. But this is about to change as the planets start shifting to the Western sector on the 23rd. The shift is not complete yet, but by next month the Western sector will be stronger than the Eastern, and thus you become more dependent on others and their good graces. Being in control (which has been the case for the past few months) is wonderful, but not being in control is also good in different ways. Learn to enjoy both.

Prosperity still seems very strong in the month ahead. Your money house is still powerful and active. Mercury in the money house until the 16th reinforces the importance of sales, marketing and media activities. Good communication about your product or service is ultra important still. On the 23rd the Sun enters your 4th house. You are spending more on the home and family than is the norm. Family support will be good.

There are financial opportunities through the family and family connections. You are keeping business activities within the family – doing business from home and with family members. There are profitable opportunities in real estate, restaurants, food and industries that cater to the home. There are some financial bumps on the road between the 28th and the 30th, perhaps sudden unplanned for expenses. Avoid speculations or other kinds of financial risk taking that period.

Health again becomes delicate after the 23rd. Refer to our discussion in the yearly report.

Power in the 4th house of home and family from the 23rd onwards is Cancerian heaven. The cosmos impels you to be involved with what you most love. If your energy were higher it would really be heaven.

## October

Best Days Overall: 7, 8, 16, 17, 24, 25, 26
Most Stressful Days Overall: 1, 14, 15, 20, 21, 27, 28
Best Days for Love: 1, 7, 12, 16, 20, 21, 24
Best Days for Money: 4, 5, 6, 9, 10, 11, 14, 15, 22, 23, 24
Best Days for Career: 1, 9, 18, 27, 28

Health still needs watching this month, especially until the 23rd, but things are improving. Saturn moves out of Libra and into Scorpio on the 5th. You have gone through the worst of the health stress, and your house of health is strong this month so you are paying more attention and this is good news. Continue to enhance your health in the ways described in the yearly report. However, you can also add a few other procedures this month. Mars in this house from the 7th onwards indicates the importance of physical exercise and good muscle tone. Head, face and scalp massage will be powerful as well. Mercury moves into your 6th house on the 29th, when the lungs, small intestine, arms, shoulders and respiratory system need more attention. Arm and shoulder massage is a powerful therapy and will be even more beneficial after the 29th. (Tension tends to collect in the shoulders and a good massage will release it.) Health is vastly improved after the 23rd as the Sun enters Scorpio – a harmonious aspect for you.

Home and family are still the dominant interests until the 23rd. Children, particularly the oldest, are especially important after the 23rd. On the 23rd you enter a yearly personal pleasure peak. Leisure activities call to you and your personal creativity is strong. This is a happy-go-lucky, holiday kind of period.

Financially the trends of last month continue until the 23rd. After that you seem more speculative and risk taking. You want to enjoy the actual act of earning money, and probably you will. You are enjoying your wealth these days and we can't always say this; generally earnings are going to pay basic expenses but now you are able to spend on fun activities. Your financial judgement is astute now, and you are a difficult person to fool or defraud.

The love life is improving this month. Saturn is now making harmonious aspects to you. If a current relationship survived the past two years, it will survive further. There is more harmony with the current love (or the new person in your life). Love is more fun. You are having fun in your relationship and with your friends. Singles are attracted to people they can have fun with and who have good sexual chemistry. Singles find love opportunities in the usual places – at parties, resorts, the theatre and places of leisure. For the past two years, family values and emotional intimacy were important in love, now it is fun and sexual magnetism.

The Sun trines Jupiter from the 7th to the 10th and this brings financial windfalls, increase and job opportunities (for those who are looking). Between the 24th and 27th, the Sun conjuncts Saturn; your spouse, friends or current love prosper and also supply both money and opportunity. They seem financially supportive.

## November

Best Days Overall: 3, 4, 5, 12, 13, 21, 22
Most Stressful Days Overall: 10, 11, 16, 17, 23, 24
Best Days for Love: 1, 3, 11, 12, 16, 17, 20, 21
Best Days for Money: 1, 2, 3, 4, 6, 7, 11, 13, 19, 23, 28, 29
Best Days for Career: 6, 7, 15, 23, 24, 26

Retrograde activity increases sharply this month (a short-term blip), so there is a need for more patience and perfection in all that you do. Slower and more methodically is the best way forward.

With two eclipses this month there is going to be much change, but the retrograde activity is suggesting that these changes will come via a 'delayed reaction'. Try not to leap into action before doing the appropriate research.

The solar eclipse of the 13th occurs in your 5th house and is basically benign to you. Still, it's best to reduce your schedule as it is probably not benign to many people around you. Children and children figures seem most affected. There are dramas in their lives. They are redefining their image and personalities now and over the next six months will be presenting a new image to the world.

This eclipse also brings needed financial changes and adjustments. (Every solar eclipse does this.) The financial thinking and strategy has to change. Generally this occurs because of an unexpected expense or some other financial disturbance, like a stock-market reversal. Each will be affected by it according to their situation and need. The eclipse brings out hidden situations to allow you to back on a healthier, more realistic track. Over time the changes work out well. They are disturbing only over the short term.

Avoid speculations and financial risk taking during this period. (It will be difficult, you seem very inclined to speculation now.)

Every lunar eclipse affects you strongly and the one on the 28th is no different. Take it easy. Spend more quiet time at home or close to home. If you are working out, take it gently. If you feel a pain or twinge somewhere, stop and rest. Listen to the body. This eclipse occurs in your 12th house of spirituality and suggests important changes in your spiritual regime or practice, perhaps in teachers and ideas. Usually this comes about through a deeper revelation and thus it is good. These revelations are causing a redefinition of the body, the image and the self-concept. Like the children, you are changing your image and presentation to the world over the next six months. Even personal desires and appetites will change.

This eclipse also indicates shake-ups in charitable organizations that you are involved with. There are dramas in the lives of the spiritual people you are involved with too.

### December

Best Days Overall: 1, 2, 10, 11, 18, 19, 30, 31
Most Stressful Days Overall: 8, 9, 14, 15, 20, 21, 22
Best Days for Love: 1, 10, 11, 14, 15, 18, 20, 28, 31
Best Days for Money: 3, 4, 8, 13, 16, 22, 25, 30, 31
Best Days for Career: 6, 15, 20, 21, 22, 24

Last month's increase in retrograde activity was an aberration. This month, by the 13th 90 per cent of the planets move forward – a huge percentage and a huge shift in one month. This is like a car in reverse suddenly going forwards to 60 mph in 10 seconds. Whoosh! The pace of life speeds up suddenly and dramatically. Stalled projects not only get going but move forward quickly.

Other shifts are happening for you this month too. On the 21st, as the Sun enters Capricorn, the planetary power is now in the upper half of your chart. Career and outer activities now become more important than home, family and emotional issues. It is time to take overt, direct action towards your career goals.

Your 6th house of health and work is very powerful this month, especially until the 21st. You are focused on health. Job seekers will have success now. Those who really want to work tend to find it. Your focus on health will stand you in good stead for later in the month when health and energy are more delicate. Rest and relax more after the 21st. Enhance your health in the ways described in the yearly report. From the 16th onwards give more attention to the kidneys and hips. As we mentioned, though your health is delicate it will not be as severe as last year or the first part of this year.

The love situation is improving day by day. Since October 5, your love planet is in a harmonious alignment with you. Also it is moving forward. And, on the 21st you enter a yearly love and social peak. So love is happier now. Many of the love trends that we discussed in October are still in effect. Fun and good sexual magnetism are the main attractions in love, but this month we also see that wealth and position are important too. Singles have romantic opportunities at the office and with superiors. However, keep in mind that the long-term 'detox' in the love and social life is still very much in effect. A new marriage, a new social circle – the love life of your dreams – is being born, and birth always involves birth pangs.

Finances are strong all month. Until the 21st your financial planet is in Sagittarius, which is a position of prosperity and expansion. Overspending is perhaps the main danger here. Sometimes under this aspect there is an unrealistic kind of optimism that can impair correct decisions. Optimism is good, but one needs to be realistic. Sometimes under this aspect people overly inflate their earnings. If they are actually making £10,000, in their mind they are making £50,000, and this can lead to problems. But in general, there is financial increase this month. On the 21st the financial planet moves into your 7th house and into the sign of Capricorn. Financial judgement becomes much sounder, more realistic and more down to earth then. The social circle seems wealthy and they seem more supportive financially.

# Leo

## ♌

---

---

## Personality Profile

### LEO AT A GLANCE

*Element* – Fire

*Ruling Planet* – Sun
   *Career Planet* – Venus
   *Love Planet* – Uranus
   *Money Planet* – Mercury
   *Planet of Health and Work* – Saturn
   *Planet of Home and Family Life* – Pluto

*Colours* – gold, orange, red

*Colours that promote love, romance and social
   harmony* – black, indigo, ultramarine blue

*Colours that promote earning power* – yellow,
   yellow–orange

*Gems* – amber, chrysolite, yellow diamond

*Metal* – gold

*Scents* – bergamot, frankincense, musk, neroli

*Quality* – fixed (= stability)

*Quality most needed for balance* – humility

*Strongest virtues* – leadership ability, self-esteem and confidence, generosity, creativity, love of joy

*Deepest needs* – fun, elation, the need to shine

*Characteristics to avoid* – arrogance, vanity, bossiness

*Signs of greatest overall compatibility* – Aries, Sagittarius

*Signs of greatest overall incompatibility* – Taurus, Scorpio, Aquarius

*Sign most helpful to career* – Taurus

*Sign most helpful for emotional support* – Scorpio

*Sign most helpful financially* – Virgo

*Sign best for marriage and/or partnerships* – Aquarius

*Sign most helpful for creative projects* – Sagittarius

*Best Sign to have fun with* – Sagittarius

*Signs most helpful in spiritual matters* – Aries, Cancer

*Best day of the week* – Sunday

# Understanding a Leo

When you think of Leo, think of royalty – then you'll get the idea of what the Leo character is all about and why Leos are the way they are. It is true that, for various reasons, some Leo-born do not always express this quality – but even if not they should like to do so.

A monarch rules not by example (as does Aries) nor by consensus (as do Capricorn and Aquarius) but by personal will. Will is law. Personal taste becomes the style that is imitated by all subjects. A monarch is somehow larger than life. This is how a Leo desires to be.

When you dispute the personal will of a Leo it is serious business. He or she takes it as a personal affront, an insult. Leos will let you know that their will carries authority and that to disobey is demeaning and disrespectful.

A Leo is king (or queen) of his or her personal domain. Subordinates, friends and family are the loyal and trusted subjects. Leos rule with benevolent grace and in the best interests of others. They have a powerful presence; indeed, they are powerful people. They seem to attract attention in any social gathering. They stand out because they are stars in their domain. Leos feel that, like the Sun, they are made to shine and rule. Leos feel that they were born to special privilege and royal prerogatives – and most of them attain this status, at least to some degree.

The Sun is the ruler of this sign, and when you think of sunshine it is very difficult to feel unhealthy or depressed. Somehow the light of the Sun is the very antithesis of illness and apathy. Leos love life. They also love to have fun; they love drama, music, the theatre and amusements of all sorts. These are the things that give joy to life. If – even in their best inter-ests – you try to deprive Leos of their pleasures, good food, drink and entertainment, you run the serious risk of depriving them of the will to live. To them life without joy is no life at all.

Leos epitomize humanity's will to power. But power in and of itself – regardless of what some people say – is neither good nor evil. Only when power is abused does it become evil. Without power even good things cannot come to pass. Leos realize this and are uniquely qualified to wield power. Of all the signs, they do it most naturally. Capricorn, the other power sign of the zodiac, is a better manager and administrator than Leo – much better. But Leo outshines Capricorn in personal grace and presence. Leo loves power, whereas Capricorn assumes power out of a sense of duty.

## Finance

Leos are great leaders but not necessarily good managers. They are better at handling the overall picture than the nitty-gritty details of business. If they have good managers working for them they can become exceptional executives. They have vision and a lot of creativity.

Leos love wealth for the pleasures it can bring. They love an opulent lifestyle, pomp and glamour. Even when they are not wealthy they live as if they are. This is why many fall into debt, from which it is sometimes difficult to emerge.

Leos, like Pisceans, are generous to a fault. Very often they want to acquire wealth solely so that they can help others economically. Wealth to Leo buys services and managerial ability. It creates jobs for others and improves the general well-being of those around them. Therefore – to a Leo – wealth is good. Wealth is to be enjoyed to the fullest. Money is not to be left to gather dust in a mouldy bank vault but to be enjoyed, spread around, used. So Leos can be quite reckless in their spending.

With the sign of Virgo on Leo's 2nd house (of money) cusp, Leo needs to develop some of Virgo's traits of analysis, discrimination and purity when it comes to money matters. They must learn to be more careful with the details of finance (or to hire people to do this for them). They have to be more cost-conscious in their spending habits. Generally, they need to manage their money better. Leos tend to chafe under financial constraints, yet these constraints can help Leos to reach their highest financial potential.

Leos like it when their friends and family know that they can depend on them for financial support. They do not mind – and even enjoy – lending money, but they are careful that they are not taken advantage of. From their 'regal throne' Leos like to bestow gifts upon their family and friends and then enjoy the good feelings these gifts bring to everybody. Leos love financial speculations and – when the celestial influences are right – are often lucky.

## Career and Public Image

Leos like to be perceived as wealthy, for in today's world wealth often equals power. When they attain wealth they love having a large house with lots of land and animals.

At their jobs Leos excel in positions of authority and power. They are good at making decisions – on a grand level – but they prefer to leave the details to others. Leos are well respected by their colleagues and subordinates, mainly because they have a knack for understanding and relating to those around them. Leos usually strive for the top positions even if they have to start at the bottom and work hard to get there. As might be expected of such a charismatic sign, Leos are always trying to improve their work situation. They do so in order to have a better chance of advancing to the top.

On the other hand, Leos do not like to be bossed around or told what to do. Perhaps this is why they aspire so for the top – where they can be the decision-makers and need not take orders from others.

Leos never doubt their success and focus all their attention and efforts on achieving it. Another great Leo characteristic is that – just like good monarchs – they do not attempt to abuse the power or success they achieve. If they do so this is not wilful or intentional. Usually they like to share their wealth and try to make everyone around them join in their success.

Leos are – and like to be perceived as – hard-working, well-established individuals. It is definitely true that they are capable of hard work and often manage great things. But do not forget that, deep down inside, Leos really are fun-lovers.

## Love and Relationships

Generally, Leos are not the marrying kind. To them relationships are good while they are pleasurable. When the relationship ceases to be pleasurable a true Leo will want out. They always want to have the freedom to leave. That is why Leos excel at love affairs rather than commitment. Once married, however, Leo is faithful – even if some Leos have a tendency to marry more than once in their lifetime. If you are in love with a Leo, just show him or her a good time – travel, go to casinos and clubs, the theatre and discos. Wine and dine your Leo love – it is expensive but worth it and you will have fun.

Leos generally have an active love life and are demonstrative in their affections. They love to be with other optimistic and fun-loving types like themselves, but wind up settling with someone more serious, intellectual and unconventional. The partner of a Leo tends to be more political and socially conscious than he or she is, and more libertarian. When you marry a Leo, mastering the freedom-loving tendencies of your partner will definitely become a life-long challenge – and be careful that Leo does not master you.

Aquarius sits on Leo's 7th house (of love) cusp. Thus if Leos want to realize their highest love and social potential they need to develop a more egalitarian, Aquarian perspective on others. This is not easy for Leo, for 'the king' finds his equals only among other 'kings'. But perhaps this is the solution to Leo's social challenge – to be 'a king among kings'. It is all right to be regal, but recognize the nobility in others.

## Home and Domestic Life

Although Leos are great entertainers and love having people over, sometimes this is all show. Only very few close friends will get to see the real side of a Leo's day-to-day life. To a Leo the home is a place of comfort, recreation and transformation; a secret, private retreat – a castle. Leos like to spend money, show off a bit, entertain and have fun. They enjoy the latest furnishings, clothes and gadgets – all things fit for kings.

Leos are fiercely loyal to their family and, of course, expect the same from them. They love their children almost to a fault; they have to be careful not to spoil them too much. They also must try to avoid attempting to make individual family members over in their own image. Leos should keep in mind that others also have the need to be their own people. That is why Leos have to be extra careful about being over-bossy or over-domineering in the home.

# Horoscope for 2012

## Major Trends

Last year, 2011, was a good year for Leo. Jupiter made fabulous aspects to the Sun in the first part of the year and moved into your 10th career house the latter part. There was prosperity and much career success and opportunity. Health too should have been good. Only one long-term planet was stressing you, but not enough to cause serious problems. Most of these positive trends continue this year. Health should be even better than last year (until October 5) as Neptune moves away from his stressful aspect to you. From February 3 until October 5, the long-term planets are either making good aspects or leaving you alone. Jupiter remains in your 10th house until June 11 and so career success is still happening. On the 11th, Jupiter will move into your house of friendships and will bring a happy social life.

On October 5, Saturn will enter Scorpio, which will be a stressful aspect for you. But again this by itself is not enough to cause serious problems. (More on this later.)

Neptune makes a major long-term move into your 8th house of transformation on February 3. You will be dealing more with death and death issues now, and gaining a spiritual understanding of these things. Also sex will be more spiritual and more refined. There are other trends with this transit that we will discuss later on.

Uranus remains in your 9th house, indicating that your religious and philosophical beliefs are undergoing radical change. Many will be tested. You will be forced to redefine and reshape this area of life, probably along more scientific lines.

Your areas of greatest interest in the year ahead are finance (until July 3); communication and intellectual interests (until October 5); home and family (after October 5); health and work; sex, personal transformation, personal reinvention, occult studies (from February 3 onwards); religion, philosophy, theology, higher education and foreign travel (all year); career (until June 11); friends, groups, group activities (from April 3 onwards).

Your paths of greatest fulfilment this year are career (until June 11); friends, groups, group activities (from June 11 onwards); personal creativity, personal pleasure and children (until August 31); home and family (after August 31).

## Health

*(Please note that this is an* astrological *perspective on health and not a medical one. In days of yore these perspectives were identical. But these days there could be quite a difference. For a medical perspective, please consult your doctor or health practitioner.)*

As we mentioned, overall health looks good this year, especially until October 5. Last year Uranus moved into a harmonious aspect with you and this year, on February 3,

Neptune moves away from a stressful aspect. So overall, health and energy looks fine.

Normally with this situation we would expect to see your 6th house empty, but it isn't. Though health is good, you are still focused here – probably because you want to make sure that it stays good.

Saturn, your health planet, was in some very stressful aspects last year and thus there could have been a few health scares. Probably these were just scares and nothing more. Energy – life force – is the greatest healer and greatest guard against disease. And this you had, and still have, in abundance.

Good though your health is, you can make it even better. Give more attention to the following organs: the heart (always important for you – avoid worry and anxiety, the main spiritual root causes of heart problems); the spine, knees, teeth, bones, skin and overall skeletal alignment (regular back and knee massage would be wonderful and regular visits to a chiropractor, osteopath or dermatologist would be a good idea, as the vertebrae need to be kept in the correct alignment – also it is advisable to give the knees more support when exercising, and therapies such as Alexander Technique or Feldenkrais are always good for you); the kidneys and hips (until October 5 – hips should be regularly massaged); and the colon, bladder and sexual organs (safe sex and sexual moderation are important for the long term, and most especially after October 5).

These are the most vulnerable areas this year and problems, if they happened, would most likely begin there. Thus keeping them healthy and fit is sound preventive medicine. Most of the time problems can be averted, and even when they can't be they can be so softened as to be merely minor inconveniences.

There are many natural, drugless therapies out there, but working with the charts we supply is also a viable way to proceed.

Pluto in your 6th house of health shows the importance of the colon, bladder and sexual organs. The health planet's

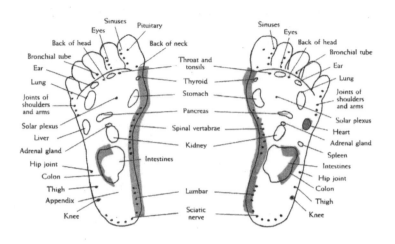

## Reflexology

*Try to massage the whole foot on a regular basis, but pay extra attention to the points highlighted on the chart. When you massage, be aware of 'sore spots', as these need special attention. It's also a good idea to massage the ankles and top side of the feet (see below).*

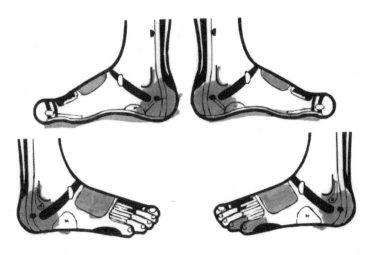

move into Scorpio (the sign that rules these organs) on October 5, reinforces this. This position also shows a tendency to surgeries. These are probably recommended, but detoxing will often do the job just as well although it usually takes longer. Detox regimes in general are good for the health and you respond well to them.

Disease affects the body, but doesn't always begin there. The physical body is not always the cause, but can manifest causes that originate on other levels such as mind and feeling.

Your chart shows that the spiritual root causes of problems are coming from a few areas – through misuse or overuse of the sexual energies, love problems, and misuse or overuse of the mental and communication faculties and family discords. Should problems arise, you will need to investigate these areas and bring them back into harmony as quickly as possible. We don't have the space here to develop this as much as we would like, but a word to the wise is sufficient.

Saturn, as we mentioned above, moves into Scorpio on October 5 and this is a stressful aspect. So you will need to watch your energy levels more after this date, and for the next two years.

## Home and Family

Your 4th house of home and family hasn't been strong for a number of years. It is pretty much empty for most of the year ahead, too. But beginning on October 5, as Saturn moves into this house, it starts to become important.

Ever since Pluto, your family planet, moved into your 6th health house in 2008 you have been focused on the overall health of the family. You have been working to make the home a healthier place to be and have probably installed much new gym or exercise equipment in the home. The home is becoming as much a health spa as a home and this trend is getting even stronger in the year ahead – especially after October 5.

The health of family members, and especially parents or parent figures, is a great concern. You seem more focused on them than on your own health.

Family is about mutual service. But this year you are doing more for them. There is a culture of 'service' in the family. If you love your family, you 'do' for them. This is the measure of family love – how much you do, how much you serve. The good news here is that it is not a one-way street. You are doing more for the family and they are doing more for you.

You have the Horoscope of someone who works from home. And this too is an important trend over the past few years. Many of you have set up home offices. The home is as much a work place as a home. This trend too is getting stronger in the year ahead.

Your family planet, Pluto, spends the year in pretty much an exact square aspect to Uranus. This indicates many dramas and shake-ups in the family unit. Often it shows sudden moves and things happening out of the blue. Often it shows splits in the family. The spouse, partner or current love is not in synch with the family and vice versa.

Emotions and passions are running high. Family members (and perhaps you as well) have extreme, sudden mood swings. These are difficult to handle. One moment there is love and harmony and the next you are at each other's throats. You don't know what to expect from family members from one moment to the next. Maintaining your personal emotional harmony – and harmony in the family unit – will be quite a challenge. You can do it, but you have to work at it.

If you are going to move, it is best to do it before October 5.

**Finance and Career**

Mars spends an unusual amount of time in your money house this year. Consider this: a normal Mars transit is approximately a month and a half. This year Mars will spend more than six months in this house. This is very significant and gives us many messages.

First off, you are developing more financial fearlessness this year. You are always a risk taker (not just in finance, but in many other areas of life) but this year (and especially until July 3) even more so. It is not so much about whether you win or lose, or whether your risks pay off or not – it is about overcoming the fear of loss, of being 'above' both profit or loss. If this is achieved, you can consider yourself successful.

You are more aggressive in financial matters now. You are into creating wealth rather than allowing it to happen. On the positive side, this brings success; on the negative side it can produce rashness and impatience in financial matters. Perhaps you are acting too quickly without giving enough thought to decisions. Perhaps you are doing too much. Not everything can be solved by action. Sometimes non-action is called for; time will resolve the situation, not more action. However you are getting much accomplished.

Mars is the ruler of your 9th house and this too gives us many messages. First off, the ruler of this house is considered one of the luckiest planets in the Horoscope. So this is another signal of good fortune, financial expansion and increased earnings. It shows that your financial goals are huge. You are after *big* wealth, not just getting by from payday to payday. Big goals tend to produce big results. But this aspect shows that you are travelling much on business; that there are financial opportunities and earnings in foreign countries, with foreigners and perhaps foreign companies. The state of the global economy plays a huge role (more than usual) on your financial life and decisions.

The 9th house rules your personal religion and philosophical beliefs. So, Mars is your religious planet. Thus religious practices enhance your wealth. Religious people in general – the members of your place of worship – are involved in your financial life, probably in a good way. (You are donating more to your place of worship as well.)

Mars in your money house indicates someone who wants financial independence, someone who wants to be in control of their financial destiny. This is one of your goals and you are likely to achieve it.

Career, as we mentioned, looks great. A banner year. Last year was good too. There have been promotions, pay rises and an overall elevation of your career and professional status. Happy career opportunities are also coming. The most important thing is that you seem to be enjoying your career. You are having fun. This tends to success.

Basically, this is a successful and prosperous year. Enjoy.

### Love and Social Life

Your 7th house of love has been powerful for many years, but now, less so. Neptune leaves that house on February 3 and it is more or less empty this year. (Only short-term planets will move through there, with short term, temporary effects.)

Normally an empty 7th house would indicate a status quo kind of love year. Married people would tend to stay married and singles would tend to stay single. But this year I'm not so sure. Your love planet Uranus spends the year more or less in square aspect to Pluto, which is a very dynamic aspect. Love is certainly challenging this year. Love is getting tested.

Much of this testing might not be because of the central relationship. The problems and challenges can be coming from personal dramas in the life of the spouse, partner or current love. He or she could be having near-death kinds of experiences, surgeries, or deaths in the family and these will impact on your relationship. (Friends could be having these kinds of experiences too.) Family disputes are also impacting on the love relationship.

Singles are not likely to marry this year; likewise those working on the second marriage. Those working on their third marriage are likely to marry or become involved in a serious relationship. This relationship seems like a lot of fun.

Leo is always a love at first sight kind of person. Love is an instantaneous kind of thing for them. But now that the love planet is in Aries (and has been since last year) this tendency is greatly magnified. And although the family seems disapproving of the love, you will go ahead anyway. Even elopements are likely. The danger now is jumping into serious relationships too quickly.

Your love planet will remain in your 9th house for many years to come. This shows various things. For students it indicates falling in love with a professor or teacher. In general you are attracted to highly educated and religious type people. Love and social opportunities happen in religious, academic or foreign settings. You seem willing to travel to the ends of the earth in search of love, and many of you will. You are in a period for 'long distance' love, conducted online, or by skyping and long trips. An existing marriage or relationship can be helped by travel. If there are problems, take a trip somewhere. Taking courses together as a couple or worshipping together will also help matters.

Leos are very sexual people. But these days good sex is not enough to hold a relationship together. There is a need for philosophical compatibility – to have a similar perspective on life, a similar world view. If this is lacking the relationship won't last very long.

In the year ahead your best and most active love periods will be January 19 to February 19; March 20 to April 5; July 23 to August 6; and November 23 to December 6.

The love life in general is very exciting, just the way you like things. Love can happen anywhere at any time. But the stability of the relationship is the issue.

**Self-improvement**

Neptune, as we mentioned, makes a major move into your 8th house on February 3 and stays there for the next 14 or so years. The sex life and sexual practice is gradually being elevated, refined and spiritualized. There is much more to sex than a 'neurological release' or fluidic discharge. In fact, from the spiritual perspective, this is the least important aspect. Sex is an energy exchange that happens on many, many levels. Sex is not evil as so many have been taught. On the contrary, it is the most sacred force in the universe – and it is precisely for this reason that its abuse can be so destructive. So you are in a period where you will be exploring the spiritual dimensions of sex.

Neptune in your 8th house also suggests that you will be more involved in personal transformation and reinvention, but in a spiritual way. The mortal human being cannot reinvent him or herself. Oh, it can make a big show of things, change the outer dress and make cosmetic changes, but not real fundamental change. Only the Spirit can do this. And this is a time for exploring these issues.

Saturn spends most of the year in your 3rd house of communication so, as in the past two years, you are in a period for disciplining the thoughts and speech. You are becoming a deeper thinker – the cosmos is demanding this of you. Best not to talk or offer opinions until you have done your homework and research. Take your time in your studies and don't be satisfied with superficial knowledge. If you follow this advice, when you *do* talk you will be listened to. Your communication will be more satisfying.

# Month-by-month Forecasts

## January

> Best Days Overall: 6, 7, 16, 17, 25, 26
> Most Stressful Days Overall: 3, 4, 17, 18, 23, 24, 30, 31
> Best Days for Love: 1, 6, 7, 10, 18, 19, 23, 24, 27, 28
> Best Days for Money: 1, 2, 3, 4, 12, 13, 21, 22, 30
> Best Days for Career: 3, 4, 6, 7, 18, 19, 27, 28, 30, 31

You begin your year with the Western, social sector of your chart totally dominant. In fact the short-term planets are in their maximum Western position this month (and next month as well). You are in a very strong social period. On the 20th you enter a yearly love and social peak. Party going and dating are much increased. Probably you are attending more weddings these days too.

When the planets are in the Western sector it means that they are 'furthest away' from you. So the cosmos is saying, 'its not about you, its about other people this period – your personal concerns are important, but we are thinking of the good of the whole and right now energy needs to flow away from you towards others'. There is nothing wrong with rational self-interest, but this is not the time for it. There is a need to put the interests of others ahead of your own. (And you seem to be doing this.) This is the kind of period where you gain your ends by attending to the needs of others. Some would call it a period of 'unselfishness'. Really, it is just a more 'enlightened' kind of selfishness. Your good will come to you but through the good graces of others. This is a time where you learn about yourself through your relationships, through your interaction with others. There are things we learn in relationships that we could never learn alone. It is good every now and then to take a vacation from ourselves, from our personal concerns, and you are in one of those periods.

Because the planetary power is 'far away' from you (you are represented by the Eastern point of the chart, the Ascendant), personal power, personal will and self-confidence are weaker than usual. It is much harder to change conditions that are uncomfortable. It can be done but with a lot more effort than usual. So, it is best to adapt to situations as best you can.

On the 20th the planetary power shifts from the lower half of your chart to the upper half. This is an important shift; day is breaking in your chart. The Sun is starting to peep over the horizon. The activities of night – sleep, dreaming, interior activity – are finished for now. It is time to be up and about and pursue your outer goals with zest. It is a time to be focused on the career and outer objectives and to make your inner dreams and visions manifest through overt physical actions. Home and family issues can be downplayed for now and energy given to the career.

Health needs more attention after the 20th. It is basically good, but this is not one of your best periods. Rest and relax more. Enhance the health in the ways mentioned in the yearly report. Happily your 6th house is strong all year, and especially until the 27th, and so you are paying attention here. Until the 27th you can enhance the health by also giving more attention to the lungs, small intestine, arms, shoulders and respiratory system; regular arm and shoulder massage will be wonderful.

**February**

>   Best Days Overall: 7, 8, 15, 16, 24, 25
>   Most Stressful Days Overall: 1, 13, 14, 19, 20, 27, 28
>   Best Days for Love: 5, 6, 7, 15, 19, 20, 24, 25
>   Best Days for Money: 1, 2, 3, 9, 10, 11, 12, 17, 22, 23, 27, 28
>   Best Days for Career: 1, 5, 6, 15, 24, 25, 27, 28

The trends that we wrote of last month are still in effect. The planetary power is still in the Western sector and the upper half of the chart is much stronger than the bottom half. Review last month's discussion of this.

Health still needs watching now, until the 19th. Enhance the health in the ways mentioned in the yearly report.

You are still in a yearly love and social peak until the 19th. After that your 8th house becomes very strong. It is not only the short-term planets that make it strong, but Neptune makes a major move into that house on the 3rd. This is a sexually active month too. Be careful not to overdo it: indulge but don't over indulge. Whatever your age or stage in life, libido is going to be stronger than usual.

Power in the 8th house show many things. On the practical level, it shows that the spouse, partner or current love is in a yearly financial peak. He or she is more generous with you. (Your financial planet will be in the 8th house from the 14th onwards, reinforcing what we say here.) There is more spousal support.

This is a good period for detoxing, and not just the physical body but all the various areas of life. Detox the mind and emotions; detox the finances (especially after the 14th). Get rid of excess possessions that you no longer use. Get rid of wasteful expenses. Consolidate bank accounts and savings. If you have good ideas this is an excellent month to attract outside investors. If you need to borrow money, this is also a good month for it. Many of you are involved with insurance claims or estates and there is good fortune now. Some of you might want to pay down existing debt and this will go easier this month. You will make more progress than usual.

So far we have been discussing practical things. But power in the 8th house indicates many deeper things. Many of you are involved in personal transformation, personal reinvention. Some call it 'self-actualization'. It is about giving birth to your 'ideal' self – to the person that you know you can be. These kinds of projects (and they are projects – sometimes full-time jobs) go well this month. Not only that, but all the knowledge that you need for the next steps will come to you. You have more energy and enthusiasm for these kings of things.

Students have been in a period of ferment and change. Schools have changed. Probably there have been changes in subjects studied and educational plans. This is all good. But Mars went retrograde on January 24 and so changes need more thought and homework now. Don't be in a rush.

Legal issues need more homework as well.

### March

Best Days Overall: 5, 6, 13, 14, 22, 23, 24
Most Stressful Days Overall: 11, 12, 18, 19, 25, 26
Best Days for Love: 5, 7, 13, 15, 16, 18, 19, 22, 25, 26
Best Days for Money: 2, 5, 7, 8, 13, 15, 16, 25, 26, 31
Best Days for Career: 7, 15, 16, 25, 26

You have all the classic ingredients for career success this month, and this year. Jupiter is right on the Mid-heaven of the Horoscope (a classic signal of success), and 60 per cent (sometimes 70 per cent) of the planets are above the horizon. Your health and energy is basically good. And, on the 5th, Venus enters your 10th house and travels with Jupiter. The two benevolent planets of the zodiac are in your house of career.

Career is peaking, but is not yet at its peak (this will happen next month). There are rises and promotions and elevations in status. There is recognition for your professional achievements, perhaps even honours. There are career opportunities as well, especially from the 11th to the 14th. (This period brings luck in speculations too.) Parents and parent figures are prospering and seem very generous with you. You have the grace and favour of the authority figures in your life. If you have issues with the government this is a good month to deal with it, they seem favourably disposed to you. If you need favours from 'on high' this is a good month to ask for them.

Your 8th house is still very powerful until the 20th, so refer to last month's discussion of this.

Your 9th house becomes more powerful than usual on the 2nd. This house is considered by Hindu astrologers to be the luckiest of all the houses. So this is a happy-go-lucky kind of month. There is travel and happy educational opportunities. Students should be successful in their studies (but with Mars still retrograde, there may be delayed reactions here). Legal matters are also favourable (though with delays as well).

Though the 9th house is not usually associated with love this is an excellent love period. Love is perhaps stormy and volatile but it is there. Your love planet is receiving very positive stimulation after the 20th. From the 23rd to the 26th there is 'sudden love' – a sudden, unexpected encounter. For marrieds this perhaps indicates unexpected social invitations or the meeting of new friends. If you are single working on the second marriage there is happy opportunity now.

When the 9th house is strong, religion, theology and philosophy become a strong interest. Often these kinds of studies and discussions are more interesting than a night out on the town. The arrival of a minister, preacher or guru is given the same weight as the arrival of the latest pop celebrity (perhaps even more). Thus there are theological and philosophical breakthroughs happening for those of you who want that.

The ruler of your Horoscope (the Sun) opposes Mars from the 1st to the 5th. Avoid risky kinds of activities, and travel plans (especially long-distance travel) are better rescheduled. Avoid confrontations. The Sun travels with Uranus from the 23rd to the 26th and while this is an exciting love period be more careful driving and avoid risky stunts. You seem to want to test the limits of the body then. The Sun squares Pluto from the 28th to the 31st. Be more patient with family members, and especially a parent or parent figure. Again, avoid confrontations and risky activities.

## April

Best Days Overall: 1, 2, 10, 19, 20, 29, 30
Most Stressful Days Overall: 8, 14, 15, 21, 22
Best Days for Love: 1, 5, 9, 10, 14, 15, 18, 19, 24, 25, 29
Best Days for Money: 4, 8, 9, 12, 13, 17, 18, 21, 22, 29, 30
Best Days for Career: 5, 14, 15, 21, 22, 24, 25

The career trends that we wrote of last month are still in effect this month, and even more strongly. The Sun crosses your Mid-heaven and enters your 10th house on the 20th, initiating a yearly career peak. Great career progress is being made. You are at the top of your chart, in control, above everyone in your life, except perhaps your children. You are in your rightful place – the lord of all you survey – the monarch sitting on your throne. (You are always the king or queen, but not always on your throne; this month you are.)

Last month was good for gaining the favour of authority figures in your life. This month *you* are the authority and you are the one who grants or denies favours. Your 9th house is still powerful until the 20th so review our discussion of this from last month.

The planetary momentum has been overwhelmingly forward since the beginning of the year. Since January 24 between 80 and 90 per cent of the planets have been moving forwards, so you have been able to achieve your goals rather quickly, with relatively few glitches or delays. The pace of life tends to be fast – the way you like things. This month retrograde activity increases a bit; Pluto joins Mars in retrograde motion. In your chart this affects the family and family issues. On the one hand the timing of this is very good. Since your focus is on the career, family issues can wait. They need time for resolution anyway. Important family decisions – home improvements, purchases for the home and such like – all need more study now. This is a time to review the home and family situation, not for overt action.

Even with Pluto retrograde, the overall momentum of the planets is still forward.

Your financial planet, Mercury, went retrograde last month on the 12th, so financial matters needed more study. This is the case until the 4th. The financial planet conjuncts Uranus from the 22nd to the 24th and this brings sudden windfalls and financial opportunities. Perhaps a business partnership or joint venture is happening. A friend is very supportive.

Health becomes more delicate after the 20th. This is not one of your best health periods, but no major problems are indicated. With your energy not up to par you could be more vulnerable to bugs and things of this nature. Rest and relax more. Enhance health in the ways mentioned in the yearly report.

## May

Best Days Overall: 7, 8, 16, 17, 26, 27
Most Stressful Days Overall: 5, 6, 11, 12, 18, 19, 20
Best Days for Love: 3, 4, 7, 11, 12, 16, 21, 22, 26, 30, 31
Best Days for Money: 1, 2, 8, 10, 18, 19, 20, 28, 29
Best Days for Career: 3, 4, 11, 12, 18, 19, 20, 21, 22, 30, 31

Every solar eclipse tends to affect you more than most people. This is because the Sun is the ruler of your Horoscope and you are more sensitive to solar transits and phenomena than other signs. But the eclipse on the 20th is a relatively mild one. Not too many other planets are affected. You've gone through many stronger ones. This eclipse occurs right on the cusp of the 10th and 11th houses and will impact on both of them. Thus there are career changes and shifts, shake-ups in the company or industry you are involved in, dramas in the lives of parents, parent figures and bosses, and perhaps in your local government as well. There are dramas in the lives of friends and friendships will get tested. Be more patient with these people this month, they are apt to be more temperamental.

Every solar eclipse tends to bring a redefinition of your image, personality and self-concept. You are changing the way you think of yourself and how you want others to see you. You will be creating a new look in the coming months. This eclipse has some unpleasant kinds of effects too: Neptune, the ruler of your 8th house is directly impacted. Thus there can be encounters with death (generally on a psychological level), near-death kinds of experiences, and perhaps surgeries. There is a need for a deeper understanding of death.

If you haven't been careful in dietary matters the eclipse will bring a detox of the body. Happily this eclipse occurs as your health and vitality improve. So health is not affected too much.

The eclipse occurs astronomically on the 20th but in life the eclipse can be felt as much as two weeks before and after. Sensitive people will feel the eclipse early. When your computer starts giving you weird error messages, or starts crashing, you will know you are in the eclipse period. The cosmos sends us forewarning of coming events. That is the time to start reducing your schedule. This eclipse will test your high-tech equipment, your hardware and software. In many cases they will need replacement.

Career is still very strong this month, until the 20th, and much progress is happening. But the interest here is waning. The Sun leaves the 10th house on that date and your career planet, Venus, will start to retrograde on the 15th. So it is time to take stock and review. Avoid major changes or decisions after the 15th.

Your 11th house becomes very strong on the 20th and so your focus is shifting to friendships, group activities, science and technology. This is a great period to expand your knowledge in these areas.

## June

   Best Days Overall: 3, 4, 12, 13, 22, 23
   Most Stressful Days Overall: 1, 2, 8, 9, 15, 16, 29, 30
   Best Days for Love: 3, 8, 9, 12, 17, 18, 22, 27, 28
   Best Days for Money: 1, 5, 6, 10, 17, 20, 21, 24, 25, 26,
      27
   Best Days for Career: 8, 9, 15, 16, 17, 18, 27, 28

In the beginning of the year the Western social sector of your chart was powerful. Last month the planetary power shifted to the East – the planets are now 'closer' to you and energy is flowing towards you rather than away from you. This trend will get even stronger in coming months. You are in a period of strong personal independence. You now have the power to change conditions and create them according to your personal specifications. No longer need you adapt to situations. The focus now is on you and your personal interests. Other people are important but your self-interest comes first these days. If others don't go along with your plans, you have the power to go it alone if need be. Most likely though, others will adapt to you rather than vice versa. This is a time for having your way in life. You are a creator, and creators create. This is your nature. If the creations are not up to par, you will pay the price for it later on when you have to live with your handiwork. But no matter – we learn from our mistakes. Create as best you can and make the necessary adjustments later.

On June 11, Jupiter makes a major move from your 10th house to the 11th. Your career focus and interest is winding down. Your career planet is still retrograde until the 27th. You have achieved much this year. Now it is time for review and to see where you want to go from here.

Your 11th house was powerful last month and now with Jupiter there it is even more so. This is a time to expand your science and technological knowledge and expertise and to master all the latest software (and many of you will be involved in writing or producing high-tech gadgetry and software now). This is a time to upgrade your equipment. Leos love the media. This is a time to get more involved with that, or perhaps get into it as a creative hobby. Jupiter rules your 5th house of creativity, so his move into the 11th house shows a shift in your personal creativity. It is more 'tech' oriented.

A lunar eclipse on the 4th occurs in your 5th house of creativity, again indicating changes there. It also shows that children in your life are having dramas. They are (like you) redefining themselves, their image and self-concept. This has profound implications down the road, for as we change ourselves we change our relationships and many other areas of life. This period is not a time for speculations. Spiritual changes are also happening, changes in practice, routine and ideas. There are dramas in the lives of the spiritual people in your life.

### July

> Best Days Overall: 1, 2, 9, 10, 11, 19, 20, 21, 28, 29
> Most Stressful Days Overall: 5, 6, 12, 13, 26, 27
> Best Days for Love: 1, 5, 6, 9, 15, 19, 20, 24, 25, 28
> Best Days for Money: 1, 2, 5, 6, 9, 10, 11, 15, 16, 19, 20, 21, 22, 23, 24, 25, 28, 29
> Best Days for Career: 5, 6, 12, 13, 15, 24, 25, 26

Your 12th house of spirituality became powerful on the 21st of last month and is still strong until the 22nd. This is a month for spiritual breakthroughs and interior growth. In nature, growth is from 'within out'. Before growth can be seen outwardly it has occurred inwardly. And so it is with you. This internal growth will lead to your outer expansion. So it is very important. This is the time to review the past year, correct mistakes (make atonement) and set your goals for the year ahead – you are approaching your personal new year, your Solar Return. You are winding down the old year and want to start the new cycle clean and in a good way.

Finance is very good this month. On June 26, your financial planet entered your own sign and will be there all of this month. Thus windfalls and happy opportunities come to you. Financial opportunities are seeking you out. You are having your way in the financial life. If you are negotiating contracts, this is favourable for you. You are dressing more expensively, spending on yourself, and projecting an image of wealth. Others see you as wealthy. The only problem is Mercury's retrograde on the 15th. Make important purchases or investments before this date. After that you should be reviewing your finances and seeing where improvements can be made. Mercury's retrograde will not stop earnings, only slow things down a little.

This month (and next) the planetary power is in its maximum Eastern position. You are in a period of maximum independence and personal power. Use it to make your life better and to create happy conditions for yourself. Refer to our previous discussion of this.

Uranus has been square to Pluto practically all year. Last month the aspect was most exact and this is the situation in the month ahead as well. So there are dramas happening at home and your attention is needed there. Family and friends are not getting along that well. The same is true with the spouse or current love. Moves could happen now. There are shake-ups in the family unit. Maintaining emotion harmony will be quite a challenge.

Health is excellent this month, especially after the 22nd. You have all the energy you need to achieve any goal you set for yourself. When the Sun enters your sign on the 22nd you enter a yearly personal pleasure peak. A happy period – no one knows how to enjoy life better than a Leo.

## August

Best Days Overall: 6, 7, 16, 17, 24, 25
Most Stressful Days Overall: 1, 2, 8, 9, 10, 22, 23, 29, 31
Best Days for Love: 1, 2, 3, 6, 13, 14, 16, 22, 23, 24, 29, 30, 31
Best Days for Money: 1, 2, 6, 7, 11, 12, 16, 17, 18, 19, 20, 21, 24, 25, 29, 30
Best Days for Career: 2, 3, 8, 9, 10, 13, 14, 22, 23, 31

You are still in a yearly personal pleasure peak. You are having your way in life and enjoying all the pleasures of the flesh now – a great period to get the body in the shape that you want. Love was happy last month, especially the end of the month, and singles had solid romantic opportunities. Love is still good this month too until the 22nd. With your 1st house strong you have more personal charisma and magnetism. The personal appearance shines. Your normal 'star quality' is even more enhanced now. This is another plus for love.

Finances are still excellent. Mercury, your financial planet, is still in your 1st house and still retrograde until the 8th. After the 8th the financial judgement improves. Leos are speculators by nature, and even more so than usual with Mercury in your own sign. But restrain this impulse during Mercury's retrograde. Impulse spending (another Leo trait) should also be restrained during Mercury's retrograde. On the 23rd as the Sun enters your money house you enter a yearly financial peak. So the good times keep rolling.

The planets are starting to shift from the upper half of the Horoscope to the bottom half. The shift is not yet complete. Right now the planets are more or less evenly distributed between the two hemispheres. You are needed at home. The family situation is still very volatile. A parent or parent figure is having many changes and dramas. He or she seems to lack direction as well.

The sages say that the number one reason that prayers are not answered or are delayed is because of emotional discord.

Thus emotional harmony is more important than just 'feeling good' – it is a factor in your inner life. With Uranus (your love planet) in square aspect to Pluto (your family and emotional planet) these past few months, this has been quite a challenge and it can be a major cause for not being able to connect to the Higher Power. The Divine has never left you. Its energy can't reach you because of the discord. So it's up to you to create the emotional harmony needed.

Your love planet went retrograde on July 13 and will remain so until December. This doesn't stop love or dating, it only slows things down. Indeed it should be slowed down a little. You have had happy romantic and social opportunities these days, but don't rush things. Let love develop as it will. Let the circumstances of life test the love. It is not good to make important love decisions one way or another now.

The Sun opposes Neptune from the 22nd to the 25th. Avoid drinking and driving, or taking strong medications while driving. Stay in your body and avoid 'dreaminess'. Be more mindful and aware in all that you do, especially if you are handling dangerous objects.

## September

Best Days Overall: 2, 3, 12, 13, 21, 22, 29, 30
Most Stressful Days Overall: 5, 6, 19, 25, 26
Best Days for Love: 1, 2, 12, 20, 21, 22, 25, 26, 29, 30
Best Days for Money: 4, 5, 7, 8, 14, 15, 16, 17, 25, 26
Best Days for Career: 1, 5, 6, 12, 21, 22, 29, 30

The family situation is still very volatile and probably there are intense conflicts going on. Your attention there is needed more than ever. Take whatever steps necessary to make the home safer. Keep dangerous objects away from children. Check all your smoke detectors and other alarm systems. Some of you might be doing major repairs or renovations in the home now, and if so the safety aspects are important. Pluto starts to move forward on the 18th so matters are clarifying there.

You are still in a yearly financial peak until the 23rd, and your financial judgement is much more reliable now than it was last month. This is a good time to shop for big ticket items. Finances seem especially favourable from the 1st to the 6th as Mercury makes beautiful aspects to Pluto. The family, and especially a parent or parent figure, is more supportive financially. You have profitable opportunities through the family and family connections in home-based businesses, real estate, restaurants, hotels or industries that cater to the home. (There are also hidden issues here that need your investigation: what you see is not what you get.) Probably you are spending more on the home and family as well, but it doesn't seem stressful to you. You have the money to spend.

On the 23rd the Sun enters your 3rd house. This indicates a month for expanding the mind, for catching up on the phone calls, emails, text messages and letters that you owe. It's also a good month for expanding your knowledge and for taking courses in subjects that interest you. The mind is sharper this period and learning goes better. Students should do well in their studies.

Mercury, your financial planet, moves into your 3rd house on the 17th. Thus sales, marketing, communication, advertising, PR and good use of the media are important financially. These issues are always important on the financial level, but this period more so. It also indicates earnings from buying, selling, trading and retailing. You have a good feeling for the short-term trends in the market place and this can translate to profit.

Venus enters your sign on the 7th and will be there all month. This is a happy transit. She brings beauty and glamour to the image, social grace and charm to the personality. Generally this is a nice aspect for love. Men are attracting young and beautiful women into their life and women are becoming more attractive. But Venus is also your career planet and this shows that happy career opportunities are seeking you out. You have an opportunity for a new car and communication equipment too.

The Sun makes stressful aspects to both Pluto and Uranus from the 28th to the 30th. Take it nice and easy while driving, working out or indulging in sports. Avoid risky daredevil-type stunts. This is not a time to try to break some athletic record. Avoid confrontations.

## October

Best Days Overall: 1, 9, 10, 11, 18, 19, 27, 28
Most Stressful Days Overall: 2, 3, 16, 17, 22, 23, 29, 30, 31
Best Days for Love: 1, 9, 12, 18, 21, 22, 23, 27
Best Days for Money: 4, 5, 6, 7, 12, 13, 14, 15, 16, 17, 22, 23, 25, 26
Best Days for Career: 1, 2, 3, 12, 21, 29, 30, 31

The main headline this month is Saturn's move into Scorpio, your 4th house, on the 5th. He will be in this house for the next two to three years so this is a major transit. Things at home and with the family have been volatile all year. We wish we could say that things were getting better, but it doesn't look that way. Family life is not very happy now. You are taking on extra burdens and responsibilities in the home. Probably you are doing your duty, doing everything right, but just going through the motions. You are not enjoying things. Your job is to make these extra burdens and responsibilities happy and joyful. You will have to work at it, but it can be done. The cosmos is going to install a 'right order' in the home and family situation. Things need to be shifted around and reorganized, as does the emotional life.

This month you see the importance of this area of life and are giving it major attention from the 23rd onwards. Leos are not depressed kinds of people. Your nature is always 'up' and optimistic. But now you have to be more careful about this. Your natural ebullience is not there. You will have to consciously project more optimism and joy into your life.

The avoidance of depression is now a big factor in your health. If health problems arise, examine the emotional and family life and bring them into harmony as best (and as fast) as you can.

On the 5th Mercury enters Scorpio and your 5th house. From the 4th to the 7th finances seem stressed. Perhaps there is an extra health or family expense that arises, but it is a short-term expense. You are spending on the home and family but can earn from this area as well. It works both ways. The financial planet in Scorpio gives you razor sharp financial intuition. You see beneath the surface of things to underlying realities.

Venus moves into the money house on the 3rd – another good financial transit. This shows that you have the financial favour and support of the authority figures in your life – bosses, parents and elders. This often indicates pay rises and earning from your good career reputation. Government payments can come as well.

On the 23rd, the planetary power shifts again to the Western, social sector of your chart, indicating a time to take a vacation from your self and your personal interests and focus on others. Now you will have to live with the conditions you created in the past six months when your personal power was strong. It is time to cultivate the social skills and attain your ends through co-operation and consensus – a wise king or queen sometimes has to do this.

### November

Best Days Overall: 6, 7, 14, 15, 23, 24
Most Stressful Days Overall: 12, 13, 18, 19, 26, 27
Best Days for Love: 1, 6, 11, 14, 18, 19, 20, 23
Best Days for Money: 1, 2, 6, 7, 8, 9, 11, 14, 15, 19, 23, 24, 28, 29
Best Days for Career: 1, 11, 20, 26, 27

Health needs watching this month so rest and relax more, especially during the period of the solar eclipse of the 13th which is stressful on you. More quiet time at home or close to home is called for now. This is a short-term blip; your health and vitality will improve after the 22nd. Enhance your health in the ways mentioned in the yearly report.

Things at home and with the family have been problematic all year, but this solar eclipse seems to bring things to a head. It occurs in your 4th house. There is a lot of pent-up emotion in the family and with family members and now it is primed to explode. Try not to make matters worse. Stay as calm as possible under the circumstances. There will be negativity, but you can maximize or minimize it – the choice is yours. This solar eclipse, like every solar eclipse, forces you to redefine yourself, your image, your self-concept, and how you want others to perceive you. Probably family members are defining you in unpleasant ways; it is up to you to define yourself the way you want to be, otherwise you will get put into some 'box' that is not pleasant. Moves and repairs in the home could happen now too.

The lunar eclipse of the 28th occurs in your 11th house and is relatively benign. The Moon (which generically rules family and emotional issues) reinforces what we have been saying above. There are dramas in the family this period. There are dramas in the lives of friends and friendships are getting tested now. Be more patient with your friends as they are apt to be more temperamental now. Every lunar eclipse brings spiritual changes and this one is no different. Your high-tech equipment, computers, software and gadgetry, gets tested and some of it will have to be replaced.

Mars makes some stressful aspects this month. From the 23rd to the 25th he squares Uranus and from the 27th to the 30th he conjuncts Pluto. These are powerful transits. Be more careful driving and avoid confrontations and temper tantrums. Both you and others are likely to overreact now. Be more mindful and alert and avoid risky activities. Your spouse, partner or current love also needs to be more careful on the physical plane. Be more patient with the beloved this period.

Your financial planet goes retrograde from the 6th to the 26th, and this shows a need for a financial review, for taking stock and for planning improvements. Big purchases or major investments are better off delayed. If you must do these things try to schedule them before the 6th or after the 26th. Earnings will increase this month; Mercury's retrograde won't stop this but there will be delays.

## December

Best Days Overall: 3, 4, 12, 13, 20, 21, 22, 30, 31
Most Stressful Days Overall: 10, 11, 16, 17, 23, 24
Best Days for Love: 1, 3, 10, 11, 12, 16, 17, 20, 30, 31
Best Days for Money: 2, 5, 6, 7, 8, 11, 16, 21, 25, 31
Best Days for Career: 1, 10, 11, 20, 23, 24, 31

On November 22 you entered another of your yearly personal pleasure peaks, and this lasts until the 21st. The timing of this is marvellous. For this is a time of year where there is more partying and carousing, so you are right in tune with the times. (The virtues of Leo are more needed now and so the cosmos impels you in this direction. Parties are not really parties without Leo – something is lacking there.)

The Western social sector of your Horoscope has been strong since October, but now the power here is increased even further. From the 1st to the 10th and the 23rd to the 31st, 80 per cent of the planets are in the West. From the 10th to the 23rd it is 90 per cent. These are huge percentages. Forget about yourself for a while and focus on others. Attain your ends through consensus and co-operation, rather than regal edicts. As you put others first, your own needs will be taken care of quite nicely by the karmic law. This behaviour 'puts the universe in your debt'. (Some people might not return your favour, but others will. It doesn't really matter.) Leos are very strong individuals, so putting others first is a challenging lesson.

Finances were good last month, but are even better this month. Your financial planet is in Sagittarius and in the 5th house. It is also moving forward now. Money is earned in happy ways. There is luck in speculations. Probably you are over spending and will have to work harder to make up the difference (after the 21st). The financial optimism is boundless now. You are enjoying your wealth now, which is the whole point of wealth. If it is merely hoarded where is the joy in it? A master is quoted as saying, 'Money is like manure, not good unless it is spread around.' This is certainly your attitude this month.

By the 21st the carousing is about over with. You enter a more serious work period. Job seekers will have good fortune now. Health should be good too – you are focused here.

Love is basically good this month. Your devotion to others makes you more popular. New friends are coming into the picture. Your love planet Uranus starts moving forward on the 13th enhancing your social confidence and bringing more clarity in your relationships. The main danger here is the tendency to have power struggles in your relationship – Mars moves into your 7th house on the 26th. Try to avoid this. The Sun is square to Uranus from the 25th to the 27th, so be more patient with the beloved. Agree to disagree. This is a challenging aspect, but very short term. It is not the trend in your overall relationship. Be more careful driving during this period (avoid drinking and driving) and risky kinds of activities. This is not a time for daredevil stunts.

# Virgo

## ♍

---

---

## Personality Profile

### VIRGO AT A GLANCE

*Element* – Earth

*Ruling Planet* – Mercury
   *Career Planet* – Mercury
   *Love Planet* – Neptune
   *Money Planet* – Venus
   *Planet of Home and Family Life* – Jupiter
   *Planet of Health and Work* – Uranus
   *Planet of Pleasure* – Saturn
   *Planet of Sexuality* – Mars

*Colours* – earth tones, ochre, orange, yellow

*Colour that promotes love, romance and social harmony* – aqua blue

*Colour that promotes earning power* – jade green

*Gems* – agate, hyacinth

*Metal* – quicksilver

*Scents* – lavender, lilac, lily of the valley, storax

*Quality* – mutable (= flexibility)

*Quality most needed for balance* – a broader perspective

*Strongest virtues* – mental agility, analytical skills, ability to pay attention to detail, healing powers

*Deepest needs* – to be useful and productive

*Characteristic to avoid* – destructive criticism

*Signs of greatest overall compatibility* – Taurus, Capricorn

*Signs of greatest overall incompatibility* – Gemini, Sagittarius, Pisces

*Sign most helpful to career* – Gemini

*Sign most helpful for emotional support* – Sagittarius

*Sign most helpful financially* – Libra

*Sign best for marriage and/or partnerships* – Pisces

*Sign most helpful for creative projects* – Capricorn

*Best Sign to have fun with* – Capricorn

*Signs most helpful in spiritual matters* – Taurus, Leo

*Best day of the week* – Wednesday

# Understanding a Virgo

The virgin is a particularly fitting symbol for those born under the sign of Virgo. If you meditate on the image of the virgin you will get a good understanding of the essence of the Virgo type. The virgin is, of course, a symbol of purity and innocence – not naïve, but pure. A virginal object has not been touched. A virgin field is land that is true to itself, the way it has always been. The same is true of virgin forest: it is pristine, unaltered.

Apply the idea of purity to the thought processes, emotional life, physical body, and activities and projects of the everyday world, and you can see how Virgos approach life. Virgos desire the pure expression of the ideal in their mind, body and affairs. If they find impurities they will attempt to clear them away.

Impurities are the beginning of disorder, unhappiness and uneasiness. The job of the Virgo is to eject all impurities and keep only that which the body and mind can use and assimilate.

The secrets of good health are here revealed: 90 per cent of the art of staying well is maintaining a pure mind, a pure body and pure emotions. When you introduce more impurities than your mind and body can deal with, you will have what is known as 'dis-ease'. It is no wonder that Virgos make great doctors, nurses, healers and dieticians. They have an innate understanding of good health and they realize that good health is more than just physical. In all aspects of life, if you want a project to be successful it must be kept as pure as possible. It must be protected against the adverse elements that will try to undermine it. This is the secret behind Virgo's awesome technical proficiency.

One could talk about Virgo's analytical powers – which are formidable. One could talk about their perfectionism and their almost superhuman attention to detail. But this would be to miss the point. All of these virtues are manifestations of a Virgo's desire for purity and perfection – a world without Virgos would have ruined itself long ago.

A vice is nothing more than a virtue turned inside out, misapplied or used in the wrong context. Virgos' apparent vices come from their inherent virtue. Their analytical powers, which should be used for healing, helping or perfecting a project in the world, sometimes get misapplied and turned against people. Their critical faculties, which should be used constructively to perfect a strategy or proposal, can sometimes be used destructively to harm or wound. Their urge to perfection can turn into worry and lack of confidence; their natural humility can become self-denial and self-abasement. When Virgos turn negative they are apt to turn their devastating criticism on themselves, sowing the seeds of self-destruction.

## Finance

Virgos have all the attitudes that create wealth. They are hard-working, industrious, efficient, organized, thrifty, productive and eager to serve. A developed Virgo is every employer's dream. But until Virgos master some of the social graces of Libra they will not even come close to fulfilling their financial potential. Purity and perfectionism, if not handled correctly or gracefully, can be very trying to others. Friction in human relationships can be devastating not only to your pet projects but – indirectly – to your wallet as well.

Virgos are quite interested in their financial security. Being hard-working, they know the true value of money. They do not like to take risks with their money, preferring to save for their retirement or for a rainy day. Virgos usually make prudent, calculated investments that involve a minimum of risk. These investments and savings usually work out well, helping Virgos to achieve the financial security they seek. The rich or even not-so-rich Virgo also likes to help his or her friends in need.

## Career and Public Image

Virgos reach their full potential when they can communicate their knowledge in such a way that others can understand it. In order to get their ideas across better, Virgos need to develop greater verbal skills and fewer judgemental ways of expressing themselves. Virgos look up to teachers and communicators; they like their bosses to be good communicators. Virgos will probably not respect a superior who is not their intellectual equal – no matter how much money or power that superior has. Virgos themselves like to be perceived by others as being educated and intellectual.

The natural humility of Virgos often inhibits them from fulfilling their great ambitions, from acquiring name and fame. Virgos should indulge in a little more self-promotion if they are going to reach their career goals. They need to push themselves with the same ardour that they would use to foster others.

At work Virgos like to stay active. They are willing to learn any type of job as long as it serves their ultimate goal of financial security. Virgos may change occupations several times during their professional lives, until they find the one they really enjoy. Virgos work well with other people, are not afraid to work hard and always fulfil their responsibilities.

## Love and Relationships

If you are an analyst or a critic you must, out of necessity, narrow your scope. You have to focus on a part and not the whole; this can create a temporary narrow-mindedness. Virgos do not like this kind of person. They like their partners to be broad-minded, with depth and vision. Virgos seek to get this broad-minded quality from their partners, since they sometimes lack it themselves.

Virgos are perfectionists in love just as they are in other areas of life. They need partners who are tolerant, open-minded and easy-going. If you are in love with a Virgo do not waste time on impractical romantic gestures. Do practical and useful things for him or her – this is what will be appreciated and what will be done for you.

Virgos express their love through pragmatic and useful gestures, so do not be put off because your Virgo partner does not say 'I love you' day-in and day-out. Virgos are not that type. If they love you, they will demonstrate it in practical ways. They will always be there for you; they will show an interest in your health and finances; they will fix your sink or repair your video recorder. Virgos deem these actions to be superior to sending flowers, chocolates or Valentine cards.

In love affairs Virgos are not particularly passionate or spontaneous. If you are in love with a Virgo, do not take this personally. It does not mean that you are not alluring enough or that your Virgo partner does not love or like you. It is just the way Virgos are. What they lack in passion they make up for in dedication and loyalty.

## Home and Domestic Life

It goes without saying that the home of a Virgo will be spotless, sanitized and orderly. Everything will be in its proper place – and don't you dare move anything about! For Virgos to find domestic bliss they need to ease up a bit in the home, to allow their partner and children more freedom and to be more generous and open-minded. Family members are not to be analysed under a microscope, they are individuals with their own virtues to express.

With these small difficulties resolved, Virgos like to stay in and entertain at home. They make good hosts and they like to keep their friends and families happy and entertained at family and social gatherings. Virgos love children, but they are strict with them – at times – since they want to make sure their children are brought up with the correct sense of family and values.

# Horoscope for 2012

## Major Trends

The first decade of the millennium has been difficult, filled with sudden and dramatic changes, shake-ups and upheavals in many areas of life; 2007 to 2009 were especially difficult. If you got through those years, 2012 will be a piece of cake. By now you are in radically different conditions and circumstances than you were 10 years ago, and I would say much improved as well. This was the purpose of the upheavals – to liberate you into better conditions.

You begin the year with all the major long-term planets either in good aspect to you or leaving you alone. Health and energy (and overall success) therefore is good. With high energy the world is your oyster; there is nothing you can't do or achieve. Things that once seemed impossible are now possible. (When energy is low, it is as if your horizons are limited and overall success is harder to achieve.)

On February 3, Neptune makes a major move from your house of health to your 7th house of love and marriage. It will stay there for the next 14 or so years. This obviously has a big impact on your marriage, current relationship and overall love life. More on this later.

This Neptune transit is also a stressful aspect to you, although not enough to cause major problems. On June 11, Jupiter moves from Taurus into Gemini, another stressful aspect. So energy levels are lower as the year progresses.

Jupiter's move into Gemini, though it is physically more taxing is a wonderful career aspect for you. You enter one of the high career points in your life (more on this later).

Saturn has been in your money house for two years and thus you felt financially squeezed. Perhaps you were taking on extra financial burdens. But happily, on October 5, Saturn leaves this house and moves into your 3rd house. Thus your finances improve.

Your areas of greatest interest this year will be the body, image and personal pleasure (until July 3); finance (until October 5); children and personal creativity; health and work (until February 3); love, romance and social activities (from February 3 onwards); sex, the deeper issues of life, personal transformation and reinvention, occult studies; religion, philosophy, theology, higher education and foreign travel (until June 11); and career (after June 11).

Your paths of greatest fulfilment this year will be home and family (until August 31); communication and intellectual interests (after August 31); religion, philosophy, theology, higher education and foreign travel (until June 11); and career (after June 11).

## Health

*(Please note that this is an* astrological *perspective on health and not a medical one. In days of yore there was no difference, these perspectives were identical. But these days there could be quite a difference. For a medical perspective, please consult your doctor or health practitioner.)*

Health is always important to you but in recent years even more so. However, this year, as Neptune leaves your 6th house of health this area is less important than usual. I read this as a positive. Your health seems basically good and thus you have no need to focus overly here. (As the year progresses though, you might want to pay more attention, especially after June 11.)

Neptune's presence in your 6th house for the past 14 years greatly shaped your health attitudes and practice. You saw how love and marital issues affected your health. There was a direct and profound connection. Also, with Neptune (the most spiritual of all the planets) involved in your health, many of you explored the spiritual dimensions of healing. Spiritual healing was a major interest. By now you have learned these lessons and are exploring other dimensions of healing.

Last year your health planet Uranus made a major move from Pisces into Aries. It will be in Aries for another six

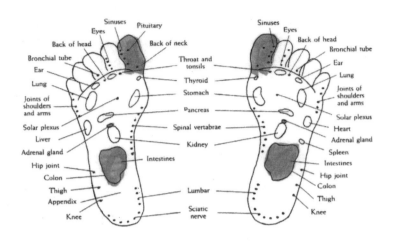

## *Reflexology*

*Try to massage the whole foot on a regular basis, but pay extra attention to the points highlighted on the chart. When you massage, be aware of 'sore spots', as these need special attention. It's also a good idea to massage the ankles and top side of the feet (see below).*

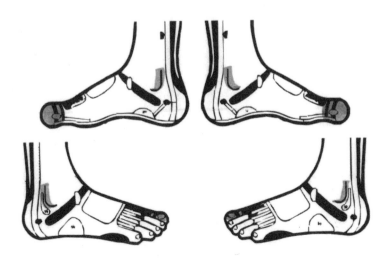

years or so and this is a long-term trend. Your health attitudes are now less spiritual and more 'hands on' – more
physical. Whereas for many years, your feet have been
important health-wise, now it is the head, face and scalp.
Regular head and face massage will be very powerful. Like
the feet, the head and face contain reflexes to the whole
body, so when you massage there, you are energizing the
whole body. Moreover, where for many years good health
was about 'spiritual fitness' now it is more about physical
fitness. Health is not just about 'no symptoms' but the ability
to run, jog or lift x amount of pounds or kilos.

Good muscle tone is very important these days. This is not
just for cosmetic reasons, it is the muscles that hold the spine
and skeleton in its right alignment and if they lose their tone
the whole alignment of the body gets knocked awry. These
days you are spending more time at the gym than in meditation. Many of you are getting into body building and body
sculpting. (However, the lessons you learned about spiritual
healing will help here too; don't just throw them out the
window.)

With head now a vulnerable organ, craniosacral therapy
will be powerful for you. Very often chronic conditions arise
because of the plates of the skull are not in alignment. The
minute they are brought into alignment the condition starts
to heal.

Uranus is now in your 8th house of transformation. Thus
you respond well to detox regimes. Good health is not about
adding more to the body, but removing material that doesn't
belong there. In many cases you see surgery as a quick fix to
a health problem. Sometimes these things are called for, but
you seem too hasty about it. Get a second opinion.

The health planet in the 8th house also shows the need
for safe sex and sexual moderation – healthy sex life.

Mars spends an unusual amount of time in your own
sign this year. His normal transit is a month and a half, but
this year he will spend more than six months in your sign
(from January 1 to July 3). You will be much more into
physical exercise and sports that period, which is basically

good. But this transit acts very much like an amphetamine. It speeds up the system. There is more energy, more aggressiveness, a tendency to rush, to want everything done in a hurry. And this can lead to accidents and injury. Often it makes people more combative than usual and can lead to fights, both physical and verbal. This is the main health danger this period. By all means exercise and achieve your goals, but watch the temper and make an effort to 'slow down'. Be more mindful when driving or indulging in sports.

## Home and Family

Ever since Pluto left Sagittarius in 2008, things should have been quieter with the family. The 15 years before that were quite turbulent. There were deaths in the family, break-ups and a whole cosmic detox going on. There were many, many dramas, surgeries, and perhaps near-death experiences as well. The lull is probably welcome now. The main detox is over with. The major changes that needed to happen have happened. Your relationship with your family is probably on a higher and better level now.

A lunar eclipse on June 4 brings a minor, short-term detox. If there are flaws in the home or secret grudges in the family, they will be revealed now for cleansing and correction. But this will be nowhere as severe as what went before in 2008.

With your 4th house empty, the year ahead is most likely to maintain the status quo. Though you have the freedom to move if you want to, you probably lack the inclination. You are more or less content with the home and family situation as it is.

Jupiter, your family planet, will be in Taurus until June 11. Taurus tends to conservatism and stability. You don't want to rock the boat then. With Jupiter in your 9th house, family members are travelling and more interested in religion, philosophy and higher education. Your family circle could expand during this period, through marriage, birth or meeting people who are like family to you. You enjoy good family support. They seem generous with you.

A parent or parent figure has wonderful job opportunities this year. This could be with their present company or a new one. They seem very devoted to the other parent too, especially after June 11. Parents are prospering, travelling and enjoying the good life. (They do need to watch their weight though.)

The family as a whole seems to rise in status in the year ahead, especially after June 11. They seem very ambitious. Children in your life could be having surgeries and near-death kinds of experiences. They are likely to have multiple moves in the year ahead (and in future years).

After October 5 siblings or sibling figures become more serious. They seem to be taking on extra burdens and responsibilities. They need to work harder to show love and warmth to others. They seem too cold and aloof. These siblings could have married in the past year (and are likely to marry or be involved in a serious relationship this year too), yet, it doesn't seem to bring them the happiness that they thought it would.

**Finance and Career**

As we have mentioned, finances have been a problem for the past two years and the trend continues for most of the year ahead. However, it seems to me that the worst is over with. There was a need to reorganize the finances and this you have been doing. Though you probably felt squeezed financially, the truth is that with some juggling you have all the resources you need.

As we have written in previous years, these past two years have been more about financial management rather than actual earnings. The cosmos has been pushing you to manage what you have in a better and healthier way – to gain control over your financial life rather than have it control you.

Pressure is rarely pleasant, but it has some good side-effects. While it reveals weaknesses (and thus you have the opportunity to correct them), it also reveals secret strengths that you never knew you had. You have received much financial insight these past few years. You are no longer afraid of financial crises. You handle them calmly and efficiently. You have become quite adept at handling financial difficulties. The landlord is often willing to wait a few days for the rent; the credit card company can be negotiated with; the banks are often willing to refinance or restructure mortgages. There is no difficulty that is insurmountable. Money that was perhaps spent frivolously or wastefully can be put to better use. Things that you thought were absolutely essential are seen as not as essential as you thought. That new outfit that you lust for will probably go on sale in a few weeks. These new insights are preparing you for the future prosperity that is to come.

Perhaps the most important thing that has been happening is that you are taking a more sober and long-term perspective on finance. You are learning that wealth is built up over time, step by step, methodically. Rarely does it happen overnight, and you have been learning how this step-by-step process is done. It is a discipline to be sure. Living within one's income doesn't necessarily mean doing without. You just might have to apply some creativity in getting what you want. As you practise this, you will develop a momentum that will lead to long-term, stable, secure wealth. Wealth will be like the tide coming in, inexorable and inescapable.

The main headline this year is in the career. Jupiter starts to cross your Mid-heaven on June 11 and will be in your 10th house of career for the rest of the year. So you are outwardly successful in your profession and in your social status. You are elevated and promoted this year. The family too seems more successful, as we mentioned, and they seem very supportive of your own career goals. Some of these career opportunities are coming from the family or through family connections.

What I especially like about your career is that it seems emotionally comfortable. It doesn't violate your emotional harmony. This tends to success. In many cases this transit indicates working from home, or making the office more 'home like'.

Though you will be experiencing career success and opportunity earlier in the year, you probably won't feel the full financial benefits of this until after October 5, as Saturn at last moves out of your money house. But no matter, the worst is over with and the trend is up.

## Love and Social Life

The love situation has been turbulent for many years now. Even long-established marriages and relationships were in trouble and there have been many a divorce and break-up. By now, you are in completely different social conditions, with a different circle of friends and different relationships. Any marriage that survived 2003 to 2010 will probably survive anything.

Ever since Uranus moved out of your 7th house last year, the love situation has calmed down and become more stable. After seven years of excitement and instability many of you welcome 'boring' these days. There is something comforting about this. There is security, a sense of being 'grounded', a sense of safety.

The main trend now is Neptune's move into your 7th house. This is a powerful position for Neptune – he will be in his own sign and house and thus more powerful on your behalf. A good signal for love. The love and social life will be good.

Your already high ideals of love become even higher. Neptune is going to refine, elevate and spiritualize your whole love life and social circle. You are going to meet spiritual and creative friends – dancers, poets, artists, psychics, astrologers, yogis.

The spiritual connection in love, always important to you, becomes even more important now. No matter how good the sexual chemistry is, if this is lacking, the relationship won't last long. When you are with your beloved you need to feel that you are close to God, that you have Divine sanction for the relationship. This is the kind of transit where the love – the marriage – is not just a mundane, physical, practical affair, but is really two people walking the same spiritual path. The love and the marriage becomes part and parcel of your spiritual discipline.

On a more mundane level, there is a need for more information in love. (And this is true for business partnerships as well.) There is much that is hidden. What you see on the surface is not the actual reality. So go slow in love. Let it develop. Learn to see behind the outward glamour.

Neptune is the planet of revelation – it parts the veil and reveals the hidden things. On a mundane level, this 'lifting of the veil' tends to produce scandals and unpleasant revelations. Neptune is not setting out to produce scandal. But when you shine a light in a dark room, whatever is there, is revealed – both the good and the bad. These hidden revelations will test your love in coming years. If the love is real, it will survive these things. If not, the relationship will probably dissolve. On the positive side, many of you will find your perfect love and romance now (with your high ideals, nothing less will satisfy you). Many of you will experience nuances in love that few mortals ever experience.

The year ahead seems sexually active. Uranus is now in your 8th house. This indicates much sexual experimentation, as if you are throwing out all the old rule books and learning for yourself what works for you. In general this is a good thing as this is how we gain real knowledge. But this experimentation needs to be kept positive and constructive.

Singles working on the first marriage are likely to marry or be in a serious relationship. Those working on the second marriage also have wonderful aspects until June 11. Those in or working on the third marriage have a status quo kind of year.

Singles find love opportunities in spiritual locales and settings, at meditation or spiritual seminars or retreats, or as they involve themselves in charitable or altruistic kinds of activities. Psychics, ministers and gurus have important love guidance these days.

## Self-improvement

Neptune in your 7th house for many years to come shows that your ideals of love are higher than ever. You know what real love is and what it is not. High ideals in love are basically good and you deserve them, but in everyday life this can create many dramas. First off, your ideals can be so high that no mortal could ever live up to them. Humans, by definition, are limited. Some have a greater capacity for love than others, but always there is some limitation. Thus when you are involved in a relationship there is always this sense of dissatisfaction and disappointment. Outwardly it is often hard to understand this feeling. The beloved might be good and caring by worldly standards, but for you this is not enough. You are comparing him or her to the Divine Ideal, and hence this feeling of dissatisfaction. Also the beloved will (consciously or unconsciously) feel your sense of disappointment and react to it, and this will further cloud your relationship.

These disappointments are not punishments. There is a spiritual agenda behind them. Little by little, disappointment by disappointment, you are being led to your ideal love – the spiritual love that comes from the Divine. This is what you have been searching for all these years and what your heart longs for. You were just looking in the wrong places. When you discover this and rely on it, you will always be loved perfectly. More importantly you will enter relationships from a different place – not as someone who is needy but as someone who can express more love in a relationship.

Neptune in the 7th house often produces confusion in love. Thus, it is good to 'cast all your love burdens on the Divine, and go free'. Surrender the marriage, the relationship and the management of your love life to the Divine. If you do this wholeheartedly your whole love life will straighten out.

# Month-by-month Forecasts

## January

Best Days Overall: 3, 4, 12, 13, 21, 22, 30, 31
Most Stressful Days Overall: 5, 6, 7, 19, 20, 25, 26
Best Days for Love: 6, 7, 15, 18, 19, 24, 25, 26, 27, 28
Best Days for Money: 3, 4, 6, 7, 12, 14, 15, 16, 17, 21, 25, 26, 30
Best Days for Career: 1, 2, 5, 6, 7, 12, 22

The art of reading a Horoscope is really the art of resolving contradictions. And here we see a beauty. Mars is in your own sign, making you very independent and self-willed – someone who wants what they want when they want it, and who doesn't suffer fools lightly. Yet, the planetary power is mostly in the Western social sector, the sector of 'other people'. There is a need to be independent but also a need to get on with others. Your own interests are very important, but the interests of others are more important. Your way is probably not the best way this period. Yet, you might feel that it is and this can produce feelings of frustration and anger. You want what you want, but other people seem in charge of your destiny. You chafe under this.

With this configuration it seems best to channel this Mars energy into other, more constructive directions. Exercise more. Get more involved in sports and athletics. This is a very good month to lose weight and detox the body (as are the next six months). Channel your personal desires in ways that don't conflict with others. Right now the cosmos is calling you to sublimate your personal desires for a while and to put others first. With Mars in your own sign, the tendency is to get things done by brute force, but this is not really a time for that. This is a time for diplomacy and tact, for getting things done through consensus and co-operation. Anger and impatience (Mars traits) are not helpful right now.

You begin your year with most of the planets below the horizon and still in the night time of your year. This is soon to change, but this is the situation this month. You are still in a period for producing the infrastructure of future career success. You are doing the inner work involved with the career. You still need to find and function from your point of emotional harmony. Home and family should take priority over the career now.

Health is good this month. Your 6th house of health is powerful all month but especially after the 20th, so you are focused here even more than usual. Job seekers seem successful this month, with many, many opportunities happening.

Love seems happy this month whether you are single or married. Venus enters your 7th house on the 14th and stays there the rest of the month. Venus will also conjunct your love planet Neptune from the 12th to the 15th. This is a very happy transit for love with the two love planets in your chart travelling together. A romantic meeting happens for singles; it seems ideal but you need to look deeper here. Give it time. The person – the situation – is not as it appears. This transit also brings opportunities for business partnerships or joint ventures. The spouse, partner or current love is financially supportive, as are friends.

### February

Best Days Overall: 1, 9, 10, 17, 18, 27, 28
Most Stressful Days Overall: 2, 3, 15, 16, 22, 23, 29
Best Days for Love: 4, 5, 6, 13, 15, 21, 22, 23, 24, 25
Best Days for Money: 1, 5, 6, 9, 11, 12, 15, 17, 24, 25, 27, 28
Best Days for Career: 2, 3, 11, 12, 22, 23, 29

The planetary power is now in its maximum Western position; the planets are now 'furthest away' from you and power should be flowing towards other people. But Mars is still in your own sign, so review last month's discussion of this.

The main headline now is the power in your 7th house of love. Venus moved in last month. Neptune (your love planet) moves in on the 3rd; Mercury on the 14th and the Sun on the 19th. Even the new Moon (on the 21st) occurs here in the 7th house. So this is where the action and the interest are. A romantic kind of month. You are in the mood for love – real, romantic, committed love. Thus singles are attracting 'marriage material' now.

The social life is very active. Singles are dating more and enjoying their dates more. One of the problems here (and it is a good one to have) is that there are so many opportunities that you feel confused. The new Moon of the 21st will clarify these issues. With the Pisces energy now very strong in the Horoscope, you are idealistic in love. You are not likely to settle for anything less than perfection. The month ahead is also more sexually active. The ruler of your 8th house is in your sign and Venus moves into your 8th house on the 8th.

Your financial planet has been in Pisces since January 14 and is there until the 8th of this month. Thus your financial intuition has been super. You just need to trust it. You have good financial support from your spouse, current love or partner (and friends too). The social connections are playing a huge role in earnings. Like last month you have opportunities for business partnerships and joint ventures, but more homework needs to be done.

On the 8th the financial planet moves into Aries and into a conjunction with Uranus. There are sudden windfalls. Job seekers have a sudden opportunity too (and have good aspects until the 19th). Finances have been tight for the past two years, but this is one of your better periods. After the 8th you will have financial opportunities with new ventures or business start-ups; perhaps you are thinking of starting your own business.

Your financial planet in the 8th house suggests a need to cut waste. You expand by cutting wasteful expenses. Your borrowing power will increase after the 8th too, but be careful not to abuse this.

Your health is basically good this month, but rest and relax more from the 19th onwards. Enhance your health in the ways mentioned in the yearly report.

## March

Best Days Overall: 7, 8, 15, 16, 25, 26
Most Stressful Days Overall: 1, 13, 14, 20, 21, 27, 28, 29
Best Days for Love: 2, 7, 11, 15, 16, 20, 21, 25, 26, 30
Best Days for Money: 7, 9, 10, 15, 16, 25, 26
Best Days for Career: 1, 2, 5, 13, 27, 28, 29, 31

Your yearly social peak is still going strong until the 20th. The love life is happy and very active. Most of the planets are still in the Western social sector of your chart, so keep in mind our previous discussions of this. Put others first (and you seem to be doing this), avoid self-will and attain your ends through your social skills. It is more difficult now to change undesirable conditions (though you probably want to), so adapt to them as best you can. This way, you can see what needs to be changed and can put these changes into effect when your personal power cycle begins in a few months.

Mercury, the ruler of your Horoscope, goes retrograde on the 12th and will be retrograde all month. Self-confidence and self-esteem are not up to their usual standards. It is a time to review your personal goals, especially those related to the body and image, and see where you can make improvements. In a way, this lack of self-confidence is endearing to others and makes you even more popular.

Last month the planets made an important shift from the lower half of your Horoscope to the upper half. Thus, you are in the daytime of your year. The activities of night are finished. You are more focused on outward goals and objectives, and career success, and you are pursuing them in overt, physical ways. Home and family are still important, but can take a back seat for now. Mercury's retrograde affects the career as Mercury is also your career planet. Thus, it is a good time to review the career and your career goals and see where improvement can be made. Also it is a time to gain more mental clarity about your goals. Once this is done, you will be in a stronger position when Mercury starts to move forward next month.

Health still needs watching until the 20th. There is nothing serious afoot, just less energy. So rest and relax more. Health will improve dramatically after the 20th.

Your 8th house was strong last month and gets even stronger after the 20th. When the 8th house is strong people are dealing with death and death issues. Perhaps there is an anniversary of someone's death – a mass or a remembrance. Often people have dreams of death or dreams where departed ones appear to them. This is most usual, but sometimes there are actual deaths or near-death kinds of experiences. Sometimes surgery is recommended as the solution to a problem. (Cosmetic surgery now wouldn't be a surprise.) All these kinds of experiences are there to help you get a deeper, more spiritual understanding of death, because if death is not understood, life is not lived properly.

Job seekers have had good aspects since the beginning of the year, and this month there are opportunities with non-profit organizations (especially from the 23rd to the 26th). If you are still looking for work you might want to donate some time to a charity or voluntary body. This will lead to opportunities.

Your financial planet travels with Jupiter from the 11th to the 14th – a very prosperous period. There is luck in speculations. Sales people make sales. Writers sell their work. Intellectual property becomes more valuable. In general, earnings increase.

## April

Best Days Overall: 4, 12, 13, 21, 22
Most Stressful Days Overall: 10, 16, 17, 24, 25
Best Days for Love: 5, 7, 14, 15, 16, 17, 24, 25, 26
Best Days for Money: 4, 5, 6, 12, 13, 14, 15, 21, 22, 24, 25
Best Days for Career: 8, 9, 17, 18, 24, 25, 29, 30

Your 8th house was strong last month and is strong all of this month. The Sun leaves there on the 20th, but the ruler of your Horoscope, Mercury, re-enters on the 17th and stays there for the rest of the month. Review last month's discussion of this. But there is more to add here.

The 8th house is the place where we renew and regenerate ourselves. We all have areas in our lives in need of resurrection and renewal. With some it is a relationship; with others it is a financial situation; with others it is some organ. This is the month to work on these things. Detox and regeneration go hand in hand. It is really one process. Before anything can be renewed, whatever it was that was causing the problem must be removed. When this occurs, resurrection just happens naturally. Nature is doing this all the time.

Thus this is a great month to get involved in detox regimes, whether for the physical body, the emotions, or the mind. There are many techniques out there and it is good to research them now. It is also a good time to go through your physical home and get rid of excess possessions that you no longer use. You will be amazed at how much lighter you feel as you do this. The financial life could use more detoxing as well. We have discussed this in previous months. If you still have waste – extraneous expenses or redundant bank, savings or credit card accounts – get rid of the ones that you don't use or need. This too will make you feel lighter. It will also make room for the new good – the new possessions and money – that wants to come to you.

Personal reinvention and personal transformation are also associated with the 8th house. Many of you are involved in these kinds of projects (and they are noble projects, the greatest work a person can do), and these projects go well now. You will see great progress here if you work at it.

On a more mundane level, this house represents the income of the spouse or partner. And so he or she is prospering this year and especially this month. He or she is in a yearly financial peak and thus is likely to be more generous with you.

Mercury conjuncts Uranus from the 22nd to the 24th, which is basically a good aspect. You are exploring personal freedom this period. Job seekers have great opportunities. There are sudden (and it seems happy) career changes and opportunities. A parent or parent figure can have a 'miraculous' healing. Perhaps he or she is travelling as well.

However there are some caveats here. You are more experimental with the body under this transit and thus likely to get involved in daredevil stunts, and you need to be more mindful about this. Experiment with the body, but in a safe way.

### May

Best Days Overall: 1, 2, 9, 10, 18, 19, 20, 28, 29
Most Stressful Days Overall: 7, 8, 13, 14, 15, 21, 22
Best Days for Love: 3, 4, 5, 11, 12, 13, 14, 15, 21, 22, 23, 30, 31
Best Days for Money: 2, 3, 4, 10, 11, 12, 19, 20, 21, 22, 29, 30, 31
Best Days for Career: 8, 18, 19, 20, 21, 22, 28, 29

Your 9th house of religion, philosophy, theology, higher education and foreign travel was powerful last month and is still strong until the 24th of this month. For students this indicates success in their studies. It is also a nice period for those applying or entering college. There is good fortune here. Whatever your age or stage in life your mind and horizons are expanding this month. There are happy educational opportunities. There is travel and travel opportunity and more interest in foreign cultures and countries. Those of you involved with religion should have groundbreaking insights and revelations here. Philosophy (though there are few who engage in it) is more important in worldly affairs than even psychology, for it is your philosophy – your personal philosophy – that will shape and mould your psychological reactions. Breakthroughs here will change the whole life. So this is an important month.

Health is good, but needs more watching after the 20th. There's nothing to fear, just be more careful with your energy. Rest and relax more. A solar eclipse on the 20th will affect you strongly, especially those of you born early in the sign. Reduce your schedule for a few days before and after this date.

The eclipse occurs right on the Mid-heaven of the Horoscope making it even more powerful for you. (The Mid-heaven is the strongest point in the chart.) Thus there are dramatic career changes happening. There are shake-ups in your company and in your industry, and probably changes in top management. There are personal dramas in the lives of authority figures – bosses, elders, superiors and parents. Perhaps they are having a detox of the body. There will be important spiritual changes over the next six months, changes of teachers, teaching, practice and the overall regime. There are dramas in the lives of aunts and uncles as well (or those who play this role in your life).

This eclipse announces the beginning of a yearly career peak. The changes that occur will probably be good for your career – doors should open for you. Many of you will have revelation about your spiritual mission too (not just your outward career). With your spiritual planet now energizing your career house from the 20th onwards, being involved with charities and altruistic causes will foster the career and your public image.

## June

   Best Days Overall: 5, 6, 15, 16, 24, 25
   Most Stressful Days Overall: 3, 4, 10, 11, 17, 18
   Best Days for Love: 1, 8, 9, 10, 11, 17, 18, 19, 27, 28, 29
   Best Days for Money: 5, 6, 8, 9, 17, 18, 26, 27, 28
   Best Days for Career: 1, 10, 17, 18, 20, 21

Last month's solar eclipse affected you powerfully, and now you have another powerful one on the 4th – this time a lunar eclipse. Health is more stressful anyway but especially around the eclipse period. Sensitive people feel these eclipses long before they happen, anything up to two weeks before. When family members or friends start getting temperamental, or when strange phenomena happen in the home, you know you are in the eclipse period and should start exercising more care. Avoid risky kinds of activities. Elective surgeries or other kinds of stressful activities are better off being rescheduled.

This eclipse brings important changes in the family situation (some of these changes are good, but very disruptive). Dirty laundry in the family relationship, long suppressed, is now being cleaned. Although this is not pleasant, it is basically good. An eclipse in the 4th house brings out hidden flaws in the home. Sometimes one finds all kinds of underworld critters – termites, mice and even bats – occupying the house. (They have probably been there a while, but now you discover them and have to deal with them.) Friendships and technology equipment get tested too. Equipment often needs replacement.

Jupiter, the family planet, makes a major move on the 11th. He moves out of your 9th house into the 10th house of career. Over the long haul this is a very positive transit, a signal for career success and elevation both for you and the family as a whole. But in the short term it shows family crisis. (Jupiter is also re-stimulating the solar eclipse point of May 20 from June 9 to the 17th, reinforcing everything we are saying.) You are in a career peak this month, but family is going to demand attention and will distract you from your outer goals.

When Jupiter crosses the solar eclipse point of May 20 it is best to avoid foreign travel if possible. Of course if you must travel, you must. In those cases pray and do your best. But elective travel should be rescheduled. Do your best to make the home as safe as possible. Are there stray nails jutting out of walls or carpets? Are your smoke detectors in good working order? Are there dangerous objects lying around unsecured? Are there loose floorboards? These are the things that should be checked.

Health and vitality improve tremendously after the 21st.

Your financial planet Venus went retrograde last month on the 15th, and is retrograde for most of the month ahead until the 27th. So major purchases, investments or financial decisions are better off delayed. You are in a period of financial review. And your goal should be mental clarity on finance. It won't happen overnight, but by the 27th it should have happened.

## July

Best Days Overall: 3, 4, 12, 13, 22, 23, 30, 31
Most Stressful Days Overall: 1, 2, 7, 8, 15, 16, 28, 29
Best Days for Love: 5, 6, 7, 8, 15, 16, 17, 24, 25, 26
Best Days for Money: 5, 6, 15, 16, 24, 25
Best Days for Career: 1, 2, 9, 10, 11, 15, 16, 19, 20, 21, 28, 29

Uranus has been square to Pluto (the ruler of your 3rd house) almost all year. But last month and this month the aspect is very exact. This is a very dynamic aspect. Cars and communication equipment probably need replacement these days. More care and mindfulness is needed when driving. Take more care in communicating to co-workers as well. Misunderstanding seems at the root of problems at work. This month Mars will activate this aspect from the 15th to the 21st, greatly reinforcing the above advice.

The upper half of the chart is still stronger than the bottom half. Your 10th house of career is much stronger than the 4th house of home and family. So career is important and seems very successful now. The two benevolent planets of the Horoscope, Jupiter and Venus, are in your 10th house. You have much help and support. The family seems supportive of career goals as well so there isn't much of a conflict between home and career.

With Venus in the 10th house (as she has been since April) you have the financial favour of the bosses and authority figures in your life. This is an aspect for a pay rise (it could have already happened, but if not it can still happen now). Mars moves into your money house on the 4th and stays there the rest of the month. Since Mars will make nice aspects to your financial planet, this is another signal for prosperity. Finances have been tight for two years now, but this month things seem much easier. Your spouse, partner or current love seems financially supportive. You have greater borrowing power now, greater access to outside money. This is a wonderful thing but be careful not to abuse this.

The Eastern sector of the self, self-interest and personal power is now the dominant sector. You have the power to have things your way. If conditions are not to your liking you can more easily create better ones. Now you have the support of the cosmos. Your personal happiness is important to others and to the cosmos. So there is no need to adapt or to settle for second best – create your own happiness; take the initiative now. The only complication is the retrograde of Mercury, which affects you personally, your career and parents or parent figures. You have the power to create, but need more mental clarity as to what you really want. And this is what you should strive for now. When Mercury goes forward next month, you will be in a good position to create whatever you want. Career opportunities (and you have some interesting ones) need more study and homework. Resolve all doubts. Strive for mental clarity. Decisions made by bosses or parents or parent figures are not written in stone now – they can change their minds.

Health is good this month. You can enhance it further in the ways described in the yearly report. Surgeries could be recommended between the 15th and the 21st, but don't be in a rush. Get other opinions.

Your 11th house of friends became powerful last month and is still strong until the 22nd.

## August

Best Days Overall: 8, 9, 10, 18, 19, 27, 28
Most Stressful Days Overall: 4, 5, 11, 12, 24, 25, 31
Best Days for Love: 2, 3, 4, 5, 13, 14, 22, 23, 31
Best Days for Money: 1, 2, 3, 11, 12, 13, 14, 20, 21, 22,
    23, 29, 30, 31
Best Days for Career: 6, 7, 11, 12, 16, 17, 24, 25

Your love planet Neptune has been retrograde since June. This doesn't stop love from happening. Singles will still be dating, but things slow down a bit. Important love decisions shouldn't be taken now. Let love develop as it will. Inner clarity is the most important thing now, especially from the 22nd to the 25th. Wait until this comes before making important love decisions one way or another. From the 7th to the 9th Venus makes beautiful aspects to the love planet and thus there are fortunate meetings and social invitations. Probably there are opportunities for business partnerships or joint ventures, but these all need more study.

Jupiter re-activates the lunar eclipse point of June 4 (this eclipse is still in effect even now) and thus there can be more family crises and dramas with parents or parent figures. This happens towards the end of the month.

Your 12th house of spirituality became powerful last month and is powerful this month too. On a mundane level this is a month for being more involved in charities and altruistic causes. There is a need for seclusion (a normal desire under this transit). There is a need and desire to 'rise above' your present conditions, to transcend them and view them from a higher perspective. Some people achieve this through sex, drugs or alcohol, but this is not the correct way. Really, this is the call of the spirit calling you into greater alignment with it. For those on the spiritual path, this brings inner growth and deep insights into life. When these things happen it is better than drugs or alcohol.

It is no accident that the spiritual 12th house becomes powerful just before your birthday – your solar return or personal new year. You are closing an old cycle (the past year) and getting ready for the new year (your birthday) to begin. So there is a need to digest the past year, to review your achievements (or non-achievements), correct mistakes (make atonement) and set your goals for the year ahead.

This spiritual period will extend well into next month. Your spiritual planet, the Sun, moves into your own sign on the 23rd. Aside from spirituality this brings 'unearthly' glamour and beauty to the image. An aura of mystery. You will learn spiritual techniques for enhancing the image (better than cosmetics). Also this initiates a yearly personal pleasure peak. You will learn that spirit is not abstract but tangible – experiential. Also it is very concerned with the seemingly minor personal details of your life. Intuition and inner guidance will guide you in issues involving the body and image.

## September

Best Days Overall: 5, 6, 14, 15, 23, 24
Most Stressful Days Overall: 1, 7, 8, 21, 22, 27, 28
Best Days for Love: 1, 9, 12, 18, 21, 22, 27, 28, 29, 30
Best Days for Money: 1, 7, 8, 12, 16, 17, 21, 22, 25, 26, 29, 30
Best Days for Career: 4, 5, 7, 8, 15, 16, 17, 25, 26

This is basically a happy month, but with a few bumps on the road to keep things interesting – to keep you on your toes!

You are still in the midst of a yearly personal pleasure peak and the desires of the flesh are being gratified. On the 23rd you enter a yearly financial peak. So there is prosperity happening as well. Health and energy are good. You have great self-confidence and more personal power and magnetism than usual. You have the energy to achieve whatever you wish to achieve. (Big goals will take more time, smaller ones happen faster.)

Though career is important and you are successful, this area is quietening down now. The planets are shifting from the upper to the lower half of the Horoscope this month. So it is time to take a breather in the career (at least overtly) and focus on the home, family and the emotional life. With night falling in your year, work on the career through inner, 'night' methods, rather than though overt, 'day' methods. This is the time to set up the 'inner conditions' for future success. This is when you gather the forces for the next career push.

Your spiritual planet enters the money house on the 23rd and your financial planet enters your spiritual 12th house on the 7th. From the 23rd onwards the Sun and Venus are in 'mutual reception' – each is a guest in the house of the other. This is considered a positive aspect. It shows mutual co-operation between these two planets, which is another signal for prosperity. The financial intuition is wonderful now and should be trusted. You are getting much inner, spiritual guidance in finance this period. It can come to you directly, via dreams and hunches, or through others such as psychics, astrologers, card readers, gurus or ministers. Sometimes simple mundane things trigger your financial intuition – for example, you are driving and you see a tortoise crossing the road ('buy Tortoise energy'). These are inner messages to you. Sometimes you pick up the newspaper and some passage will leap out at you – it seems to have a heightened significance. Pay attention. Each will get the message in the way that they can understand.

Mercury, the ruler of your Horoscope, also enters the money house this month on the 17th. The ruler of the Horoscope is always your helper and friend. It is considered fortunate.

Personal power is still very strong. The planets are in their maximum Eastern position so you can create conditions according to your liking in the ways that please you. If you make mistakes, you will find out down the road and they can be corrected. Learning to create properly is like learning anything else: one learns through one's mistakes.

### October

Best Days Overall: 2, 3, 12, 13, 20, 21, 29, 30, 31
Most Stressful Days Overall: 4, 5, 6, 18, 19, 24, 25, 26
Best Days for Love: 1, 7, 12, 16, 21, 24, 25, 26
Best Days for Money: 1, 4, 5, 6, 12, 14, 15, 21, 22, 23
Best Days for Career: 4, 5, 6, 7, 16, 17, 25, 26

Jupiter is still more or less camped out on the lunar eclipse point of June 4. There is continued turbulence and crises in the home and family situation. A parent or parent figure needs to be more careful and avoid risky kinds of activities these days. There are many dramas in his or her personal life right now.

Finances are still very good. You are still in the midst of a yearly financial peak until the 23rd but there are some financial dramas in finance this month, perhaps some unexpected expenses. These happen from the 1st to the 5th (Venus re-activates the solar eclipse point of May 20) and from the 14th to the 18th (when Venus re-activates the lunar eclipse point of June 4). These events are not going to stop your prosperity, but they will force changes.

Venus moves into your own sign on the 3rd, which is another prosperity signal. Financial opportunities are opening up for you. You don't need to do anything except show up. Expensive clothing, jewellery and personal items are coming to you. Regardless of how much you have in the bank, you look rich and live richly (perhaps above your income level). You spend on yourself. Your personal appearance and overall presentation is a big factor in your earnings.

We see improvement in the finances in other ways too. Saturn is finally leaving the money house on the 5th. This will be a huge relief. The feeling of financial tightness and of restriction will leave. Also, after two and a half years in your money house you are no doubt financially healthier than you were at the beginning of the Saturn transit; Saturn is a genius at this sort of thing.

Your love planet is still retrograde so love is more or less on hold. Certainly, singles will be dating and having fun, but serious love is on hold for a while. Love improves after the 23rd and perhaps even a few days before the 23rd. There is a happy love experience or meeting from the 4th to the 7th, but the permanence of this is in question.

Health is good all month. You can enhance it in the ways described in the yearly report. Venus in your own sign enhances the personal appearance. Whatever the actual state of your health, you look attractive and more glamorous than usual.

## November

Best Days Overall: 8, 9, 16, 17, 26, 27
Most Stressful Days Overall: 1, 2, 14, 15, 21, 22, 28, 29
Best Days for Love: 1, 3, 11, 12, 20, 21, 22
Best Days for Money: 1, 2, 8, 11, 12, 13, 16, 19, 26, 28, 29
Best Days for Career: 1, 2, 6, 7, 14, 15, 23, 24, 28, 29

Your 3rd house of communication and intellectual interests became powerful last month (after the 23rd) and is powerful until the 22nd of this month. Saturn is now in this house for the long term.

This is a month for expanding the knowledge base – for taking courses in subjects that interest you, for attending lectures, seminars and workshops. It is also good for sales, marketing, PR, advertising and media activities. The only problem with media activities or mass mailings is Mercury's retrograde (until the 11th). It is probably better to do these things after the 11th. This is a month to catch up on all the reading you need to do – the reports, the newsletters and magazines that you get. It's good also to catch up on all the letters, emails and texts that you owe people.

The 3rd house also relates to dividend and interest income (income from your assets). This month this seems to increase, but over the long term, they will probably decrease. (You probably need to find other ways to supplement your income.)

Learning – real learning – is a joy when it happens. This month you get the opportunity to enjoy learning. Over the long term though, you (and especially students) need to work harder to learn. You have to learn to study even when you don't feel like it, to take a disciplined approach to it.

Jupiter is still camped out on the lunar eclipse point of June 4. The good news is that you are more focused on home and family and are more in a position to be a help here.

There are two eclipses this month, a solar eclipse on the 13th and lunar eclipse on the 28th. This is a near repeat of the previous two in May and June. The solar eclipse occurs in your 3rd house and is basically benign to you. For students it shows changes in schools or educational plans. Cars and communication equipment often need to be replaced. There are dramas in the lives of siblings (and this is only the beginning – they have two years of drama coming up; the eclipse is preparing them for it). As always, there are spiritual changes and upheavals in spiritual or charitable organizations that you belong to. There are dramas in the lives of the spiritual people in your life.

The lunar eclipse of the 28th affects you more strongly. Arrange a nice easy schedule for that period. Avoid risky or stressful kinds of activities. Spend more quiet time at home. This eclipse shows career changes, and changes in your company or industry. A parent has financial shake-ups. Friendships and high-tech equipment get tested.

## December

Best Days Overall: 5, 6, 7, 14, 15, 23, 24
Most Stressful Days Overall: 12, 13, 18, 19, 25, 26, 27
Best Days for Love: 1, 10, 11, 18, 19, 20, 28, 31
Best Days for Money: 1, 8, 9, 10, 11, 16, 20, 25, 31
Best Days for Career: 2, 11, 21, 25, 26, 27, 31

Your love planet went forward on the 11th of last month after many months of retrograde motion. The current love situation is starting to clarify. You are clearer about your next moves, and so is the spouse, partner or current love. As long as you are clear as to your motives and desires, the love decisions will be good. Even mistakes will turn out well; they will just be learning experiences.

Last month the planetary power shifted to the Western social sector of the Horoscope – another good signal for love as you are becoming more 'other' conscious. Good relations with others – social acceptance – is more important than usual and so you are willing to overcome all the various challenges that arise. Now you are in a period where you have less personal control, and there are many lessons to be learned with this. Personal power (which you have had for the past six or so months) is wonderful, but can produce negative karma if it is misapplied. Now, one learns to allow a higher power to be in control. Downplay the self and focus on others.

On the 23rd of last month, your financial planet entered the 3rd house and will be there until the 16th of this month. So sales, marketing, advertising, mass mailings and media activities are all very important financially. You need to create a buzz around your product or service. Buying, selling, retailing and trading are also paths to profit. On the 16th the financial planet enters Sagittarius, your 4th house. Thus you are spending more on the family but you can also earn from here, from family connections and people who are like family to you. The family is more financially supportive during this period, especially a parent. Investors will find profit opportunities in property, restaurants, the food business and lodgings, and also industries that deal with the home. Foreign investments also look good.

The 4th house (where power is most of the month) is concerned with more than just home and family. These are important, but this house is about your emotional life, your everyday moods and feelings. So when the 4th house is powerful, deep psychological insights come. You can see how a certain behaviour or pattern was born and developed and this consciousness allows you to change it if need be. These insights help you deal with family members, employees and other people in general.

In the subconscious (ruled by the 4th house) is the 'memory body' – the record of all past events that you have experienced (from this life or past lives). Thus the memory is sharper and there is a greater interest in the past.

History, personal and collective, is more interesting this month.

On the 21st, the Sun enters your 5th house and you enter another one of your yearly personal pleasure peaks. Enjoy.

# Libra

$\simeq$

---

THE SCALES
*Birthdays from
23rd September to
22nd October*

---

## Personality Profile

### LIBRA AT A GLANCE

*Element* – Air

*Ruling Planet* – Venus
  *Career Planet* – Moon
  *Love Planet* – Mars
  *Money Planet* – Pluto
  *Planet of Communications* – Jupiter
  *Planet of Health and Work* – Neptune
  *Planet of Home and Family Life* – Saturn
  *Planet of Spirituality and Good Fortune* –
    Mercury

*Colours* – blue, jade green

*Colours that promote love, romance and social
  harmony* – carmine, red, scarlet

*Colours that promote earning power* –
  burgundy, red–violet, violet

*Gems* – carnelian, chrysolite, coral, emerald, jade, opal, quartz, white marble

*Metal* – copper

*Scents* – almond, rose, vanilla, violet

*Quality* – cardinal (= activity)

*Qualities most needed for balance* – a sense of self, self-reliance, independence

*Strongest virtues* – social grace, charm, tact, diplomacy

*Deepest needs* – love, romance, social harmony

*Characteristic to avoid* – violating what is right in order to be socially accepted

*Signs of greatest overall compatibility* – Gemini, Aquarius

*Signs of greatest overall incompatibility* – Aries, Cancer, Capricorn

*Sign most helpful to career* – Cancer

*Sign most helpful for emotional support* – Capricorn

*Sign most helpful financially* – Scorpio

*Sign best for marriage and/or partnerships* – Aries

*Sign most helpful for creative projects* – Aquarius

*Best Sign to have fun with* – Aquarius

*Signs most helpful in spiritual matters* – Gemini, Virgo

*Best day of the week* – Friday

# Understanding a Libra

In the sign of Libra the universal mind – the soul – expresses its genius for relationships, that is, its power to harmonize diverse elements in a unified, organic way. Libra is the soul's power to express beauty in all of its forms. And where is beauty if not within relationships? Beauty does not exist in isolation. Beauty arises out of comparison – out of the just relationship between different parts. Without a fair and harmonious relationship there is no beauty, whether it in art, manners, ideas or the social or political forum.

There are two faculties humans have that exalt them above the animal kingdom: their rational faculty (expressed in the signs of Gemini and Aquarius) and their aesthetic faculty, exemplified by Libra. Without an aesthetic sense we would be little more than intelligent barbarians. Libra is the civilizing instinct or urge of the soul.

Beauty is the essence of what Librans are all about. They are here to beautify the world. One could discuss Librans' social grace, their sense of balance and fair play, their ability to see and love another person's point of view – but this would be to miss their central asset: their desire for beauty.

No one – no matter how alone he or she seems to be – exists in isolation. The universe is one vast collaboration of beings. Librans, more than most, understand this and understand the spiritual laws that make relationships bearable and enjoyable.

A Libra is always the unconscious (and in some cases conscious) civilizer, harmonizer and artist. This is a Libra's deepest urge and greatest genius. Librans love instinctively to bring people together, and they are uniquely qualified to do so. They have a knack for seeing what unites people – the things that attract and bind rather than separate individuals.

## Finance

In financial matters Librans can seem frivolous and illogical to others. This is because Librans appear to be more concerned with earning money for others than for themselves. But there is a logic to this financial attitude. Librans know that everything and everyone is connected and that it is impossible to help another to prosper without also prospering yourself. Since enhancing their partner's income and position tends to strengthen their relationship, Librans choose to do so. What could be more fun than building a relationship? You will rarely find a Libra enriching him- or herself at someone else's expense.

Scorpio is the ruler of Libra's solar 2nd house of money, giving Libra unusual insight into financial matters – and the power to focus on these matters in a way that disguises a seeming indifference. In fact, many other signs come to Librans for financial advice and guidance.

Given their social grace, Librans often spend great sums of money on entertaining and organizing social events. They also like to help others when they are in need. Librans would go out of their way to help a friend in dire straits, even if they have to borrow from others to do so. However, Librans are also very careful to pay back any debts they owe, and like to make sure they never have to be reminded to do so.

## Career and Public Image

Publicly, Librans like to appear as nurturers. Their friends and acquaintances are their family and they wield political power in parental ways. They also like bosses who are paternal or maternal.

The sign of Cancer is on Libra's 10th house (of career) cusp; the Moon is Libra's career planet. The Moon is by far the speediest, most changeable planet in the horoscope. It alone among all the planets travels through the entire zodiac – all 12 signs and houses – every month. This is an important key to the way in which Librans approach their careers, and also to what they need to do to maximize their career potential. The Moon is the planet of moods and feelings – Librans need a career in which their emotions can have free expression. This is why so many Librans are involved in the creative arts. Libra's ambitions wax and wane with the Moon. They tend to wield power according to their mood.

The Moon 'rules' the masses – and that is why Libra's highest goal is to achieve a mass kind of acclaim and popularity. Librans who achieve fame cultivate the public as other people cultivate a lover or friend. Librans can be very flexible – and often fickle – in their career and ambitions. On the other hand, they can achieve their ends in a great variety of ways. They are not stuck in one attitude or with one way of doing things.

## Love and Relationships

Librans express their true genius in love. In love you could not find a partner more romantic, more seductive or more fair. If there is one thing that is sure to destroy a relationship – sure to block your love from flowing – it is injustice or imbalance between lover and beloved. If one party is giving too much or taking too much, resentment is sure to surface at some time or other. Librans are careful about this. If anything, Librans might err on the side of giving more, but never giving less.

If you are in love with a Libra, make sure you keep the aura of romance alive. Do all the little things – candle-lit dinners, travel to exotic locales, flowers and small gifts. Give things that are beautiful, not necessarily expensive. Send cards. Ring regularly even if you have nothing in particular to say. The niceties are very important to a Libra. Your relationship is a work of art: make it beautiful and your Libran lover will appreciate it. If you are creative about it, he or she will appreciate it even more; for this is how your Libra will behave towards you.

Librans like their partners to be aggressive and even a bit self-willed. They know that these are qualities they sometimes lack and so they like their partners to have them. In relationships, however, Librans can be very aggressive – but always in a subtle and charming way! Librans are determined in their efforts to charm the object of their desire – and this determination can be very pleasant if you are on the receiving end.

## Home and Domestic Life

Since Librans are such social creatures, they do not particularly like mundane domestic duties. They like a well-organized home – clean and neat with everything needful present – but housework is a chore and a burden, one of the unpleasant tasks in life that must be done, the quicker the better. If a Libra has enough money – and sometimes even if not – he or she will prefer to pay someone else to take care of the daily household chores. However, Librans like gardening; they love to have flowers and plants in the home.

A Libra's home is modern, and furnished in excellent taste. You will find many paintings and sculptures there. Since Librans like to be with friends and family, they enjoy entertaining at home and they make great hosts.

Capricorn is on the cusp of Libra's 4th solar house of home and family. Saturn, the planet of law, order, limits and discipline, rules Libra's domestic affairs. If Librans want their home life to be supportive and happy they need to develop some of the virtues of Saturn – order, organization and discipline. Librans, being so creative and so intensely in need of harmony, can tend to be too lax in the home and too permissive with their children. Too much of this is not always good; children need freedom but they also need limits.

# Horoscope for 2012

## Major Trends

Last year was a stressful, even dangerous year. Three, and sometimes four, long-term planets were in stressful alignment with you. There were times when the short-term planets also joined the fray and it seemed to you that the whole universe was against you. Just getting through 2011 with your health and sanity intact should be considered an achievement. The fury of the storm is a bit weaker than last year, but the storm is still there. By now, you have developed the mental and spiritual muscles to withstand it, and you are in a better survival position than last year. Keep in mind that, intense though the challenges are, the cosmos won't give you more than you can handle. It might push you to the edge, but not over it.

Three powerful long-term planets are still in stressful alignment with you – Saturn, Uranus and Pluto. After October 5, Saturn will leave your sign, and things should get a lot easier. The Category 5 hurricane gets downgraded to a mere tropical storm. After what you have been through this will be a walk in the park.

It is only through the buffeting and hammering of life that we learn what we are made of, and this has been the main positive of the past year. You are a stronger and wiser person now.

Your areas of greatest interest this year are the body and image (until October 5); finance (from October 5 onwards); home and family; children, creativity and personal pleasure (until February 3); health and work (from February 3 onwards); love, romance and social activities; sex, personal transformation, personal reinvention; occult studies (until June 11); religion, theology, philosophy, foreign travel and higher education (from June 11 onwards); and spirituality (until July 3).

Your paths of greatest fulfilment are sex, personal transformation, personal reinvention, occult studies (until June

11); religion, theology, philosophy, foreign travel and higher education (from June 11 onwards); communication and intellectual interests (until August 31); and finances (from August 31 onwards).

## Health

*(Please note that this is an* astrological *perspective on health and not a medical one. In days of yore there was no difference, these perspectives were identical. But these days there could be quite a difference. For a medical perspective, please consult your doctor or health practitioner.)*

Health is very delicate and needs much watching. Last year was especially difficult, but you still need to be careful this year. As we mentioned, the hurricane has been downgraded to a tropical storm, but tropical storms can also do damage if one is not careful.

Aside from the difficult aspects last year, your 6th house of health was empty and so the main danger was that you would ignore things. In this respect the year ahead is better. Your 6th house becomes powerful from February 3 onwards. Thus you are more likely to pay attention to health and do the things that are necessary.

There is more good news. There is much you can do to enhance your health and even prevent problems from developing. Even if they can't be totally prevented, they can be 'softened' to a great degree. Give more attention to the following organs: the heart (avoid worry and anxiety, the main root causes of heart problems – if there is something constructive that can be done in a situation, by all means do it, but worry and anxiety do nothing to help you and only sap energy and damage your body); the kidneys and hips (hips should be regularly massaged); and the feet (feet should be regularly massaged; keep them warm in the winter and wear sensible shoes that fit and don't knock you off balance).

Neptune is your health planet. As our regular readers know, he is the most spiritual of all the planets. Not only

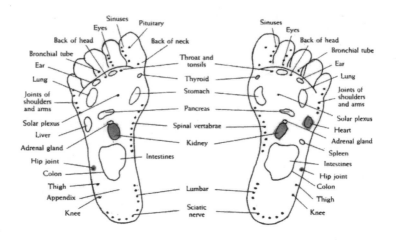

## Reflexology

*Try to massage the whole foot on a regular basis, but pay extra attention to the points highlighted on the chart. When you massage, be aware of 'sore spots', as these need special attention. It's also a good idea to massage the ankles and top side of the feet (see below).*

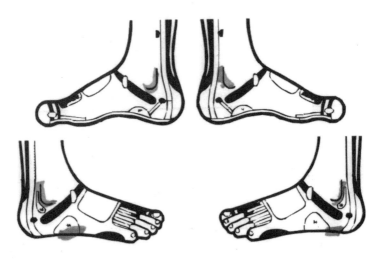

that, but he is moving into his own sign and house where he will be even more 'Neptunian' than usual. Thus you benefit greatly (even more than usual) from spiritual therapies – prayer, meditation, reiki, the laying on of hands, the manipulation of subtle energies and so forth. Though many of you already know much about spiritual healing, you are going to go much deeper into it over the coming years; more on this later.

Your health planet will be in a water sign all year (and for many years to come). So you will benefit greatly from water-based therapies. It is probably a good idea to drink more water than usual. Being around water is healthy. Boating, swimming, water skiing – activities that bring you close to water are healthy kinds of exercises. Soaking in a natural spring or in a tub or whirlpool is also very good. A long soak starts to relax the muscles and cleanses the emotional body. These things are especially good if you feel under the weather.

Perhaps even more important is maintaining high energy levels. Don't be embarrassed to take a nap during the day or when you feel tired (no matter your age). Try to work more rhythmically, alternating activities and organizing them better. Delegate or outsource tasks as much as possible.

There are so many ways that energy is frivolously wasted. If you think about it you will see it for yourself. Excessive thinking (and especially negative thinking) is a huge waste of energy; negative emotions likewise. There are so many physical motions that aren't necessary and which only drain the batteries. Humans are truly prodigal. When the aspects are kind they can get away with it, but when the aspects get stressed, they can't, and it becomes a health issue.

## Home and Family

Pluto entered your 4th house of home and family in 2008 and will be there for many years to come. Thus this is a 'house of power' this year and for many years. There is great focus here.

The trends we are writing of are long term. They were true for the past few years too. A cosmic detox is taking place in the family over the long term. This is happening on many levels – in the physical home, in the family relationships and in your emotional and domestic life.

Detox is all about health and purification. Material that doesn't belong comes to the surface for cleansing and correction. This is a deliberate process. It will happen whether you co-operate or not, but it is best to co-operate as the process will go more smoothly. The cosmic object here is not punishment (though it can feel this way) but health – emotional and family health. You are in the process of giving birth to your ideal home and family situation. All that is less than the ideal is being purged.

On the purely mundane level this works itself out as major renovations going on in the home such as new plumbing and wiring – not superficial work, but deep renovations. Many of you will completely change the shape of your home, tearing down walls, eliminating rooms and creating new ones, for example. Since Pluto is also your financial planet, you are spending money on the home and family; investing in the home. Perhaps a home office is being created as well.

Your family planet Saturn has been in your own sign for the past two years, and will be there for most of the year ahead. This reinforces the focus on the home and family. You have been taking on extra burdens and responsibilities in the home and with the family. Perhaps you are supporting a parent, or taking more responsibility for this person. There are extra family expenses these days and this seems stressful.

The family seems devoted to you, especially one of your parents, but perhaps over-controlling. Often you feel that you are 'owned' by them and are not your own person. (Family can also be very supportive these days too, and in a financial way as well. But again there is a feeling that there is a price tag on this largesse. Your freedom is severely limited.)

Pluto is the planet of death, surgery and near-death kinds of experiences. Thus these things have been happening in the family. This is all part of the detox that is going on. The whole family relationship is being transformed. You will not lose your family but the old 'instinctive' ties will be broken and you will relate to them on a new and better level. The restrictions you are feeling now will lead to greater freedom in the future.

Pregnant Librans need to be more careful during the pregnancy; there is a greater tendency to miscarriage or abortion with this aspect. Pregnancy seems more complicated this year. There are more dramas involved and it is not a smooth ride.

## Finance and Career

A stormy financial year ahead is indicated. Fasten your seat belts. Uranus spends the year pretty much in square aspect (a stressful aspect) with your financial planet. Saturn is also in stressful aspect with your financial planet but this is not as strong as last year. Achieving your financial goals will require more effort than usual. There are many, many challenges to deal with.

Uranus squaring Pluto shows that the year ahead is full of dramatic financial changes – major financial changes – and these happen suddenly and unexpectedly. These are not things that one can prepare for. By the time the year is over with you will be in a whole different kind of financial situation. The changes are not just material – how you earn, how you spend, how you invest, where you bank, etc. – they are also attitude changes in your financial thinking and planning, and in your financial strategy. The old rules don't seem to work this year and you are searching for new ones.

The truth underneath all the drama is that the cosmos is in process of setting you free financially. It is breaking the old chains, the old attachments that are holding you back. It's hard to see this while the process is happening, but in hindsight it will be clear.

When finances are stormy there is a tendency to indulge in reckless speculation, but this is not advisable this year. Resist the temptation; it will only deepen the problem. Speculation in general is not advisable this year.

As we mentioned, home, family and children expenses seem the main stress. Perhaps you are overspending there. But these same drains can also be sources of supply. Family members can be supportive and have good financial ideas.

It is good to enjoy one's wealth – a great blessing. But this year, be careful about overspending on leisure kinds of activities. Keep within budget.

Saturn enters the money house on October 5, so you will be reorganizing and restructuring the financial life. This is not generally pleasant, but it will be good in the long term. It is a time for good financial management, for gaining control over your money rather than letting it control you, and for setting the foundation for long-term wealth. You will find, that if you reorganize your assets, spending and investments, you will have all the resources that you need. The resources are already there, you just have to shift things around a little. Family will be more financially co-operative that period as well.

### Love and Social Life

Last year, Uranus entered your 7th house for the long term. It will be there for the next six years or so. This tests existing marriages and relationships. Love and friendships are highly unstable these days. Good relationships will survive (although even good ones will require more work and effort) but the flawed ones will probably dissolve. By the time Uranus leaves this house you will be in totally different social conditions and circumstances than you are now. You will have a new circle of friends too. (Business partnerships are unstable as well and are getting tested.)

Again it is important to understand that the cosmos is not punishing you. Basically it is setting you free on a social level, to enter the social life and marriage of your dreams. In order to do this it sometimes resorts to dramatic, spectacular methods. These days, it is best to give your spouse, partner or current love as much freedom as possible, so long as it isn't destructive. Over-control (and you have a tendency to this these days) is not advisable.

No one in the zodiac is more loving and gracious than Libra. But ever since Saturn entered your sign in 2010, this natural love and warmth might not be coming through. You have seemed to be cold, aloof and separate, probably without meaning to. You will have to consciously project more love and warmth to others. This will be an effort this year but worth it.

For singles this is an exciting love period. Love can happen at any time in any place or condition. There is much dating. There are new and exciting people coming into your life. But there is also instability. Love comes suddenly and can leave suddenly. Marriage is not likely nor is it advisable right now. Uranus in the 7th house is an aspect for serial love affairs, rather than marriage. Singles (and even those of you who are married) are more experimental in love. You are learning about love through trial and error and experimentation, not from the rule books. There are no rules for you; it is strictly what works for you that determines the issue.

When Uranus is in the 7th house people often express rebellion in the arena of love. We all have ways that we express rebellion and it is different for every person, but for you it is the love arena. Thus you are attracted to unconventional types of people and relationships; the more unconventional (and socially unacceptable) the better. The problem with this is that making 'political points' is not the basis for a long-term relationship, and if that is the motive, it is doubtful that the relationship will last very long.

Those of you who are working on the second marriage have excellent opportunities after June 11. Those working on the third marriage have a status quo kind of year.

**Self-improvement**

As we mentioned earlier you are in a period (for at least the next 14 or so years) where you will be going deeper into the spiritual dimensions of healing. This is a huge subject and you should study as much as you can on this theme. The works of Emmet Fox and Ernest Holmes are good places to begin. There are many other wonderful books on this subject as well. But these are 'classics' and will lead you to other books. A good grasp of this, and your persistent application, will turn your whole health situation around. It will not only clear up symptoms but also the spiritual root causes of those symptoms.

The premises of spiritual healing are as follows. There is one and only one healer – the Divine. Everything that happens in a healing – the therapies, the doctors, the pills – are only the instruments that the Divine may choose to use. They are not the causes of healing, but the side effects. The Divine healer generally acts through instruments, but not always. It can act directly on the body if it chooses without any human intervention at all. How it will act is not really our business, but it will do so if we turn to it. This is the main point.

Health problems this year are probably coming from spiritual disconnection, and so it is important for you to stay connected to the Divine and in a state of grace. This is always good of course, but these days, it is an actual health issue.

It is also very important to be open to intuition. The inner guidance will lead unerringly to healing if one follows it. When intuition comes it seems to us (to the human mind) that it is irrational or illogical, because intuition is seeing far into the future. In hindsight, it is always seen to be perfectly logical and rational. Intuition is the short cut to good health these days.

Saturn in your own sign is making you feel your physical limits. Self-esteem and self-confidence are not up to their usual standards. Your ego is getting a reality check through cosmic adjustments. If your self-esteem has been irrationally high, Saturn will adjust it. If irrationally low (which is more likely these days) Saturn will raise it. When Saturn is finished doing his job you will have a more realistic perspective on yourself and your abilities. Thus you will make better decisions.

Saturn in your money house after October 5 also brings a reality check to the financial realm. If your financial ideas or plans are unrealistic, Saturn will adjust things. If your standards and expectations have been too high, Saturn will make them realistic. If too low, Saturn will raise them. The financial pressure that he puts on you will bring out many hidden talents and insights that you never knew you had. You will discover financial possibilities that were hidden from you when times were good. This is the agenda here.

# Month-by-month Forecasts

### January

Best Days Overall: 5, 6, 7, 14, 15, 23, 24
Most Stressful Days Overall: 1, 2, 8, 9, 21, 22, 28, 29
Best Days for Love: 1, 2, 3, 4, 6, 7, 12, 13, 18, 19, 21, 22, 27, 28, 29, 30, 31
Best Days for Money: 3, 4, 12, 17, 18, 21, 30
Best Days for Career: 3, 4, 8, 9, 12, 13, 23, 24

Your year begins with most of the planets below the horizon in the lower hemisphere of the Horoscope. Not only that, they are in the maximum of their lower position. Your 4th house of family is very powerful, while your 10th house of career is mostly empty (only the Moon visits there on the 8th and 9th). This gives the very clear message that career can be (and probably will be) downplayed and the main focus should be on the home, family and emotional issues. This is a period for inner, psychological growth, rather than external growth. You are in the night time of your year and this is when a person builds up the forces for the next day. Many powerful, invisible processes are happening when a person sleeps. The outer body is inactive, but inwardly much is going on. And so it is with you.

Last month, the planets made an important shift from the independent Eastern sector to the social Western sector of the Horoscope. You are always a social person, but now even more so. In your case this is a happy shift. You get to exercise your natural social genius more and thus will tend to be more successful. Personal power and independence is lessened now, and you are more reliant on others (and their good graces) for your good. But this is something you enjoy and are good at. This is a time where you learn about who you are through your interactions with others.

Health is stressful now, especially until the 20th. Keep in mind our discussion of this in the yearly report. You are in one of the most stressful health periods of your year (and perhaps of your life), so take it nice and easy now. Do whatever it is possible to do and then rest. I have found that by breaking up the day – working for two hours, then resting, then working, then resting – energy is maximized. One can be productive without getting overtired. Health improves after the 20th, but still needs watching. The short-term planets become more harmonious to you, but the long-term ones are still stressing you. Venus travels with Neptune from the 12th to the 15th and enters your house of health on the 24th. This shows a greater focus on health (a good thing) and also the power of spiritual healing methods on your health.

Job seekers have wonderful opportunities during this period.

## February

Best Days Overall: 2, 3, 11, 12, 19, 20, 29
Most Stressful Days Overall: 4, 5, 17, 18, 24, 25
Best Days for Love: 1, 5, 6, 9, 10, 15, 17, 18, 24, 25, 27, 28
Best Days for Money: 1, 9, 13, 14, 17, 18, 27, 28
Best Days for Career: 2, 3, 4, 5, 11, 12, 21, 22

Many of the trends of last month are very much in effect now. The planetary power is still in the lower half of the chart and mostly in the social West. Keep in mind our discussion of this last month. The ruler of your Horoscope, Venus, enters your 7th house of love on the 8th reinforcing the social nature of the month ahead.

Your 5th house of pleasure and creativity became powerful on January 20 and is powerful until the 19th. You are in a yearly personal pleasure peak. Happiness, enjoying your life, is a powerful antidote to disease. Librans are always creative but in this period even more so.

Love is challenging this month. Your love planet went retrograde on January 24 and stays that way all of this month. Not only that but it is receiving stressful aspects. It is your focus on the beloved – putting him or her first – that will salvage a current relationship. The love challenges might not be stemming from problems in the relationship itself; your spouse, partner or current love is having personal challenges and thus is more difficult to deal with. He or she lacks direction these days and so can say or do things from a place of uncertainty.

Singles have happy romantic opportunities from the 8th onwards, and especially between the 8th and 10th. But the stability of these meetings and experiences are in question. These can be one night stands. They seem to lack 'staying power'. However they are happy one night stands. Important love decisions should be avoided. Your love and social life should be being reviewed to attain mental and emotional clarity. When this happens (and it will take some time) the decision-making will be easy. With the love planet in your spiritual 12th house since the beginning of the year, there are many hidden things that will come to light. In love, what you see is not what you get. Be patient and slow down.

With the above alignment, love opportunities happen in spiritual settings – in meditation seminars, spiritual lectures, at the yoga, tai chi or chi qong studio – as you involve yourself in charity or altruistic kinds of activities.

Your house of health becomes very powerful this month, a very good development. Health does need more focus and you are giving it priority. This is a very nice position for job seekers and they should have success this month. Those of you who employ others are adding to the work force.

When Venus travels with Uranus from the 8th to the 10th you will be more experimental with the body, testing its limits. This is basically a good thing, but it should be done mindfully. Carelessness can produce accidents or injury.

Finances (and there are many dramatic changes afoot) were better last month than now. But after the 20th you should see improvement here.

### March

Best Days Overall: 1, 9, 10, 18, 19, 27, 28, 29
Most Stressful Days Overall: 3, 4, 15, 16, 22, 23, 24, 30, 31
Best Days for Love: 7, 8, 15, 16, 22, 23, 24, 25, 26
Best Days for Money: 7, 11, 12, 15, 16, 25, 26
Best Days for Career: 3, 4, 11, 12, 22, 23, 30, 31

The planets move into their maximum Western position this month, and your 7th house of love is the most powerful in the Horoscope from the 20th onwards. You are in a yearly social peak. However, though there is more dating and more romantic meetings for singles (the 11th to the 17th is very strong for this), the love planet is still retrograde all month. Sure, enjoy the social whirl, have fun, but avoid making important love decisions one way or another. As we mentioned last month, there are many hidden things coming to light and you need to know these things before making decisions.

Until the 20th the focus is on health. But even after this date health needs watching even more than before. This is a stressful health period. Keep in mind our previous discussions on this. When energy is low, your aura weakens, and your aura is your spiritual immune system. When this happens, you become more vulnerable to opportunistic invaders (microbes, viruses, destructive kinds of bacteria, fungi, parasites, etc.) But other things also happen. The faculties tend to be less sharp than usual and thus accidents can happen. So take it nice and easy after the 20th. The good news is that the cosmos will never give you more than you can handle. It might push you to the edge, but never over the edge. This will be a more sexually active kind of month as well. Venus and Jupiter are in your 8th house of regeneration. While this is basically good, the danger is overdoing a good thing. You need all your energy now.

Finances are much more stressful this month. It won't stop earnings, but there are more complications involved here. You will need to work harder than usual to achieve your financial goals. The good news here is that your spouse, partner or current love is very prosperous (he or she might lack direction in the personal life, but financially things are good). He or she will be more generous with you. You will have good access to outside money, to credit or to outside investors. This will pick up the slack in your personal earnings. Venus will conjunct Jupiter from the 11th to the 14th, which will be a nice financial period. Regardless of actual earnings, you live 'as if' earnings were high. You are likely to get a new car and communication equipment that period. Sales people make important sales then. Writers sell their work.

If the aspects were easier, the wealth would be greater from these things. But these events relieve some of the stress at least.

## April

Best Days Overall: 6, 14, 15, 24, 25
Most Stressful Days Overall: 12, 13, 19, 20, 26, 27
Best Days for Love: 3, 4, 5, 12, 14, 15, 19, 20, 21, 24,
    25
Best Days for Money: 4, 8, 12, 13, 21, 22
Best Days for Career: 1, 2, 10, 11, 20, 21, 26, 27

Last month the planets made an important shift. The power moved from the lower half to the upper half of the Horoscope. Dawn is breaking in your year. It is now time to be up and about your business in the world. The whole purpose of night is to give birth to the day. So now you will make the dreams of the night manifest in tangible reality. You will start to pursue your career objectives in outer, objective, more physical kinds of ways. By now (hopefully) you have found your point of emotional harmony and can now give your attention to the outer life, to your ambitions and the purposes of your incarnation.

You are still in the midst of a yearly social peak and this month things seem happier and clearer. Your love planet starts to move forward on the 14th. You know what you have to do now. It is safe to make love decisions after the 11th.

Your 8th house was powerful last month and becomes even more powerful after the 20th. Aside from indicating increased libido and more sexual activity, the 8th house rules over issues of personal transformation. It is about giving birth to the self that you long to be, your ideal self. But before this can happen, the old self, the old personality, the old mentality has to die. And thus this house is also associated with death. Generally the death that happens is more on a psychological level. Those advanced on the spiritual path experience the death of the ego or of certain qualities of the ego. Those less advanced experience the death of certain mental or emotional patterns, perhaps the death of some old habit. If you go through an 8th house transit and nothing in you has died, well, you haven't really succeeded. Just as the new day can't begin until the old day is dead, so the new you cannot be born until the old you (the one that has been creating all the problems and dramas) is gone. Generally this is a process and doesn't happen all at once. But now you make progress here.

Sometimes power in the 8th house brings actual confrontations with death: life and death kinds of crises, near-death kinds of experiences, or a need to deal with the death of someone close. The purpose here is to gain a greater understanding of death. It is never punishment.

People often have dreams of death under these transits. This is another way of confronting death on the psychological level. As we mentioned, old aspects of yourself are dying and thus it is quite natural to have dreams of death.

Your personal finances are improving – there is increase this month (both Jupiter and Saturn are making nice aspects to Pluto, your financial planet) – but there are still complications. Pluto goes retrograde on the 10th (and will be that way for many more months). Double-check your finances and avoid short cuts. Be perfect in all that you do, and, of course, do your homework before making major purchases or investments. Your financial life is now under review for many more months. Your goal is clarity. Once this is attained, your financial decision making will be easy. Your spouse, partner or current love is still in a yearly financial peak and still seems more generous with you than usual.

Health still needs a lot of watching and care. Until the 20th you are still in one of the most stressful health periods in your year. So keep in mind our previous discussions.

**May**

Best Days Overall: 3, 4, 11, 12, 23, 24, 25, 30, 31
Most Stressful Days Overall: 9, 10, 16, 17, 23, 24, 25
Best Days for Love: 1, 2, 3, 4, 9, 10, 11, 12, 16, 17, 19, 20, 21, 22, 28, 29, 30, 31
Best Days for Money: 1, 2, 5, 6, 9, 10, 19, 20, 28, 29
Best Days for Career: 1, 2, 9, 10, 20, 21, 23, 24, 25, 30

Last month, the ruler of your Horoscope, Venus, entered your 9th house, where she stays for an unusually long time, until August 8. So this is an important interest for many months. But there is more to this; your 9th house is even more prominent this month. The Sun enters there on the 20th and Mercury on the 24th. After the 20th it is the strongest house in your chart, both quantitatively and qualitatively. A solar eclipse on the 20th also occurs in this House, further highlighting it. This is the main headline of the month.

Power in the 9th house is read on many levels. On the mundane level, it shows foreign travel, a jet-setting kind of life (each according to their level), and a greater interest in foreign affairs and cultures. It shows a 'happy-go-lucky', optimistic kind of period. When this house is strong even people of modest means manage to take expensive trips. They might be on minimum wage but somehow they manage. The cosmos arranges the finances.

The house is considered lucky by astrologers because in the 9th house the horizons – physical, emotional and mental – are expanded, and when this happens it causes great euphoria. Suddenly you discover, yes, I can have that thing that I want, I can have that career, that house, that lifestyle that I dream about. Perhaps before the transit, you felt 'cut off' from it; now it is a real possibility.

Travel expands the physical horizons. Higher education (another 9th house concern) expands the mind and the knowledge base. Religion, philosophy and theology expand the mind and the spirit. All these interests are important now. There is much more to say about this, but space doesn't permit.

The solar eclipse of the 20th occurs right on the cusp of the 9th house, so your religious and philosophical beliefs, your personal religion, are getting tested. Generally this happens through a crisis of faith: events happen that contradict your beliefs and now you must re-evaluate these things. Fine tune them. Discard the beliefs that are merely superstition disguised as religion or philosophy and keep the ones that are true. This is a healthy exercise and should be done on regular basis anyway. But now the eclipse forces the issue.

Students at college or postgraduates make important changes in their education. There are shake-ups in the hierarchy of the schools as well. Students entering college could have a few surprises too – the college they want is not available, and they wind up somewhere else (usually in a better place). Or, they intended study one thing but end up pursuing another course. Though there are shake-ups, students are successful in their studies and educational plans for the year ahead and especially for the next few months.

Friendships and high-tech equipment get tested now too. Often there is need for replacement. This eclipse is benign to you, but it won't hurt to reduce your schedule around it anyway.

## June

Best Days Overall: 8, 9, 17, 18, 27, 28
Most Stressful Days Overall: 5, 6, 12, 13, 20, 21
Best Days for Love: 5, 6, 7, 8, 9, 12, 13, 15, 16, 17, 18, 25, 26, 27, 28
Best Days for Money: 1, 2, 5, 6, 17, 26, 27, 29, 30
Best Days for Career: 8, 9, 18, 19, 20, 21, 29, 30

The power in your 9th house is even stronger this month than last month. On June 11, Jupiter makes a major move into this house and will stay there for the rest of the year. Keep in mind our discussion of this last month.

This month we have a lunar eclipse on the 4th that occurs in your 3rd house of communications. This eclipse is basically benign to you, but it might not be so benign to people around you. This eclipse brings career changes. I feel it is setting up conditions for greater progress and success – you are entering a yearly career peak on the 21st. Good luck often comes disguised as some disturbance or shake-up and only later, in hindsight, do we realize that the event was actually lucky. So it is with this eclipse. There are shake-ups in your company and industry, and perhaps in your local government. There are dramas in the lives of parents, bosses and authority figures. Last month your high-tech gadgetry got tested – computers or software or website – this month the car or communications equipment get tested. There are dramatic events in the lives of siblings or sibling figures in your life. Perhaps a marriage is happening – a good thing, but disruptive.

On the 15th of last month, the ruler of your Horoscope, Venus, made one of her rare retrogrades. (Where most of the planets go retrograde for months every year, Venus only retrogrades once every two years; Mars too.) So it is time to slow down a bit and take stock of your life and personal goals. It's good to think about the meaning of your life and its ultimate purpose (Venus is retrograde in your 9th house). Perhaps the recent changes in your beliefs are contributing to this review. Self-confidence and self-esteem might not be up to their usual standards, but this is normal. There is nothing wrong with you; this is the way that most people feel when the ruler of their Horoscope is retrograde. Your personal appearance, your image and your self-concept are also under review now. See what areas can be improved and make the changes when Venus starts to move forward on the 27th. The good news is that this month we are in the maximum of retrograde activity for the year (until the 25th 40 per cent of the planets are moving backwards), so the pace of life is slower and you have more time for this.

Health again needs special attention after the 21st. Watch the energy levels now and enhance the health in the ways described in the yearly report.

Major financial changes have been brewing all year. This month (and last month) Uranus' square to Pluto has become more exact. The changes are dramatic but are leading you to greater financial freedom and independence.

## July

> Best Days Overall: 5, 6, 15, 16, 24, 25
> Most Stressful Days Overall: 3, 4, 9, 10, 11, 17, 18, 30, 31
> Best Days for Love: 4, 5, 6, 9, 10, 11, 15, 16, 24, 25
> Best Days for Money: 3, 5, 6, 12, 15, 16, 22, 24, 25, 26, 27
> Best Days for Career: 7, 8, 17, 18, 19, 28

Your 9th house is still very strong, and with two benevolent planets (Venus and Jupiter) there, the affairs of this house are very fortunate. Students are successful in school and in their studies; there are happy travel and educational opportunities; and there is much philosophical progress and many breakthroughs in understanding. In general there is an optimism about life. With health still stressful, this optimism is a big help. I have noted that health crises tend to open spiritual doors. They are never what they seem. The crisis is an actual 'doorway' – a 'star gate' – into higher consciousness. And this is what is happening with you these days. The insights and knowledge that you need to deal with health issues is coming to you now. If you apply these things (and not just talk about them) your health will improve; more than that, your whole life will improve.

You are still in the midst of a yearly career peak. There is much progress here and many demands on you. (And this is part of the health issue.) You have friends in high places who are opening doors for you. Friends, in general, are supportive of career goals. Your technological expertise seems very important. Stay up to date with the latest developments. Your innovations, your ability to 'think out of the box', are noted by your superiors and are helpful in the career. Being involved with groups and organizations also helps the career.

Though you are a loving person (and more so than usual these days) actual, real-life relationships are stormy. Be patient. There is a love crisis from the 15th to the 21st. Passions are high, tempers flare – the relationship hangs by a thread. Try not to make matters worse. The conflict seems to involve finance, children, disagreements about leisure activities and perhaps real or imagined infidelity. Light not heat is needed now.

Your love planet, Mars, moves into your own sign on the 4th. Generally this is good for love. Your spouse, partner or current love tends to be devoted to you and puts your interests ahead of his or her own. Love opportunities seek you out (a reversal of the situation earlier in the year) and you don't need to do anything special to attract love. But Mars is making dynamic aspects with both Uranus and Pluto (not powers to take lightly) and this is causing the ruckus. In general both you and your partner need to avoid confrontations. The tendency now is to overreact and this can have negative consequences. Both of you also need to be more careful driving and more mindful on the physical plane.

Your overall health improves after the 22nd, but still needs watching.

## August

    Best Days Overall: 1, 2, 11, 12, 20, 21, 29, 30
    Most Stressful Days Overall: 6, 7, 13, 14, 15, 27, 28
    Best Days for Love: 1, 2, 3, 6, 7, 11, 12, 13, 14, 20, 21, 22,
       23, 31
    Best Days for Money: 1, 2, 8, 11, 12, 18, 20, 21, 22, 23,
       27, 29, 30
    Best Days for Career: 6, 7, 13, 14, 15, 17, 18, 27

On June 21 the planets started to shift from the West (the social sector) to the East. On July 4, Mars entered your sign. On the 8th of this month, Venus, the ruler of your Horoscope moves from the West to the East. So you are now in a cycle of personal power and independence. You can have your way now (and are probably getting it). And this is part of the problem in love. Perhaps you are being too assertive, or too demanding. (Perhaps you are not, but you are just being perceived that way.) You have less need of others these days and if they don't agree with your plans, you can go on your own.

Venus crosses the Mid-heaven on the 8th and enters your 10th house of career. Though technically your yearly career peak ended on July 23, it is revived now. You seem very successful. You are elevated, recognized and perhaps even honoured. You are above everyone in your world these days. This situation won't last for ever, so don't ride rough-shod over others; use your power and authority wisely and in a measured way. You will pay a price for any misuse later on.

Being on top is fun. But this also seems part of the love problem. Not everyone can handle being on the bottom in a relationship. Also, as you will see, being on top makes you an automatic target for the wrath of others. They tend to lash out at what they can see.

Uranus and Pluto have been in a pretty exact square for months now (these are very slow-moving planets). So there is much financial change and upheaval going on. Some of these changes are quite dramatic and the twists and turns of fortune can be very extreme – and this month even more so. Venus starts to enter this planetary picture from the 14th to the 17th. Avoid speculations and other kinds of financial risk taking. In fact *all* kinds of risk taking should be avoided during this period. Be more careful driving or exercising. Nice, light, relaxed workouts are called for; this is not a time for trying to break records. If you feel twinges or pain, stop and rest. Get the ego out of the way and listen to the body. Though you are in power now, avoid confrontations. Exercise power softly.

The good news financially is that you have the whole-hearted support of your spouse, partner, current love and friends. They are very active on your behalf, especially after the 24th. The love life in general will improve after the 24th. Either the current relationship harmonizes or you meet someone new who is harmonious to you.

Your 11th house is powerful until the 23rd. Thus you are in a social period. This is not necessarily romantic, more about friendship, being involved with groups and group activities.

On the 23rd you enter a very spiritual period.


**September**

Best Days Overall: 7, 8, 16, 17, 25, 26
Most Stressful Days Overall: 2, 3, 10, 11, 23, 24, 29, 30
Best Days for Love: 1, 2, 3, 10, 11, 12, 18, 19, 21, 22, 27, 28, 29, 30
Best Days for Money: 5, 7, 8, 14, 16, 17, 18, 19, 23, 25, 26
Best Days for Career: 5, 6, 10, 11, 14, 15, 25


Finances are improving – stabilizing – this month. Your financial planet is receiving good aspects from the Sun and Mercury in the first half of the month, and starts to move forward on the 18th (it has been retrograde since April 10). If you have been reviewing your finances, striving for clarity, it is starting to happen now. With mental clarity, the financial decision making will always be good. Your spouse, partner or current love (and friends in general) are still very supportive financially. There are opportunities for business partnerships or joint ventures this month. There are some bumps on the road at the end of the month as the Sun makes stressful aspects to the financial planet from the 28th (perhaps there is a financial dispute with a friend or organization), but this is short term. Try not to make matters worse. The problem will pass very quickly, unless you yourself extend it.

Venus moves out of your house of career on the 7th and enters your 11th house of friends. So the 11th house which was powerful last month continues to be powerful. This is a time to be more involved with groups and organizations. It is also good for expanding your knowledge of science, technology, astrology and astronomy. Being powerful was exciting, but now you enjoy the social pleasures more. In a group, everyone is equal, no one person dominates, and you kind of like it this way.

Your 12th spiritual house became powerful last month and is even more powerful this month – Mercury joins the Sun in this house on the 1st. You are undoubtedly more intuitive these days, receiving spiritual messages and having a more active dream life. But from the 1st to the 3rd your spiritual planet (Mercury) is in opposition to Neptune (the generic spiritual planet). Thus you need to verify your intuitions and dreams. They may not mean what you think. These inner messages always have multi-dimensional meanings. Give them more thought. Pray for the correct interpretation.

Since you are getting ready for your personal new year, this is an excellent time to review the past year, to rationally assess your situation, and to set goals for what you want for the coming year. What have you achieved this past year? What was left undone? What could have been improved? What mistakes were made? This is the time to correct them and prepare for the new cycle coming up.

Health has been delicate all year, but you are in one of your best health periods this year now and health problems are in abeyance. Probably they are still there, but they are much less severe.

As we mentioned, the Sun makes stressful aspects with both Uranus and Pluto from the 28th to the 30th. Friendships get tested now. There are probably dramatic events in the lives of friends. Children are having love and social dramas. Friends and children need to avoid risky activities. Your high-tech equipment gets tested. This is annoying but in the end leads to upgrades and improvements.

### October

Best Days Overall: 4, 5, 6, 14, 15, 22, 23
Most Stressful Days Overall: 1, 7, 8, 20, 21, 27, 28
Best Days for Love: 1, 9, 12, 18, 21, 27, 28
Best Days for Money: 2, 4, 5, 6, 12, 14, 15, 16, 17, 20, 22, 23, 29
Best Days for Career: 4, 5, 7, 8, 14, 15, 24

On the 23rd of last month you entered one of your yearly personal pleasure peaks and this continues until the 23rd of this month. This month there will be even more personal pleasure – more sense and carnal gratification – than last month. Saturn, after more than two years in your sign, moves out of Libra and into Scorpio. For two years, you have been more stoic and Spartan with your self. Personal pleasures were severely limited, but now the brakes are off, and you can indulge again. In the past two and a half years your probably lost weight, perhaps you overdid it. Now you can start gaining more pounds. Self-esteem and self-confidence were not what they should have been during this period, either; but now (and especially this month) you will see big improvements. Health is much improved now. Health problems of the past are either gone or in abeyance. But you still need to continue watching your health.

Since September 23 the planets have been in their maximum Eastern position, so you are in a period of maximum personal power and independence. Take advantage of this by creating conditions and circumstances according to your liking. Many of you will be surprised to learn that the cosmos is very interested in your personal happiness and is furnishing its means these days.

On the 23rd, as the Sun moves into your money house, you enter a yearly financial peak. Earnings will be strong. But with Saturn also in your money house you have a need to manage what you have in a better way. Though your earnings are strong now, you need to be conservative in finances and not spend in profligate ways. Money represents 'energy' and needs due respect.

The good news this month is that Saturn and Pluto are in 'mutual reception' for many years to come. Each planet is now a guest in the house of the other. This shows good co-operation between the planetary energies – each is helping the other – which is a good prosperity signal. You have help, especially from the family, parents and parent figures and those who are 'like family' to you. Finances have been erratic this year and there have been many dramatic changes. Now is a time to create more stability here, from reorganizing and restructuring your finances. In the past year you have been perhaps attracted by easy or fast money. This could have led to many problems. Now you will start to create stable, long-term wealth.

In your chart Jupiter is your communication planet. He goes retrograde on the 4th so you need to be more careful communicating. Though Mercury is moving forward this month, you will have many 'Mercury retrograde' kinds of experiences – letters not getting delivered, calls not going through or getting cut off, emails bouncing back and things of this nature. Miscommunication and misunderstanding can be expensive financially and time-wise, so more care in the beginning will minimize problems later on. If you are thinking of buying a car do more homework. Avoid, if possible, signing contracts, completing on a house, or entering into long-term financial commitments. All these things need more research.

## November

Best Days Overall: 1, 2, 10, 11, 18, 19, 23, 24
Most Stressful Days Overall: 3, 4, 5, 16, 17, 23, 24
Best Days for Love: 1, 6, 7, 11, 15, 20, 23, 24, 26
Best Days for Money: 1, 2, 8, 11, 12, 13, 16, 19, 26, 28, 29
Best Days for Career: 3, 4, 5, 13, 23

The lower half of your Horoscope has been dominant since September. This dominance has increased month by month since then. Last month, on the 28th, Venus crossed over from the upper to the lower half of the Horoscope, and this month 70 per cent (sometimes 80 per cent) of the planets are below the horizon of the chart. You've done well career-wise this year and now it is time to handle your emotional, inner needs. Your emotions and moods are the infrastructure upon which career success rests. Any building needs a good foundation. You can safely downplay the career now and focus on the home, family and emotional life.

Librans always have a natural sense of style. They always know how to dress and present themselves in a beautiful way, and this month even more so. If you are buying clothing, jewellery or accessories, this is the time to do it.

Health is much improved now, but you can enhance it further in the ways mentioned in the yearly report.

There are two eclipses this month and this guarantees change and excitement. In your case these eclipses seem mild, but read the newspapers – they are not so mild for the world at large.

The solar eclipse of the 13th occurs in your money house. Finances have been unstable all year and there have been dramatic financial changes. The eclipse shows that you are not finished with the changes. This eclipse will test your friendships and high-tech equipment. Both might need replacing. There are dramas in the lives of your friends. Children of appropriate age have crisis in their marriages or relationships.

The lunar eclipse of the 28th occurs in your 9th house. It is almost a repeat of the solar eclipse of May 20. There are crises of faith and your beliefs will get tested. If they are good, they will survive, but if not, they will get more refinement and fine tuning. Students make important educational changes. There are upheavals at your place of worship and dramas in the lives of the religious people in your life. There are career changes as well and shake-ups in your corporate hierarchy and industry. There are dramas in the lives of parents, bosses and authority figures. (It is at times like this that you learn that merely being in a high position doesn't guarantee stability or ease. Those with authority are subject to the same trials and tribulations as everyone else.)

## December

Best Days Overall: 8, 9, 16, 17, 25, 26
Most Stressful Days Overall: 1, 2, 14, 15, 20, 21, 22, 28, 29
Best Days for Love: 1, 6, 10, 11, 15, 20, 21, 22, 24, 31
Best Days for Money: 6, 8, 10, 11, 14, 16, 23, 25
Best Days for Career: 1, 2, 3, 13, 22, 28, 29

Your yearly financial peak technically ended on the 23rd of last month. But on November 28 Venus entered the money house, so this peak is extended. Finances are turbulent and being reorganized, but earnings are good this period. You are very focused here and this is 90 per cent of your success. You are paying attention. Good personal appearance seems a factor in earnings. Family and a parent figure are still supportive, and your intuition is good, especially until the 11th. The Sun travels with your financial planet at the end of the month from the 29th, but you will feel the beneficial effect of this even earlier. Friends are helpful financially and are co-operating with your financial goals. You are probably spending on high-tech equipment but you can also earn from this. All in all this is a prosperous month. You have good financial judgement and are not likely to overspend. You will get good value for money.

Your 3rd house of communication and intellectual interests is powerful all month, so this is the time to catch up on all the letters, emails and texts that you need to do. Since Jupiter is still retrograde, give more care to the quality of your communication. Avoid carelessness and be as clear as you know how to be. Spell things out. And if you are in doubt about what someone else is writing or saying, ask and get clarification. This will save a lot of heartache later on. The retrograde of your communication planet is good for certain things. It is good for taking courses, attending lectures and writing, although it is not such a good time for buying a car or communication equipment, for signing contracts or making long-term commitments.

Generally when communication is awry, we merely experience glitches and inconveniences. But sometimes these glitches can actually be life threatening, for example when a pharmacist misreads a prescription and gives the patient the wrong medication. So you want to avoid activities where good communication is a must. Elective kinds of surgeries and elective travel are probably best avoided now too.

Your love planet has been in your 4th House since November 17. There is more socializing with the family and family members and from home in general. A nice romantic evening at home seems preferable to a night out on the town. Emotional intimacy and emotional support are important in love (and you seem to be getting that). This is how you feel loved and how you show love. Singles need to go slowly in love, especially until the 26th. Let love develop as it will. On the 26th Mars moves into your 5th house and love seems happier. You are having fun with your spouse, partner or current love. Singles are attracted to good times, not just emotional support. The person who can show them a good time is the one they prefer.

Health needs more watching after the 21st, but you have gone through the worst of it. Health issues will not be as severe as earlier in the year (or last year).

# Scorpio

♏

---

THE SCORPION

*Birthdays from*
*23rd October to*
*22nd November*

---

## Personality Profile

### SCORPIO AT A GLANCE

*Element* – Water

*Ruling Planet* – Pluto
  *Co-ruling Planet* – Mars
  *Career Planet* – Sun
  *Love Planet* – Venus
  *Money Planet* – Jupiter
  *Planet of Health and Work* – Mars
  *Planet of Home and Family Life* – Uranus

*Colour* – red–violet

*Colour that promotes love, romance and social*
  *harmony* – green

*Colour that promotes earning power* – blue

*Gems* – bloodstone, malachite, topaz

*Metals* – iron, radium, steel

*Scents* – cherry blossom, coconut, sandalwood, watermelon

*Quality* – fixed (= stability)

*Quality most needed for balance* – a wider view of things

*Strongest virtues* – loyalty, concentration, determination, courage, depth

*Deepest needs* – to penetrate and transform

*Characteristics to avoid* – jealousy, vindictiveness, fanaticism

*Signs of greatest overall compatibility* – Cancer, Pisces

*Signs of greatest overall incompatibility* – Taurus, Leo, Aquarius

*Sign most helpful to career* – Leo

*Sign most helpful for emotional support* – Aquarius

*Sign most helpful financially* – Sagittarius

*Sign best for marriage and/or partnerships* – Taurus

*Sign most helpful for creative projects* – Pisces

*Best Sign to have fun with* – Pisces

*Signs most helpful in spiritual matters* – Cancer, Libra

*Best day of the week* – Tuesday

# Understanding a Scorpio

One symbol of the sign of Scorpio is the phoenix. If you meditate upon the legend of the phoenix you will begin to understand the Scorpio character – his or her powers and abilities, interests and deepest urges.

The phoenix of mythology was a bird that could recreate and reproduce itself. It did so in a most intriguing way: it would seek a fire – usually in a religious temple – fly into it, consume itself in the flames and then emerge a new bird. If this is not the ultimate, most profound transformation, then what is?

Transformation is what Scorpios are all about – in their minds, bodies, affairs and relationships (Scorpios are also society's transformers). To change something in a natural, not an artificial way, involves a transformation from within. This type of change is a radical change as opposed to a mere cosmetic make-over. Some people think that change means altering just their appearance, but this is not the kind of thing that interests a Scorpio. Scorpios seek deep, fundamental change. Since real change always proceeds from within, a Scorpio is very interested in – and usually accustomed to – the inner, intimate and philosophical side of life.

Scorpios are people of depth and intellect. If you want to interest them you must present them with more than just a superficial image. You and your interests, projects or business deals must have real substance to them in order to stimulate a Scorpio. If they haven't, he or she will find you out – and that will be the end of the story.

If we observe life – the processes of growth and decay – we see the transformational powers of Scorpio at work all the time. The caterpillar changes itself into a butterfly; the infant grows into a child and then an adult. To Scorpios this definite and perpetual transformation is not something to be feared. They see it as a normal part of life. This acceptance of transformation gives Scorpios the key to understanding the true meaning of life.

Scorpios' understanding of life (including life's weak-nesses) makes them powerful warriors – in all senses of the word. Add to this their depth, patience and endurance and you have a powerful personality. Scorpios have good, long memories and can at times be quite vindictive – they can wait years to get their revenge. As a friend, though, there is no one more loyal and true than a Scorpio. Few are willing to make the sacrifices that a Scorpio will make for a true friend.

The results of a transformation are quite obvious, although the process of transformation is invisible and secret. This is why Scorpios are considered secretive in nature. A seed will not grow properly if you keep digging it up and exposing it to the light of day. It must stay buried – invisible – until it starts to grow. In the same manner, Scorpios fear revealing too much about themselves or their hopes to other people. However, they will be more than happy to let you see the finished product – but only when it is completely unwrapped. On the other hand, Scorpios like knowing everyone else's secrets as much as they dislike anyone knowing theirs.

**Finance**

Love, birth, life as well as death are Nature's most potent transformations; Scorpios are interested in all of these. In our society, money is a transforming power, too, and a Scorpio is interested in money for that reason. To a Scorpio money is power, money causes change, money controls. It is the power of money that fascinates them. But Scorpios can be too materialistic if they are not careful. They can be overly awed by the power of money, to a point where they think that money rules the world.

Even the term 'plutocrat' comes from Pluto, the ruler of the sign of Scorpio. Scorpios will – in one way or another – achieve the financial status they strive for. When they do so they are careful in the way they handle their wealth. Part of this financial carefulness is really a kind of honesty, for

Scorpios are usually involved with other people's money – as accountants, lawyers, stockbrokers or corporate managers – and when you handle other people's money you have to be more cautious than when you handle your own.

In order to fulfil their financial goals, Scorpios have important lessons to learn. They need to develop qualities that do not come naturally to them, such as breadth of vision, optimism, faith, trust and, above all, generosity. They need to see the wealth in Nature and in life, as well as in its more obvious forms of money and power. When they develop generosity their financial potential reaches great heights, for Jupiter, the Lord of Opulence and Good Fortune, is Scorpio's money planet.

## Career and Public Image

Scorpio's greatest aspiration in life is to be considered by society as a source of light and life. They want to be leaders, to be stars. But they follow a very different road than do Leos, the other stars of the zodiac. A Scorpio arrives at the goal secretly, without ostentation; a Leo pursues it openly. Scorpios seek the glamour and fun of the rich and famous in a restrained, discreet way.

Scorpios are by nature introverted and tend to avoid the limelight. But if they want to attain their highest career goals they need to open up a bit and to express themselves more. They need to stop hiding their light under a bushel and let it shine. Above all, they need to let go of any vindictiveness and small-mindedness. All their gifts and insights were given to them for one important reason – to serve life and to increase the joy of living for others.

## Love and Relationships

Scorpio is another zodiac sign that likes committed clearly defined, structured relationships. They are cautious about marriage, but when they do commit to a relationship they tend to be faithful – and heaven help the mate caught or even suspected of infidelity! The jealousy of the Scorpio is legendary. They can be so intense in their jealousy that even the thought or intention of infidelity will be detected and is likely to cause as much of a storm as if the deed had actually been done.

Scorpios tend to settle down with those who are wealthier than they are. They usually have enough intensity for two, so in their partners they seek someone pleasant, hardworking, amiable, stable and easy-going. They want someone they can lean on, someone loyal behind them as they fight the battles of life. To a Scorpio a partner, be it a lover or a friend, is a real partner – not an adversary. Most of all a Scorpio is looking for an ally, not a competitor.

If you are in love with a Scorpio you will need a lot of patience. It takes a long time to get to know Scorpios, because they do not reveal themselves readily. But if you persist and your motives are honourable, you will gradually be allowed into a Scorpio's inner chambers of the mind and heart.

## Home and Domestic Life

Uranus is ruler of Scorpio's 4th solar house of home and family. Uranus is the planet of science, technology, changes and democracy. This tells us a lot about a Scorpio's conduct in the home and what he or she needs in order to have a happy, harmonious home life.

Scorpios can sometimes bring their passion, intensity and wilfulness into the home and family, which is not always the place for these qualities. These traits are good for the warrior and the transformer, but not so good for the nurturer and family member. Because of this (and also because of their need for change and transformation) the Scorpio may be prone to sudden changes of residence. If not carefully constrained, the sometimes inflexible Scorpio can produce turmoil and sudden upheavals within the family.

Scorpios need to develop some of the virtues of Aquarius in order to cope better with domestic matters. There is a need to build a team spirit at home, to treat family activities as truly group activities – family members should all have a say in what does and does not get done. For at times a Scorpio can be most dictatorial. When a Scorpio gets dictatorial it is much worse than if a Leo or Capricorn (the two other power signs in the zodiac) does. For the dictatorship of a Scorpio is applied with more zeal, passion, intensity and concentration than is true of either a Leo or Capricorn. Obviously this can be unbearable to family members – especially if they are sensitive types.

In order for a Scorpio to get the full benefit of the emotional support that a family can give, he or she needs to let go of conservatism and be a bit more experimental, to explore new techniques in child-rearing, be more democratic with family members and to try to manage things by consensus rather than by autocratic edict.

# Horoscope for 2012

## Major Trends

Neptune has been in your 4th house of home and family for many years. This year he makes a major move out of Aquarius and into Pisces, your 5th house. He will be in this house for many years to come. Your leisure preferences and personal creativity are now becoming more refined. You will gravitate to more 'spiritual' kinds of entertainment. The drumming or chanting circle will replace the club or bar. Classical music will replace pop. You will start to have inspired creative ideas too. The children in your life are more spiritual these days too.

Last year was a banner love year and many of you married or entered into serious love relationships and perhaps business partnerships as well. This trend continues in the year ahead, especially until June 11. The year ahead also seems more sexually active. More on this later.

Pluto, the ruler of your Horoscope, has been in your 3rd house of communication since 2008 and will be there in the year ahead and for many years to come. So communication and intellectual interests – the expanding of the mind and the acquisition of knowledge – are important long-term interests. Pluto will in a square aspect with volatile Uranus all year. So this is a year to be more mindful when driving. There is need to avoid risky activities. Saturn has been in your 12th house of spirituality for the past two years and will be there for most of the year ahead. On October 5, he will enter your own sign of Scorpio. This is generally a stressful kind of transit but of itself not enough to cause ill health. Energy is not up to its usual standards, but your health will be OK. But this is a time for taking a lower profile; a time for shining 'quietly'. New burdens and responsibilities are being placed on you and you can't seem to avoid this. This transit initiates a two-year cycle of 'character building'.

Your major interests in the year ahead (and there are many) are communication and intellectual interests (and this will become even stronger after October 5); home and family (until February 3); children, creativity and personal pleasure (from February 3 onwards); health and work; love and romance (until June 11); sex, personal transformation, personal reinvention and occult studies (from June 11 onwards); friends, groups, group activities, science and astrology (until July 3); and spirituality (until October 5).

Your paths of greatest fulfilment are love, romance and social activities (until June 11); sex, personal transformation, personal reinvention and occult studies (from June 11 onwards); finances (until August 31); the body, image and personal pleasure (after October 31).

## Health

*(Please note that this is an* astrological *perspective on health and not a medical one. In days of yore these perspectives were identical. But these days there could be quite a difference. For a medical perspective, please consult your doctor or health practitioner.)*

Though health is basically good (and for most of the year seems improved over 2011), your 6th house of health is very strong. You are focused here. But your chart is showing that the focus is not coming from health problems (which is usually the case) but more from a desire to maintain health and to prevent future problems.

Neptune has been in stressful aspect with you for many years and this year, on February 3, he starts to make a harmonious aspect. Jupiter is in stressful aspect with you until June 11, but then moves away. The only long-term stress is when Saturn enters your sign on October 5.

Uranus, as we have mentioned, will be in your 6th house for many years to come. So you are becoming more experimental in health matters. You will tend to gravitate to alternative types of therapies rather than the orthodox ones. In fact, the latest and the trendiest therapies are what appeal to you these days. But the main point of having Uranus involved in your health is that you are engaged in a project that everyone should be doing: you are learning how you function. You are learning the health rules that apply to you and you alone. Everyone is wired up differently and things that work for others might not work for you, and therapies that work for you might not work for others. So this is a trial and error learning process.

Good though your health is, you can make it even better. Give more attention to the following organs: the heart (after October 5); the colon, bladder and sexual organs (safe sex and sexual moderation is very important); the head, face and scalp (regular scalp and face massage will be very powerful); the muscles (vigorous physical exercise is wonderful; muscles need to be toned up properly); the adrenals (anger and fear tend to stress the adrenals, so avoid

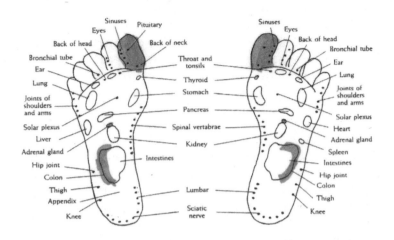

## Reflexology

*Try to massage the whole foot on a regular basis, but pay extra attention to the points highlighted on the chart. When you massage, be aware of 'sore spots', as these need special attention. It's also a good idea to massage the ankles and top side of the feet (see below).*

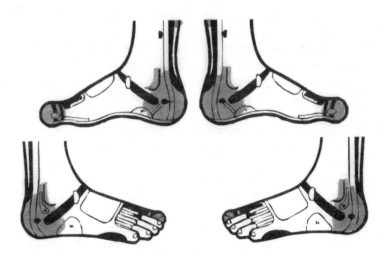

these negative emotions as much as possible); and the ankles and calves (these should be regularly massaged, and the ankles should be given more support when exercising).

Uranus also happens to be your family planet. It also rules your emotional life. The message is very clear; good health for you also means good emotional health, good family relations, and harmony in the home and the feelings. If problems arise you will need to explore this area and bring it into harmony as quickly as you can.

Uranus, as we mentioned, is in square aspect with Pluto all year. This is a very dynamic aspect. You could be experimenting with the body in reckless kinds of ways, testing its limits recklessly, and this could lead to accident or injury. This is not a year for daredevil stunts. Drive more carefully and be more mindful on the physical plane.

### Home and Family

Your 4th house of home and family has been powerful for many years, but this year it is less so. On February 3, Neptune leaves here and moves into the 5th house for the long term. Last year, Uranus, your family planet, made a major move into Aries, your house of health. So the family situation is undergoing much change these days. Attitudes are changing. The family dynamic is very different nowadays. The family as a whole seems more health conscious. And you seem more focused on the health of family members than on your own (especially the health of a parent or parent figure in your life).

For years you were making the home more of a 'playground' or entertainment centre. Now it is becoming more like a health spa. You are installing health gadgets, exercise equipment, saunas, whirlpools, things of this nature. You are also removing health hazards from the home and property. Perhaps your property has toxic paint or roofing. This is a time where you correct these things.

Many of you moved in recent years. This year you are more likely to stay put. However, in June and July there are opportunities to move, to purchase or sell a home. Whether you take the opportunity is a matter of free will.

The main trend this year is the Uranus–Pluto square that is in effect the whole year. This shows conflict with the family. You and the family (and especially a parent) are not seeing eye to eye. The danger here is emotional discord, which can create health problems. It's OK to disagree, but when the passions get involved it's another story. Keeping harmony with the family is going to be your main challenge in the year ahead.

There can be deaths or near-death kinds of experiences with family members, parents or parent figures. Sometimes this indicates surgeries. Sometimes the family unit as a whole has a near-death kind of experience – a collapse or dissolution. These things don't have to actually happen, but there is confrontation indicated with these kinds of events. The possibility is there, but with more work and effort it can be avoided.

A parent or parent figure could have moved last year, and if not, it could still happen this year. This looks like a happy move. Siblings in your life have much domestic instability now. They are likely to move many times, or perhaps live in different places for a long period. They are constantly upgrading the home. Children are likely to move after June 11. This is also a happy move.

**Finance and Career**

Your money house is not a house of power this year, so the tendency is to the status quo in earnings. You have no need to make major changes in the financial life; the cosmos neither pushes you one way nor another. (A lunar eclipse on June 4 will produce some short-term financial changes, but the overall status quo remains.)

In June 2011, your financial planet, Jupiter, entered your 7th house, and will remain there until June 11 this year. This produces various kinds of phenomena. For singles it indicates a wealthy marriage. For marrieds it shows earning from the marriage – spousal support. Often this transit shows a business partnership or joint venture, something very lucrative. In general, social connections are playing a huge role in earnings. Friends seem supportive financially and provide opportunities.

Since Jupiter moved into your 7th house you have been working to integrate your social and financial life. It's almost as they are one thing. You do business with the people you socialize with. You socialize with the people involved in your business. Much of the social activity this year is related to finance.

There seems to be great instability job-wise this year. Probably there will be job changes, and perhaps multiple job changes. Sometimes people don't actually leave their present company; they move to a different position. Also the conditions at work seem to be constantly changing. Those of you who employ others have high employee turnover this year. And even with the ones that stay with you, it is hard to know who will be available when. Job seekers have opportunities through family, family connections and people who are like family to you.

Your 10th house of career is basically empty this year – only the short-term planets will move there on a temporary basis. This suggests a status quo kind of career year. Two solar eclipses this year will help you fine tune your career. Flaws and problems in it get revealed so that you can make corrections and change course.

Jupiter will move into your 8th house on June 11. This is a very beautiful financial transit for the spouse, partner or current love. (Finances are good for them even before June but now they get even better.) He or she is more generous with you. This is an aspect for inheritance, although no one need actually die. You can be named in a will or appointed to some position in someone's estate. If you have insurance claims, this aspect shows good fortune. If you are looking for outside investors there is good fortune here too. Your ability to borrow is strong (regardless of wider economic conditions). Many people earn money through creative kinds of financing. They borrow at one rate and use the money to earn a higher rate in some business or venture. They borrow and then refinance at lower, more favourable rates. These kinds of opportunities are open for you this period. Probably you will pay more taxes this year, but this means that you are earning more.

You need to be careful not to abuse debt during this period. Don't overdo it.

Your financial planet in the sign of Gemini after June 11 also has other messages. Sales, marketing, PR, advertising and good use of the media are all important in finances. And these are major interests in your life anyway. Communication skills are important financially.

### Love and Social Life

As we mentioned, last year was a very strong love year, and the trend continues in the year ahead, especially until June 11. Jupiter in the 7th house shows marriage or relationships that are like a marriage; serious kinds of relationships. If it hasn't happened yet, it is still likely in the year ahead. It also shows more social activity – more parties and gatherings, and more dating than usual. New and important friends enter your social circle too.

As we mentioned, you are socializing with the people that you do business with. There is an integration of the love and financial life happening now. This position also shows that you are mixing with wealthy people. Friends and your spouse tend to be wealthy (more than usual) and they are supportive of you.

Your love planet is Venus and she is the best love planet to have as this is her natural domain. But Venus is a fast-moving planet. Over the course of the year, she will move through all the signs and houses of your Horoscope. Thus there are many short-term trends in love that are best dealt with in the monthly reports. Much depends on where Venus is and the kind of aspects that she is receiving at a given time.

Venus does spend an unusual amount of time in Gemini and your 8th house this year. Normally she stays in a sign for about a month, but she will be in Gemini for four. Again this indicates that the spouse or current love is very involved in finance – a money person. It also shows that two things are important in love during that period (April 3 to August 7): the sexual chemistry (always important to you) and the mental compatibility. One without the other won't work for very long. Often it shows dramas in the love life – the relationship seems threatened but often it can be regenerated and renewed.

**Self-improvement**

Saturn has been in your spiritual 12th house for some years now, and remains there until October 5. You have been in a period for taking on spiritual disciplines and regimes, and for taking a very practical approach to your spiritual life. Because spiritual phenomena are above the human mind, many have the idea that it is all vague and nebulous. You will (and probably have) discovered that this is not so. It is just a higher order of rationality and just as scientific in its way as physics or chemistry.

Your spiritual life – your spiritual ideas, ideals and attitudes – has been getting a reality check these days. Many of you discover abilities that you never knew you had. Many pretend they have abilities, and they will be found out revealed under the testing. By the time Saturn leaves your 12th house you will have a more realistic understanding of where you are on the spiritual path and where you need to go. This is invaluable for further progress.

Saturn is the ruler of your 3rd house of communication and intellectual activities. His position in the 12th house shows that the lower mind, your intellect, is becoming more refined and spiritualized. The intellect is not your enemy as so many spiritual paths claim. It is the impurities there, the false ideas that are the enemy. Remove the impurities and the intellect becomes your friend and ally on the path. You are in a period where this kind of work goes better. The intellect has its practical uses – it is through the intellect we can plan and organize our daily functions. So it is not advisable to nullify it. It is merely a question of letting the intellect do the job it was designed for and no more.

# Month-by-month Forecasts

### January

Best Days Overall: 8, 9, 17, 18, 25, 26
Most Stressful Days Overall: 3, 4, 10, 11, 23, 24, 30, 31
Best Days for Love: 3, 4, 6, 7, 18, 19, 27, 28, 30, 31
Best Days for Money: 3, 4, 12, 19, 20, 21, 30
Best Days for Career: 3, 4, 10, 11, 12, 13, 23, 24

Your year begins with the planetary power shifting from the independent East to the social West. Personal power and independence are weakening. Unpleasant conditions can be changed, but with much more effort than usual, and it is best now to adapt to situations as much as you can. In the past six months you have created life conditions for yourself, and now is when you 'road test' them, when you have to live with them, until the next cycle of independence happens. Now you are coming into a more social period, and it is time to cultivate the social skills and to take a vacation from the personal self and the personal interests. It is time to put other people first.

You begin your year at the 'midnight hour'. Most of the planets are below the horizon and your 4th house of home and family is very powerful. Many wonderful interior processes are happening. At night the outer body sleeps, but it is being recharged and rejuvenated for the next day. So it is with you. Career and outer activities are in a temporary lull and it is best to work on them internally. Visualize your career goals and live in them as if they already existed –

creative, conscious daydreaming is very powerful. In due course when day breaks in your year, your physical actions to attain your career goals will be natural and powerful, side effects of your interior work.

In order to get the most from sleep, there is a need for emotional harmony. If this is lacking, the sleep is affected and the processes that should happen won't happen correctly. Thus you are in a period where you need to cultivate this. You need to first find, and then function from your personal point of emotional harmony. In fact this, and the family, is your actual spiritual mission from the 20th onwards.

Many of you will be working from home and this is in line with the Horoscope. Family connections and the family itself are helpful career-wise. Solutions to career problems are close at hand.

Your 3rd house of communication and intellectual interests is powerful until the 20th. With all the planets moving forward until the 24th (very unusually) this is a good time for mass mailings, marketing projects and ad campaigns. It is also a good period for expanding your knowledge base, for taking courses in subjects that interest you. It is a time to take care of your 'mental body'.

You are in a very powerful year for love and romance. Singles are likely to marry this year. Until the 14th, your love planet is in your 4th house and thus family is playing cupid. A romantic evening at home is more enjoyable than a night out on the town. This changes after the 24th. Then you prefer a night out on the town to staying at home. Your love planet travels with Neptune from the 12th to the 15th. This brings a romantic meeting, but don't rush into anything; things are not as they seem.

**February**

> Best Days Overall: 4, 5, 13, 14, 22, 23
> Most Stressful Days Overall: 1, 7, 8, 19, 20, 27, 28
> Best Days for Love: 1, 5, 6, 15, 24, 25, 27, 28
> Best Days for Money: 1, 9, 15, 16, 17, 27, 28
> Best Days for Career: 2, 3, 7, 8, 11, 12, 21, 22

Though health has been basically good, and gets even better this month, you have been experimenting and making important changes to the health regime. But now with your health planet (Mars) retrograde for the next few months (the retrograde began on January 24), be more cautious with your experiments and changes.

Health needs more watching until the 19th. There is nothing serious afoot, but overall energy is not up to the usual standard. So rest and relax more then. After the 19th there is much power in Pisces and your 5th house and health will improve dramatically. Not only that, but you enter a yearly personal pleasure peak. This is a happy-go-lucky kind of period.

The world looks at leisure and fun as something 'frivolous', and perhaps as irresponsible. But with Neptune now in your 5th house for the long haul, you are learning the spiritual value of fun, of joy, and of happiness. There is much more to it than meets the eye. In fact learning to enjoy life, to take an easy attitude to it, is part of the spiritual mission of the month from the 19th onwards. Children in your life are also part of your mission.

Love was happy last month and is happy this month too. Last month the love planet entered your 5th house of fun and it remains there until the 8th. Married couples are having fun in the marriage. Singles have many love affair opportunities. You are enjoying your friendships more and are involved in fun activities with your friends, spouse, partner or current love. Fun, tenderness and sensitivity are important attractions in a relationship. With the love planet in Pisces you are experiencing nuances in love that few people experience. Singles find love opportunities in the usual places – parties, resorts, at the theatre, and places of entertainment; after the 8th romantic opportunities happen at work, with co-workers, or with people involved in your health.

Venus in Aries from the 8th onwards tends to rashness in love; there is a tendency to fall in love at first sight. But the staying power of this ardour is in question. However, so intense are the love feelings that you would consider elopement.

Venus travels with Uranus from the 8th to the 10th. This brings sudden, unexpected, out of the blue love meetings. But these things seem unstable. There is extreme moodiness in love that period – sudden and swift mood changes. You need to be more patient with the current love or spouse.

Though finance is not a major priority, earnings are good this month. Your financial planet makes beautiful aspects with the ruler of the Horoscope, Pluto. There is luck in speculations as well. You catch the lucky breaks. The social connections are playing a huge role in earnings. Your spouse, partner or current love is highly supportive and generous with you.

### March

Best Days Overall: 3, 4, 11, 12, 20, 21, 30, 31
Most Stressful Days Overall: 5, 6, 18, 19, 25, 26
Best Days for Love: 7, 15, 16, 25, 26
Best Days for Money: 7, 13, 14, 15, 16, 25, 26
Best Days for Career: 3, 4, 5, 6, 11, 12, 22, 23

In your Horoscope, Saturn is your communication planet. He takes on Mercury's role in your chart. Saturn went retrograde on February 4. On the 12th of this month Mercury (the generic ruler of communication) also goes retrograde. So both the planets that rule communication are retrograde at the same time. You need to be more careful in your communication. Slow things down and get it right. Now is not the time for mass mailings or advertising campaigns. Avoid signing contracts, exchanging on homes or entering into long-term commitments. Major purchases are better off delayed. The information you read in the newspapers or see on TV, or that you receive about products, might not be what you think. Sales and special events might not be such bargains in hindsight. An apparent decision from a company or government agency is not written in stone, and it can be reversed – which can either be a positive thing or a negative. Many of the things that happen can't be prevented. But we can minimize much of the negative effect through proper planning. Avoid unnecessary travel. If you must travel, insure your ticket and allow more time to get to your destination. The fine print on all contracts should be studied, especially contracts involving debt – loans, mortgages, or credit cards. If you must make a major purchase make sure the store has a good returns policy. The main thing is to be sure you are saying or writing what you really mean and that you are hearing what is being said to you. Don't take it for granted that the other person or company will understand what you mean. You have to remove ambiguity. If you are not sure of a message that you receive ask questions. Miscommunication and misunderstanding is the main challenge this month.

Health is good this month and you seem very focused here as well. You can make it even better in the ways mentioned in the yearly report.

Until the 20th you are still in a yearly party period. Afterwards, you seem 'partied out' and are in a more serious work-oriented period. Your 6th house of health and work becomes powerful. This is a wonderful position for job seekers. (However, with Mars still retrograde all month job offers and job changes need more research. Resolve all doubts before deciding. The same is true if you are hiring employees. Changes in the health regime also require more homework.)

Love is great this month. Venus enters your house of love on the 5th and stays there all month. She will travel with

Jupiter from the 11th to the 14th – a very powerful love and financial transit. There are happy romantic meetings. Singles meet wealthy suitors. There are happy opportunities for business partnership and joint ventures. A company that you own could be sold or merged under this transit too.

### April

Best Days Overall: 8, 16, 17, 26, 27
Most Stressful Days Overall: 1, 2, 14, 15, 21, 22, 29, 30
Best Days for Love: 5, 10, 14, 15, 21, 22, 24, 25
Best Days for Money: 4, 8, 9, 12, 13, 21, 22
Best Days for Career: 1, 2, 10, 11, 20, 21, 29, 30

The communication problems we saw last month, the missed phone calls, the messages or letters never delivered, the glitches with communication equipment, will start easing up after the 4th as Mercury starts to move forward. But Saturn is still retrograde, and you still have to contend with these kinds of things, albeit to a lesser degree. It is a good idea to continue to exercise care in communication.

The planetary power moves into its maximum Western position on the 20th. You enter a yearly love and social peak. Marriages and business mergers or partnerships are very likely now. (And if they don't actually happen, there is great progress towards these things.) You are in the mood for romance. This is the time for exercising 'soft power' rather than 'hard power', for getting your way through consensus and co-operation rather than overt force. The time for 'hard power' will come, but not now. Pluto, the ruler of your Horoscope, also starts to move backwards as this is happening (on the 10th), so personal power and self-confidence are not as strong as usual. This month it seems like a good thing. Your personal vulnerability seems attractive to the opposite sex. When you are weak, your spouse, partner or current love is strong and your friends are strong. So this makes up for the deficiency. Your way is probably not the best way this period. Let others have their way instead.

Your spiritual mission is other people after the 20th. You are there for them.

Health needs watching after the 20th. The good news is that your 6th house of health is strong and so you are paying attention. With attention you can avert problems from developing. Enhance the health in the ways mentioned in the yearly report, but this month you can also pay attention to the lungs, arms, shoulders and heart.

Your love planet enters your 8th house on the 3rd. This indicates a more sexually active kind of month. Sexual magnetism seems the most important attraction, but wealth and status are also important. This is a month for mixing with people of higher status than you. Romances can happen with these kinds of people as well. Power is very alluring now.

There is another important development this month. On the 20th the planetary power shifts from the lower to the upper half of the chart. By now you have achieved some emotional harmony and you are ready to start focusing on the career and outward objectives. Your friends, spouse or current love seem supportive here. This is a month for advancing your career by social means, by attending or hosting the right kinds of parties and by cultivating the right kind of contacts. Until the 20th it is your work ethic that matters, but afterwards it is not your work but who you know that is important.

**May**

> Best Days Overall: 5, 6, 13, 14, 15, 23, 24, 25
> Most Stressful Days Overall: 11, 12, 18, 19, 20, 26, 27
> Best Days for Love: 3, 4, 11, 12, 18, 19, 20, 21, 22, 30, 31
> Best Days for Money: 2, 7, 8, 10, 19, 20, 29
> Best Days for Career: 1, 2, 9, 10, 20, 21, 26, 27, 30

It is good now that personal power and self-will are not up to their usual standards. Your personal goals and desires, especially those that relate to the body, image and personal appearance, should be under review now. Mental clarity is the main aim and it will come with time. Avoid making major wardrobe or image changes now. Your motives have to be right with these things.

A solar eclipse on the 20th affects you strongly. Reduce your schedule and avoid risky kinds of activities. This eclipse occurs in your 8th house and can bring 'near-death' kinds of experiences or surgeries – encounters with death, physically or psychologically. Every solar eclipse brings career changes – shake-ups in your company and industry, and dramas in the lives of bosses, parents or authority figures. This eclipse is no different. If you are involved with estate or insurance issues, these take a dramatic turn one way or another. Important decisions are often made under the eclipse.

Children and children figures in your life are affected by this eclipse. They should also take it easy and avoid risk taking. If they have not been careful in dietary matters, there can be a detox of the body. They are changing their image, their persona and self-concept over the next six months, with the process beginning now. Your spouse, partner or current love makes important financial changes now. (Their finances are good and so the changes will be good.)

Love has been wonderful the past few months and is still happy this month. You are still in a yearly love peak. But on the 15th Venus will start to retrograde, so perhaps it is time to step back a bit from the social whirl and review it all. Many of you are contemplating marriage now, and while it's fine to contemplate it, it's not so good to do it. Important love decisions are better off delayed. This is a time for gaining mental and emotional clarity about your relationships. Once this happens, resulting decisions will be good. Singles are still meeting new people, but let love develop at its own pace.

The retrograde of Venus will not stop your love life, but will tend to slow things down a bit.

Health improves after the 20th.

Finances and career also look good. The Sun travels with Jupiter from the 11th to the 14th and this brings financial windfalls, opportunities or expensive items to you. There are also happy career opportunities. A pay rise or promotion wouldn't be a surprise.

## June

Best Days Overall: 1, 2, 10, 11, 20, 21, 29, 30
Most Stressful Days Overall: 8, 9, 15, 16, 22, 23
Best Days for Love: 8, 9, 15, 16, 17, 18, 27, 28
Best Days for Money: 3, 4, 5, 6, 17, 26, 27
Best Days for Career: 8, 9, 18, 19, 22, 23, 29, 30

Major financial changes are happening this month, Scorpio. A lunar eclipse on the 4th occurs in your money house. Jupiter, your financial planet, will re-activate the solar eclipse point of last month. These bring changes that long needed to be made, but now you are forced into it. In the end these things are good. Your financial thinking and strategy gets an overhaul now.

We see other changes happening as well. Jupiter moves into your 8th house on the 11th, so your spouse, partner, or current love is in an excellent financial period and will undoubtedly be more generous with you. He or she entered a yearly financial peak on the 20th of last month and it is still going on until the 21st.

The lunar eclipse brings educational changes for students: changes of school, changes of courses, changes of plans and of strategy. It tends to produce crises of faith too; belief systems, personal philosophies and religion get tested. Superstitions are revealed for what they are and get thrown overboard. In the end (and this will be a six-month process) you will have a new and healthier view of the world and life and this will make all the difference in the world in your outer affairs. There are dramas (personal dramas) in the lives of academics and religious people in your life.

Your 8th house was powerful last month and is powerful this month as well, especially until the 21st. This is Scorpio heaven. The cosmos impels you to things that you most love to do. It is a period of increased sexual activity (regardless of your age and stage in life). You have greater access to outside money, to credit or investors. You prosper personally by prospering others. There is inheritance, insurance monies or royalties coming to you. You are more of a money manager this period, managing the assets of others. Probably you are attending more funerals these days. You are always fascinated by death and have a deep and abiding interest in this subject – and this month even more so. Probably there are more encounters with death (usually on a psychological level).

Uranus has been square to Pluto all year, but this month the aspect is very exact. So be more mindful on the physical plane. Avoid risky kinds of activities. If you must test the limits of your body, do it in a safe and mindful manner. Watch your driving and avoid confrontations. These are the main health dangers now. But overall health and energy are good.

Most likely you are experimenting with your image, upgrading it constantly. But since Pluto is retrograde, you don't really seem satisfied. This process will continue for some more months.

## July

Best Days Overall: 7, 8, 17, 18, 26, 27
Most Stressful Days Overall: 5, 6, 12, 13, 19, 20, 21
Best Days for Love: 5, 6, 12, 13, 15, 24, 25
Best Days for Money: 1, 2, 5, 6, 15, 16, 24, 25, 28, 29
Best Days for Career: 7, 8, 18, 19, 20, 21, 28

Retrograde activity is pretty much at its peak level for the year. It reached its peak last month (40 per cent of the planets retrograde until June 25). Then it receded a bit to 30 per cent until the 15th of this month. And after that we're back at 40 per cent. We will never exceed this level in 2012. You are not personally affected that much, but others are. The pace of life slows down. Progress is slower and one must learn patience. If you are a manager or parent, this is a time to instil in your employees or children the 'slow way'. Make sure they avoid short cuts and stress the importance of being perfect. Better to be a little late finishing a project but to do it perfectly than to complete it sooner with flaws. Any time savings will be an illusion as the work will have to be redone.

Your family planet, Uranus, goes retrograde on the 13th. In your case, this seems a good thing. You are entering a yearly career peak (beginning on the 22nd) and so your focus is on the outer world and your outward objectives. The timing here is beautiful. There's not much you can do about certain family issues, only time will resolve them, so you are set free to concentrate on your career goals.

Health is good until the 22nd; after that, try to rest and relax more. Yes, you will be very busy that period – career obligations weigh heavy on you – but with some creativity you can be productive in a more 'restful' way. You can delegate and outsource wherever possible. You can break up your day with short cat naps and then go back to work. You can keep your mind on priorities and let lesser things go. It is also possible through meditation to 'charge the body' with infinite energy. Your health planet moves into the spiritual

12th house on the 4th and so spiritual healing will be very powerful this month. You will get good results from it.

Until the 22nd you are preparing for career advancement. Now's a good time to take courses or seminars related to your career. There is career-related travel happening as well. Be a mentor to those below you and a disciple to those above you. These attitudes and practices help the career and are noted by superiors.

Mars makes highly stressful aspects with both Uranus and Pluto from the 15th to the 21st. This affects you and family members. Risk taking should be avoided; confrontations likewise. People tend to overreact under these aspects and trivialities can be magnified into violent behaviour. Drive more carefully and make the home as safe as possible.

### August

Best Days Overall: 4, 5, 13, 14, 15, 22, 23, 31
Most Stressful Days Overall: 1, 2, 8, 9, 10, 16, 17, 29, 31
Best Days for Love: 2, 3, 8, 9, 10, 13, 14, 22, 23, 31
Best Days for Money: 1, 2, 11, 12, 20, 21, 24, 25, 29, 30
Best Days for Career: 6, 7, 16, 17, 18, 27

Retrograde activity is still at its yearly high until the 8th, so keep in mind our discussion of this last month. After the 8th, as Mercury goes forward, the percentage drops a little. You are still in a yearly career peak and much progress is being made. The authority figures in your life – bosses, parents, superiors and elders – seem supportive here.

Continue to watch your health until the 23rd. Review our discussion of last month. Health and energy will seem to magically improve after the 23rd. Perhaps the credit will be given to some new pill, herb or therapy, but the truth is that the planetary power shifted into a more harmonious alignment with you. Your health planet, Mars, moves into your own sign on the 24th and this tends to boost energy too. Vigorous exercise is always good for you, but even more so after this date. You are very much into physical fitness then.

Mars in your sign has its good points and negative points. On the positive side, you have more energy, more zeal, more courage. You are a much more dynamic kind of personality. You get things done in a fraction of the normal time. (However with many planets retrograde, you will have to learn more patience.) You will excel in sports and exercise regimes. The negative side of this transit needs to be watched though. You can be more impatient, and more in a hurry. Rashness can lead to accident or injury. You tend to be more argumentative and combative, perhaps unconsciously, and this provokes these kinds of responses in others. However, with Mars in your sign, you are more focused on health.

Your love planet makes a major move out into your 9th house on the 8th. She has been in your 8th house since April 3, so this is a major move. There is a shift in love attitudes. For the past few months the sexual chemistry has been the most important thing in love. It is still important, but now you see that it isn't enough. You want emotional intimacy as well as physical intimacy. The sharing of feelings is important. Family values are important. Philosophical compatibility is important. Singles find love opportunities in foreign lands or with foreigners, in educational or religious-type settings. Love will tend to be happy this month – the 9th house is always fortunate.

## September

    Best Days Overall: 1, 10, 11, 19, 27, 28
    Most Stressful Days Overall: 5, 6, 12, 13, 25, 26
    Best Days for Love: 1, 5, 6, 12, 21, 22, 29, 30
    Best Days for Money: 7, 8, 16, 17, 21, 22, 25, 26
    Best Days for Career: 5, 6, 12, 13, 14, 15, 25

In July, the planetary power began to shift to the East from the West, and with Venus moving into the Eastern sector this month, the shift is complete. The Eastern sector of the chart will be dominant for the rest of the year. You should have a clearer picture of what needs changing in your life after a few months of having to adapt to others, and now is the time to do it.

Personal power, personal initiative, personal will is very strong now (and especially with Mars in your own sign too). You have the power to change things, to create conditions as you like them, and now is the time to exercise that power. Cosmic energy is moving towards you. Others are always important, but don't neglect your own needs or interests. This is the time to think of number one. Some might call this selfish, but it is an 'enlightened self-interest'. If you are not in emotional harmony you can't really be of service to others. If others don't go along with your plans, you can go it alone if necessary.

Your love planet crosses your Mid-heaven on the 7th and enters your 10th house of career. The Mid-heaven is the most prominent and powerful position in the Horoscope so this gives us many messages. Though you are more independent these days, love and the social life is still high on your priorities. You are mixing with people of status and power this month. Singles will have opportunities for an office romance – romantic opportunities with superiors. This is a time to further your career by social means, by attending or hosting the right parties or gatherings or by befriending people who can help you career-wise. Your social graces, your ability to get on with others is probably more important career-wise than your actual abilities.

We see the social connection with the career in other ways too. On the 23rd, your career planet enters Libra. So Venus and the Sun (the love planet and the career planet) are in 'mutual reception'. Each is a guest in the sign and house of the other. There is great co-operation between these two planets. Friends, your spouse or current love and the social circle in general are helping the career. Singles find love opportunities as they pursue their career goals and with people involved in the career.

This month is not only strong romantically but socially as well. Your 11th house of friends is very powerful until the 23rd.

Finances are a bit stormy until the 23rd. You need to work harder to attain your goals. Perhaps there are financial disagreements with bosses, authority figures, parents, or elders, and perhaps even with the government. But these pass. On the 23rd, as the Sun enters Libra, there is better financial co-operation with these people. Earnings will increase. Be patient until that date.

## October

Best Days Overall: 7, 8, 16, 17, 24, 25, 26
Most Stressful Days Overall: 2, 3, 9, 10, 11, 22, 23, 29, 30, 31
Best Days for Love: 1, 2, 3, 12, 21, 29, 30, 31
Best Days for Money: 4, 5, 6, 14, 15, 18, 19, 22, 23
Best Days for Career: 4, 5, 9, 10, 11, 14, 15, 24

You have done well financially so far this year. Now it is time to take a breather and take stock. Jupiter, your financial planet, starts to retrograde on the 4th and will remain that way for the rest of the year. This retrograde won't stop earnings, only slow things down a bit. The financial life should be under review now. Your financial thinking and judgement is not up to its usual standard. Probably there are trends happening that you don't know about yet – developments behind the scenes. Thus normal logic (which reasons from the known and the visible) is not very reliable now. The need now is for mental clarity. Avoid making important purchases, major investments or financial decisions until this clarity is obtained. This is not a time for financial short cuts or get-rich-quick schemes.

Dealing with the retrograde of the financial planet is a challenge for those who live in Western societies. The belief is in growth, growth, growth. The pauses in the growth, so necessary for further development, are not valued. But this is a violation of cosmic law. Expansion and contraction are two sides of a coin. During contractions or slow downs, the forces are built up for the next expansion, and thus the next expansion is healthier. The great fortunes are made during the contractions and not the expansions. Nathan Rothschild is quoted as saying, 'The time to buy is when there is blood in the streets.' So it is important for you to use this 'slow down' properly, in line with its cosmic intent, to prepare for the next expansion.

Love is more delicate this month too. Venus will be in Virgo from the 3rd to the 28th. You and your spouse, partner or current love can both be more critical in love. You can over-analyse and over-mentalize, and this tends to kill any mood of romance. Avoid this as much as possible. If there is imperfection correct it as quickly as you can with minimum negativity. Avoid destructive forms of criticism – this never helps. You deserve perfection in love, but you need to go about it in the right way.

Venus' move into Virgo indicates another shift in love attitudes. Last month, power and position was the turn on. Now, it is friendship. You want to be friends with the beloved as well as lovers. Singles find love opportunities in groups, group activities and organizations. Friends are playing cupid this period.

On the 23rd the Sun enters your 1st house initiating another yearly personal pleasure peak. Personal independence is even stronger than last month, so keep in mind our previous discussion of this. You are not only enjoying yourself, but career opportunities – good ones – are coming to you as well.

## November

Best Days Overall: 3, 4, 5, 12, 13, 21, 22
Most Stressful Days Overall: 6, 7, 18, 19, 26, 27
Best Days for Love: 1, 11, 20, 26, 27
Best Days for Money: 1, 2, 11, 14, 15, 19, 28, 29
Best Days for Career: 3, 4, 6, 7, 13, 23

Last month was a significant and important month. Saturn moved into your sign on October 5 and will be there for the next two to two and a half years. So you are taking on more responsibilities now. The outlook on life is becoming more serious. Whatever your age and stage in life, you feel older than your years. Even young people are thinking and planning for old age. Your normal warmth is probably not there. You will need to consciously project more warmth to others. Often this transit brings feelings of loneliness, even among married people or people involved in love relationships. Outwardly you are in relationship, but in your inner heart, you feel alone. The relationship can bring certain pleasures but not assuage the deeper issues of the soul. This you have to handle alone.

Also last month, the planetary powers shifted from the upper (career) half of the Horoscope to the lower half. You have attained your career objectives for a while. You are seen as successful this period. Now it is time to set up the conditions for future career success. Career is important, but you pursue it differently now (and for the rest of the year). You pursue it by dreaming, visualizing, imagining and setting goals. If you can attain the inner feeling of 'being where you want to be' you can consider yourself successful, for although something hasn't happened outwardly, it will happen in the future, by cosmic law.

There are two eclipses this month. The first, a solar eclipse on the 13th, occurs in your own sign and affects you powerfully. A reduced schedule is called during that period, even though health is basically good. Risky types of activities should be avoided. You are redefining your image, your personality and self-concept now (and with Saturn in your own sign, this is a healthy thing). You are facing your 'physical limitations' these days and thus unrealistic expectations based on physical prowess are thrown out the window.

Every solar eclipse brings career changes and dramas with the authority figures in your life – bosses, parents and elders – and this one is no different. There are crises and shake-ups in your company, your industry and your local government. These things force you to make appropriate changes to your career strategy and thinking.

A lunar eclipse on the 28th occurs in your 8th house – again, avoid risky kinds of activities. This eclipse can bring encounters with death (usually on the psychological level), surgeries or near-death kinds of experiences. Your spouse, partner or current love is forced to make dramatic financial changes, usually because of a crisis. Issues involving estates, taxes and insurance claims take a dramatic turn. Students make important changes in educational plans. Foreign travel is best avoided during this period. Once again your religious and philosophical beliefs get tested. If you made the appropriate changes in May, you will sail through this. This is a re-testing to see your progress.

### December

Best Days Overall: 1, 2, 10, 11, 18, 19, 30, 31
Most Stressful Days Overall: 3, 4, 16, 17, 23, 24, 30, 31
Best Days for Love: 1, 10, 11, 20, 23, 24, 31
Best Days for Money: 8, 12, 13, 16, 25
Best Days for Career: 3, 4, 13, 22, 30, 31

The planetary power is overwhelmingly in the lower half of the Horoscope. At least 70 per cent (and sometimes 80 per cent) of the planets are below the horizon of your Horoscope. Your family planet, Uranus, starts to move forward on the 13th, so family matters are more clear now. Give the focus to the home and family and downplay the career. With so many planets below the horizon and the

10th house basically empty, career success is measured in different ways now. If you can attain the feeling of success, and hold the image of where you want to be, then you are successful, regardless of what is happening in so-called 'objective reality'. You have created your future and the rest will be 'automatic side-effects' of your visualization. You need not concern yourself about ways and means – these will unfold when day breaks in your year in 2013.

You will find that visualization and inner work goes best when there is emotional harmony. Thus this is your need these days. Feeling right is more important than doing right. If you feel right, the doing will also be right.

Last month on the 22nd, the Sun entered your money house and is there until the 21st of this month. You are in a yearly financial peak. Earnings should increase. Only keep in mind that your financial planet is still retrograde, so caution and review are still necessary. (Review our discussion of this in the October report.) Personal financial confidence might not be that strong, but this month you have the financial support and favour of your bosses and superiors, and of your spouse or current love and friends. In other words you have a lot of external help. The new Moon of the 13th also occurs in your money house and this brings some temporary clarity in the financial realm.

Love has been much happier recently. Venus crossed the Ascendant and moved into your 1st house on November 22. Love was seeking you out and most likely found you. You are having your way in love. The personal appearance shines; there is more glamour and beauty and the opposite sex takes notice. The spouse, partner or current love seems very devoted to you, putting you first. Though you still need to project more warmth to others (a long-term trend) this month it is easier to do. Singles need only go about their daily business and love will find them.

On the 16th Venus moves into your money house. Thus your spouse, partner or current love (and friends too) supports your financial goals and is personally active in a good way in your financial life. There are happy opportunities for business partnerships and joint ventures, but these require more study and homework. You shouldn't just jump into these things. You are seeing how to combine your financial and social life, to make these two areas support each other. (Usually, with this aspect, people do business with the people they socialize with – thus they kill two birds with one stone.)

# Sagittarius

♐

---

---

## Personality Profile

### SAGITTARIUS AT A GLANCE

*Element* – Fire

*Ruling Planet* – Jupiter
  *Career Planet* – Mercury
  *Love Planet* – Mercury
  *Money Planet* – Saturn
  *Planet of Health and Work* – Venus
  *Planet of Home and Family Life* – Neptune
  *Planet of Spirituality* – Pluto

*Colours* – blue, dark blue

*Colours that promote love, romance and social
  harmony* – yellow, yellow–orange

*Colours that promote earning power* – black,
  indigo

*Gems* – carbuncle, turquoise

*Metal* – tin

*Scents* – carnation, jasmine, myrrh

*Quality* – mutable (= flexibility)

*Qualities most needed for balance* – attention to detail, administrative and organizational skills

*Strongest virtues* – generosity, honesty, broad-mindedness, tremendous vision

*Deepest need* – to expand mentally

*Characteristics to avoid* – over-optimism, exaggeration, being too generous with other people's money

*Signs of greatest overall compatibility* – Aries, Leo

*Signs of greatest overall incompatibility* – Gemini, Virgo, Pisces

*Sign most helpful to career* – Virgo

*Sign most helpful for emotional support* – Pisces

*Sign most helpful financially* – Capricorn

*Sign best for marriage and/or partnerships* – Gemini

*Sign most helpful for creative projects* – Aries

*Best Sign to have fun with* – Aries

*Signs most helpful in spiritual matters* – Leo, Scorpio

*Best day of the week* – Thursday

# Understanding a Sagittarius

If you look at the symbol of the archer you will gain a good, intuitive understanding of a person born under this astrological Sign. The development of archery was humanity's first refinement of the power to hunt and wage war. The ability to shoot an arrow far beyond the ordinary range of a spear extended humanity's horizons, wealth, personal will and power.

Today, instead of using bows and arrows we project our power with fuels and mighty engines, but the essential reason for using these new powers remains the same. These powers represent our ability to extend our personal sphere of influence – and this is what Sagittarius is all about. Sagittarians are always seeking to expand their horizons, to cover more territory and increase their range and scope. This applies to all aspects of their lives: economic, social and intellectual.

Sagittarians are noted for the development of the mind – the higher intellect – which understands philosophical and spiritual concepts. This mind represents the higher part of the psychic nature and is motivated not by self-centred considerations but by the light and grace of a Higher Power. Thus, Sagittarians love higher education of all kinds. They might be bored with formal schooling but they love to study on their own and in their own way. A love of foreign travel and interest in places far away from home are also noteworthy characteristics of the Sagittarian type.

If you give some thought to all these Sagittarian attributes you will see that they spring from the inner Sagittarian desire to develop. To travel more is to know more, to know more is to be more, to cultivate the higher mind is to grow and to reach more. All these traits tend to broaden the intellectual – and indirectly, the economic and material – horizons of the Sagittarian.

The generosity of the Sagittarian is legendary. There are many reasons for this. One is that Sagittarians seem to have an inborn consciousness of wealth. They feel that they are rich, that they are lucky, that they can attain any financial goal – and so they feel that they can afford to be generous. Sagittarians do not carry the burdens of want and limitation which stop most other people from giving generously. Another reason for their generosity is their religious and philosophical idealism, derived from the higher mind. This higher mind is by nature generous because it is unaffected by material circumstances. Still another reason is that the act of giving tends to enhance their emotional nature. Every act of giving seems to be enriching, and this is reward enough for the Sagittarian.

### Finance

Sagittarians generally entice wealth. They either attract it or create it. They have the ideas, energy and talent to make their vision of paradise on Earth a reality. However, mere wealth is not enough. Sagittarians want luxury – earning a comfortable living seems small and insignificant to them.

In order for Sagittarians to attain their true earning potential they must develop better managerial and organizational skills. They must learn to set limits, to arrive at their goals through a series of attainable sub-goals or objectives. It is very rare that a person goes from rags to riches overnight. But a long, drawn-out process is difficult for Sagittarians. Like Leos, they want to achieve wealth and success quickly and impressively. They must be aware, however, that this over-optimism can lead to unrealistic financial ventures and disappointing losses. Of course, no zodiac sign can bounce back as quickly as Sagittarius, but only needless heartache will be caused by this attitude. Sagittarians need to maintain their vision – never letting it go – but they must also work towards it in practical and efficient ways.

**Career and Public Image**

Sagittarians are big thinkers. They want it all: money, fame, glamour, prestige, public acclaim and a place in history. They often go after all these goals. Some attain them, some do not – much depends on each individual's personal horoscope. But if Sagittarians want to attain public and professional status they must understand that these things are not conferred to enhance one's ego but as rewards for the amount of service that one does for the whole of humanity. If and when they figure out ways to serve more, Sagittarians can rise to the top.

The ego of the Sagittarian is gigantic – and perhaps rightly so. They have much to be proud of. If they want public acclaim, however, they will have to learn to tone down the ego a bit, to become more humble and self-effacing, without falling into the trap of self-denial and self-abasement. They must also learn to master the details of life, which can sometimes elude them.

At their jobs Sagittarians are hard workers who like to please their bosses and co-workers. They are dependable, trustworthy and enjoy a challenge. Sagittarians are friendly to work with and helpful to their colleagues. They usually contribute intelligent ideas or new methods that improve the work environment for everyone. Sagittarians always look for challenging positions and careers that develop their intellect, even if they have to work very hard in order to succeed. They also work well under the supervision of others, although by nature they would rather be the supervisors and increase their sphere of influence. Sagittarians excel at professions that allow them to be in contact with many different people and to travel to new and exciting locations.

## Love and Relationships

Sagittarians love freedom for themselves and will readily grant it to their partners. They like their relationships to be fluid and ever-changing. Sagittarians tend to be fickle in love and to change their minds about their partners quite frequently.

Sagittarians feel threatened by a clearly defined, well-structured relationship, as they feel this limits their freedom. The Sagittarian tends to marry more than once in life.

Sagittarians in love are passionate, generous, open, benevolent and very active. They demonstrate their affections very openly. However, just like an Aries they tend to be egocentric in the way they relate to their partners. Sagittarians should develop the ability to see others' points of view, not just their own. They need to develop some objectivity and cool intellectual clarity in their relationships so that they can develop better two-way communication with their partners. Sagittarians tend to be overly idealistic about their partners and about love in general. A cool and rational attitude will help them to perceive reality more clearly and enable them to avoid disappointment.

## Home and Domestic Life

Sagittarians tend to grant a lot of freedom to their family. They like big homes and many children and are one of the most fertile signs of the zodiac. However, when it comes to their children Sagittarians generally err on the side of allowing them too much freedom. Sometimes their children get the idea that there are no limits. However, allowing freedom in the home is basically a positive thing – so long as some measure of balance is maintained – for it enables all family members to develop as they should.

# Horoscope for 2012

## Major Trends

The first decade of the millennium has been fraught with sudden and dramatic changes. You were constantly dealing with the unexpected. Your main lesson was to be comfortable with change and instability, to be at peace with it. And by now you have learned this. Things have quietened down the past two years. There is more stability in the life now. And this trend continues in the year ahead.

Children and children figures in your life have been difficult to deal with. They seem very rebellious these days and this trend continues in the year ahead. Your job is to channel their rebellion (which is really an urge to innovation mis-expressed) into positive directions.

Jupiter has been in your 6th house of health since June of last year and will be there until June 11. This is a very good signal for health. If there have been health problems there has been good news about them. This is also a very nice transit for job seekers. Many of you have found dream jobs in the past year, and if not, will be able to find them this year. More on this later.

Jupiter will move into your 7th house on June 11. Venus, the planet of love, spends four months in this house. Thus the year ahead is a very strong love and social year. Those of you looking for that special someone are likely to find him or her this year.

Mars spends an unusual amount of time in your 10th house of career (more than six months). Thus you are in a very active career period. You are working unusually hard, fending off rivals and competitors. But you seem to be enjoying all of this. (More details below.)

This year the planets, and especially the long-term ones, are dispersed all over your chart. This is true for everyone, but for you it has special significance. It shows many interests in your life. However, your tendency will be to disperse your energy and attention. It will be harder to keep your focus on your main objectives. It will take some discipline.

Your areas of greatest interest this year are finance; communication and intellectual interests (until February 3); home and family (from February 3 onwards); children, creativity and personal pleasure; health and work (until June 11); love, romance and social activities (from June 11 onwards); career (until July 3); friends, groups and group activities (until October 5); and spirituality (from October 5 onwards).

Your paths of greatest fulfilment in the year ahead are health and work (until June 11); love, romance and social activities (from June 11 onwards); the body and image (until August 31); and spirituality (from August 31 onwards).


## Health

*(Please note that this is an* astrological *perspective on health and not a medical one. In days of yore these perspectives were identical. But these days there could be quite a difference. For a medical perspective, please consult your doctor or health practitioner.)*

Two planets are making stressful aspects on you early in the year: Neptune (from February 3 onwards) and Mars (until July 3). But the other long-term planets are either in harmonious aspect or leaving you alone. Health is reasonable now. Happily, your health house is very strong – Jupiter, your ruling planet, is there until June 11. So you are focused on health and staying on top of things, which is good news.

The peak health stress time is from June 11 to July 3, so you need to rest and relax more then. On July 3 Mars will leave his stressful aspect and start to make harmonious aspects with you, so your health and energy will start to improve for the rest of the year.

There is much you can do to improve health and prevent problems from developing. Pay more attention to the follow-ing organs: the heart (avoid worry and anxiety); the kidneys and hips (hips should be regularly massaged); the neck and

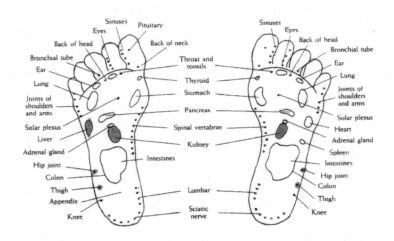

## Reflexology

*Try to massage the whole foot on a regular basis, but pay extra attention to the points highlighted on the chart. When you massage, be aware of 'sore spots', as these need special attention. It's also a good idea to massage the ankles and top side of the feet (see below).*

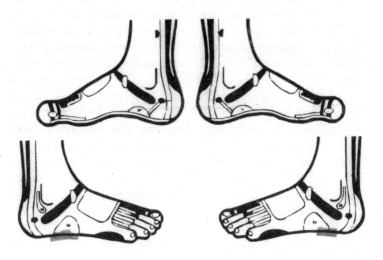

throat (regular neck massage is powerful as tension tends to collect in the back of the neck and needs to be released); the liver and thighs (until June 11); and the lungs, arms, shoulders and respiratory system (from April 3 to August 7, massage the arms and shoulders more regularly to release tension).

Since your health planet, Venus, moves very quickly – in the course of the year she will move through all the signs and houses of your Horoscope – there are many short term trends in health that are best dealt with in the monthly reports.

Venus is the generic planet of love. Her role as your health planet shows that discords in the marriage, the current relationship or with friends can be a root cause of health problems. Thus, if problems arise you will need to explore this area and restore harmony. Love issues are especially important from April 3 to August 7, as Venus is occupying the 7th solar house.

Jupiter is the ruler of your Horoscope. His position in your 6th house until June 11 shows that good health for you means much more than just no symptoms – it means looking good as well. There is a vanity component to good health. Your state of health dramatically affects your physical appearance (and this is not so for everyone). Staying healthy will do more for your physical appearance than hosts of cosmetics and lotions. This factor can also be used in healing. If you feel under the weather do something to enhance the appearance – have the hair done, buy a new outfit, or jewellery or accessory. You should start to feel better physically.

Good health is a form of beauty and with Venus as your health planet you understand this better than most. Beauty is the natural state of a healthy person, for the cosmos is beauty and created by beauty. Beauty itself is a powerful healing force and you more than most respond to it. Thus if you feel unwell listen to beautiful music, visit an art gallery, or spend time in parks or other places of natural beauty. You will immediately start to feel better.

## Home and Family

Uranus spent many years in your 4th house and this was a period of great instability in the home, with the family, and in your emotional life. Probably there were multiple moves. Many a family broke up. You were plagued by extreme mood swings, both personally and with family members, and there were many dramas with the parents or parent figures. In 2011 Uranus finally left your 4th house and things are a bit quieter in the home and with the family. Your emotional life also seems more stable. On February 3, Neptune moves into this house and will spend the next 14 years or so there. This is a major cosmic change.

There is more idealism about the family. Family members are under very intense spiritual influences now. Many are entering a spiritual path or being exposed to spiritual teachings. Many of you are meeting up with your true spiritual family, which might not be your biological family. (We all have a spiritual family – a family that loves and supports us unconditionally. Sometimes they are incarnate and sometimes not, but now is the time to discover this family.)

The home is becoming a more spiritual kind of place, as much a shrine as a home. Many of you will be setting up private altars in the home, and many will be hosting spiritual meetings there. The home is becoming spiritualized and refined.

Neptune is the planet of revelation. Here in the 4th house he is bringing spiritual revelation to the affairs of this house. His impersonal light reveals what is: the good, the bad, the ugly. Thus, in many cases there are scandals or unpleasant revelations about family members. But there are also revelations of secret good too. Family members need to be more careful of drug or alcohol abuse these days too. There is a stronger tendency to these things.

If you are buying or selling a home you need to do a lot more homework than usual. Your judgement could be unrealistic. There are things hidden behind the scenes that you need to be aware of. Hidden things in the home need to be checked out. So take your time and get all the facts.

Children are more rebellious these days, as we have mentioned. You can't just use 'blind authority' with them. They need to understand the 'whys and wherefores' of what is expected of them. Communication with them should improve after June 11.

**Finance and Career**

Pluto has been in your money house since late 2008 and will be there for many more years to come. There is a cosmic detox going on in the financial life. There is a need to expand by cutting back. This sounds like an oxymoron, yet it is not. It is much akin to a detox of the body. Just as the body is purged of material that was clogging up the works, and thus the natural health of the body returns, the financial life is purged of waste and duplication and thus the natural financial health is restored. Do you have excess possessions that you don't use? Now is the time to get rid of them. Do you have redundant bank or savings accounts? Now is the time to consolidate them. Are you spending wastefully? Now is the time to eliminate the waste.

Sometimes detoxing is quite dramatic. Many of you will face financial 'near-death' kinds of experiences – you will feel that you are face to face with 'ruin' – but this is part of the detox and what you imagine is not really likely to happen. It is the fear of it that you are dealing with. These fears were obstructing the financial life and financial decision making. You are giving birth to the financial life of your dreams and these are the birth pangs.

Pluto in the money house has other meanings. Often this shows inheritance. Often it indicates earnings from insurance claims or royalties. Debt needs to be managed properly. Constructive debt – borrowing for things or investments that will increase in value – will make you rich. Destructive debt – borrowing for things that will be worthless down the road – can wreak havoc on you. This is a time for getting clear about these things. Perhaps the main message of Pluto in the money house is that you are exploring the spiritual dimensions of wealth, a long-term trend. Pluto is your spiritual planet. There are spiritual laws involved with wealth and now is the time to discover this.

When your financial planet, Saturn, moves into your 12th house on October 5, this issue, the spirituality of wealth, becomes even more prominent for you. Your intuition is very important and needs to be trusted. This is the true short cut to wealth.

Saturn spends most of the year in Libra, your 11th house. Thus your social connections are very important financially. You have rich friends and they seem supportive. It is also important that you stay up to date with the latest technology. Your technological expertise is important in your earnings – a marketable commodity. You are probably spending more on technology, and can earn from this field as well. This position favours online kinds of businesses. (Even if you are not in an online business, online activities seem to be important in the financial life.)

Being more involved with trade or professional organizations is important financially too.

## Love and Social Life

If you are single working on your first marriage, the year ahead brings a special someone to you. (More likely you will be chasing him or her.) And whatever marriage you are into, the year ahead is a strong and happy social year. You are going out more, attending more parties, gatherings, weddings and the like. New and important friendships are happening and you find that your whole social circle is greatly expanded.

Serious, committed romance is definitely in the air. Venus, the planet of love, will be in your 7th house of love for four months, an unusually long transit for her. (Her normal transit is one month.) So it is like taking 'love pills'; your mood is more romantic and you attract people who are more romantic. You attract the 'beautiful' people this year. Jupiter, the ruler of your Horoscope, moves into your 7th house on June 11 and stays there for the rest of the year. Thus your house of love is active and powerful and this tends to success in this department.

Jupiter in this house makes you socially popular too. The reason is very simple. You are going out of your way for others. You are putting others first, ahead of your own interests. Whoever you are with feels this. They know that you are in their corner, solidly supportive and behind them. If more people were like this, many a troubled marriage would be cured – spiritual healers affirm that the main root cause of failed marriages is not incompatibility or personality clashes but selfishness.

Jupiter in your 7th house also shows that you are more aggressive, more proactive in love and social matters. You are not waiting around for the phone to ring but are actively creating your own social life by organizing events, hosting parties, and cultivating the friends that you want. If you like someone that person will know it very clearly. You go after what you want, and this year you are likely to get it.

This year you basically follow your Natal pattern. Intellectual compatibility is very important to you. You like smart people – writers, teachers, journalists, media people. You need to fall in love with the beloved's thought process as well as the body. You like someone you can talk to, and exchange ideas and information with. Mental intimacy is as important as the other intimacies. Good communication is a form of sexual foreplay, and perhaps is more important than the other foreplays. You are turned on by love talk.

You find love and social opportunities in educational settings, at lectures and seminars and perhaps at a book store or library – also at the work place, with fellow workers, the health spa, the doctor's surgery or with people involved in your health.

Those in or working on their second marriage will have an active social year, but serious relationships seem the status quo. Singles will tend to remain single; married couples will tend to stay married. Those in the third marriage have been having their relationships tested for two years now, and many did not make it. This trend continues in the year ahead. Those working towards their third marriage are better off not marrying this year.

## Self-improvement

Neptune, as we mentioned, moves into your 4th house this year. The 4th house is not only associated with the home and family, but also with your emotional life. The feeling nature is becoming more spiritualized. You are only feeling the beginnings of this; it will get much stronger as the years go by. (Neptune will be in this house for another 14 years.)

Sagittarians are generally not emotionally sensitive (nothing compared to say a Pisces or a Cancer), but now you will start becoming more sensitive. Other signs, especially the water signs (Cancer, Scorpio and Pisces), have long experience in dealing with this, but for you it will be new. There are adjustments to be made. There are many good points to this sensitivity. You will be more in touch with your own and other people's feelings. Probably you will become more popular because of this. You will be more nurturing to others. You will have increased psychological insight both for yourself and for others. You will become more psychic and more creative, and more musical and poetic. You will start to experience nuances of feeling that you never experienced before.

The downside of this kind of sensitivity is that you are more easily hurt. You are more sensitive to little slights that perhaps never bothered you before. And if you are around the wrong people, this can be quite painful. Normally you are a very 'up' kind of person, always on the go, always ready for action. Now you are more moody and more prone to melancholy and depression (if you are not careful). These changes are as dramatic as the changes of puberty. It's as if a new faculty is being born in you.

The best way to handle this is to become an observer of your feelings. See the emotional body as kind of meter that registers different vibrations. You will still feel and have emotions, but you will be above them and more able to direct them in a positive way. The pain will alert you that you are in a 'negative' state and need to get out of it. This is the good part of it – in the old days, you could have been in a negative state without being aware of it.

I feel this new emotional sensitivity is going to produce very profound spiritual changes, something that we see in other ways too. Uranus is square to Pluto, your spiritual planet, all year (in different degrees of exactness). You are changing your spiritual practice, your teachers and your whole approach.

It is said that we can't 'think our way into the Kingdom of Heaven' – it is beyond thought, beyond logic. We can only 'feel' our way into it, and you are being given the faculty with which to do this.

# Month-by-month Forecasts

### January

Best Days Overall: 8, 9, 17, 18, 25, 26
Most Stressful Days Overall: 5, 6, 7, 12, 13, 25, 26
Best Days for Love: 1, 2, 5, 6, 7, 12, 18, 19, 22, 27, 28
Best Days for Money: 3, 4, 6, 7, 12, 15, 16, 21, 22, 24, 30
Best Days for Career: 1, 2, 12, 13, 22

Your year begins with most of the planets below the horizon. In your personal year, this is night-time, soon to approach the midnight hour. The activities of night are favourable now. Night is for resting, dreaming, visualizing, and building up the forces necessary for the next day. Night is for the home and family and for love and emotional harmony. You have done your work at the office and now you need to get into your point of emotional harmony. Career seems hectic now. Do whatever needs to be done, but pay more attention to the home and family. If the night is not used properly, the preparations for the coming day will not be completed.

Most of the planets are still in the Eastern sector of your chart (this is soon to change), and so you are still in a period of independence and personal power. Creating new life conditions is easier now than later. So, if there is something that needs changing, this is the time to do it. Later on it will be more difficult.

You begin the year in the midst of a financial peak – in a period of peak earnings and peak interest in finance. Thus you are successful. You have a lot of financial help this month from friends, the social circle and from your spouse, partner or current love. Also from parents, parent figures, bosses and the government. You have the financial favour of the authority figures in your life. You seem able to integrate the social life and the financial life this period. Usually this indicates that you do business with friends and people that you socialize with. There are opportunities for business partnerships or joint ventures after the 8th. If you have issues with the government this is a good month to deal with it (especially after the 8th). Job seekers have good aspects all month, but especially until the 20th.

Health is good this month. You can enhance it further by giving more attention to the ankles and calves (until the 24th) and to the feet afterwards. All of these should be regularly massaged. You are very focused on health this year; it is one of your strong interests. This is not because you are ailing but comes from a 'cosmetic' interest. Good health enhances the personal appearance.

Children and children figures in your life are more difficult to deal with. If you are involved in a love affair (not a marriage) it is getting tested this month.

The year ahead is going to be a wonderful love year and now you are sort of preparing yourself for it. Until the 8th love opportunities find you, there is nothing much you need to do. Your spouse, partner or current love is very devoted to you. After the 8th love opportunities happen as you pursue your financial goals and with people involved in your finances. Love is very practical after the 8th. You are turned on by wealth and material gifts.

### February

Best Days Overall: 7, 8, 15, 16, 24, 25
Most Stressful Days Overall: 2, 3, 9, 10, 22, 23, 29
Best Days for Love: 2, 3, 5, 6, 11, 12, 15, 22, 23, 24, 25, 29
Best Days for Money: 1, 3, 9, 12, 17, 18, 21, 27, 28
Best Days for Career: 2, 3, 9, 10, 11, 12, 22, 23

Last month the planetary power was in the independent East. This month it shifts to the social Western sector from the 19th onwards. From here on in it is more difficult to change conditions. It is a time for adapting to things as best you can. Personal power and independence is weakened to develop other parts of the character – the social graces and the ability to get on with others. The cosmos creates scenarios of 'dependence' so that you are forced to get on with others and cultivate their grace. Your needs are important, but the needs of others are more important right now. Your way might not be the best way these days.

Your 3rd house of communication and intellectual interests was powerful last month and still powerful until the 19th. The planets that rule communication in your Horoscope, Mercury and Uranus, are moving forward (as are 80 per cent of the planets this month). So this is a great month for mass mailings, advertising campaigns and communication projects. (Good sales and marketing – good PR – is important financially as well, more so than usual.) As our regular readers know, this is a good time to take courses in subjects that interest you and to expand your knowledge base in general. Learning is easier. Students (especially below college level) have more success in their studies.

Your 4th house of home and family is the strongest in the

Horoscope this month. Half of the planets are either there or moving through it this month. This shows great activity and great focus. You are in the midnight hour of your year now, the point of deepest internal, subjective activity. The inner life, the life of mood and feeling, is more important than the outer life. Feeling right is more important than doing right. Right feeling – emotional peace and harmony – will lead, inevitably, to right doing. To overly engage in outer activities is equivalent to depriving yourself of a good night's sleep. Of course, do what needs to be done in the outer world and in your career, but shift more focus to the home, family and the emotional life.

Your financial planet goes retrograde on the 6th. It will be retrograde for many more months, so you are in for a period of financial review. Your goal is to attain mental clarity on personal finances, goals and the general financial picture of your environment. So the really big financial decisions – big purchases, investments and so on – need more homework and are better off delayed. Saturn's retrograde will not stop earnings but it will slow things down a bit. This is a time for building up the forces for the next financial expansion.

Health is more delicate from the 19th onwards. As usual this means you should rest and relax more. Do your best to maintain high energy levels. Until the 8th you can enhance your health by giving more attention to the feet (foot massage is very powerful and energizes the whole body). Spiritual healing methods are powerful then too. After the 8th head, face and scalp massage is powerful. Vigorous physical exercise is good too.

**March**

>  Best Days Overall: 5, 6, 13, 14, 22, 23, 24
>  Most Stressful Days Overall: 1, 7, 8, 20, 21, 27, 28, 29
>  Best Days for Love: 1, 2, 5, 7, 13, 15, 16, 25, 26, 27, 28, 29, 31
>  Best Days for Money: 2, 7, 10, 15, 16, 19, 25, 26, 29
>  Best Days for Career: 2, 5, 7, 8, 13, 31

Love was a bit bumpy until the 14th of last month. But things improved afterwards. Your love planet Mercury moved into Pisces on February 14 and is there this month (on and off) as well. Love is more idealistic these days, more spiritual. Practical concerns are not the issue now: it is the feeling of love that matters. In January wealth and material gifts turned you on, now it is emotional intimacy, emotional sharing, emotional support that you crave. This is how you feel loved and also how you show it.

There was more socializing from the home last month with family members and with those who are like family to you, and this trend continues (on and off) in the month ahead. Singles are likely to meet old flames from the past in order to resolve old issues. Sometimes this doesn't happen literally – you can meet someone new who has the same or similar patterns as the old flame. This is another way that the cosmos resolves old issues.

Mercury goes retrograde on the 12th. This doesn't stop love or social activities, but it slows things down a bit. A breather is in order. Current relationships (and your general social agenda) need a review. Mercury spends some time in Aries, from the 3rd to the 23rd, and this often produces 'rashness' in love – love-at-first-sight kinds of experiences. But with Mercury going retrograde, rashness in love is not advisable. Venus travels with the ruler of your Horoscope from the 11th to the 14th and this brings a happy love meeting or social experience.

Health still needs watching until the 20th, but afterwards it improves dramatically. The ailments (probably minor) that were bothering you until then magically disappear. The sense of fatigue and lethargy also disappear. You are brimming with energy and can achieve any goal you set for yourself. You feel the spring fever strongly.

Your 4th house of home and family is still powerful until the 20th, so review our discussion of this last month. On the 20th, your 5th house becomes strong and you enter one of your yearly personal pleasure peaks. This is a time for enjoying life. Sure you are working hard, but you are also having fun. Life is not all about fun and games – it is serious business – but we are to enjoy life, even the duties and responsibilities. This is the spiritual message of the 5th house.

Speculations seem favourable this month (but as always don't indulge in this blindly; follow intuition). Your personal creativity seems more marketable as well.

Elective foreign travel is best avoided between the 1st to the 5th, the 23rd to the 26th and the 29th to the 31st. There can be dramas in the lives of the religious figures in your life, and perhaps with people in your place of worship. Legal matters are best delayed these periods as well.

### April

Best Days Overall: 1, 2, 10, 19, 20, 29, 30
Most Stressful Days Overall: 4, 16, 17, 24, 25
Best Days for Love: 5, 8, 9, 14, 15, 17, 18, 24, 25, 29, 30
Best Days for Money: 4, 6, 7, 12, 13, 15, 21, 22, 25
Best Days for Career: 3, 4, 8, 9, 17, 18, 29, 30

Children in your life have been very ambitious (and successful) so far this year. But since January 24, when Mars went retrograde, they have lacked direction and seem unsure about their next moves. By the 11th mental clarity returns to them and they proceed with confidence. Your love planet starts moving forward on the 4th and thus the pace of social activity quickens. By now you should have more mental clarity about your relationships and social life and are in a better position to make important decisions. The love planet is in Pisces, your 4th house, until the 17th. This shows 'nostalgia' in love, a desire to return to the past and to old flames, old experiences and the 'good old days'. (Often it is necessary to resolve the past before we can go forward, and this is what is happening now.) Emotional support, emotional intimacy and sharing are still important in love. Practical concerns are not the issue now. It is the feeling of love that matters. You could be happy in a shack, so long as the feeling of love was there.

On the 17th, Mercury moves into Aries, your 5th house. This is a major mood shift in love. Like last month you will have love-at-first-sight experiences, but this month it is safer to indulge. Love is about fun now. Relationships are to be enjoyed. You are having more fun – more leisure kinds of activities – with your spouse, partner, current love and friends this month. Love is honeymoonish. With Mercury in Aries, you (and the people you attract) are good at the honeymoon aspects of love, but not so good at the other parts. When tough times come, you want out. Mercury travels with Uranus from the 22nd to the 24th and this brings 'unexpected' love, unexpected romance and unexpected social invitations. But the stability of these things is in question. Sudden and unexpected career opportunities are likely that period as well. Also there can be career changes and dramas in the lives of parents, parent figures or bosses.

Venus, the generic planet of love enters your 7th house of love on the 3rd and will be there all month, which is a good romantic signal. This shows romantic opportunity at the work place, with co-workers, and with people involved in your health. Health professionals are especially attractive for singles.

Health is good this month, yet you are still very focused here. The focus doesn't seem to be coming because of sickness, but from the cosmetic perspective. You want to look good. Also, with Venus in your house of love, there is a romantic component to it as well. The focus on health enhances romance.

You can enhance your already good health this month by giving more attention to the heart (from the 20th onwards) and to the lungs, arms, shoulders and respiratory system from the 3rd onwards.

## May

Best Days Overall: 7, 8, 16, 17, 26, 27
Most Stressful Days Overall: 1, 2, 13, 14, 15, 21, 22, 28, 29
Best Days for Love: 3, 4, 8, 11, 12, 18, 19, 20, 21, 22, 28, 29, 30, 31
Best Days for Money: 2, 4, 9, 10, 12, 19, 20, 22, 29, 31
Best Days for Career: 1, 2, 8, 18, 19, 20, 28, 29

There are many changes and shifts in the life this month. There is a solar eclipse on the 20th right on the cusp of your 7th house of love. The planetary power shifts from the lower half of the Horoscope to the upper half, and Venus makes one of her rare retrograde moves on the 15th.

The solar eclipse of the 20th has a strong effect you, particularly on those of you born early in the sign of Sagittarius (November 21–25). Reduce your schedule during this period. This eclipse is heralding major changes in love. There are many scenarios that happen. Sometimes the person is in an existing relationship that isn't right and the eclipse explodes it. Sometimes problems in the existing relationship are brought to the surface to be resolved. The marriage or relationship is reborn. Sometimes the person decides to change the marital status – singles decide that they want to be married, and marrieds decide that they want to be single. You are about to enter a very happy love cycle and old debris – blockages and obstructions – needs to be cleared away in order for this to happen. And this is what is happening this month.

Foreign travel is best avoided around this eclipse period. Legal matters take dramatic turns, and students make important educational changes. This eclipse is a direct hit on

Neptune, your family planet. Thus there are family crises and dramas. Be more patient with family members as they are apt to be more temperamental now.

On the 20th, the day of the eclipse, you enter a yearly social peak. Next month will be even better, but it's beginning now. Love is in the air now, but old issues need resolution.

The retrograde of Venus suggests that you avoid making dramatic changes to the diet or health regime. Study these things more carefully. Job seekers also need to do more homework about potential job offers. Those already working should avoid making job changes just yet, as the thinking and planning behind them are probably unrealistic.

Aside from the stresses of the eclipse, health needs more watching from the 20th onwards. Continue to enhance the health by giving more attention to the lungs, respiratory system, arms and shoulders, and also to the ways mentioned in the yearly report. Breathing exercises are good too. Air purity is more important health-wise than usual.

### June

Best Days Overall: 3, 4, 12, 13, 22, 23
Most Stressful Days Overall: 10, 11, 17, 18, 24, 25
Best Days for Love: 1, 8, 9, 10, 17, 18, 20, 21, 27, 28
Best Days for Money: 5, 6, 9, 17, 18, 26, 27, 28
Best Days for Career: 1, 10, 20, 21, 24, 25

The month ahead is a bit challenging and stressful, but if you watch your energy many nice things will happen, especially in the area of love.

Last month there was a strong solar eclipse in your 7th house. You will still be feeling this eclipse for the rest of this month, as Jupiter, the ruler of your Horoscope, is re-activating the eclipse point all month as he transits this point. So you need to avoid risky kinds of activities and take it nice and easy. On the 4th there is a strong lunar eclipse in your own sign. Again the same advice applies. Add to this the stressful aspects being made by the short-term planets – the Sun, Mercury and Venus (and the Moon a few times a month) – and everything we are saying is reinforced.

The lunar eclipse of the 4th will bring a redefinition of the image and self-concept. Jupiter's re-activation of the solar eclipse point also brings the same. A major love relationship could be the cause behind all this, as there is nothing like love to make people redefine themselves. It can also bring encounters with death (usually on the psychological level), near-death experiences and surgeries. Dreams of death are common with such an eclipse but they shouldn't be taken too seriously right now. In a dream, a death is usually showing some dramatic change in the life. Your spouse, partner, or current love is making major financial changes. Friends are having their marriages or relationships tested.

Health needs attention all month, especially until the 21st. Enhance the health in the ways mentioned in the yearly report and in last month's discussion. Your health planet, Venus, is still retrograde until the 27th so avoid making major changes to the diet or health regime just yet. This is a time for study and research. After the homework is done, and more clarity is attained, then you can make the changes.

Jupiter, as we mentioned, enters your house of love on the 11th and is there for the rest of the year. This is a classic indicator of love and marriage. Venus in your 7th house is another important indicator. You are more personally popular these days, and this will be the case for the rest of the year. You seem to be taking the advice of putting others first and they respond to this. You are more proactive in love and you are creating the social life of your dreams.

The financial changes that your spouse, partner or current love is making seem good. On the 21st he or she enters a yearly financial peak and is likely to be more generous with you.

Elective travel should be avoided all month, but especially around the eclipse period, and from the 28th to the 30th. Be more careful driving from the 28th to the 30th as well.

Love is happy this month but can be tempestuous (with some bumps on the road) from the 10th to the 13th. Be more patient with the beloved then. The spouse, partner or current love needs to avoid risky activities that period; avoid confrontations, arguments and take more care driving.

## July

Best Days Overall: 1, 2, 9, 10, 11, 19, 20, 21, 28, 29
Most Stressful Days Overall: 7, 8, 15, 16, 22, 23
Best Days for Love: 1, 2, 5, 6, 9, 10, 11, 15, 16, 19, 20, 21, 24, 25, 28, 29
Best Days for Money: 3, 4, 5, 6, 15, 16, 24, 25, 30, 31
Best Days for Career: 1, 2, 9, 10, 11, 19, 20, 21, 22, 23, 28, 29

Last month planetary retrograde activity hit its maximum for the year; 40 per cent of the planets were retrograde until June 25. This month we again hit the maximum from the 15th onwards. These retrograde affect you strongly, and involve love, communication, career, home and family. All these issues should be under review now. Life still goes on, but the pace of life slows down. With so many retrograde planets there are no short cuts now. Take your time and do everything as perfectly as you can. Ultimately (because you won't have to redo shoddy or careless work) this will be the short way.

Communication especially needs more care. On the 13th your communication planet, Uranus, goes retrograde (remaining so until December). On the 15th, Mercury goes retrograde. Thus the two planets that rule communication in your chart are retrograde at the same time. This is not a time for mass mailings or major advertising campaigns. (It is good to plan these things, but not to actually do them.) It's best to avoid signing contracts or making major purchases this period too. Everyone has Mercury-retrograde stories to tell – letters that never reach their destination, credit card companies that take two payments out of your account when you only authorized one, phone calls that don't get through, and so on. Usually the events that happen are merely inconvenient, but in certain circumstances they can be life threatening – a doctor prescribes the wrong medication, for instance. So it is best to avoid elective kinds of surgeries or elective travel as well, although obviously things that you have to do, you must do.

Many of the problems you face in love, career and in the family are coming from miscommunications and misunderstandings this period. A little more care in the beginning can save a lot of heartache later on. Make sure you say what you mean and that the other person gets what you are saying. Don't take communications for granted. Make sure you understand what the other person is saying too. Don't be afraid to ask questions to clarify things.

Love is happy this month, but under review. Avoid major love decisions one way or another. In spite of the retrograde of your love planet, love is in the air now.

Health is good too. Enhance the health in the ways described in previous reports.

### August

Best Days Overall: 6, 7, 16, 17, 24, 25
Most Stressful Days Overall: 4, 5, 11, 12, 18, 19, 31
Best Days for Love: 2, 3, 6, 7, 11, 12, 13, 14, 16, 17, 22, 23, 24, 25, 31
Best Days for Money: 1, 2, 11, 12, 20, 21, 27, 28, 29, 30
Best Days for Career: 6, 7, 16, 17, 18, 19, 24, 25

Retrograde activity is still at its yearly peak until the 8th, so keep in mind our discussion of this last month. You are generally a 'fast lane' kind of person. You like the fast pace of life, so now your challenge is patience, patience, patience.

On July 22 the Sun entered your 9th house and is there until the 23rd of this month. This is Nirvana for the Sagittarian. The cosmos impels you to do what you most love to do – travel, indulge in higher education, religion, philosophy and theology. Many of you are travelling. With all the retrograde planets, allow more time to get to your destination. Don't schedule connecting flights too closely and insure your tickets. Protect yourself as much as possible. This is good advice all month, but especially before the 8th. Try to avoid travel from the 22nd to the 25th.

This is a month for religious and philosophical insights and breakthroughs in your understanding. These breakthroughs will eventually affect every area of life in a positive way.

The planetary power is mostly above the horizon of your chart now. On the 23rd the Sun crosses the Mid-heaven and enters your 10th house of career, so you enter a yearly career peak. Happily, your career planet Mercury will be moving forward by then and so there will be mental clarity and good decision making. Great career progress is happening now. There is career-related travel from the 23rd onwards too.

Your health is basically good, but rest and relax more after the 23rd. Your health planet has spent many months in Gemini, your 7th house, and on the 8th she moves on into Cancer, your 8th house, so there are some changes happening in the health regime and needs. Now you need to give more attention to the stomach and breasts (for women). Diet is more of an issue now too. The stomach is more sensitive. Detox regimes are more powerful for you. Safe sex and sexual moderation become important. The sign of Cancer rules moods and emotions. Thus you need to make sure that these are constructive and positive. Over-indulgence in depressive or self-pitying states can actually cause physical pathologies, so avoid them as much as possible. If you find yourself in such a state (and it can happen) get out of it as quickly as possible. Don't wallow in it. If problems arise examine these things. Also examine family relationships and bring them into harmony as quickly as you can.

With the health planet in the 8th house there is an indication of surgery. Surgery is seen as the quick fix to a problem.

Sometimes this is justified, but don't rush into things; get a second opinion.

## September

> Best Days Overall: 2, 3, 12, 13, 21, 22, 29, 30
> Most Stressful Days Overall: 1, 7, 8, 14, 15, 27, 28
> Best Days for Love: 1, 4, 5, 7, 8, 12, 15, 16, 17, 21, 22, 25, 26, 29, 30
> Best Days for Money: 7, 8, 9, 16, 17, 18, 23, 24, 25, 26
> Best Days for Career: 4, 5, 14, 15, 16, 17, 25, 26

Retrograde activity lessens this month; until the 18th 30 per cent of the planets are retrograde, and afterwards it's only 20 per cent. So the pace of life quickens now. There is faster forward progress towards your goals. Career progress (and you are still in the midst of a yearly career peak) should happen faster now too.

The lunar eclipse of June 4 is still very much in effect in your Horoscope. Last month Jupiter, your ruling planet, was camping out on this point all month. And the situation is pretty much the same this month. It is as if you are getting a re-enactment of the eclipse. Avoid risk-taking activities. Do whatever needs to be done, but elective things that are stressful or risky are best avoided.

Your redefinition of your personality and image is very intense now. Perhaps others are trying to label you and the only way out is for you to define yourself. On the positive side, this redefinition can be coming from your career success. There is nothing that will change our image better than a dose of success. Success, which is happening now (each according to their level and stage in life) tends to make one a target of those less blessed, and this seems an issue these days as well.

Although the solar eclipse of May happened months ago, it is also very much in effect. Neptune, the family planet, makes a very exact aspect on this point this month. So there are dramas in the family, the home and with parents or parent figures. Changes need to happen in the home, but be more cautious with them as Neptune is retrograde. The emotional life can be confused now. You are not sure what you are feeling or why you are feeling what you feel. In spite of all these things keep the focus on the career as much as possible.

Try to avoid travelling from the 28th to the 30th. If you can't avoid it, protect yourself as best you can.

Your health improves after the 23rd, but until then needs some attention. Until the 7th your health planet is still in the sign of Cancer, so keep in mind our discussion of this last month. On the 7th, it moves into Leo, your 9th house. This again changes the health needs. Start giving more attention to the heart. Avoid worry and anxiety, the root causes of health problems. If there is something constructive to be done about a situation, by all means take action. But avoid worry, it achieves nothing.

Secret machinations in the love live and career get exposed early in the month. This might not be so pleasant, but in the end it is good. Avoid major career or love decisions then.

## October

Best Days Overall: 1, 9, 10, 11, 18, 19, 27, 28
Most Stressful Days Overall: 4, 5, 6, 12, 13, 24, 25, 26
Best Days for Love: 1, 4, 5, 6, 7, 12, 16, 17, 21, 25, 26
Best Days for Money: 4, 5, 6, 7, 14, 15, 16, 20, 21, 22, 23, 24
Best Days for Career: 5, 7, 12, 13, 16, 17, 25, 26

Ever since Jupiter moved into Gemini on June 11, finances have been good. Sure there have been ups and downs, but the basic trend has been positive. This month on the 5th, your financial planet, Saturn, makes a major move out of Libra (where it has been for two and a half years) into Scorpio – from your 11th house into your 12th. It is moving away from its positive aspect with Jupiter for a while, so finances are a bit more difficult than usual. This doesn't mean poverty or lack, only more work to achieve the financial goals. (Next year, when Jupiter enters Cancer, you once again have very nice financial aspects. This is sort of a lull, not a disaster.)

The Sun travels with your financial planet from the 24th to the 27th bringing windfalls, opportunities and financial increase. From the 2nd to the 14th Saturn makes nice aspects to Neptune. This brings good family support, spending on the family, and perhaps investments in the home.

Your spiritual planet, Pluto has been in your money house for some years now. Saturn will now be in your spiritual 12th house for the next couple of years. These two planets will thus be in 'mutual reception' – each is a guest in the house of the other. This is considered very positive. There is good co-operation between these two planets. This highlights the need to go deeper into the spiritual dimensions of wealth; to learn the spiritual laws involved in wealth and to apply them. You will be making great progress in this area now. Most of you already have a natural understanding of this (Sagittarius more than most grasp this), but it is time to go deeper. When you understand that there is one and only one source of supply – the Divine – you will know true financial freedom and independence. This seems the cosmic agenda these days.

Some of you might be taking jobs in charitable or non-profit type organizations. There is a need now to earn money in 'spiritually correct' kinds of ways. Just getting rich is not enough for you – it has to be spiritual, idealistic, meaningful, and in ways that bless others and life.

Your 12th house of spirituality becomes powerful on the 23rd, so you will be making good progress in understanding these things.

Last month the planetary power shifted back to the East, from the West. Though other people are still very important to you (and you are putting others first) it is good now to think of yourself and your own needs. You have more personal power and independence, and this is getting stronger until the end of the year. It is easier to make changes to conditions and circumstances now. The only thing you need to be aware of is Jupiter's retrograde beginning on the 4th. You have the power to change conditions, but need more mental clarity before you do it.

## November

Best Days Overall: 6, 7, 14, 15, 23, 24
Most Stressful Days Overall: 1, 2, 8, 9, 21, 22, 28, 29
Best Days for Love: 1, 2, 6, 7, 11, 14, 15, 20, 23, 24, 28, 29
Best Days for Money: 1, 2, 3, 11, 12, 16, 17, 19, 21, 28, 29
Best Days for Career: 6, 7, 8, 9, 14, 15, 23, 24

Most of the planets are now in the Eastern sector and Mars entered your sign on the 7th of last month. Personal power and independence are super high now. You have abundant energy and drive. You can conquer the world. After doing the appropriate homework, you can create the conditions of your life according to your personal specifications. Though you are devoted to others you are not dependent on them. You can and should have your own way, which is the best way these days. You have the energy and the power; you just need more mental clarity. It's like you are sitting in a super-charged sports car capable of going 150 miles per hour, but you lack the road map. You have the power but lack the direction. Once you get the right direction – look out!

The only problem with Mars in your own sign is that you might be too much in a hurry. With retrograde activity temporarily increasing this month, make haste slowly. Impatience can lead to accidents or personal injury. Also you need to watch the temper. It is not anger really, but perhaps frustration that bothers you – you want things done, and when delays happen, you explode. Tone this down.

There are two eclipses this month. Only one of them has a strong effect on you – the lunar eclipse of the 28th. The solar eclipse of the 13th is mostly benign to you. This eclipse occurs in your house of spirituality, announcing major changes in your spiritual practice, ideas and ideals. If you are involved in charities or voluntary organizations, there are shake-ups here, and dramas in the lives of the gurus, spiritual mentors and the spiritual people in your life. As with the last solar eclipse of May 20, there is a crisis of faith. Belief systems and your personal philosophy get tested and refined. Students make important changes in educational plans.

The lunar eclipse occurs in your 7th house – the second eclipse to occur in this house this year. It will test marriages, partnerships and love relationships. The good ones survive and get even better; the flawed ones tend to dissolve. Like the last eclipse, it brings changes in the marital status. Singles often decide to marry under such an eclipse. Since the eclipsed planet, the Moon, is ruler of your 8th house, this eclipse can bring encounters with death, near-death kinds of experiences, surgeries and things of this nature. There is a need to understand death on a deeper level and overcome fear of it here. Relax during this period and avoid risk taking.

Eclipse periods tend to be volatile. Add to this Mars square to Uranus (between the 23rd and the 25th) and its conjunction with Pluto (from the 27th to the 30th), and you have even greater volatility. Be more careful driving. Avoid risk and confrontations (people tend to overreact under this transit) and speculations. Children and children figures also need to be more careful.

## December

Best Days Overall: 3, 4, 12, 13, 20, 21, 22, 30, 31
Most Stressful Days Overall: 5, 6, 7, 18, 19, 25, 26, 27
Best Days for Love: 1, 2, 10, 11, 20, 21, 25, 26, 27, 31
Best Days for Money: 1, 8, 10, 14, 15, 16, 18, 25, 28
Best Days for Career: 2, 5, 6, 7, 11, 21, 31

In spite of the recent eclipses, health and vitality seem very good. If there have been surgeries or injury (God forbid) your recuperative power is very strong now. Last month on the 22nd you entered another of your yearly personal pleasure peaks. The Sun crossed the Ascendant and entered your 1st house. It is there until the 21st of this month. It is interesting that your personal pleasure peak coincides with the holiday season. The holidays are more festive than usual. You are in the peak of personal power and personal independence. There is no need to rely on others or to adapt to them, at least as far as your personal happiness is concerned. You have the power to design your life as you please and should be exercising this power.

With the Sun in your 1st house you are travelling now and enjoying the good life. Sagittarians of appropriate age are much more fertile these days than usual. The personal appearance shines. You emanate both beauty and star quality and the opposite sex takes notice.

Your love planet Mercury enters your sign on the 11th and will be there for the rest of the month. Love opportunities come to you. Love is seeking you. You are more or less having your way in love. What is most beautiful here is that Jupiter (your personal planet) and Mercury are in 'mutual reception' from the 11th onwards. Thus there is wonderful co-operation between the two planets. Yes, you and the beloved are very different people and have opposite perspectives on things, but in spite of this, you are for the beloved and the beloved is for you. You are each putting each other first. You might disagree about things, but you are mutually devoted.

Finances are strong this month, especially after the 21st. As the Sun enters the money house you enter a yearly financial peak. You are having much personal pleasure and you have the wherewithal to indulge. Career opportunities are coming to you as well. You have the image of the successful person this month, especially after the 11th, and people see you this way.

Health as we mentioned is good. But you can enhance it even further through spiritual means (meditation, spiritual healing methods, the laying on of hands, reiki and the manipulation of subtle energies) until the 16th. Detox is also powerful then. After the 16th you can enhance your health by giving more attention to the liver and thighs. Though health is good you seem more focused on it than usual this month. This seems to be because of the cosmetic value of health rather than a need to deal with any pathology. When you are healthy you look good. And you want to look good.

# Capricorn

♑

---

THE GOAT

*Birthdays from
21st December to
19th January*

---

## Personality Profile

### CAPRICORN AT A GLANCE

*Element* – Earth

*Ruling Planet* – Saturn
  *Career Planet* – Venus
  *Love Planet* – Moon
  *Money Planet* – Uranus
  *Planet of Communications* – Neptune
  *Planet of Health and Work* – Mercury
  *Planet of Home and Family Life* – Mars
  *Planet of Spirituality* – Jupiter

*Colours* – black, indigo

*Colours that promote love, romance and social
  harmony* – puce, silver

*Colour that promotes earning power* –
  ultramarine blue

*Gem* – black onyx

*Metal* – lead

*Scents* – magnolia, pine, sweet pea, wintergreen

*Quality* – cardinal (= activity)

*Qualities most needed for balance* – warmth, spontaneity, a sense of fun

*Strongest virtues* – sense of duty, organization, perseverance, patience, ability to take the long-term view

*Deepest needs* – to manage, take charge and administrate

*Characteristics to avoid* – pessimism, depression, undue materialism and undue conservatism

*Signs of greatest overall compatibility* – Taurus, Virgo

*Signs of greatest overall incompatibility* – Aries, Cancer, Libra

*Sign most helpful to career* – Libra

*Sign most helpful for emotional support* – Aries

*Sign most helpful financially* – Aquarius

*Sign best for marriage and/or partnerships* – Cancer

*Sign most helpful for creative projects* – Taurus

*Best Sign to have fun with* – Taurus

*Signs most helpful in spiritual matters* – Virgo, Sagittarius

*Best day of the week* – Saturday

## Understanding a Capricorn

The virtues of Capricorns are such that there will always be people for and against them. Many admire them, many dislike them. Why? It seems to be because of Capricorn's power urges. A well-developed Capricorn has his or her eyes set on the heights of power, prestige and authority. In the sign of Capricorn, ambition is not a fatal flaw, but rather the highest virtue.

Capricorns are not frightened by the resentment their authority may sometimes breed. In Capricorn's cool, calculated, organized mind all the dangers are already factored into the equation – the unpopularity, the animosity, the misunderstandings, even the outright slander – and a plan is always in place for dealing with these things in the most efficient way. To the Capricorn, situations that would terrify an ordinary mind are merely problems to be managed, bumps on the road to ever-growing power, effectiveness and prestige.

Some people attribute pessimism to the Capricorn sign, but this is a bit deceptive. It is true that Capricorns like to take into account the negative side of things. It is also true that they love to imagine the worst possible scenario in every undertaking. Other people might find such analyses depressing, but Capricorns only do these things so that they can formulate a way out – an escape route.

Capricorns will argue with success. They will show you that you are not doing as well as you think you are. Capricorns do this to themselves as well as to others. They do not mean to discourage you but rather to root out any impediments to your greater success. A Capricorn boss or supervisor feels that no matter how good the performance there is always room for improvement. This explains why Capricorn supervisors are difficult to handle and even infuriating at times. Their actions are, however, quite often effective – they can get their subordinates to improve and become better at their jobs.

Capricorn is a born manager and administrator. Leo is better at being king or queen, but Capricorn is better at being prime minister – the person actually wielding power.

Capricorn is interested in the virtues that last, in the things that will stand the test of time and trials of circumstance. Temporary fads and fashions mean little to a Capricorn – except as things to be used for profit or power. Capricorns apply this attitude to business, love, to their thinking and even to their philosophy and religion.

**Finance**

Capricorns generally attain wealth and they usually earn it. They are willing to work long and hard for what they want. They are quite amenable to foregoing a short-term gain in favour of long-term benefits. Financially, they come into their own later in life.

However, if Capricorns are to attain their financial goals they must shed some of their strong conservatism. Perhaps this is the least desirable trait of the Capricorn. They can resist anything new merely because it is new and untried. They are afraid of experimentation. Capricorns need to be willing to take a few risks. They should be more eager to market new products or explore different managerial techniques. Otherwise, progress will leave them behind. If necessary, Capricorns must be ready to change with the times, to discard old methods that no longer work.

Very often this experimentation will mean that Capricorns have to break with existing authority. They might even consider changing their present position or starting their own ventures. If so, they should be willing to accept all the risks and just get on with it. Only then will a Capricorn be on the road to highest financial gains.

**Career and Public Image**

A Capricorn's ambition and quest for power are evident. It is perhaps the most ambitious sign of the zodiac – and usually the most successful in a worldly sense. However, there are lessons Capricorns need to learn in order to fulfil their highest aspirations.

Intelligence, hard work, cool efficiency and organization will take them a certain distance, but will not carry them to the very top. Capricorns need to cultivate their social graces, to develop a social style, along with charm and an ability to get along with people. They need to bring beauty into their lives and to cultivate the right social contacts. They must learn to wield power gracefully, so that people love them for it – a very delicate art. They also need to learn how to bring people together in order to fulfil certain objectives. In short, Capricorns require some of the gifts – the social graces – of Libra to get to the top.

Once they have learned this, Capricorns will be successful in their careers. They are ambitious hard workers who are not afraid of putting in the required time and effort. Capricorns take their time in getting the job done – in order to do it well – and they like moving up the corporate ladder slowly but surely. Being so driven by success, Capricorns are generally liked by their bosses, who respect and trust them.

**Love and Relationships**

Like Scorpio and Pisces, Capricorn is a difficult sign to get to know. They are deep, introverted and like to keep their own counsel. Capricorns do not like to reveal their innermost thoughts. If you are in love with a Capricorn, be patient and take your time. Little by little you will get to understand him or her.

Capricorns have a deep romantic nature, but they do not show it straightaway. They are cool, matter of fact and not especially emotional. They will often show their love in practical ways.

It takes time for a Capricorn – male or female – to fall in love. They are not the love-at-first-sight kind. If a Capricorn is involved with a Leo or Aries, these Fire types will be totally mystified – to them the Capricorn will seem cold, unfeeling, unaffectionate and not very spontaneous. Of course none of this is true; it is just that Capricorn likes to take things slowly. They like to be sure of their ground before making any demonstrations of love or commitment.

Even in love affairs Capricorns are deliberate. They need more time to make decisions than is true of the other signs of the zodiac, but given this time they become just as passionate. Capricorns like a relationship to be structured, committed, well regulated, well defined, predictable and even routine. They prefer partners who are nurturers, and they in turn like to nurture their partners. This is their basic psychology. Whether such a relationship is good for them is another issue altogether. Capricorns have enough routine in their lives as it is. They might be better off in relationships that are a bit more stimulating, changeable and fluctuating.

## Home and Domestic Life

The home of a Capricorn – as with a Virgo – is going to be tidy and well organized. Capricorns tend to manage their families in the same way they manage their businesses. Capricorns are often so career-driven that they find little time for the home and family. They should try to get more actively involved in their family and domestic life. Capricorns do, however, take their children very seriously and are very proud parents – particularly should their children grow up to become respected members of society.

# Horoscope for 2012

## Major Trends

Saturn, your ruling planet, has been in your 10th house of career for a number of years now, so you have been personally very ambitious and successful. You seem above everyone in your life, calling all the shots. This trend continues for most of the year ahead. On October 5, Saturn leaves your 10th house and enters the 11th, and this shows a shift of focus; career goals have been attained and now you want the fruits of your career success – good friendships.

Though you have been working hard and been very dedicated to your career, with Jupiter in your 5th house last year and until June 11 this year, you are managing to have some fun too. Enjoy this while you can. Jupiter will enter your 6th house on June 11 and again work becomes important. There are job changes in the year ahead, but it looks to me like they are good ones. More on this later.

Uranus moved into your 4th house of home and family last year. This indicates moves – perhaps a few of them – and turmoil in the family. There's more on this later too.

Pluto has been in your 1st house since 2008 and will be there for many more years to come. Thus there is a detox (long term and on various levels) going on in the body. This is a very good period to lose weight if you need to. It shows cosmetic kinds of surgeries as well.

Neptune enters your 3rd house of communication and intellect on February 3 and will stay there for the next 14 or so years. Your mind, your thinking, your taste in reading are being elevated and spiritualized. For many people the intellect is a blockage to spiritual progress, and the cosmos is now dealing with this. The mind is more intuitive now.

Your areas of greatest interest in the year ahead are the body and image; finance (until February 3); communication and intellectual interests (after February 3); home and family; children, creativity, leisure activities and personal pleasure (until June 11); health and work (from April 3 onwards); religion, philosophy, theology, foreign travel and higher education (until July 3); career (until October 5); friends, groups, group activities and organizations (from October 5 onwards).

Your paths of greatest fulfilment in the year ahead are children, creativity and personal pleasure (until June 11); health and work (after June 11); spirituality (until August 31); friends, groups, group activities and organizations (from August 31 onwards).

## Health

*(Please note that this is an* astrological *perspective on health and not a medical one. In days of yore these perspectives were identical. But these days there could be quite a difference. For a medical perspective, please consult your doctor or health practitioner.)*

You have three long-term planets in stressful aspect to you, Capricorn, so health needs watching. The good news is that this is an improvement over last year when there were four long-term planets stressing you. Further, as the year goes on, the health stresses will ease: Saturn will move away from its stressful aspect on October 5.

In the meantime, you need to pay more attention here. Your 6th house of health is strong from April 3 onwards, so you are paying attention. But you need to focus here from the beginning of the year. The first four months of the year are crucial. Force yourself to focus on health even when you don't feel like it. The danger is that you will ignore things until it is too late, until something major happens.

You have (as do all the signs) many areas of interest this year. But with your energy not up to its usual standards perhaps you need to narrow down your interests. Stick to the really important ones. The danger is that you will disperse your energies in too many directions.

If you got through last year, you will get through this one too. Still, there is much you can do to improve and enhance your health and energy. Pay more attention to the following

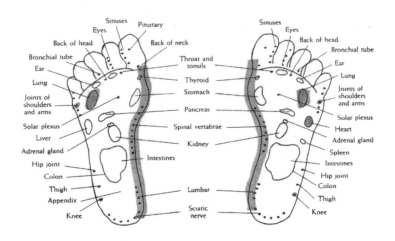

## Reflexology

*Try to massage the whole foot on a regular basis, but pay extra attention to the points highlighted on the chart. When you massage, be aware of 'sore spots', as these need special attention. It's also a good idea to massage the ankles and top side of the feet (see below).*

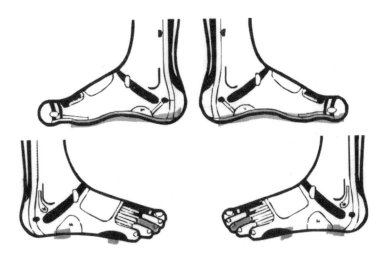

organs: the heart (avoid worry and anxiety – if there is
something positive that can be done in a given situation by
all means do it, but eliminate the worry as it doesn't help
you and puts stress on the heart); the spine, knees, teeth,
bones, skin and overall skeletal alignment (regular back
massage, visits to a chiropractor or osteopath, will be very
good, and give the knees more support when exercising);
the lungs, small intestine, arms, shoulders and respiratory
system (arms and shoulders should be regularly massaged);
the liver and thighs (from June 11 onwards; thighs should
be regularly massaged).

With a few timely steps most problems can be prevented.
And even if they can't be totally prevented, they can be lessened to a huge extent. Something that should be devastating
becomes a minor inconvenience.

The most important thing is maintaining high energy
levels. Rest when tired. Don't be ashamed to take a nap
when you feel tired. Work with a rhythm and alternate
different activities. Delegate and outsource wherever possible.

With Pluto in your own sign, detox regimes are good and
you respond well to them. Perhaps you are too quick these
days to jump into surgery. It may or may not be called for,
but get a second opinion.

There are many short-term trends in health and these are
best covered in the monthly reports. Your health planet
Venus moves quickly and month to month your health
needs change.

## Home and Family

As we mentioned earlier, your 4th house is now a 'house of
power' for the next six years or so. This becomes a very
important and tumultuous area of life, and will be very challenging.

Uranus in the 4th house indicates many, many things,
and over the next six years all of them are varied. First off, it
shows moves, perhaps multiple moves. Sometimes people

don't actually sell up and move but they live in different places for long periods of time and it is as if they have moved. Sometimes they buy second or third homes and shuttle back and forth between them. There is a need for change in the home, constant change. No sooner do you find your dream home or dream dwelling when you discover a new and better one and so you move there. When you move to the new and better one you find another new and better home and so you want to move there. This goes on and on and on.

Often the urge to move, the urge to change, manifests as a constant upgrading of the home. You redecorate, are satisfied for a time, and then see a better way to decorate and go through the process again. The home is upgraded much in the same way that you upgrade your software or computer.

You are also installing new high-tech gadgetry in the home. The home will have all the latest and the best equipment. You seem to be spending a lot of money here these days.

You are more experimental in the home and in the way you conduct your domestic life. You are throwing out all the old rule books (you are probably fed up with the 'how-to's) and learning what works for you and your family through trial and error.

Uranus in the 4th house often indicates break-ups in the family unit. This doesn't need to happen (it is only a tendency) but holding the family unit together, maintaining harmony will be quite a challenge.

Family is nature's survival mechanism. It is very important. But sometimes the bonds of family are excessive and unreasonable. In those cases (and it is always a case by case judgement) a break-up of the family unit is a form of liberation. The soul is free to follow the true life purpose.

Emotionally this transit is very stressful. It shows that feelings and moods (both personally and with family members) are volatile, extreme and unpredictable. There are sudden and inexplicable mood swings and shifts. Some of you will benefit from medication. This will not cure the problem but will calm the symptoms and in this respect it is good. However prayer and meditation – spiritual therapies – will effect a cure although they take longer and require more effort and commitment.

It may seem as if you don't know where you stand with family members (and especially parent figures) from moment to moment. A parent or parent figure (in the case of a woman, this shows the father, in the case of a man, it is the mother) is having many personal dramas in the year ahead. He or she wants to explore personal freedom and change and seems fed up with obligations and responsibilities. He or she is very restless and is probably more nomadic in the year ahead. He or she could be having surgery as well.

## Finance and Career

It looks like a stormy but exciting financial year ahead. Your financial planet Uranus spends the year ahead in square aspect with Pluto. Thus there are many, many changes happening. A cosmic detox is happening in the financial life. Impurities there (poverty in thinking, lack, wrong planning and strategies) are being brought to the surface so that you can correct them. While they are hidden, there's not much you can do about them. So the surfacing of these things are not really challenges (though it seems that way) but the beginning of the cure. It is the kind of year where you face many a 'near-death' financial experience, or encounters with ruin (or what you believe is ruin). These need not actually happen, but you are confronting the fear and the possibility of these things. This too is part of the detox.

You seem in financial conflict with friends. Friends don't seem as supportive as they once were. Friends seem devoted to you (and this is curious) but not financially supportive. Perhaps you are called on to help them and this is a stress. You need to be careful of too much debt, and too much of the wrong kind of debt.

You are spending on the home as we mentioned, and spending on the family. You can also earn from them too.

You have the aspects of someone who earns from the family business or from family connections. Probably you will work more from home. Real estate investments seem very attractive too. Start ups seem very attractive this year. And many of you will be starting your own business now. The financial planet in the 4th house shows earnings and earning opportunities from the food business, restaurants, hotels, home improvement and industries that cater to the home. Uranus also indicates high-tech industries, computers, software, new inventions and companies that are involved with these things.

Earnings seem more volatile than usual in the year ahead. The highs are very high, but the lows are extreme as well. Smoothing out earnings will be a major challenge.

Last year you didn't seem too comfortable with the way you were earning. Probably you weren't enjoying it; perhaps you felt it was 'beneath' you. But this year that has passed. You seem much more personally comfortable with the way you earn.

Capricorns are generally not financial risk takers. They are conservative. But ever since your financial planet moved into Aries last year you seem much more speculative. In life, risks are unavoidable; even the safest investments carry some form of risk. The issue is one of degree. These days you are taking on higher degrees of risk. The secret agenda here is to learn to overcome financial fear and to develop more courage.

Though finances are volatile, your career – your status professionally and in your industry – is very good. If you work for others there should have been promotions in the past two years and more are likely this year. If you are in your own business, the business seems elevated in stature. If it hasn't happened yet, it is still likely to happen in the year ahead.

## Love and Social Life

Your 7th house of love and marriage is not a 'house of power' this year. Thus the year ahead maintains more or less the status quo. Marrieds will tend to stay married; singles will tend to stay single. Your empty 7th house (only the Moon moves through there for a few days every month, and the short-term planets move through there temporarily) gives you much freedom and latitude in this area. Those who really desire to marry will have more freedom to do it, but usually the desire for change or marriage is much less under this aspect.

The Moon is your love planet and is the fastest of all the planets. Where Mercury or Venus will move through the whole zodiac in a year, the Moon does so every month. So there are many short-term trends in love that are best dealt with in the monthly reports. In general though, your enthusiasm for social activities – and your personal social magnetism – will be stronger when the Moon waxes than when she wanes. Thus you can schedule your social life accordingly.

While marriage doesn't seem likely, there is still much dating and love affairs for singles. Jupiter has been in your 5th house since June of 2011 and will be there until June 11 this year. So there is love in your life, but probably not serious love. More like entertainment. Probably most of you prefer it that way.

Those in their second or third marriages are having their marriages tested this year. The second marriage seems stormy, but can survive. The third marriage will need a miracle to survive (although miracles do happen). If the fourth marriage survived last year, it will probably survive the year ahead, but it is not a smooth ride.

Parents are having their marriages tested too. They need to give each other a lot of space, a lot of freedom. Siblings and sibling figures have storms in their marriages, but they seem survivable. If they get past July 3, their relationships can survive further. Children of marriageable age are better off not marrying this year. If they are already married the marriage is very stormy and its survival is in question. Grandchildren of appropriate age have love in the life, but more homework needs to be done before they marry. There are many secret things in the relationship that need to come out.

### Self-improvement

Discord in the feeling body is the number one reason that prayers are not answered or delayed, according to the sages. If your spiritual practice doesn't seem to be working, you need to explore this area. The problem is not with the Divine (it always stands ready to help) but with the discord in the emotional life, which is blocking the answers and the help.

The emotional life, as we mentioned, is unusually volatile. Your job is to bring it under control through positive direction. Your goal should be 'peace and harmony' in the feeling nature. This is a complex subject, but this year you need this peace and harmony more than ever.

Your spiritual planet spends the first part of the year in your 5th house. Thus you are receiving many creative, artistic or musical ideas in the year ahead. Your personal creativity is unusually strong this year and you should give it expression. Getting into a good creative flow is a cure for depression, but also one of the most enjoyable, euphoric experiences a person can have.

Neptune, as we mentioned, will be in your 3rd house of communication for many years to come. Your intellect is getting refined and spiritualized. You will be better able to communicate your spiritual ideas and ideals. Rather than being an impediment to you, the intellect will now become part of your spiritual journey, an ally and friend.

Your spiritual planet, Jupiter, will move into your 6th house of health on June 11. Thus, this is a period for exploring the spiritual dimensions of healing. This too is a huge subject, but very interesting and you should read as much as you can on this subject. You will start to get good practical results from spiritual healing techniques after June 11. You respond very well to these things.

When Saturn, your ruling planet, moves into your 11th house on October 5, you will start to have a greater appreciation and understanding of astrology, science, astronomy and technology. Your knowledge in these fields will start to expand.


# Month-by-month Forecasts

## January

> Best Days Overall: 3, 4, 12, 13, 21, 22, 30, 31
> Most Stressful Days Overall: 1, 2, 8, 9, 14, 15, 28, 29
> Best Days for Love: 3, 4, 6, 7, 8, 9, 12, 13, 18, 19, 23, 24, 27, 28
> Best Days for Money: 1, 3, 4, 10, 12, 19, 21, 23, 24, 28, 30
> Best Days for Career: 6, 7, 14, 15, 18, 19, 27, 28

Last month the planetary power shifted to the lower half of your Horoscope. The planetary power is now below the horizon of your chart and you are in the night time of your personal year. This situation is in effect until late June. Though the activities of night, which tend to happen on the inner, invisible levels, are not very much valued in our culture, they are nevertheless important. This is when the forces are built up for the next day. The body and mind rest, repair, and recreate themselves. The activities of the day are born in the night. Career success is happening now, but on the invisible levels; you are getting yourself ready for the next cycle of outward success. It is important now to set up the right conditions for your career, to get the family, domestic and emotional life in order. When this is done, you will have a solid foundation for future career growth.

Most of the planets are in the Eastern sector of the self. In fact this month they are in their maximum Eastern position. It means that the short-term planets are 'closest' to you and cosmic energy flows towards you, not away from you. You have maximum personal power and independence. You are a self-rolling wheel these days, a being of 'cause' not of 'effect'. You make things happen rather than respond to things. Since your personal power is strong now, you can more easily create conditions as you like them. The world adapts itself to you rather than vice versa. Build your life as you desire it to be. You are in a period of 'making karma'.

Since the 21st of last month, you are in a yearly personal pleasure peak. This is a time for enjoying all the carnal delights, and for getting the body and image in right shape.

On the 20th, as the Sun enters your money house, you enter a yearly financial peak. You have the resources for personal pleasure and for getting into emotional harmony. On the 8th Mercury crosses your Ascendant and enters the 1st house, which is a very nice aspect for job seekers. Job opportunities come to you. There's no need to scour the wanted ads or pound the pavements, jobs will find you. Travel opportunities are also coming to you.

Health is good this month and you can enhance it further in the ways mentioned in the yearly report. You are more focused on health this month (especially from the 8th to the 27th) but it seems to be from a cosmetic kind of perspective. Good health enhances your appearance. So a health regime and right diet is seen as another cosmetic. The good news here is that your interest is not because of any pathology.

Love is status quo this month. You will tend to have more energy and enthusiasm for social matters as the Moon waxes from the 1st to the 9th and from the 23rd onwards. Social magnetism is strongest then. You can adjust your schedule accordingly.

**February**

Best Days Overall: 1, 9, 10, 17, 18, 27, 28
Most Stressful Days Overall: 4, 5, 11, 12, 24, 25
Best Days for Love: 2, 3, 4, 5, 6, 11, 12, 15, 21, 22, 24, 25
Best Days for Money: 1, 7, 9, 15, 17, 19, 20, 24, 27, 28
Best Days for Career: 5, 6, 11, 12, 15, 24, 25

Home, family and emotional issues are an important focus this month. The only problem now is that your family planet, Mars, is retrograde (it went retrograde on January 24). There is a lack of clarity and direction here. Many issues will need time to resolve. By all means give attention to the family but avoid making major decisions now, unless you have researched them thoroughly.

You are still in the midst of a yearly financial peak until the 19th. Money is earned through work, communications, sales, marketing, PR and also through creative kinds of financing. It is easy to borrow now. Outside money is easily accessed. Your spouse, partner or current love is supportive financially. This is a good month to expand by cutting back, by cutting waste in the financial life. A good detox of the financial life is in order. When you get rid of the waste, lo and behold, you discover that you have enough resources for every need. Your career planet travels with your financial planet from the 8th to the 10th. This brings luck in speculations – happy money – money that is earned in happy, fun kinds of ways. It also brings the financial favour of bosses, parents or parent figures – pay rises could also happen.

Your 3rd house of communication becomes very powerful this month. Neptune moves in for the long term on the 3rd, and half the planets are either in this house or moving through here this month. So this is a time to launch that advertising campaign, mass mailings or other marketing projects.

Students are more successful in their studies. Learning comes easily and is more enjoyable, and it is a good month to take courses in subjects that interest you and to expand your knowledge base. If you are a trader, you are more active in the month ahead.

Though siblings or sibling figures in your life are having marriage and relationship problems (this will take time to sort out), they are having a good month. Health seems good. There is self-confidence and self-esteem. And they seem to be enjoying their lives. Their finances are good, but in need of review.

Your health is still good. You can enhance it further by giving more attention to the ankles and calves (massage them regularly) until the 14th and to the feet (also massage them) afterwards. Spiritual healing methods are especially powerful for you after the 14th. Mercury travels with Neptune from the 13th to the 15th and the Sun travels with Neptune from the 18th to the 21st. Avoid elective kinds of surgeries then.

Saturn, the ruler of your Horoscope, goes retrograde on the 7th. Personal goals and issues involving the body, image and personal appearance are under review for the next few months. Many of you are contemplating cosmetic surgery these days. Do more homework now.

### March

Best Days Overall: 7, 8, 15, 16, 25, 26
Most Stressful Days Overall: 3, 4, 9, 10, 22, 23, 24, 30, 31
Best Days for Love: 3, 4, 7, 11, 12, 15, 16, 22, 23, 25, 26, 30, 31
Best Days for Money: 5, 7, 13, 15, 16, 18, 19, 22, 25, 26
Best Days for Career: 7, 9, 10, 15, 16, 25, 26

The planets make an important shift this month from the independent Eastern to the social Western sector. This happens on the 20th, but you will probably feel this even before then. Your personal power and independence are being reduced. It is more difficult (though it can be done) to create conditions to suit you now. Better to adapt to conditions as best you can. Now is the time where you live with your creations of the past six months. If you created well, life is good. If not, you are 'paying the karma' now. This will lead to better creations down the road, when the Eastern sector gets powerful again. With Saturn retrograde now, personal confidence is a bit weaker. This is perhaps a good thing. Let others have their way provided it isn't destructive or in violation of your moral principles.

Your career has been successful for some years now, but now you are in a lull – your 4th house of home and family is where the focus is this month. It's been that way since the beginning of the year, but now more so than ever. This is a month for psychological progress and psychological break-throughs and insights. These insights enable to you to rede-fine your past, to rewrite (from a higher level) your personal history. There is a greater interest in the past this month, both the collective past and your personal past. This is a time where you enjoy reading history or watching historical films or TV shows.

Though career is in a lull, there are happy opportunities from the 11th to the 14th. There is also spiritual guidance available for the career then, either through dreams or through psychics, ministers, gurus or spiritual channels.

Those on the spiritual path will have revelations of their past incarnations. Sometimes this happens through sponta-neous dreams (which are really past memories being played back) or through past life regression. With Mars still retro-grade these revelations need verification. Don't be too quick to jump to conclusions.

Health needs your attention after the 20th. Enhance the health by maintaining high energy levels and by head and scalp massage (from the 2nd to the 24th), and by foot massage after the 24th. Many planets are in stressful align-ment with you after the 20th, so pay attention here. Be aware of the messages that the body is sending you. If you are working out and feel a pain, stop and rest. If you feel very fatigued, likewise stop and rest. Many of you will be tempted to make important changes to the health regime this month, but with your health planet retrograde from the 11th onwards, it's best to avoid this. Do more homework instead.

**April**

Best Days Overall: 4, 12, 13, 21, 22
Most Stressful Days Overall: 6, 19, 20, 26, 27
Best Days for Love: 1, 2, 5, 10, 11, 14, 15, 20, 21, 24, 25, 26, 27
Best Days for Money: 1, 4, 9, 10, 12, 13, 14, 15, 18, 19, 21, 22, 29
Best Days for Career: 5, 6, 14, 15, 24, 25

Finances were good last month, especially the latter part of the month. They are reasonably good this month as well. There has been good financial co-operation with your spouse, partner or current love this past month and it is still good in the month ahead. Mercury will travel with your financial planet from the 22nd to the 24th and this brings good financial ideas and information to you. Job seekers have work opportunities. There are financial opportunities in foreign lands, with foreign companies and with foreigners in general. After the 20th there is luck in speculations and the spouse or current love seems prosperous and generous.

Continue to watch the health until the 20th. Review our discussion of this last month. The main thing is to keep your energy as high as possible. With your health planet still retrograde until the 4th (it began on March 12) medical assessments of your condition might not be accurate or will need verification. They are not written in stone and are subject to change when Mercury starts to move forward on the 4th. Spiritual healing techniques (and foot massage) are powerful until the 17th. Afterwards head, face and scalp massage are powerful. Physical exercise and good muscle tone are important after the 17th too. States of fear and anger should be avoided as much as possible as these stress the adrenals, which are more vulnerable after the 17th. Good emotional health and family harmony are important after the 17th.

Your health will improve dramatically after the 20th. The good news about all this health drama is that it seems to bring more clarity to the family and emotional life. The family situation is still highly unstable, but at least there is more clarity now. After the 11th as Mars starts moving forward, you can start implementing plans for the home and family. Decisions are likely to be better.

After the 20th, as the Sun enters your 5th house you enter another yearly personal pleasure peak. Joy itself is a great healing force and happily it is available to all – one just needs to be open to it, and during this period you are. Capricorns are very 'duty' oriented. Life is a serious business to them. But there is a season for everything, and this is a season for being less serious and for having fun. Serious, serious, serious – duty, duty, duty – all the time is not good. Take a holiday from this now. Don't worry; you will pick up your responsibilities later on.

Love is status quo this month, but social magnetism will be strongest from the 1st to the 6th and from the 21st to the 30th, as the Moon waxes.

## May

Best Days Overall: 1, 2, 9, 10, 18, 19, 20, 28, 29
Most Stressful Days Overall: 3, 4, 16, 17, 23, 24, 25, 30, 31
Best Days for Love: 1, 2, 3, 4, 9, 10, 11, 12, 20, 21, 22, 23, 24, 25, 30, 31
Best Days for Money: 2, 7, 10, 11, 12, 16, 19, 20, 26, 29
Best Days for Career: 3, 4, 11, 12, 21, 22, 30, 31

Though you need to watch your health all year, this is one of your better months. Health and overall vitality are good. Your ability to enjoy life and to be more involved in leisure activities is helping the health as well. You can enhance the health further by giving more attention to the head, face, scalp and adrenals until the 9th and to the neck and throat afterwards. Tension tends to collect in that region and should be massaged out. Vigorous physical exercise is still good until the 9th, afterwards a creative hobby would be therapeutic. The kidneys and hips are also important until August; make sure you massage the hips regularly (feel for sore spots and massage them out).

You are very focused on health this month, especially after the 20th. This is good. Extra focus now will help you get through next month when health once again becomes more stressful.

Job seekers seems successful this month; those who employ others likewise. Until the 9th job seekers have opportunities through the family and family connections. From the 9th to the 24th, job opportunities come as you are having fun at leisure activities. (You can also find work at these kinds of places too.)

A solar eclipse on the 20th affects you strongly, so reduce your schedule a bit. The Sun is the ruler of your 8th house so solar eclipses tend to be dramatic in your chart. There can be encounters with death (generally on the psychological level), near-death experiences, surgeries and things of this nature. Near-death kinds of experiences don't always have to be dramatic. The cosmic intent is not to kill you but to deliver a message: life here on earth is short and can end at any time; time to get on with the serious business of life, the purposes for which you were born.

The eclipse occurs right on the cusp of your 6th house so there are job changes afoot. The conditions at the place of work are changing dramatically. If you employ others, there is employee turnover. There can be health scares and important changes in the health regime as well. Your spouse, partner or current love is making dramatic financial changes now (and for the next six months); children likewise. Neptune, your communication planet, is very affected by this eclipse, thus communication equipment will get tested and much of it might need replacement.

If you are involved with estates, insurance claims or tax issues there is good fortune from the 11th to the 14th. There is more sexual activity that period too (each according to their age and stage in life).

Speculations have been favourable for you so far this year, but avoid this from the 15th onwards as Venus makes one of her rare retrograde moves. Career opportunities will also need much more study as well. They can be good, but get more facts – don't leap without looking.

## June

Best Days Overall: 5, 6, 15, 16, 24, 25
Most Stressful Days Overall: 12, 13, 20, 21, 27, 28
Best Days for Love: 8, 9, 17, 18, 19, 20, 21, 27, 28, 29, 30
Best Days for Money: 3, 5, 6, 8, 9, 12, 17, 22, 26, 27
Best Days for Career: 8, 9, 17, 18, 27, 28

There is a lunar eclipse on the 4th that occurs in your 12th house of spirituality. It is basically benign for you but you will be feeling the effects of this for months to come. There are important (and probably dramatic) changes in your spiritual regime and practice. Those not on a spiritual path can start to embark on one. Those already on it can change their path, their teachers and teachings. People often convert from one religion to another under this kind of eclipse. There are shake-ups and upheavals in charitable or spiritual organizations that you are involved with. Sometimes this eclipse brings scandals or unpleasant revelations. Most importantly it tests love – the marriage, business partnerships, or a current love relationship. Friendships of the heart get tested. Often it is not the relationship itself that is the problem but dramas in the personal lives of friends, the spouse, partner or current love. Good relationships survive these things and even get better. The shaky ones, the ones that are inherently flawed, are the ones that don't survive.

The changes in your spiritual life are seen in other ways too. Jupiter, your spiritual planet, will be re-activating last month's solar eclipse all month.

Last month's eclipse announced job changes, and now Jupiter moving into your 6th house shows the reason for this – only the best will do for you. If your job situation was not up to standard, it dissolved. Now, new and better job opportunities are coming. Losing a job is considered bad, but if it happens now, it is luck in disguise.

Jupiter's move into your 6th house also shows changes in the health regime. First off, from now until the end of the year (and well into 2013) the liver and thighs need more attention. Regular thigh massage will be powerful for you. Also it indicates that you will respond very well to spiritual healing techniques, prayer, meditation, energy medicine, the manipulation of subtle energies, laying on hands, etc. You will be going deeper into the spiritual dimensions of health and healing both for yourself and for others.

Children in your life will be very prosperous nowadays. (They do need to be careful not to abuse debt.) Parents or parent figures are getting new cars and communication equipment over the next six months.

From the 21st onwards, health becomes more delicate. But now you have the tools – the spiritual tools – to deal with things. Rest and relax more and stay 'prayed up'.

On the 21st you enter a yearly love and social peak. Singles are more likely to find a special someone now. Singles are dating more. Married people are attending more social functions. Your spouse, partner or current love enters a yearly financial peak as well. There are financial windfalls coming to them.

**July**

Best Days Overall: 3, 4, 12, 13, 22, 23, 30, 31
Most Stressful Days Overall: 9, 10, 11, 17, 18, 24, 25
Best Days for Love: 5, 6, 7, 8, 15, 17, 18, 19, 24, 25, 28
Best Days for Money: 1, 5, 6, 9, 15, 16, 19, 20, 24, 25, 28
Best Days for Career: 5, 6, 15, 24, 25, 26

Health still needs watching until the 22nd. Continue to enhance the health in the ways described last month. Your interest in spiritual healing will give you new tools to deal with health issues. Perhaps the most important one is the ability to charge the body with energy and vitality. This is something you need right now. If you are making important changes to the health regime or diet, or buying expensive health equipment, try to do it before the 15th when Mercury is still moving forward. After that, it's best to delay these kinds of things. When Mercury is retrograde after the 15th health information, even diagnoses, are not very reliable. Take them with a few grains of salt. They are subject to change.

The planets are starting to shift from the lower half of your Horoscope to the upper half. Dawn is breaking in your year. Time to be up and about and focused on your outer, career objectives. The shift is not yet complete but you are feeling it now. Mars crosses the Mid-heaven and enters your 10th house of career on the 4th and spends the rest of the month here. Career is active and hectic; it needs your attention. There are competitors who want your position and you must fend them off. There are competitors in your industry that need dealing with as well. Mars also happens to be your family planet. So family is also important. You are trying to merge a successful career with a happy and harmonious home life. Family members, especially a parent or parent figure, are ambitious now and seem successful in their careers. They seem supportive of your career goals as well.

You are still in a yearly love and social peak until the 22nd. You have had stronger peaks in previous years (and next year's peak will be stronger than this one) but this is the peak for the year. The marriage of the parents or parent figures in your life is stressful this month and getting tested. One of them is trying very hard to keep things together, but it might not be enough.

Finances are reasonable this month. The financial planet receives very nice aspects after the 22nd and earnings will increase. Speculations will become more favourable. But before this happens there are some bumps in the road. Mars makes dynamic aspects with Uranus and Pluto from the 15th to the 21st. This can bring unexpected expenses or financial hits, perhaps because of family or issues involving friends. It could happen because of computer breakdowns or glitches as well. Family members need to be more careful driving and should avoid risky types of activities. The home needs to be made safer during this period as well.

### August

Best Days Overall: 8, 9, 10, 18, 19, 27, 28
Most Stressful Days Overall: 6, 7, 13, 14, 15, 20, 21
Best Days for Love: 2, 3, 6, 7, 13, 14, 15, 17, 18, 22, 23, 27, 31
Best Days for Money: 1, 2, 6, 11, 12, 16, 20, 21, 24, 29, 30
Best Days for Career: 2, 3, 13, 14, 20, 21, 22, 23, 31

On the 8th, as Venus shifts to the upper half of the Horoscope, the upper half becomes stronger than the lower half (both in quantity and quality). Though you are not likely to downplay family issues, the focus should be more on the career. With Mars still in your career house your family life and career tend to co-operate with each other. It is not an 'either or' kind of situation. You can handle both.

Though your yearly love and social peak ended last month, Venus' move into your 7th house of love on the 8th is still good for romance. You are in a more romantic mood and that makes all the difference in the world. The love that happens this month seems more of the 'fun and games' variety rather than serious, committed love. Still, love seems happy. You are enjoying your relationships this month, scheduling fun kinds of activities with friends, your spouse, partner or current love.

Speculations are basically favourable this month but avoid them from the 14th to the 17th. Your partner or current love has had a few solid months of prosperity. He or she is still in a yearly financial peak until the 23rd. There are some financial shake-ups from the 21st to the 24th as their financial planet re-activates an eclipse point. Changes that perhaps should have been made earlier are now made. Children in your life are in a period of great prosperity. From the 14th to the 17th there is some conflict either with the government or with bosses.

Be more careful driving from the 21st to the 24th. Cars and communication equipment can be temperamental that period. Siblings and sibling figures need to avoid risky activities then.

Health is much improved this month. Your health planet starts to move forward on the 8th so there is more clarity here. Enhance the health in the ways described in the yearly report. The heart and circulation need special attention now. Detox regimes are also powerful, and in many cases they can replace surgery.

Job seekers still have great aspects. Charities or non-profit organizations are interesting places to work, and often they have leads for other kinds of jobs.

## September

Best Days Overall: 5, 6, 14, 15, 23, 24
Most Stressful Days Overall: 2, 3, 10, 11, 16, 17, 29, 30
Best Days for Love: 1, 5, 6, 10, 11, 12, 14, 15, 21, 22, 25, 29, 30
Best Days for Money: 2, 7, 8, 12, 16, 17, 20, 21, 25, 26, 29
Best Days for Career: 1, 12, 16, 17, 21, 22, 29, 30

Uranus, your financial planet, went retrograde on July 13 and will be retrograde until December. This will not stop earnings, but will slow things down a bit. It is the pause that refreshes. Your finances are now under review. There are areas that can be improved and this is the time to find them and make plans for improvement. Normally your financial judgement is astute – no-one is better at this than Capricorn (perhaps Taurus can give you a run for your money) – but now it is not up to its usual standard. This is the time to prepare for the next financial expansion that will begin in December. There is nothing wrong with you. You are merely experiencing the natural rhythms of life. When slow downs are used properly, the expansions are healthier.

Ever since your financial planet moved into Aries last year, you have been kind of rash (by your standards) and taking risks in finance. But now is not the time for this.

In July and August the planets were at their maximum retrograde activity for the year. This too contributed to some of the slow down. The pace of life in general slows down. This month retrograde activity temporarily lessens, but finances are still under review.

Your spouse, partner or current love faces some financial challenges from the 28th to the 30th and should avoid financial risk taking. You and he or she are not in financial agreement this period. Computers and high-tech equipment seem more temperamental now too, and might need replacement. Friends need to avoid risky activities and you should take a nice, easy and relaxed schedule.

Your 9th house became strong last month and is still strong until the 23rd. Thus you are travelling (or have wonderful opportunities to do so). Students do well in their studies. There are religious, philosophical and theological breakthroughs happening too. This is a period where the 'mental horizons' are expanded. And when this happens every other department of life improves as well.

On the 23rd, the Sun crosses the Mid-heaven and enters your 10th house. You begin a yearly career peak. Though there might be delays in financial affairs, the career is moving forward at a good clip. Push forward boldly here. You have a lot of support.

## October

Best Days Overall: 2, 3, 12, 13, 20, 21, 29, 30, 31
Most Stressful Days Overall: 1, 7, 8, 14, 15, 27, 28
Best Days for Love: 1, 4, 5, 7, 8, 12, 14, 15, 21, 24
Best Days for Money: 4, 5, 6, 9, 14, 15, 18, 22, 23, 27
Best Days for Career: 1, 12, 14, 15, 21

Health needs watching this month. However, you have come through the worst. Health should start to improve on a long-term basis from the 23rd onwards. In the meantime keep in mind our previous discussions. You can enhance the health by giving more attention to the kidneys and hips (until the 5th), to the colon, bladder and sexual organs (from the 5th to the 29th) and to the liver and thighs (after the 29th). Until the 5th try to maintain love and career harmony; after the 5th detoxing is powerful. Safe sex and sexual moderation also become more important. After the 29th, spiritual healing (important ever since June) becomes even more important.

Saturn, the ruler of your Horoscope and the most important planet in your chart makes a major move out of Libra and into Scorpio – out of your 10th house and into the 11th – on the 5th. This shows a major change of focus for the long term. You are still in a yearly career peak (a peak career year). But career goals have likely been attained (or at least you have made good progress towards them), and now it is time to get more involved in social issues – more involved with groups, organizations and networking.

The fruits of career success are social, the kind of friends and contacts you make at the top. Career success leads to the attainment of 'fondest hopes and wishes' and this is what is happening for you over the next few years. You seem very good at the social level now. Pluto, the ruler of your 11th house of friends, has been in your own sign for some years now. And now Saturn is in the 11th house the two planets are now in 'mutual reception'. There is wonderful co-operation happening here, and thus success. You could be named to head a group or organization now, or to be in some powerful position. You seem perfect for this.

Your technological expertise expands this month and for many years to come. You are more innovative and inventive now. This is a sea change for you. Normally you are a conservative kind of person, a traditionalist. Not any more.

This new embracing of change and innovation is having very good effects on your health. Part of your health problems arose from resisting change. Now you are flowing with it.

You are still feeling the effects of the last two eclipses. Jupiter is re-activating the lunar eclipse of June 4 all month. Thus there are important changes still happening in your spiritual life. Mars re-stimulates the solar eclipse point of May 20 from the 6th to the 10th. There are family crises. Family members need to avoid risky kinds of activities. There are dramas with parents and parent figures. Make sure there are no health hazards in the home. Mercury re-activates this point from the 28th to the 31st. Be more careful driving and avoid foreign travel if possible. There are job changes or instability with your employees.

**November**

Best Days Overall: 8, 9, 16, 17, 26, 27
Most Stressful Days Overall: 3, 4, 5, 10, 11, 23, 24
Best Days for Love: 1, 3, 4, 5, 11, 13, 20, 23
Best Days for Money: 1, 2, 6, 11, 14, 18, 19, 23, 28, 29
Best Days for Career: 1, 10, 11, 20

Though your health and vitality are much improved, the month ahead seems volatile, turbulent and bumpy. Two eclipses this month practically guarantee this. But Mars (not a power to be trifled with) also makes dynamic aspects at the end of the month.

In September the planetary power began to shift from the West (the social sector) to the East. Last month, on the 28th, Venus also moved from the West to the East and the Eastern sector is now very much dominant. Once again you enter a period of enhanced personal power and independence. For the past six or so months you had to adjust and adapt to existing conditions, but now with the planetary power moving in your direction, you have the power to make conditions to suit you. This shouldn't create fear in you, only give you some pause. You have the power to create, but you are held responsible for the nature and quality of your creation. So create wisely, happily and well. Whereas for the past six or so months, your good came through the good graces of others, now you can create your own good. Personal initiative – personal ability – matters now.

The solar eclipse of the 13th occurs in your 11th house (which has been powerful and prominent anyway). Thus there are dramas in the lives of your friends and major shake-ups and upheavals in trade or professional organizations that you belong to. Your high-tech equipment – computers, software and gadgets – are more temperamental and will get tested. Some of it will need replacement. (Your equipment will probably be temperamental a couple of weeks before the eclipse, and when this starts to happen you will know that you are in your eclipse period and can start to slow down.)

As we mentioned earlier, in your chart solar eclipses tend to be dramatic. The Sun rules your 8th house. The Angel of Death comes visiting. He is not after you *per se*, but lets you know that he is around. It is time to be more serious about life, and to get on with the really important things of life.

The spouse, partner or current love is forced to make important financial changes, probably because of some crisis.

The lunar eclipse of the 28th occurs in your 12th house of spirituality, announcing even more spiritual changes coming up. This has been an area of ferment for some months. Many changes have already been made, but more are in store. If you made the appropriate changes this eclipse will have little impact, it will merely test these changes. Every lunar eclipse tests the love life and friendships and this one is no different. You go through this twice every year, so it is not the end of your relationship necessarily; it gets put into a 'crisis' so that flaws can be corrected.

Mars squares Uranus from the 23rd to the 25th and conjuncts Pluto from the 27th to the 30th. There are family crises to deal with and more dramas in the lives of friends. Do your best to make the home safer. Family members and friends need to avoid risky kinds of activities. If you read the newspapers this period, you will see how dynamic this transit is.

## December

Best Days Overall: 5, 6, 7, 14, 15, 23, 24
Most Stressful Days Overall: 1, 2, 8, 9, 20, 21, 22, 28, 29
Best Days for Love: 1, 2, 3, 10, 11, 13, 20, 22, 28, 29, 31
Best Days for Money: 3, 8, 12, 16, 17, 20, 25, 30
Best Days for Career: 1, 8, 9, 10, 11, 20, 31

Most of the planets are in the East and Mars entered your sign on the 17th of last month. Mars is in your sign until the 26th. This is a period of maximum personal power and independence; review our discussion of this last month. You make rapid progress towards your goals. You achieve much very quickly. You are personally more dynamic and charismatic. You excel at sports and exercise. The only problem here is 'too much of a good thing'. You can be in too much in a hurry and this can lead to accidents or injury. You could, unconsciously, be appearing too combative to others and this can lead to conflict and argument. You could be seen as a bully if you are not careful. Still, this is a period where you get your way in life.

Your 12th house is very powerful this month (as it was last month). So this is a very spiritual kind of month; a month where much interior growth is happening. For those on the spiritual path, there are breakthroughs in understanding. For those not on the path, there are 'weird coincidences' that can't be explained rationally and a hyper-active dream life. Sometimes these events are not fully understood until years later, but keep them in your mental filing cabinet.

For those on the spiritual path this is a period for more meditation and spiritual practice. For those not on the path this is time for being more involved with charity work, non-profit organizations and altruistic causes. There is much satisfaction in these things now.

You are all having breakthroughs in spiritual healing this month, especially after the 11th. Mercury, your health planet, is in 'mutual reception' with Jupiter, your spiritual planet. Each is a guest in the house of the other. Thus each is co-operating with the other. Spiritual healing has been important since June, but now even more so. If you have applied these insights, your health is much improved.

Capricorns are unique among the signs in that their personal new year (the solar return) coincides (more or less) with the collective New Year. So this month you are preparing for two new years. It is good now to review the past year, assess your performance, correct mistakes, and set your goals and intentions for the year ahead. This requires some quiet time with yourself, and until the 21st the cosmos is supplying this.

On the 21st the Sun enters your own sign and you begin a yearly personal pleasure peak – a time for enjoying all the pleasures of the body, good food, good wine and other sensual delights. It is also good for losing weight (if you need to).

It is never a good idea to drink and drive, or to take drugs or medication and drive, but this is especially so this holiday season. The Sun makes dynamic aspects with both Uranus and Pluto from the 25th onwards. Yes, there are more festivities that period, but if you have had a bit too much, take a cab home or have someone drive you.

# Aquarius

~~~

---

## THE WATER-BEARER
*Birthdays from*
*20th January to*
*18th February*

---

## Personality Profile

### AQUARIUS AT A GLANCE

*Element* – Air

*Ruling Planet* – Uranus
   *Career Planet* – Pluto
   *Love Planet* – Venus
   *Money Planet* – Neptune
   *Planet of Health and Work* – Moon
   *Planet of Home and Family Life* – Venus
   *Planet of Spirituality* – Saturn

*Colours* – electric blue, grey, ultramarine blue

*Colours that promote love, romance and social
   harmony* – gold, orange

*Colour that promotes earning power* – aqua

*Gems* – black pearl, obsidian, opal, sapphire

*Metal* – lead

*Scents* – azalea, gardenia

*Quality* – fixed (= stability)

*Qualities most needed for balance* – warmth, feeling and emotion

*Strongest virtues* – great intellectual power, the ability to communicate and to form and understand abstract concepts, love for the new and avant-garde

*Deepest needs* – to know and to bring in the new

*Characteristics to avoid* – coldness, rebelliousness for its own sake, fixed ideas

*Signs of greatest overall compatibility* – Gemini, Libra

*Signs of greatest overall incompatibility* – Taurus, Leo, Scorpio

*Sign most helpful to career* – Scorpio

*Sign most helpful for emotional support* – Taurus

*Sign most helpful financially* – Pisces

*Sign best for marriage and/or partnerships* – Leo

*Sign most helpful for creative projects* – Gemini

*Best Sign to have fun with* – Gemini

*Signs most helpful in spiritual matters* – Libra, Capricorn

*Best day of the week* – Saturday

# Understanding an Aquarius

In the Aquarius-born, intellectual faculties are perhaps the most highly developed of any sign in the zodiac. Aquarians are clear, scientific thinkers. They have the ability to think abstractly and to formulate laws, theories and clear concepts from masses of observed facts. Geminis might be very good at gathering information, but Aquarians take this a step further, excelling at interpreting the information gathered.

Practical people – men and women of the world – mistakenly consider abstract thinking as impractical. It is true that the realm of abstract thought takes us out of the physical world, but the discoveries made in this realm generally end up having tremendous practical consequences. All real scientific inventions and breakthroughs come from this abstract realm.

Aquarians, more so than most, are ideally suited to explore these abstract dimensions. Those who have explored these regions know that there is little feeling or emotion there. In fact, emotions are a hindrance to functioning in these dimensions; thus Aquarians seem – at times – cold and emotionless to others. It is not that Aquarians haven't got feelings and deep emotions, it is just that too much feeling clouds their ability to think and invent. The concept of 'too much feeling' cannot be tolerated or even understood by some of the other signs. Nevertheless, this Aquarian objectivity is ideal for science, communication and friendship.

Aquarians are very friendly people, but they do not make a big show about it. They do the right thing by their friends, even if sometimes they do it without passion or excitement.

Aquarians have a deep passion for clear thinking. Second in importance, but related, is their passion for breaking with the establishment and traditional authority. Aquarians delight in this, because for them rebellion is like a great game or challenge. Very often they will rebel strictly for the fun of rebelling, regardless of whether the authority they defy is right or wrong. Right or wrong has little to do with the rebellious actions of an Aquarian, because to a true Aquarian authority and power must be challenged as a matter of principle.

Where Capricorn or Taurus will err on the side of tradition and the status quo, an Aquarian will err on the side of the new. Without this virtue it is doubtful whether any progress would be made in the world. The conservative-minded would obstruct progress. Originality and invention imply an ability to break barriers; every new discovery represents the toppling of an impediment to thought. Aquarians are very interested in breaking barriers and making walls tumble – scientifically, socially and politically. Other zodiac signs, such as Capricorn, also have scientific talents. But Aquarians are particularly excellent in the social sciences and humanities.

**Finance**

In financial matters Aquarians tend to be idealistic and humanitarian – to the point of self-sacrifice. They are usually generous contributors to social and political causes. When they contribute it differs from when a Capricorn or Taurus contributes. A Capricorn or Taurus may expect some favour or return for a gift; an Aquarian contributes selflessly.

Aquarians tend to be as cool and rational about money as they are about most things in life. Money is something they need and they set about acquiring it scientifically. No need for fuss; they get on with it in the most rational and scientific ways available.

Money to the Aquarian is especially nice for what it can do, not for the status it may bring (as is the case for other signs). Aquarians are neither big spenders nor penny-pinchers and use their finances in practical ways, for example to facilitate progress for themselves, their families, or even for strangers.

However, if Aquarians want to reach their fullest financial potential they will have to explore their intuitive nature. If they follow only their financial theories – or what they believe to be theoretically correct – they may suffer some losses and disappointments. Instead, Aquarians should call on their intuition, which knows without thinking. For Aquarians, intuition is the short-cut to financial success.

## Career and Public Image

Aquarians like to be perceived not only as the breakers of barriers but also as the transformers of society and the world. They long to be seen in this light and to play this role. They also look up to and respect other people in this position and even expect their superiors to act this way.

Aquarians prefer jobs that have a bit of idealism attached to them – careers with a philosophical basis. Aquarians need to be creative at work, to have access to new techniques and methods. They like to keep busy and enjoy getting down to business straightaway, without wasting any time. They are often the quickest workers and usually have suggestions for improvements that will benefit their employers. Aquarians are also very helpful with their co-workers and welcome responsibility, preferring this to having to take orders from others.

If Aquarians want to reach their highest career goals they have to develop more emotional sensitivity, depth of feeling and passion. They need to learn to narrow their focus on the essentials and concentrate more on the job in hand. Aquarians need 'a fire in the belly' – a consuming passion and desire – in order to rise to the very top. Once this passion exists they will succeed easily in whatever they attempt.

## Love and Relationships

Aquarians are good at friendships, but a bit weak when it comes to love. Of course they fall in love, but their lovers always get the impression that they are more best friends than paramours.

Like Capricorns, they are cool customers. They are not prone to displays of passion or to outward demonstrations of their affections. In fact, they feel uncomfortable when their other half hugs and touches them too much. This does not mean that they do not love their partners. They do, only they show it in other ways. Curiously enough, in relationships they tend to attract the very things that they feel uncomfortable with. They seem to attract hot, passionate, romantic, demonstrative people. Perhaps they know instinctively that these people have qualities they lack and so seek them out. In any event, these relationships do seem to work, Aquarian coolness calming the more passionate partner while the fires of passion warm the cold-blooded Aquarius.

The qualities Aquarians need to develop in their love life are warmth, generosity, passion and fun. Aquarians love relationships of the mind. Here they excel. If the intellectual factor is missing in a relationship an Aquarian will soon become bored or feel unfulfilled.

### Home and Domestic Life

In family and domestic matters Aquarians can have a tendency to be too non-conformist, changeable and unstable. They are as willing to break the barriers of family constraints as they are those of other areas of life.

Even so, Aquarians are very sociable people. They like to have a nice home where they can entertain family and friends. Their house is usually decorated in a modern style and full of state-of-the-art appliances and gadgets – an environment Aquarians find absolutely necessary.

If their home life is to be healthy and fulfilling Aquarians need to inject it with a quality of stability – yes, even some conservatism. They need at least one area of life to be enduring and steady; this area is usually their home and family life.

Venus, the planet of love, rules the Aquarian's 4th solar house of home and family as well, which means that when it comes to the family and child-rearing, theories, cool thinking and intellect are not always enough. Aquarians need to bring love into the equation in order to have a great domestic life.

# Horoscope for 2012

## Major Trends

Like last year, the long-term planets are kind to you in the year ahead. Only Jupiter is in stressful aspect until June 11. From June 11 to October 5 all the long-term planets are either leaving you alone or in harmonious aspect. On October 5, however, Saturn will move into a stressful aspect. Thus health and energy should be good in the year ahead, provided you don't waste it, and it spells success in your goals. (More on this later.)

Uranus' move into Aries last year was a significant transit for you as Uranus rules your Horoscope. While Uranus was in Pisces you were into personal glamour and otherworldly beauty. Now, you are more into physical fitness, exercise and physical activity. You are cultivating the beauty of this world. In previous years spiritual types of exercise, yoga, tai chi, chi qong, were alluring; now it is the gym, the track and the sports field.

You are always an innovative communicator. I would wager that the Internet, texting, social networking and all these modern ways of communicating were pioneered by Aquarians (or people strong in the sign). But with Uranus now in your 3rd house you are taking it to new levels. Some of the ways you are communicating might not yet be invented at the time of this writing! This is a long-term trend.

Neptune, your financial planet, makes a major move out of your sign (where he has been for 14 years) into Pisces, your 2nd house. This move reinforces trends that we have been seeing for a number of years, such as the importance of intuition and spirituality in your financial life. (More on this later.)

As with all the signs, your interests are many and widespread. It will be a challenge to maintain your focus on the really important things. (Perhaps you consider everything equally important!)

Your areas of greatest interest this year are the body and image (until February 19); finance (from February 3 onwards); communication and intellectual interests; home and family (until June 11); children, creativity and personal pleasure (from April 3 onwards); sex, personal transformation, personal reinvention and occult studies (until July 3); religion, philosophy, theology, foreign travel and higher education (until October 5); and career (from October 5 onwards).

Your paths of greatest fulfilment this year are home and family (until June 11); children, creativity and personal pleasure (from June 11 onwards); friends, groups and group activities (until August 31); and career (from August 31 onwards).


## Health

*(Please note that this is an* astrological *perspective on health and not a medical one. In days of yore these perspectives were identical. But these days there could be quite a difference. For a medical perspective, please consult your doctor or health practitioner.)*

As we mentioned, health and energy look good in the coming year. The long-term planets are basically kind to you now. Further, your 6th house of health is not at all strong. You are not paying too much attention here, because you have no need to. You are sort of taking good health for granted. If there have been health problems in the past, you should hear good news about it now.

Good though your health is, you can make it even better. Give more attention to the following organs: the ankles and calves (these should be regularly massaged and ankles should be given more support when exercising); and the

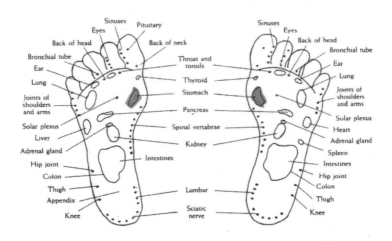

## Reflexology

*Try to massage the whole foot on a regular basis, but pay extra attention to the points highlighted on the chart. When you massage, be aware of 'sore spots', as these need special attention. It's also a good idea to massage the ankles and top side of the feet (see below).*

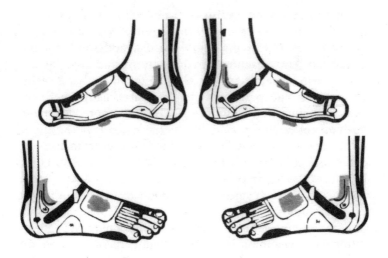

stomach and breasts (diet is always an important issue for you; meals should be taken in a calm, relaxed way to enhance the digestion).

With the Moon as your health planet, there is a strong need for emotional, domestic and family harmony. This is important for everybody, but for you it is an actual health issue. If problems arise, you need to explore these areas and bring them into harmony as quickly as you can.

Moods need to be kept positive and constructive. A negative mood, such as depression, should be considered the first symptom of disease. Nip it in the bud, before it gets too serious.

With the Moon as the health planet, the memory body (ruled by the Moon) plays a huge role in health. If problems arise, chances are that an old unresolved memory has been activated and needs to be cleared. In some cases, past life regression therapy might be appropriate as well.

Our regular readers know that the Moon is the fastest of all the planets. Where even the other fast-moving planets will take a year to go through all your signs and houses, the Moon will do this every month. So there are many short-term trends in health that are best covered in the monthly reports.

Good though your health is, there will be periods in the year where health is less easy than usual. These are temporary issues caused by planetary transits, not trends for the year ahead. This year these periods are April 20 to May 20; July 22 to August 22; and October 23 to November 22 (this last period is the most severe in the year ahead). These are the times when you need to rest and relax more and avoid wasting energy.

Your main health challenge this year comes from a strong square aspect between Uranus and Pluto, which is in effect all year. It was in effect last year too, but this year it is more exact. This shows a need to be more 'mindful', more alert and conscious on the physical plane while driving, while handling knives or sharp objects, or while doing risky kinds of things. Dreaminess is a virtue in meditation and while seeking inner guidance, but not while you are doing physical things.

## Home and Family

Jupiter moved into your 4th house of home and family in June 2011 and is there until June 11 this year, so home and family are more important and a greater focus than usual. This is basically a happy transit. It brings moves, happy ones, renovations in the home and the enlargement of the home and the family unit.

Often people don't actually move under this transit. Sometimes they buy additional homes. Sometimes they enlarge and renovate the home so that it is 'as if' they have moved. Almost always they acquire expensive items for the home. The home becomes happier and more enjoyable.

Jupiter in your 4th house shows that the family circle is enlarged in the year ahead, usually through births or marriage. Sometimes it happens through meeting people who become like family to you, so it is as if your family circle has expanded.

Aquarians of child-bearing age are much more fertile than usual these days, and this will be so even after June 11. Family members also seem more fertile. The family as a whole seems more prosperous and they seem generous with you. This is especially so for a parent or parent figure. Family support is good now.

Jupiter is the ruler of your 11th house and his position in your 4th house indicates other things as well. First off, you are installing expensive high-tech gadgetry in the home. Your friends and your family seem to be getting along. Friends are supportive of the family and home goals. You are successfully creating a 'team spirit' in the family and are realizing 'fondest hopes and wishes' for the family and the home this year.

Children and children figures are having a very spiritual period. Their growth is more internal and invisible rather than overt. You can't see it, but you can sense it. If they are of appropriate age, there is love and romance happening after June 11. A marriage wouldn't be a surprise either. There are renovations going on in their homes as well.

Siblings are having a status quo home and family year. Probably they are more nomadic than usual. They will be living in different places for long periods of time. Also there is much personal drama happening in their lives. Though you are very devoted to your siblings they seem distant with you for most of the year. This will change in October, as more harmony is established.

One parent or parent figure is prospering as we have mentioned. He or she needs to watch the weight more this year. The other needs to watch their overall energy after October 5. They seem to be taking on more responsibility.


### Finance and Career

Many of the trends that we have see in the past are still in effect in the year ahead. For years you have been exploring the spiritual dimensions of wealth, the use of the intuition, inner guidance and the role of the spirit in your finances, and this is still going on. In fact it should become even stronger. Neptune, your financial planet and the most spiritual of all the planets, will be in his own sign and house and even more 'Neptunian' than before. Neptune's energies will be more pronounced. Aquarian financiers will often make a big show of studying profit and loss statements, financial reports, market analyses – the normal tools of modern business decision making – but in the end they will base their decision on a dream, the reading of a psychic, the layout of the tarot cards, or the I Ching.

Your financial intuition has been good for many years, and now will get even better. As our regular readers know this is the short cut to wealth. One instant, one millisecond of true intuition is worth many years of hard labour. Your challenge has been to access the supernatural sources of supply rather than the natural ones. There are definite spiritual laws behind this. You already know much, but you are exploring more deeply.

With Neptune involved in your finances, nothing is the way it appears. There are many secret, behind the scenes activities going on in your business and financial dealings, and thus you need to do more homework before making important decisions or investments. (Perhaps this is why the intuition is so important; nothing is hidden from intuition.)

There are scandals and unpleasant revelations with those involved in your finances in the coming years. And, probably, there will be revelations of secret good there too. Both kinds of revelations are likely now. What is hidden will come to light.

On a mundane level, Neptune rules oil, natural gas, shipping, shipbuilding, water utilities and industries involving water. It also rules certain pharmaceuticals – mood enhancers, narcotics and pain killers. All of these industries are interesting as jobs, businesses or investments.

There is one important change that we see here. For years you have been spending on yourself, investing in yourself, in your image and appearance and cultivating the image of wealth. This seems to have died down. Perhaps you have already achieved this image and don't need to pay too much attention any more. You are cultivating the image of the 'intellectual' rather than the 'rich person' these days.

Mars spends an unusual amount of time (more than six months) in the sign of Virgo, your 8th house, this year. This suggests some protracted conflict with estates, taxes, or debt. Your spouse or partner has a protracted financial conflict. He or she needs to slow down before making important financial decisions. He or she seems too much in a rush and liable to make errors.

Spirituality has been important career-wise for many years. Your career planet has been in your 12th house since 2008 and will be there for many more years. But this year, Saturn, the spiritual planet of your Horoscope and ruler of the 12th house, crosses the Mid-heaven and enters your house of career on October 5. This makes spirituality even more important in your career than before. (More on this later.)

## Love and Social Life

Your 7th house of love and romance is not a 'house of power' this year (and hasn't been for some years). Thus the status quo is likely to prevail. Singles are likely to remain single; marrieds are likely to remain married. The cosmos is neither pushing you one way nor another. You seem to have little need or inclination to make any dramatic changes here.

For singles this seems a year for love affairs rather than committed relationships. This is especially so from April 3 onwards. On April 3, Venus moves into your 5th house of love affairs and stays there for an unusually long time – more than four months, and Jupiter moves in there too on June 11. So there is much dating and fun, but these things are not very serious.

Your love planet is the Sun. In the course of a year, he will move through all the signs and houses of your Horoscope. Thus there are many short-term trends in love that are best dealt with in the monthly reports.

Those working towards their first marriage will have very good opportunities from March 20 to March 31, July 22 to August 1 and from September 6 to September 14. These are short-term windows of opportunity. Generally what happens is that important meetings happen, sometimes with new people and sometimes with old flames.

Those into their second marriages have had their relationships tested these past few years. If they survived last year (which was very stressful) they will survive the year ahead. Singles working on their second marriage are better off not marrying this year. Avoid rushing into marriage or committed relationships now. Let love grow and develop as it will. Singles working to their third marriage have very nice opportunity from June 11 to August 9.

The marriages of siblings have been tested for the past two years, and the trend continues. They need to reignite the spark of romance; things have become too cold and mechanical.

Children of appropriate age are very likely to marry or be involved in a relationship that is 'like a marriage'. Grandchildren of appropriate age are better off not marrying for a few years. The love life and love attitudes are too unstable. They have exciting love lives, but should avoid commitment for a while.

## Self-improvement

Your spiritual planet, Saturn, will cross the Mid-heaven and enter your 10th house on October 5. This makes the spiritual life even more important than usual. It is very high on your priorities and this tends to spell success. You are learning that the spiritual life is not something vague or abstract but is very tangible in 'bottom line' kinds of ways.

This transit makes you very idealistic about your career. Much depends on where you are on the spiritual path. More advanced people will probably opt for a 'spiritual' career, such as in ministry, a charity or healing. Others might be involved in a worldly kind of career but very involved in altruistic causes and charities on the side. In fact, even from the worldly perspective, this is good practice, and will advance the worldly career. Many of you will be attracted to careers with non-profit organizations.

The values of the world and the values of spirit are generally at odds. And this is your main challenge in the year ahead (and for the next few years): how to be successful and yet maintain your spiritual integrity; how to be successful and yet do something really meaningful. Everyone works this out in their own way and you will too. There are no rules to this.

What we said about finance – learning the spiritual dimensions of it – also applies to the career. You are learning the spiritual dimensions of it this year and in coming years. Your intuition not your logic becomes important in career decisions. Intuition sees far into the future; logic looks only at the past and projects from that.

In astrology the 10th house rules your career, your life work in the world. On a deeper level, it shows the *dharma* or the purpose of the incarnation – the spiritual mission for the life. And so you are delving deeper into these things. You came to this Earth to do something very specific that only you can do. And this is a time to discover what it is and to get on with it. The good news is that this will be revealed to you over the coming years. Perhaps not in its totality – the spiritual mission is really an 'unfoldment' – but what you need for the next steps will be revealed. (This will happen though your personal meditations or through psychics, gurus, spiritual channels or ministers, or perhaps in dreams.)

A good prayer-meditation this year would be: 'The Divine idea of my career is manifest now and I fulfil my destiny under grace.'

## Month-by-month Forecasts

### January

Best Days Overall: 5, 6, 7, 14, 15, 23, 24
Most Stressful Days Overall: 3, 4, 10, 11, 17, 18, 30, 31
Best Days for Love: 3, 4, 6, 7, 10, 11, 12, 13, 18, 19, 23, 24, 27, 28
Best Days for Money: 3, 4, 7, 12, 15, 21, 24, 25, 26, 30
Best Days for Career: 3, 12, 17, 18, 21, 30

You begin your year in a rare window of opportunity. The Eastern sector of your chart is dominant; your 1st house is very powerful; and you are in a period of maximum personal power and independence. The planetary energies are flowing towards you rather than away from you. Your personal happiness, the way you like to do things, is supported by the cosmos now. You have the power to create happy conditions for yourself and to do this on your own. There is little need to compromise; you can and should have things your own way. Also, until the 24th, 100 per cent of the planets are in forward motion. This will not happen again this year. So, your creations and personal progress is likely to be quick.

Adding to this is good health. Energy and vitality are high – at their optimum – especially after the 20th. You have the energy to achieve any goal that you set for yourself.

With power comes responsibility. There is a cosmic accounting for the use of power. If you create wrongly, or misuse your forces, you will have to deal with this later on. But no matter, we learn to create by creating, and by making mistakes.

This month the planetary power shifts from the upper to the lower half of your chart. The demands of the career are less. The focus should be on home, family and emotional issues – your personal happiness, your personal emotional comfort zone. There are no excuses now for emotional discord. If things are not the way you want them, change them.

It is good that your year begins with your 12th house of spirituality powerful. You need adequate preparation to create. You need to make sure that your creations are in harmony with the Higher Power in you. This takes more prayer, meditation and communion.

Love is very happy this month. Until the 20th singles find love in spiritual-type settings – at the yoga studio, the prayer meeting, the charity event, the meditation seminar or spiritual lecture. Love is also very idealistic. (Perhaps overly so; your standards are so high that no mortal human could ever live up to them.) After the 20th, love is more physical and down to earth. There is nothing that singles need to do to attract love. It finds them. Just go about your daily routine and love will find you.

Finances are good this month too. On the 8th Venus enters the money house. The family as a whole prospers and family support is good. There are happy financial opportunities from home, with family members and through family connections.

## February

> Best Days Overall: 2, 3, 11, 12, 19, 20, 29
> Most Stressful Days Overall: 1, 7, 8, 13, 14, 27, 28
> Best Days for Love: 2, 3, 5, 6, 7, 8, 11, 12, 15, 21, 22, 24, 25
> Best Days for Money: 1, 4, 9, 13, 17, 21, 22, 23, 27, 28
> Best Days for Career: 9, 13, 14, 17, 18, 27

Last month on the 20th, you entered a yearly personal pleasure peak. For the past two months you have been enjoying 'spiritual pleasures' and otherworldly delights. But now, you are enjoying the pleasures of the flesh – good food, good wine, good restaurants, and other forms of physical 'pampering'. This is still going on until the 19th.

It is no accident that the 1st house becomes powerful only after power in the 12th house. This is the way things happen every year, and shows that personal, physical happiness is the result of spiritual causes. Spiritual harmony results in physical harmony.

On the 19th (and you will probably feel this even earlier) you enter a yearly financial peak. Half of the planets are either in your money house or moving through it this month. Earnings soar and financial goals are attained easily. Financial intuition is at all time highs now; you just need to trust it. You have the financial support of family, friends, children and your spouse, partner or current love. Speculations are favourable after the 14th. There are opportunities for business partnerships or joint ventures as well. But merely 'getting rich' is not enough for you these days. There is a strong idealism in the financial life. You have a compelling need to earn in socially and spiritually responsible ways. Making money is not your challenge – this will just happen. It is doing it in the proper way, in a spiritually correct way that challenges you now.

In your chart Mars is your communication planet, and he went retrograde on January 24. There can be all kinds of communication glitches now, so take more care in communicating. Allow more time for things to get done and for getting to various destinations. Don't take information you receive at face value (especially what you read in the newspapers). Major purchases and contracts need more homework done on them.

You are still having your way in love, especially until the 19th. There's still no need to do anything special to attract or find love; it finds you. Those who are married have the doting devotion of their spouse this period. After the 19th, singles find love opportunities as they pursue their financial goals and with people involved in their finances. Love is still idealistic, but wealth doesn't hurt either.

### March

> Best Days Overall: 1, 9, 10, 18, 19, 27, 28, 29
> Most Stressful Days Overall: 5, 6, 11, 12, 25, 26
> Best Days for Love: 3, 4, 5, 6, 7, 11, 12, 15, 16, 22, 23, 25, 26
> Best Days for Money: 2, 7, 11, 15, 16, 20, 21, 25, 26, 30
> Best Days for Career: 7, 11, 12, 15, 25

You are still in a yearly financial peak until the 20th. Review our discussion of this from last month. Health and vitality are still excellent and personal power (though not as strong as in the past two months) is still good. The major challenge now is Mercury's retrograde on the 12th. This is going to be a lot stronger than a typical Mercury retrograde, for now, *both* of the planets that rule communication in your Horoscope are retrograde at the same time – Mercury and Mars. We discussed some of the issues of Mars' retrograde last month, but now it is even stronger.

These retrogrades will not stop earnings or love, only slow things down a bit. There are more glitches and delays to deal with. Mental mistakes tend to increase. Letters either don't get delivered or are delayed. Phone calls are missed. Emails bounce. Deliveries don't happen on time. It takes longer than you expect to get from one place to another. Most of the problems you face this month arise from miscommunication and misunderstandings.

Generally the things that happen are merely annoying and inconvenient. But in certain circumstances they can be life threatening. The doctor writes the wrong prescription, or the pharmacist misreads the doctor's prescription and so the patient gets the wrong medication, for example. Or the pilot loses contact with ground control and so makes the wrong kind of landing. Thus it is good to avoid elective kinds of surgeries and elective kinds of travel these days. If there are flaws in your car or communications equipment, you will certainly find out about it now.

The main thing is to communicate better right from the start. More care in the beginning can save much time and heartache later on. Say what you mean. Don't take things for granted. Make sure the other party got your true message. And also make sure that you understood what the other person was saying, and don't be afraid to ask questions. This is especially important when communicating with children.

The interesting thing here is that these retrogrades happen as your 3rd house of communication becomes very powerful (after the 20th). Normally this would be a great time for mass mailings, advertising campaigns and media activities. But now, it's better just to plan these things, rather than actually do them.

Love is basically happy, but there are some bumps on the road. From the 1st to the 5th the love planet Venus opposes Mars. This can bring arguments and conflict with the beloved. Avoid power struggles now as they are likely to escalate out of control. Venus squares Pluto from the 28th to the 31st and the same advice applies. The beloved needs to be more careful while driving or handling dangerous objects.

The love planet conjuncts Uranus from the 23rd to the 26th. This brings sudden love and romantic meetings, sudden social invitations. However, the stability of these affairs is open to question.

**April**

Best Days Overall: 6, 14, 15, 24, 25
Most Stressful Days Overall: 1, 2, 8, 21, 22, 29, 30
Best Days for Love: 1, 2, 5, 10, 11, 14, 15, 20, 21, 24, 25, 29, 30
Best Days for Money: 4, 7, 12, 13, 16, 17, 21, 22, 26
Best Days for Career: 4, 8, 12, 21

The communication problems of the past month are easing up now. Mercury starts to move forward on the 4th and Mars on the 14th. Often we are cleaning up the mess caused by these problems for a long time after they happen. However, your 3rd house of communication is still very powerful until the 20th, so mass mailings, advertising campaigns, and media activities get the green light after the 14th. Hopefully, you've got good solid plans in place and so their execution will go well. Health is good, but needs more attention after the 20th. Nothing major will happen unless you allow yourself to get overtired or burn the candle at both ends. This is not one of your best health periods but this is not a trend for the year ahead or your life. It's just a temporary situation caused by the short-term transits. Rest and relax more and enhance the health in the ways mentioned in the yearly report.

In general, your health and energy are strongest when the Moon waxes, from the 1st to the 6th this month, and from the 21st onwards.

You are now in the midnight hour of your year. The planetary power is at its maximum 'unconscious' position. In other words it is operating on the unconscious, inner level rather than the outer level. At midnight, usually, the body sleeps, but powerful inner activities, hidden from sight and consciousness, are happening. Career might seem in a lull, but important developments are happening behind the scenes. The stage is being set for future career growth – for the coming day. In our culture, people tend to panic when there is a lull in the career. But this is unfounded. There is a wonderful natural rhythm to these things that needs to be understood.

You are in a period for psychological progress now. Those involved in therapy will have good results. The time is also favourable for getting the home and domestic life in order. These are the foundations upon which a healthy career is based. Feeling right is more important than doing right. If you feel right, your actions will naturally be good.

This month the planetary power shifts from the East to the West. Thus, personal power, personal independence is less than usual. The cosmos is impelling you to become more 'other oriented' and to put the needs of others ahead of your own. Now it is more difficult to create the life conditions that you desire. You basically have to live with the conditions you created since the beginning of the year. Best to adapt to situations as best you can. The Higher Power is strong when the personal ego is weak.

## May

Best Days Overall: 3, 4, 11, 12, 23, 24, 25, 30, 31
Most Stressful Days Overall: 5, 6, 18, 19, 20, 26, 27
Best Days for Love: 1, 2, 3, 4, 9, 10, 11, 12, 20, 21, 22, 26, 27, 30, 31
Best Days for Money: 2, 5, 10, 13, 14, 15, 19, 20, 23, 29
Best Days for Career: 1, 2, 5, 6, 9, 10, 19, 20, 28, 29

Retrograde activity increases this month. Pluto, the career planet, went retrograde on April 12 and will be retrograde for many more months. Career is under review. Many issues there will not be resolved by personal effort. Only time will resolve them. In the meantime, with your 4th house of home and family still very powerful this month, this is where energy and attention should flow. Review our discussion of this from last month.

Venus, your family planet, will start one of her rare retrogrades on the 15th. Give attention to the home and family, but avoid making major family decisions now; these all need more research. The domestic situation, like the career, is under review. The emotional life can be a bit confusing under this aspect; you feel something, but you don't know why you feel as you feel. Often there is much wasted time trying to figure this out. It is OK not to know; knowledge will come with time.

Both the parent figures in your life lack direction this period. You seem in conflict with one of them.

A solar eclipse on the 20th, though benign to you, impacts on the finances. Big financial changes are happening and this will continue for many more months. Perhaps love issues, or actions of your spouse or partner are causing these changes. You and the spouse or current love are basically harmonious now, but not in financial matters. This seems a source of conflict. This eclipse will test the love life, as every solar eclipse does. You have gone through this many times and so it is nothing to fear. Good relationships endure and get even better, for now the problems reveal themselves and you can correct them. But flawed relationships can dissolve. Be more patient with the beloved this period as he or she is apt to be more temperamental.

Since this eclipse occurs in your 5th house avoid speculations this period. (This will be difficult as the speculative fever is upon you.) Children in your life should avoid risky kinds of behaviours and should relax more. They have dramas in their lives now and are undergoing image and personality changes. They are redefining themselves in a new way. This will go on for the next six months or so.

Health improves dramatically after the 20th. In spite of the eclipse you enter another of your yearly personal pleasure peaks. Troubled relationships can be corrected by getting into fun kinds of activities together. Laugh more. Go to the theatre or a concert. Loosen up a bit. Stop taking things so seriously.

In general health and vitality will be strongest as the Moon waxes from the 20th onwards. The Moon waxes from the 1st to the 6th too, but the other aspects are stressful.

Avoid elective foreign travel from the 15th onwards. If you must travel, allow more time to get to your destination and insure your tickets.

### June

Best Days Overall: 8, 9, 17, 18, 27, 28
Most Stressful Days Overall: 1, 2, 15, 16, 22, 23, 29, 30
Best Days for Love: 8, 9, 17, 18, 19, 22, 23, 27, 28, 29, 30
Best Days for Money: 1, 5, 6, 10, 11, 17, 19, 26, 27, 29
Best Days for Career: 1, 2, 5, 15, 24, 29, 30

A lunar eclipse on the 4th is also basically benign to you. It occurs in your 11th house and so friendships get tested. Often there is nothing wrong with the relationship *per se*, but there are dramas in the lives of friends: are you there for them? Computer equipment, software and hardware, will get tested. In many cases it needs replacement.

This eclipse brings job changes. Your job can change within your present company or with a new one. Often we enter a job with a kind of half-hearted attitude – 'I'll take it for now, I need a job.' These kinds of jobs are in jeopardy and this might be the time to make changes. But in many cases people take jobs from a sense of commitment. These jobs will probably endure though there will be changes in the working conditions. Lunar eclipses tend to produce health scares too. But your health looks good this month (and for the year ahead), so these will just be scares and nothing more. You will probably wind up making changes in your diet and health regime.

We see the problems with friends in another way as well. Jupiter, the planet of friends, re-activates last month's solar eclipse from the 7th to the 17th. High-tech equipment is temperamental again too.

Jupiter makes a major move into your 5th house on the 11th and will be there for the rest of the year. Basically this is a happy transit. This month (you are still in the middle of a yearly personal pleasure peak) and the rest of the year ahead are more fun. There are parties and entertainments and all kinds of fun-type activities in store. Aquarians of appropriate age are more fertile this year (and especially this month). The children in your life enter a happy period, a period of prosperity and good fortune. Speculations are favourable for the rest of the year ahead (though the favourability will wax and wane with the planetary transits and aspects.)

Unattached singles have love opportunities in the usual places until the 21st – at night clubs, places of entertainment, resorts, parties, etc. After the 21st romantic opportunities happen at work, with co-workers or as you pursue your health goals. Healers and health professionals are particularly attractive after this date.

Love is about fun until the 21st. You (or your partner) are good at the honeymoon aspects but not so good when the tough times hit. But after the 21st this changes. Love is about service to the beloved. Service is love in action.

Retrograde activity increases this month and hits the maximum for the year. (This maximum will be hit a few more times in coming months as well.) The pace of life slows down and it is a time for learning patience. Avoid short cuts. The long way – the thorough way – is the real short cut. Mental clarity is the most important thing now. You might not have it yet, but it is worth striving for.

## July

Best Days Overall: 5, 6, 15, 16, 24, 25
Most Stressful Days Overall: 12, 13, 19, 20, 21, 26, 27
Best Days for Love: 5, 6, 7, 8, 15, 18, 19, 20, 21, 24, 25, 28
Best Days for Money: 5, 6, 7, 8, 15, 16, 17, 24, 25, 26
Best Days for Career: 3, 12, 22, 26, 27

Retrograde activity increases this month. After the 15th we hit the maximum for the year once again, with 40 per cent of the planets moving backwards. Patience, patience, patience. Smile at delays. There is nothing wrong with you; it is just the astrological weather. Use the delays to improve your products or services.

Though your overall energy could be much better, still, many nice things are happening this month. On the 22nd you enter a yearly love and social peak. Your 5th house is strong and filled with benevolent planets. You are having a lot of fun, going to parties, and enjoying your life. A spat with the beloved from the 12th to the 15th might not be what you think. He or she is probably not feeling well. It passes.

Your 6th house of health is powerful until the 22nd, which is a good thing. Your focus on health will help you get through the low energy cycle that begins on the 22nd. Preventive measures that you take now will have a long-term effect.

Power in the 6th house is also good news for job seekers. Social connections are very helpful, probably more helpful than the wanted ads or the standard job search ways. Those who employ others also have good fortune now.

When the 6th house is powerful it is good to achieve work goals. It is especially good to achieve those tedious, detail-oriented goals like accounting and bookkeeping. The mind more easily handles details. (This is a month where you see that the little details are important too.)

Finances were good last month, especially later in the month, and they are good now. Only keep in mind that your financial planet went retrograde on June 5 and so your financial life is under review now. You have excellent financial intuition, but now it needs more verification. You are in a very speculative frame of mind after the 22nd, but restrain yourself. With Mercury retrograde, it's best to avoid speculations. If you must indulge, do it with small sums.

Mars makes stressful aspects with both Uranus and Pluto from the 15th to the 21st. Be more careful driving and be more mindful on the physical plane. Guard the tongue and do your best to avoid arguments; people overreact under this transit. Siblings should also avoid risky activities.

## August

Best Days Overall: 1, 2, 11, 12, 20, 21, 29, 30
Most Stressful Days Overall: 8, 9, 10, 16, 17, 22, 23
Best Days for Love: 2, 3, 6, 7, 13, 14, 16, 17, 18, 22, 23, 27, 31
Best Days for Money: 1, 2, 3, 4, 5, 11, 12, 13, 20, 21, 22, 29, 30, 31
Best Days for Career: 8, 18, 22, 23, 27

The ruler of your Horoscope, Uranus, went retrograde last month on the 13th, and will be retrograde for many more months. Your personal life (as well as your finances) is under review. Issues involving the body and image need more homework. It's not such a good time to buy a new wardrobe or accessories (especially if they are expensive) or for cosmetic surgery. Study things further. In a way this is good. Personal confidence and personal will is weakened with this retrograde, but with planets now in their maximum Western position, it is good that your will is weak. Personal vulnerability only heightens your social appeal. And besides, you need to take a break from thinking about yourself now. Others come first, so let them have their way.

You are still in the midst of a yearly love and social peak. You are in the mood for romance and thus it is more likely to happen. Singles are unlikely to marry just yet, but they meet people they would consider marrying. Uncommitted love seems more interesting these days.

When the 7th house of love is strong, we learn about ourselves through our relationships. While it seems that we are engaged in romance, we are really in the classroom of relationship school. No matter the outward outcome of a relationship, the real prize is the self-knowledge and insight that is gained. A dispute with the beloved from the 22nd to the 25th seems to involve finance. Compromise.

From the 7th to the 11th there is good family support financially – a parent seems eager to help. But this same person seems to conflict with you from the 14th to the 17th. He or she is helpful financially, but disapproving personally.

Cars and communication equipment are more temperamental between the 11th and 17th. If you are making a long drive, have the car checked out before you leave. There are probably more traffic delays that period as well. Allow more time to get to your destination.

Very good financial information comes to you from the 24th to the 27th. You have good financial ideas too. The money people in your life are receptive to your ideas. Only keep in mind that your financial planet is still retrograde, so study and digest things further.

## September

Best Days Overall: 7, 8, 16, 17, 25, 26
Most Stressful Days Overall: 5, 6, 12, 13, 19
Best Days for Love: 1, 5, 6, 12, 13, 14, 15, 21, 22, 25, 29, 30
Best Days for Money: 1, 7, 8, 9, 16, 17, 18, 25, 26, 27, 28
Best Days for Career: 5, 14, 18, 19, 23

Retrograde activity weakens this period. This month, 30 per cent of the planets are retrograde, and after the 18th only 20 per cent. The pace of life quickens dramatically.

Mars crossed your Mid-heaven on the 24th of last month, and the planetary power shifted from the lower to the upper half of your Horoscope. This month the shift increases even further as Venus moves from the lower hemisphere to the upper. So you are in the daytime of your year – early morning. The activities of the night have worked their magic and now it is time to be involved in the activities of the day – your outer life and goals, your career. And you pursue them by the methods of the day, not by dreaming or visualizing but through concrete actions. Hopefully by now you are in your point of emotional harmony. Feeling right is not so important now – it's doing right that's important.

Mars in your career house shows that you are very active career-wise – perhaps overactive. The career seems hectic. There are competitors to your position, and you must fend them off one way or another. Your company's competitors are strong too, and thus the company (and you as part of it) need to work harder. You are communicating well with superiors. They seem open to your thinking, ideas and thought process and this is helping your career.

Your career planet, Pluto, has been retrograde for many months, but this month on the 18th it starts to move forward again. After all these months, you have attained clarity in career matters and so you are strong now. You know where you want to go – you have a good road map – and you are heading there.

Your 8th house is powerful this month, as it was last month too. This will be a more sexually active kind of period, regardless of your age or stage in life. (Each will experience heightened libido according to their age.)

Be more patient with the beloved from the 28th to the 30th as he or she is apt to be more temperamental and to overreact. He or she should avoid risky kinds of activities that period. Daredevil stunts are out of the question.

Your 9th house becomes powerful after the 23rd, signifying a time for travel, higher education and the pursuit of religious, philosophical and theological interests.

### October

Best Days Overall: 4, 5, 6, 14, 15, 22, 23
Most Stressful Days Overall: 2, 3, 9, 10, 11, 16, 17, 29, 30, 31
Best Days for Love: 1, 4, 5, 9, 10, 11, 12, 14, 15, 21, 24
Best Days for Money: 4, 5, 6, 7, 14, 15, 16, 22, 23, 24, 25, 26
Best Days for Career: 2, 12, 16, 17, 20, 29

Saturn crosses your Mid-heaven on the 5th and enters your 10th house of career. This house becomes even more powerful after the 23rd as you enter a yearly career peak. This is the main headline of the month ahead.

Saturn on the Mid-heaven shows that you are working hard. You are earning your success. Yes, you are being helped by friends and social connections (especially after the 23rd) but you are earning your way the hard way, through sheer merit. Sometimes this transit is experienced as a tough, demanding boss who enters the picture. This person is difficult to please. Yet, you must. There is a hidden agenda here. You have the capacity to do more and be more and this is just the cosmos' way of stretching you. No, it is not pleasant, and you feel stretched to the limit. No matter. Stretch even further and go the extra mile. Do more than the person requires. This will work magic in your career.

Saturn is your spiritual planet. His position at the Mid-heaven shows that even as you pursue your worldly career, spiritual values matter. It shows that the challenges and extra work that is happening have a spiritual agenda behind them, ultimately for your good.

Aside from going the extra mile in your work, it is good to enhance the career by getting involved in charities and altruistic kinds of activities. Many of you will have career opportunities with non-profit organizations now. This can happen in a direct way (i.e. working for one) or indirectly – the organization is an important customer or client.

Love is happier and more romantic this month. Your love planet is in the romantic sign of Libra until the 23rd. Singles find love opportunities in foreign lands, with foreigners or in educational and religious settings. Last month, the love needs were sexual; this month other needs enter the picture. You like refinement and education. You like someone you can learn from – a mentor or teacher; someone you can look up to and respect. This is so even when the Sun moves into Scorpio on the 23rd. Status, power and prestige are turn-ons. (Indeed the present love interest is more successful this period and seems elevated in status.) After the 23rd, singles find love opportunities as they pursue their normal career goals and with people involved in the career. (You are very busy this period and thus you are trying to combine career and love.) You are socializing more with people that you work with or who are involved in your career.

Health needs more watching after the 23rd. Enhance the health in the ways mentioned in the yearly report. Saturn is now making stressful aspects with you (especially those of you born early in your sign, between January 19 and January 23), and so your energy needs more watching from here on in.

When Saturn is in stressful aspect we learn that we are held accountable for the use of our energy. Yes, we have free will and can use our energies as we see fit, but there is a price tag attached.

## November

Best Days Overall: 1, 2, 10, 11, 18, 19, 23, 24
Most Stressful Days Overall: 6, 7, 12, 13, 26, 27
Best Days for Love: 1, 3, 4, 6, 7, 11, 13, 20, 23
Best Days for Money: 1, 2, 3, 11, 12, 19, 21, 22, 28, 29
Best Days for Career: 8, 12, 13, 16, 26

Health needs still needs attention until the 22nd. Do your best to maintain high energy levels. Keep your focus on the really important things in your life and let lesser things go. You have to take a more business-like approach with your energy. Only invest it where the returns are high.

You are still in a yearly career peak until the 22nd so keep in mind our discussions of last month. The career gets complicated by a solar eclipse in your 10th house on the 13th. You need to relax more from the 1st to the 22nd anyway, and especially around the eclipse period. This eclipse is showing career changes. Perhaps your career – your position – has a 'near-death' kind of experience. Sometimes people actually change their career path or make important modifications here. There will be shake-ups in the management of your company and in your industry in general. There are dramas in the lives of bosses and parent figures. There can be shake-ups in your local government as well.

Every solar eclipse tests the love life and the current relationship. And so this is happening as well. Your spouse, partner or current love can be having a career crisis. Be more patient with the beloved this period as he or she is going to be more temperamental. This eclipse affects you strongly so avoid risk taking or stressful kinds of activities. Elective kinds of surgeries or travel are better off rescheduled now.

A lunar eclipse on the 28th is more benign to you. This one occurs in your 5th house and can test a love affair. Children are more temperamental this period so be more patient with them. There are personal dramas happening in their lives. They are redefining their image, personality and self-concept. (A parent or parent figure is also doing this.) Sometimes this produces a detox of the body – not sickness but a cleansing and clearing. (The symptoms often seem the same as sickness, but they are not.) You could have health scares or changes in your health regime and diet. Job changes could happen as well. (This reinforces the career change that we see indicated by the solar eclipse.)

Once the dust settles from the solar eclipse you enter the Elysian Fields of Aquarius. Your 11th house of friends becomes powerful on the 22nd and so the cosmic forces are impelling you to do the things that you most love to do: be involved with groups, friends and organizations and be involved with networking, science, technology and astrology. You are always an innovative and inventive type of person, and this month even more so than usual. You become a super Aquarius.

Love becomes happier and more harmonious after the 22nd as well. Your current relationship either improves or you enter a new and better one.

## December

Best Days Overall: 8, 9, 16, 17, 25, 26
Most Stressful Days Overall: 3, 4, 10, 11, 23, 24, 30, 31
Best Days for Love: 1, 3, 4, 10, 11, 13, 20, 22, 30, 31
Best Days for Money: 1, 8, 10, 16, 18, 19, 25, 28
Best Days for Career: 6, 10, 11, 14, 23

In October the planetary power shifted from the social West to the independent East. Personal power, personal initiative and self-confidence began to increase. This month, we see a further increase, as Uranus, the ruler of your Horoscope, starts to move forward after many months of being retrograde. The timing is perfect. By now you have attained mental clarity as to what you want – the kind of conditions that you want to be in – and now you also have the power to make it happen. Until October the planetary power was far away from you; now it is moving towards you. You have cosmic support. Trust yourself and create your life as you want to be. Take personal responsibility for your happiness. Mars will move into your sign on the 26th increasing your personal power and independence even more. Moreover, the planetary momentum is forward now (after the 13th 90 per cent of the planets will be moving forward), so you will make rapid progress towards your goals. Your desires will manifest more quickly.

Health is much improved over last month. You have all the energy you need to achieve your goals (only don't fritter it away wastefully).

Your love planet Venus is in your 11th house until the 21st. Singles find love opportunities in groups, group activities or organizations. Friends will tend to play cupid. Friendship in general is important in love. You want to be friends with the beloved. You are always experimental in love (as in all things) but this month more so. Love is enhanced by doing unconventional kinds of things with the beloved. Do the 'kooky' things – he or she will love it.

After the 21st Venus moves to the 12th house and love becomes more idealistic and spiritual. You need to feel that you have the divine stamp of approval on your relationship; that there is some 'higher agenda' involved in your relationship. Singles find love opportunities in spiritual settings – in prayer meetings, yoga studios, meditation seminars, spiritual lectures or at charity events.

Be more patient with the beloved from the 25th onwards; he or she seems more temperamental. He or she should avoid risk-taking activities then. Drinking and driving is never a good idea, but especially this period as the Sun makes stressful aspects with Uranus and Pluto. The spouse, partner or current love has a wonderful career opportunity during this period, perhaps a pay rise or promotion.

Finances are OK early in the month; nothing special one way or another. But you will see improvement from the 20th onwards.

# Pisces

)(

## Personality Profile

PISCES AT A GLANCE

*Element* – Water

*Ruling Planet* – Neptune
   *Career Planet* – Pluto
   *Love Planet* – Mercury
   *Money Planet* – Mars
   *Planet of Health and Work* – Sun
   *Planet of Home and Family Life* – Mercury
   *Planet of Love Affairs, Creativity and Children*
      – Moon

*Colours* – aqua, blue–green

*Colours that promote love, romance and social
   harmony* – earth tones, yellow,
   yellow–orange

*Colours that promote earning power* – red,
   scarlet

*Gem* – white diamond

*Metal* – tin

*Scent* – lotus

*Quality* – mutable (= flexibility)

*Qualities most needed for balance* – structure and the ability to handle form

*Strongest virtues* – psychic power, sensitivity, self-sacrifice, altruism

*Deepest needs* – spiritual illumination, liberation

*Characteristics to avoid* – escapism, keeping bad company, negative moods

*Signs of greatest overall compatibility* – Cancer, Scorpio

*Signs of greatest overall incompatibility* – Gemini, Virgo, Sagittarius

*Sign most helpful to career* – Sagittarius

*Sign most helpful for emotional support* – Gemini

*Sign most helpful financially* – Aries

*Sign best for marriage and/or partnerships* – Virgo

*Sign most helpful for creative projects* – Cancer

*Best Sign to have fun with* – Cancer

*Signs most helpful in spiritual matters* – Scorpio, Aquarius

*Best day of the week* – Thursday

# Understanding a Pisces

If Pisces have one outstanding quality it is their belief in the invisible, spiritual and psychic side of things. This side of things is as real to them as the hard earth beneath their feet – so real, in fact, that they will often ignore the visible, tangible aspects of reality in order to focus on the invisible and so-called intangible ones.

Of all the signs of the zodiac, the intuitive and emotional faculties of the Pisces are the most highly developed. They are committed to living by their intuition and this can at times be infuriating to other people – especially those who are materially, scientifically or technically orientated. If you think that money or status or worldly success are the only goals in life, then you will never understand a Pisces.

Pisces have intellect, but to them intellect is only a means by which they can rationalize what they know intuitively. To an Aquarius or a Gemini the intellect is a tool with which to gain knowledge. To a well-developed Pisces it is a tool by which to express knowledge.

Pisces feel like fish in an infinite ocean of thought and feeling. This ocean has many depths, currents and undercurrents. They long for purer waters where the denizens are good, true and beautiful, but they are sometimes pulled to the lower, murkier depths. Pisces know that they do not generate thoughts but only tune in to thoughts that already exist; this is why they seek the purer waters. This ability to tune in to higher thoughts inspires them artistically and musically.

Since Pisces is so spiritually orientated – though many Pisces in the corporate world may hide this fact – we will deal with this aspect in greater detail, for otherwise it is difficult to understand the true Pisces personality.

There are four basic attitudes of the spirit. One is outright scepticism – the attitude of secular humanists. The second is an intellectual or emotional belief, where one worships a far-distant God-figure – the attitude of most modern churchgoing people. The third is not only belief but direct personal spiritual experience – this is the attitude of some 'born-again' religious people. The fourth is actual unity with the divinity, an intermingling with the spiritual world – this is the attitude of yoga. This fourth attitude is the deepest urge of a Pisces, and a Pisces is uniquely qualified to pursue and perform this work.

Consciously or unconsciously, Pisces seek this union with the spiritual world. The belief in a greater reality makes Pisces very tolerant and understanding of others – perhaps even too tolerant. There are instances in their lives when they should say 'enough is enough' and be ready to defend their position and put up a fight. However, because of their qualities it takes a good deal to get them into that frame of mind.

Pisces basically want and aspire to be 'saints'. They do so in their own way and according to their own rules. Others should not try to impose their concept of saintliness on a Pisces, because he or she always tries to find it for him- or herself.

## Finance

Money is generally not that important to Pisces. Of course they need it as much as anyone else, and many of them attain great wealth. But money is not generally a primary objective. Doing good, feeling good about oneself, peace of mind, the relief of pain and suffering – these are the things that matter most to a Pisces.

Pisces earn money intuitively and instinctively. They follow their hunches rather than their logic. They tend to be generous and perhaps overly charitable. Almost any kind of misfortune is enough to move a Pisces to give. Although this is one of their greatest virtues, Pisces should be more careful with their finances. They should try to be more choosy about the people to whom they lend money, so that they are not being taken advantage of. If they give money to charities they should follow it up to see that their contributions are put to good use. Even when Pisces are not rich, they still like to spend money on helping others. In this case they should really be careful, however: they must learn to say no sometimes and help themselves first.

Perhaps the biggest financial stumbling block for the Pisces is general passivity – a *laissez faire* attitude. In general Pisces like to go with the flow of events. When it comes to financial matters, especially, they need to be more aggressive. They need to make things happen, to create their own wealth. A passive attitude will only cause loss and missed opportunity. Worrying about financial security will not provide that security. Pisces need to go after what they want tenaciously.

### Career and Public Image

Pisces like to be perceived by the public as people of spiritual or material wealth, of generosity and philanthropy. They look up to big-hearted, philanthropic types. They admire people engaged in large-scale undertakings and eventually would like to head up these big enterprises themselves. In short, they like to be connected with big organizations that are doing things in a big way.

If Pisces are to realize their full career and professional potential they need to travel more, educate themselves more and learn more about the actual world. In other words, they need some of the unflagging optimism of the Sagittarius in order to reach the top.

Because of all their caring and generous characteristics, Pisces often choose professions through which they can help and touch the lives of other people. That is why many Pisces become doctors, nurses, social workers or teachers. Sometimes it takes a while before Pisces realize what they really want to do in their professional lives, but once they find a career that lets them manifest their interests and virtues they will excel at it.

## Love and Relationships

It is not surprising that someone as 'otherworldly' as the Pisces would like a partner who is practical and down to earth. Pisces prefer a partner who is on top of all the details of life, because they dislike details. Pisces seek this quality in both their romantic and professional partners. More than anything else this gives Pisces a feeling of being grounded, of being in touch with reality.

As expected, these kinds of relationships – though necessary – are sure to have many ups and downs. Misunderstandings will take place because the two attitudes are poles apart. If you are in love with a Pisces you will experience these fluctuations and will need a lot of patience to see things stabilize. Pisces are moody, intuitive, affectionate and difficult to get to know. Only time and the right attitude will yield Pisces' deepest secrets. However, when in love with a Pisces you will find that riding the waves is worth it because they are good, sensitive people who need and like to give love and affection.

When in love, Pisces like to fantasize. For them fantasy is 90 per cent of the fun of a relationship. They tend to idealize their partner, which can be good and bad at the same time. It is bad in that it is difficult for anyone to live up to the high ideals their Pisces lover sets.

## Home and Domestic Life

In their family and domestic life Pisces have to resist the tendency to relate only by feelings and moods. It is unrealistic to expect that your partner and other family members will be as intuitive as you are. There is a need for more verbal communication between a Pisces and his or her family. A cool, unemotional exchange of ideas and opinions will benefit everyone.

Some Pisces tend to like mobility and moving around. For them too much stability feels like a restriction on their freedom. They hate to be locked in one location for ever.

The sign of Gemini sits on Pisces' 4th solar house (of home and family) cusp. This shows that the Pisces likes and needs a home environment that promotes intellectual and mental interests. They tend to treat their neighbours as family – or extended family. Some Pisces can have a dual attitude towards the home and family – on the one hand they like the emotional support of the family, but on the other they dislike the obligations, restrictions and duties involved with it. For Pisces, finding a balance is the key to a happy family life.

# Horoscope for 2012

**Major Trends**

The spiritual life is always important to you Pisces, but now that Neptune is moving into your sign on February 3 (and will stay for many years) it is even more so. The danger now is of losing your connection with the earth. Your feet hardly touch ground. More on this later.

Uranus moved into your money house last year (for the long term) and this is creating many exciting financial opportunities and changes. Finances are unstable now, either ultra high or ultra low (and sometimes one or the other), but are basically happy. More details later.

Saturn has been in your 8th house for some years and will be there until October 5. Friendships have been severely tested in the past year and the process continues, although a bit easier, in the year ahead. Some friendships have actually died. You also had a need to set some limits on sexual expression last year and the trend continues in the year ahead. Quality is preferable to quantity.

Jupiter moved into your 3rd house last year and will be there until June 11. Your ability to communicate is much expanded. Probably this comes from new and high-tech kinds of communication equipment, but also from an expanded knowledge base. With more knowledge you have more to say and others listen.

Love is stormy until July 3. Marriages and partnerships are being tested. Avoid power struggles in love. Venus spends more than four months in your 4th house of family this year, and Jupiter enters this house on June 11. So there are moves and marriages in the family. More on this later on.

Your areas of greatest interest (and you have many in the year ahead) are the body and image (from February 3 onwards); finance (for many years to come); communication and intellectual interests (until June 11); home and family (from April 3 onwards); love, romance and social activities (until July 3); sex, personal transformation, personal rein-vention and occult studies (until October 5); religion, philos-ophy, theology, foreign travel and higher education (from October 5 onwards); friends, groups and group activities.

Your paths of greatest fulfilment in the year ahead are communication and intellectual interests (until June 11); home and family (from June 11 onwards); career (until August 31); religion, philosophy, theology, foreign travel and higher education (from August 31 onwards).


## Health

*(Please note that this is an* astrological *perspective on health and not a medical one. In days of yore these perspectives were identical. But these days there could be quite a difference. For a medical perspective, please consult your doctor or health practitioner.)*

Health looks basically good in the year ahead Pisces. Until June 11 all the long-term planets are either in harmonious aspect or leaving you alone. On June 11 Jupiter makes a stressful aspect to you, but by himself this is not a serious issue. More serious, however, is Mars in Virgo from the beginning of the year until July 3. You need to be more care-ful on the physical plane and more alert, especially when driving or doing risky kinds of things. The danger is more of accident than lack of health.

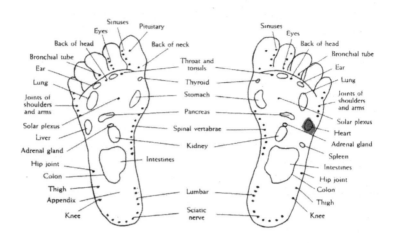

## Reflexology

*Try to massage the whole foot on a regular basis, but pay extra attention to the points highlighted on the chart. When you massage, be aware of 'sore spots', as these need special attention. It's also a good idea to massage the ankles and top side of the feet (see below).*

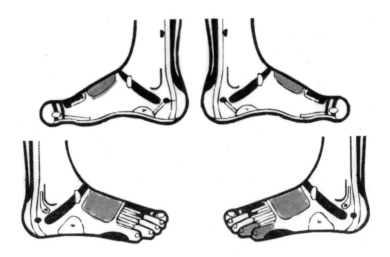

Your empty 6th house of health reinforces the ease we see in health. You are taking good health for granted and have no need to put too much effort into it. Good though your health is you can make it even better. Give more attention to the following organs: the feet (regular foot massage is powerful for you, as are foot baths and hydro-massage, and feet should be kept warm in winter – shoes should fit properly and not knock you off balance; comfort is more important than fashion, although if you can have both, so much the better!); the heart (avoid worry and anxiety, the main root causes of heart problems, and damaging from the spiritual perspective – if there is something constructive to be done in a situation, do it, of course, but eliminate the worry as it doesn't help the situation or your health).

Your health planet, the Sun, is one of the fast-moving planets. In the course of the year he will move through all the signs and houses of your Horoscope. Thus there are many short-term trends in health that are best dealt with in the monthly reports.

Twice a year, the Sun gets eclipsed. For you this can create health disturbances or scares. With overall vitality basically good, these will most likely be scares and nothing more. However, these eclipses (on May 20 and November 13) are times to make changes in the health regime, to fine tune it.

In general you tend to have a finely tuned, sensitive kind of body. With Neptune moving into your 1st house, this will become even more pronounced. The body is becoming even more refined and spiritualized than usual. You will find that your dietary needs are changing. A lighter, more vegetarian kind of diet seems called for. This doesn't mean that you have to become totally vegan, but little by little you'll find that your craving for red meat and other rich food will lessen, and you will start enjoying lighter fare. Alcohol and drugs should be avoided as much as possible. These things will affect a refined system more dramatically than a non-refined one. Other people may be able to get away with it, but not you. There's more about this below.

Though your health is good there are periods in the year where the health and energy are not up to their usual standards. This is due to temporary stressful transits. They are not trends for the year. This year these periods are May 20 to June 21, August 23 to September 22 and November 22 to December 21.

### Home and Family

As we mentioned, your 4th house becomes strong on April 3 as Venus enters for four months (an unusually long transit) and Jupiter moves into this House on June 11. So this is an active and basically happy area of life. Though there are a few challenges – there are two eclipses in this House – your interest and focus here gives you the energy and drive to overcome them. A successful area of life this year.

First off, the home is being redecorated and made more beautiful. There is more socializing and entertaining at home, and more socializing with family members in general. If there have been problems with family members in recent years you have a good opportunity to create harmony now, and it is more likely to happen. You seem able to lift the family relationship to a new and better level, a happier level. Probably there are marriages in the family too, and this fits with the symbolism of both Venus and Jupiter.

Moves, renovations and expansions of the home are likely in the year ahead. Sometimes people don't actually move; sometimes they buy additional homes, or renovate the home so that it is 'as if' they have moved. You will acquire expensive items for the home as well. The home is a happier place in many ways. If you don't move this year, you can move next year as well. Jupiter will be in your 4th house in 2013 too.

If you are looking to sell a home there is good fortune this year. There is good family support and it works both ways. You are supportive of family members and they are supportive of you. The family as a whole rises in status and stature this year. Family members are more ambitious than usual and seem successful.

Jupiter is your career planet. Thus you are either setting up a home office or enlarging and expanding the present one. You are furthering the career from home. (Career opportunities are coming from family members and family connections too.)

The family circle expands this year. This happens in various ways. Often it is through birth or marriage. Sometimes it happens by meeting people who are 'like family' to you (and these can be more supportive than biological family members in many cases).

There are some bumps on the road this year. Two eclipses (one on May 20 and the other on November 28) will bring up hidden, long-festering problems either with the physical home or with family members. When the dust settles, you will be in a better position to clear up the problem – at least you know what it is and can address it rationally.

## Finance and Career

There is a very exciting, but also very volatile financial year ahead. Many dramatic financial changes are happening. Moreover, it is not just a one-off change and you continue after it; rather it is a constant process of change, a constant upgrading of the financial life that is going on. Every time you think you have things just the way you want them, a new idea, a new investment, a new method appears and again you are making changes.

Cosmically speaking, you are being set free on a financial level. The cosmos is leading you to financial freedom, but in the process many old attachments and ways of thinking and doing things have to be shaken up and broken and this is where the drama comes from. By the time Uranus is finished with you – it is a seven-year process and you are only in year two – you will have a new sense of financial freedom and independence.

Uranus in your money house shows a penchant for start-ups and new ventures. Many of you will be starting your own business. Many of you will be working for start-up type companies in experimental kinds of fields. These businesses might not be in the mainstream right now, but in the future they will be. You seem on the ground floor. Uranus rules science, the Internet, the electronic media – the new high-tech communication systems that keep coming out year after year. So these kinds of businesses and investments are calling to you and you have a flair for them. Also the high-tech side of the health field – health gadgets and the new cutting-edge therapies that are emerging.

The interesting thing here is that you are on a financial adventure. The old financial rule books, though they have some validity, are not for you. You are learning what works for you through trial and error and experimentation. Your experiments will take you to the heights, but also through many valleys. Earnings can go sky high, but also ultra low. It would be nice if the high times lasted forever, but this is not the way Uranus works. Be sure to set aside funds from the highs to cover the lean times.

Money and financial opportunity come to you suddenly and unexpectedly. Wealth can happen for you at any time and this is exciting.

Your financial planet, Mars, spends many months in Virgo, your 7th house. This suggests that a business partner-ship is happening. This will be quite a challenge as Uranus in Aries likes to be independent. But a partnership that allows for personal autonomy could work.

In general the spouse, friends and the social circle are playing a huge (more than normal) role in earnings. You seem to be spending more on social matters too. Your part-ner or spouse seems more financially supportive than usual.

This is not an especially strong career year. You derive satisfaction from it, but you seem more focused on the home and family and your emotional life. Your mission this year involves the family – being there for them – and keeping your emotional harmony.

## Love and Social Life

Mars spends an unusual amount of time in your 7th house of love and marriage. Generally this is not a great transit for love. Existing relationships tend to get tested now. There are tendencies to power struggles in the relationship, and you should avoid this as much as possible. Mars transiting the 7th house doesn't spell divorce or break-ups; he goes through this house every year and many a marriage and long-term relationship has weathered this transit. It just tends to bring conflict. This year though, with Mars spending so much time here (over six months) break-ups are more probable. Keep in mind though that this transit doesn't last for ever and a good relationship will easily withstand it.

For singles this transit shows more aggression in love, a more proactive kind of approach. If you like someone you will let them know and go after them (albeit in a mellow, Piscean way). You tend to be a 'love at first sight' kind of person under this transit, and perhaps too quick to jump into serious relationships. You are developing courage in love, fearlessness. (This is happening in finance too.) Yes, rashness often leads to mistakes, but no matter, you pick yourself up and jump back into the fray. Mars is not afraid to fail. He doesn't like failure, doesn't believe in it, but if it happens, he is not unduly perturbed.

Mars in the 7th house is not especially conducive for marriage, so marriage is not likely this year. (In India if a person has Mars in the 7th house by birth, astrologers counsel against marriage.) But love is there, and business kinds of partnerships.

Singles are attracted to the wealthy this year. Wealth is an aphrodisiac, and you seem to be mixing more with the wealthy until July 3. Material gifts, tangible things, are turn-ons. Singles find love opportunities as they pursue their normal financial goals and with people who are involved in their finances.

Since your love planet, Mercury, is a very fast-moving planet, there are many short-term trends in love that are best dealt with in the monthly reports.

Mercury goes retrograde three times a year. You have dealt with this many, many times. It is nothing to fear, only to be understood. These times are not good for making long-term romantic decisions to marry or divorce. These are times to review the relationship (and you social life in general) and see where improvements can be made. The time for action comes later on, when mental clarity is achieved. Also, love seems to go backwards during these times and more patience is needed. This year Mercury will be retrograde from March 12 to April 5. July 15 to August 7, and November 6 to November 25.

### Self-improvement

Your ruling planet, Neptune, moves into your 1st house on February 3, as we mentioned. We discussed some of the mundane impact of this earlier. But there is much more to it. Generally this is a positive transit for you. The personal appearance will shine. You will have an unearthly, supernatural kind of beauty. In general this is good for self-confidence and self-esteem. But there are spiritual dimensions to this transit as well.

The body, as we have said, is becoming highly sensitized and refined (this process has been going on for a number of years). Your psychic abilities (already the best in the zodiac) will become even stronger. You will feel psychic vibrations (supposedly non-physical energies) in a very physical way. This is intended as a great blessing, but it needs to be understood and used properly. If not understood, it can be quite painful and lead to many unnecessary adventures. With a little training and practice, you will be able to hold an object in your hand and know all kinds of things about the owner of the object. You will feel the psychic impressions from the object in your hand. You can be near a person and immediately discern the state of health (and also the psychological state). Your body will tell you. On the other hand, you might be near a person with a heart problem and feel it as if it were your own. It feels so real that many needless surgeries have happened because of this phenomenon. So there is a need now (and for the next 14 years) to become more 'impersonal' with the body. Think of the body as an instrument that 'registers' phenomena, but don't identify with what is registered. You will discover that the body can manifest symptoms though there is no pathology in the body. It is much the same as a television showing graphic images of violence, death and destruction – there is nothing wrong with the television itself, it is merely picturing the broadcast on the screen.

Also, it will become necessary to be more choosy about who you associate with. You need to be around positive, uplifting people. Being around the wrong kind of people can be quite painful, in a physical kind of way. I have seen sensitive people being affected by sitting at the wrong table in a restaurant. There was nothing wrong with the food or service, but the people at a nearby table were troubled and the sensitive picked up on it – much like you pick up a virus – and had headaches and trouble sleeping.

Uranus is your personal spiritual planet. He rules your 12th house. His move into your money house opens new vistas in your spiritual life. Hitherto, you have thought that spirituality was 'unworldly' and not concerned with matters of Earth. Now (since last year) you will be seeing how practical it is, and how it can affect your earnings and bottom line. The Divine wants you to be rich, but in its way not yours. It will respond to your financial needs and problems, if called upon and given permission to operate. So this is a time for making your spirituality practical in the day-to-day world.

# Month-by-month Forecasts

## January

Best Days Overall: 8, 9, 17, 18, 25, 26
Most Stressful Days Overall: 5, 6, 7, 12, 13, 19, 20
Best Days for Love: 1, 2, 6, 7, 12, 13, 18, 19, 22, 27, 28
Best Days for Money: 1, 2, 3, 4, 12, 13, 21, 22, 28, 29, 30, 31
Best Days for Career: 3, 12, 19, 20, 21, 30

Your year begins with most of the planets in the Eastern sector of personal power and independence. Until the 24th all of the planets are moving forward. A clear message – this is a time to take the initiative and make things happen. You have the power to design your life according to your specifications, with little need to adapt or compromise. So long as you are not hurting others, why not have things your way? This is a time where who you are and what you can do matters. Who you know is much less important. As you take personal initiative, you will make rapid progress to your goals. Improvements will happen quickly.

Your year also begins with most of the planets above the horizon. You are in the day of your year, although late in the day. It is still good to focus on the outer life, your career and worldly goals. You are just coming off a yearly career peak and Mercury is in your career house until the 8th. Career is still a focus but less so than in previous months.

Love is delicate this month. Mars in your 7th house shows a tendency to power struggles in the marriage or current relationship, and you need to avoid this as much as possible. Sometimes it makes you or your partner overly competitive in love. The cosmic purpose of this transit is to learn fearlessness in love. Indeed where true love is present there is never any fear. If fear arises, there is something amiss in the love – perhaps it is lust or covetousness or possessiveness masking itself as love. Your love planet squares Uranus between the

8th and the 10th, so be more patient with the beloved. He or she is apt to be more temperamental. Mood changes in love are swift and extreme. The beloved (and family members as well) need to be more careful driving and avoid risky activities that period. Take extra safety precautions in the home.

Venus moves into your sign on the 24th. This is generally good for love. You look glamorous and more beautiful than usual. You dress well and with style. You are attracting the opposite sex. Your overall demeanour is graceful and charming. The love challenges are not related to these things, but to the actual relationship.

Mars is your financial planet. His position in the 7th house for many more months shows that a business partnership or joint venture is happening. Your social circle is important in finance. You are combining the social life with the financial life, and generally this means that you prefer to do business with friends and tend to socialize with the people you do business with. On the 24th Mars goes retrograde, so try to make important purchases, investments or any long-term financial commitments before then.

Health is good and you can enhance it further by giving more attention to the spine, knees, teeth, bones, skin and overall skeletal alignment until the 20th, and to the ankles and calves afterwards.

**February**

Best Days Overall: 4, 5, 13, 14, 22, 23
Most Stressful Days Overall: 2, 3, 9, 10, 15, 16, 29
Best Days for Love: 2, 3, 5, 6, 9, 10, 11, 12, 15, 21, 22, 24, 25
Best Days for Money: 1, 9, 10, 17, 18, 24, 25, 27, 28
Best Days for Career: 1, 9, 15, 16, 17, 27, 28

You are always a spiritual person. Your spiritual life is always important, and even more so last month and this month. Your spiritual 12th house is very powerful now. Not only that but Neptune, the ruler of your Horoscope and the most spiritual of all the planets moves into your sign on the 3rd. Your own sign is the strongest sign this month. Your challenge this month is to keep your feet on the ground. You are more comfortable in the spiritual world than in the material, everyday world. The dream life is so active, so vivid, so interesting that everyday life seems drab in comparison. You don't need drugs or alcohol this month (or ever): you are naturally high.

The intuition and extra-sensory perception, always good, are very strong this month. If you trust your intuition, you will avoid many of the discords of the outer world.

You are in the maximum period of personal power and independence this month. You can and should have things your way. Your way is the best way (at least for you). Others are important and to be respected, but your way is best for you. Follow it fearlessly.

This month, the planets shift from the upper to the lower half of your Horoscope. You are in the sunset of your year. The activities of day are pretty much over with and you are getting ready for the activities of the night. Day and night are not equal, but are equally important. They are two radically different modes of functioning. In the day we are 'outwardly' oriented. We achieve objectives by physical, outer motions. During the night, we are inwardly oriented and we achieve objectives by inner means, by dreaming, visualizing, and attaining the 'mood-feeling' of that which we desire. And thus right feeling is more important than right doing. In fact, right feeling *is* right doing, for it leads to right doing. So, it is important to find and function from your personal point of emotional harmony. Get the home and family life in order. Career is important and you will do whatever needs to be done, but give more attention to the home, family and your emotional life.

Your financial life is still under review. Business partner-ship or joint ventures need more study. The retrograde of your financial planet doesn't stop earnings, but slows things down a bit. When used properly it is the pause that refreshes. There are many improvements that can be made in your financial condition and now is the time to look for them and make plans. You will act on the plans later on. The most important thing now is the attainment of mental clar-ity about finances. When this happens, everything else will fall into place.

Health is good this month. You have plenty of energy. The personal appearance shines. You have all the energy you need to achieve any goal you set for yourself.

## March

Best Days Overall: 3, 4, 11, 12, 20, 21, 30, 31
Most Stressful Days Overall: 1, 7, 8, 13, 14, 27, 28, 29
Best Days for Love: 2, 5, 7, 8, 13, 15, 16, 25, 26, 31
Best Days for Money: 7, 8, 15, 16, 22, 23, 24, 25, 26
Best Days for Career: 7, 13, 14, 15, 16, 25, 26

With most of the planets still in the East, your personal effort and initiative achieves much. But when it comes to love and family, this is not so. You need more patience here, especially after the 15th when Mercury starts to retrograde. Time will solve family and love issues, not personal effort. It is good now to focus on the family and to give them more attention, but avoid making long-term family decisions after the 15th. Home projects are best done before then too.

Love and money are under review this month. Mars is still retrograde, and is joined on the 15th by Mercury, your love planet. With Neptune in your own sign now you have an unearthly kind of glamour. Regardless of your age or stage in life, this beauty shines through the body. And people are attracted to it (though they don't know why). However, this can also complicate the love life. You are a mystery to others. For the life of them, they can't figure you out.

There are good spiritual reasons for the aura of mystery about you. A part of you knows that it is 'infinite' and refuses to be put in any box or category. This baffles those in the 3D world. For them everything is defined and categorized, and you cannot be defined.

On February 19th you entered a yearly personal pleasure peak. And you are still in it until the 20th. Health is a focus this month, more from a cosmetic perspective than from an actual health perspective. When you are healthy you look good. Good health is better than any cosmetic or accessory.

This month, on the 20th, you enter a yearly financial peak. You are active in the financial realm, but keep in mind the retrograde of Mars. The retrograde of a financial planet doesn't mean that we stop all financial activity; this would be impossible. But you need to avoid financial short cuts (they are not really short cuts) and be as perfect as you can in your financial dealings. Better to be a little late and perfect, than early and mediocre. It also shows that though financial good is happening, it comes with a 'delayed reaction'.

The Sun opposes Mars from the 1st to the 15th and this can bring some conflicts at work. It also conjuncts Uranus from the 23rd to the 26th, which can bring job changes and upheavals at the workplace. If you employ others there is instability in the workforce and dramas in the lives of employees.

## April

Best Days Overall: 8, 16, 17, 26, 27
Most Stressful Days Overall: 4, 10, 24, 25
Best Days for Love: 3, 4, 5, 8, 9, 14, 15, 17, 18, 24, 25, 29, 30
Best Days for Money: 3, 4, 12, 13, 19, 20, 21, 22
Best Days for Career: 4, 10, 12, 13, 21, 22

Mercury, your love and family planet, starts to move forward on the 4th. So there is more mental clarity in these matters and it is safer to make important decisions then.

You are still very much in a yearly financial peak until the 20th. Mars, your financial planet, also starts to move forward on the 14th. The financial picture and strategy is much clearer and thus success is more likely. Very often when one is in a financial peak and the financial planet is retrograde, earnings increases still happen, but later than expected.

There was turbulence at the job last month and perhaps job changes but have no fear. Your work planet, the Sun, starts to travel with Jupiter after the 20th and this brings very happy job opportunities – dream job opportunities and prestigious kinds of jobs. This can be within your present company or with a new one. This month you feel the beginning of the aspect; next month it will be more exact. If there have been health problems, you will hear good news about them. Health is good this month. You seem to be spending more on health and health gadgets until the 20th. Financial health is as important to you as physical health. In fact, financial worries can create actual physical health problems if you allow this. Physical exercise enhances the health, scalp and head massage as well. After the 20th, enhance the health through neck massage. Craniaosacral therapy is powerful too (even before the 20th).

Love is happier this month. You still have to be careful of conflict and power struggles, but you seem to have things your way. Your love planet is in your own sign until the

17th. Singles don't need to do much to attract love – just go about your daily routine and it will find you. After the 17th Mercury enters your money house and goes into 'mutual reception' with Mars, the financial planet. Each is a guest in the house of the other. This is considered very positive; it shows co-operation between the planets and thus between these two departments of life. This reinforces what we have written earlier. You do business with the people you socialize with (your friends) and you become friends and socialize with the people you do business with. Business partnerships and joint ventures are even likelier now than early in the year. If you are the owner of company, this aspect can indicate a merger or friendly takeover.

Love is idealistic and spiritual until the 17th. Only the feeling of love matters. You could be happy in a shack with a leaky roof so long as the feeling of love is present. But after the 17th you seem more practical. Wealth is a turn-on in love. The person who can provide physical and material comforts is alluring to you.

Be more patient with the beloved from the 22nd to the 24th as he or she is apt to be more temperamental – family members too.

**May**

Best Days Overall: 5, 6, 13, 14, 15, 23, 24, 25
Most Stressful Days Overall: 1, 2, 7, 8, 21, 22, 28, 29
Best Days for Love: 1, 2, 3, 4, 8, 11, 12, 18, 19, 20, 21, 22, 28, 29, 30, 31
Best Days for Money: 1, 2, 9, 10, 16, 17, 19, 20, 28, 29
Best Days for Career: 2, 7, 8, 10, 19, 20, 29

Health needs watching from the 20th onwards, and being more careful before that won't hurt either. There is a solar eclipse on the 20th that affects all of you very strongly, especially those born early in the sign of Pisces (February 19–22). This eclipse occurs right on the cusp of your 4th house and impacts powerfully on Neptune, your ruling planet. Take it easy and avoid taking risks a few days before and after. This eclipse brings family crises, major changes in the family situation and with family members (perhaps dramas in their personal lives). Do your best to make the home safer. If there are hidden problems in the home, this is the time you find out about them so that you can make corrections. Family members are apt to be more temperamental this period too so be more patient with them. The good news here is that you are very focused on the family now and so you are on the case, on top of things.

Every solar eclipse affects the job and those who work under you. There are job changes and changes in the working conditions. But have no fear; you have fabulous job aspects this period. (This eclipse could also be indicating a recent job change that has already occurred.) Health scares also tend to happen with this kind of eclipse. Again, there's no need to panic, but get more information. There are changes in your health regime and diet as well. A physical detox wouldn't be a surprise now.

You will feel the effects of this eclipse for many months. You are redefining your image, personality and self-concept for the next six months, changing your look and overall presentation, the way you want others to see you. Usually this results in major wardrobe changes.

You are strong in the 3rd house of communication this month until the 20th. Yet your communication planet, Venus, begins retrograde motion on the 15th. If you are doing mass mailings or advertising campaigns (or other big communication projects), it will be best to do them before the 15th. After then it is better to plan these things rather than actually doing them.

Enhance the health by giving more attention to the neck and throat until the 20th and to the lungs, arms and shoulders afterwards. Good emotional health is very important after the 20th as well. If physical problems happen (God forbid), check on the family situation and bring harmony there as quickly as you can. Diet is more of an issue after the 20th as well.

Love is close to home this month – in the neighbourhood. There's no need to travel far for it.

## June

Best Days Overall: 1, 2, 10, 11, 20, 21, 29, 30
Most Stressful Days Overall: 3, 4, 17, 18, 24, 25
Best Days for Love: 1, 8, 9, 10, 17, 18, 20, 21, 24, 25, 27, 28
Best Days for Money: 5, 6, 7, 12, 13, 15, 16, 17, 25, 26, 27
Best Days for Career: 3, 4, 5, 6, 17, 26, 27

Your health still needs watching until the 21st. You are feeling the after-effects of last month's eclipse from the 8th to the 17th as Jupiter starts to move over this point, re-activating it. (It is as if you are experiencing the eclipse anew.) This brings career changes and shake-ups in your corporate hierarchy or industry. It also brings dramas in the lives of parents, parent figures or bosses. The family situation still seems volatile and perhaps a move could be happening as well.

In addition to this, there is a lunar eclipse on the 4th which affects career. It occurs in your 10th house and reinforces what we said earlier. You, family members and parent figures should take a nice, relaxed and easy schedule. Stressful activities that can be put off are better off rescheduled. Pisceans of appropriate age are super fertile now. (This would fit the other symbolism of image changes too.)

Jupiter, your career planet, moves into your 4th house of home and family on the 11th and will be there for the rest of the year. Family and the family situation is your real mission these days. Sure, many of you will have an outer career, but that is just for the world; your spiritual mission is your family. In many cases, it shows a focus on parenthood and parenting. Avoid speculations around the lunar eclipse period.

By the 21st, things quieten down a bit. Health and energy improve. Life is sunny and fun again. The storms

are temporarily abated. You enter a yearly personal pleasure peak – a happy-go-lucky period for enjoying your life.
Your 4th house is ultra-powerful this month, especially
until the 21st. This house is more than just about home
and family. It is about your emotional life, your moods and
feelings. It is about your history, the forces that shaped
who you are today (and this history goes far beyond your
childhood, it embraces many, many life times). Your 10th
career house represents your future – your aspirations and
purposes; your 4th house your past. These are intimately
related. In a given year, both of these houses will get ener-
gized at different times. Sometimes in order to go forward,
we need to go backward. That is, we need to review the
past and clear out blockages, resolve old issues. When this
happens we can start moving forward. There as a film
called *Back to the Future* and this sort of captures what the
4th house is all about. We go back and thus can move
forward.

When the 4th house is strong people become nostalgic.
They remember the 'good old days', often with a desire to
go back to them. This nostalgia is 'natural order' – subcon-
sciously you are resolving old issues.

Those of you involved in therapy will have many psychological breakthroughs this month (and there will be many in
the year ahead as well).

**July**

Best Days Overall: 7, 8, 17, 18, 26, 27
Most Stressful Days Overall: 1, 2, 15, 16, 22, 23, 28, 29
Best Days for Love: 1, 2, 5, 6, 9, 10, 11, 15, 19, 20, 21, 22, 23, 24, 25, 28, 29
Best Days for Money: 4, 5, 6, 9, 10, 11, 15, 16, 24, 25
Best Days for Career: 1, 2, 5, 6, 15, 16, 24, 25, 28, 29

Retrograde activity hit its high for the year last month; 40 per cent of the plants were retrograde until June 25. This month there is a lull until the 15th and then once again 40 per cent of the planets are retrograde. The pace of life slows down, both on a personal and collective level. It's good that your 5th house is strong. You may as well enjoy yourself as not much is happening in the world.

Neptune, the ruler of your Horoscope, went retrograde last month, and Uranus, your spiritual planet, goes retrograde on the 13th. They will be retrograde for many more months. This affects your spiritual life. The two spiritual planets in your chart are retrograde at the same time now. Dreams, intuitions, spiritual messages and instruction need much more verification these days. They are probably true on their level but might not mean what you think they mean. Wait for inner clarity before acting.

The retrograde of Mercury, from the 15th onwards, affects the love and emotional life, and the family life as well. These are now under review. Avoid making major decisions one way or another. It is a time for fact-gathering and research, a time for resolving doubts. Observe your moods and feelings without judgement and clarity will eventually come.

Mercury's retrograde doesn't stop the love life, only slows things down. Take more care in communicating with the beloved. Many of the problems between you stem from miscommunication and misunderstanding (and the same is true with family members). These misunderstandings take a huge toll on our energy. There are hurt feelings, recriminations and emotional back and forth. A little more care in the beginning can save you heartache (not to mention time) later on. Don't even try to communicate important ideas if the beloved or the family member is not in 'right state' – they are sure not to get the right message. You have to be alert for communication opportunities when things are calm and they are ready to listen.

Health is much improved over last month. If there have been health problems you hear good news about them now. You are more focused on health after the 22nd. Enhance the health in the ways described in the yearly report. This month you can also give more attention to the lungs, small intestine, arms, shoulders and respiratory system. Arm and shoulder massage is good. It is also important to maintain harmony in the family and with the beloved; discords here can create physical pathologies.

Mars has been in your house of love since the beginning of the year, but now makes a major move into your 8th house on the 4th. A good time to cut out waste in the financial life, to expand by reducing expenses and getting rid of possessions that you no longer need. Tax issues are influencing your financial decisions these days.

## August

Best Days Overall: 4, 5, 13, 14, 15, 22, 23, 31
Most Stressful Days Overall: 11, 12, 18, 19, 24, 25
Best Days for Love: 2, 3, 6, 7, 13, 14, 16, 17, 18, 19, 22, 23, 24, 25, 31
Best Days for Money: 1, 2, 6, 7, 11, 12, 20, 21, 29, 30, 31
Best Days for Career: 1, 2, 11, 12, 20, 21, 24, 25, 29, 30

Mars remains in your 8th house until the 20th, so review our discussion of last month. This position also indicates that this is a good time to pay down debt and to make debt if you need to. You have better access to outside money. Often lines of credit increase under this kind of transit. There are financial opportunities through creative kinds of financing.

If you have good ideas, money is not the issue – there is plenty of outside money available. Money can come to you through insurance claims or involvement with estates. Perhaps the most important thing is that you have a special ability now to see value where others see only death and decay. Thus you can profit from distressed companies or properties. People under this transit will often walk into a junk shop and spot a valuable antique. You see the value in what others see as 'junk'. There is some brief financial challenge from the 11th to the 17th – perhaps a sudden expense or some unexpected delay. Be patient, this is a short-term problem.

Mars leaving your 7th house marks an improvement in the love life. There is less conflict and competitiveness there and more harmony. The love planet is still retrograde until the 8th so keep in mind our discussion of this last month. On the 23rd you enter a yearly love and social peak. And with Mercury moving forward and Mars no longer in the 7th house it should be a happy social period. Your love planet is in your 6th house of health this month, while and the ruler of this house is in your 7th house after the 23rd; thus the two planets are in 'mutual reception', each a guest in the house of the other. There is great co-operation between these two planets and the areas of life that they rule. Thus there are love opportunities at work, or with the people involved in your health. You have the aspects for the office romance this period. Love can find you at the doctor's surgery, or gym, or yoga studio as you pursue your health goals. Good health enhances your love life and a happy love life enhances your health. A romantic date this period is not necessarily a night out on the town; it is more likely a mutual jog, or attending aerobics or yoga classes together.

Love is shown by service this period. When you love someone you do things for them and this is how you feel loved as well.

Health needs more watching after the 23rd. Enhance the health in the ways mentioned last month.

Venus squares Uranus from the 14th to the 17th. Be more careful driving and avoid risky activities. Be more mindful on the physical plane. Cars and communication equipment are likely to be more temperamental.

## September

Best Days Overall: 1, 10, 11, 19, 27, 28
Most Stressful Days Overall: 7, 8, 14, 15, 21, 22
Best Days for Love: 1, 4, 5, 12, 14, 15, 16, 17, 21, 22, 25, 26, 29, 30
Best Days for Money: 1, 2, 3, 7, 8, 10, 11, 16, 17, 18, 19, 25, 26, 27, 28, 29, 30
Best Days for Career: 7, 8, 16, 17, 21, 22, 25, 26

When Mercury moves into Virgo on the 1st, the planetary power makes an important shift from the lower to the upper half of your Horoscope. You are entering the daytime of your year. By now, you have found your point of emotional harmony. Hopefully you have been making the inner preparations for your career, visualizing your goals, day-dreaming (in a conscious way) about them and experiencing the feeling of their attainment. Now comes the time when the physical, outer motions have to be made. These dreams are now to become tangible reality. If you have been working correctly, the actions you take will be very natural, unforced, harmonious and spontaneous – side-effects of your inner work. Action is called for now. The daytime is for outer action.

Career has been undergoing many changes since the eclipses of May and June. Last month Jupiter (your career planet) was re-activating the lunar eclipse point of June 4. This is happening this month as well. In some cases this is producing actual career change – a change of job or change of career direction. In other cases, it is creating career change within your present situation. Shake-ups at the top are creating opportunities for you. Now is the time to start taking advantage of these things.

Authority figures are not as secure as you would think. Major dramas are happening in their lives. Working from home seems an interesting proposition. Even if you work in an office, you are probably taking more work home.

Your financial planet spends the month in the 9th house – a very bullish signal for a prosperous month. Much of what we said over the past two months is still valid now. Mars is in the sign of Scorpio, the 'natural' 8th house, but there are a few changes. Mars in this position shows financial opportunities in foreign countries, foreign investments, foreign companies and foreigners in general. You are probably spending more on travel as well. The religious people in your life – clerics, ministers, those at your place of worship – seem financially more supportive and perhaps have good ideas or connections for you. There are financial opportunities that happen through them.

Health needs watching until the 23rd. This month, enhance the health through more attention to the kidneys and hips (hip massage will be powerful on the energetic level) from the 7th onwards. Detoxing also seems good.

You are still in a yearly love and social peak until the 23rd. You still have the aspects for the office romance. There is more socializing with the family this month. Family members enjoy playing cupid and they seem very involved in your love life. Avoid being overly perfectionist in love. Your job this month is to come from the heart rather than the head.

## October

Best Days Overall: 7, 8, 16, 17, 24, 25, 26
Most Stressful Days Overall: 4, 5, 6, 12, 13, 18, 19
Best Days for Love: 1, 6, 7, 12, 13, 16, 17, 21, 25, 26
Best Days for Money: 1, 4, 5, 6, 14, 15, 22, 23, 27, 28
Best Days for Career: 4, 5, 6, 14, 15, 18, 19, 22, 23

The upper half of your chart becomes even more powerful this month as Venus crosses from the lower half to the upper half on the 3rd. So you are in a career period now. However there are complications. Your career planet goes retrograde on the 4th and will be retrograde for the rest of the year. Yes, you have to focus on your career now, but more cautiously. Take a step by step, methodical approach to it. Avoid short cuts. The long way, the perfect way, is really the short way now. The tortoise seems to lag behind the hare but in the end the tortoise wins the race. The important thing is to attain mental clarity now. This will take time.

Though your yearly love peak technically ended last month, love is still very active and prominent this month. Until the 5th the love planet is in the sign of Libra in the 8th house, indicating a sexually active period. After the 5th the love planet moves into the 9th house. This brings an increase in social activity and new friends are coming into the picture. Love opportunities happen in foreign lands, with foreigners, at educational or religious settings. On the 29th Mercury crosses the Mid-heaven, a very good aspect for love. The Mid-heaven is really the most powerful abstract point in the Horoscope, thus the love planet is at maximum power then. The social magnetism is very strong. This tends to success in love. You are socializing with the high and the mighty. There are love opportunities as you pursue your normal career goals, or with people involved in your career. The social circle and the current love are supportive career-wise too.

Mars, the financial planet, also crosses the Mid-heaven on the 7th and then enters your 10th house, indicating prosperity. Earning power is at a powerful position at the top of the chart. You have the financial favour of the powers that be – bosses, authority figures, parents, parent figures and elders. Rises often happen under this transit. Your good professional reputation enhances your income as referrals come to you. The money people in your life are supporting the career.

Mars squares Neptune from the 6th to the 9th. Do more homework on finance that period. Deals and projects are not what they seem. Don't take things at face value. Mars makes wonderful aspects to Uranus from the 13th to the 17th and the financial intuition is very good. There is spiritual guidance available about money matters.

Be more careful communicating with elders, parents and bosses from the 15th to the 18th. Problems with them (and with the government) are probably stemming from miscommunication and misunderstanding. Better communication would prevent this.

Be more careful driving from the 3rd to the 5th and definitely avoid drinking and driving. Overall, health is good this month.

### November

Best Days Overall: 3, 4, 5, 12, 13, 21, 22
Most Stressful Days Overall: 1, 2, 8, 9, 14, 15, 28, 29
Best Days for Love: 1, 6, 7, 8, 9, 11, 14, 15, 20, 23, 24
Best Days for Money: 1, 2, 6, 7, 11, 15, 19, 23, 24, 26, 28, 29
Best Days for Career: 1, 2, 11, 14, 15, 19, 28, 29

Retrograde activity spikes briefly to its yearly maximum 40 per cent between the 6th and the 11th but this is its 'last gasp' for the year. By the end of the month only 20 per cent will be retrograde, and next month the planetary power will be 90 per cent forward. The delays and glitches are only temporary.

The two generic planets of travel, Mercury (short-term local travel) and Jupiter (foreign travel), are both retrograde at the same time from the 6th to the 26th. You are very much into travel this month, but perhaps it might be better to plan foreign trips than actually take them. Your personal travel planets are moving forward, but still this is not the best time to be travelling. If you must travel follow our usual advice; allow more time to get to your destination, insure your tickets and protect yourself as best you can.

We have two eclipses this month. The first is a solar eclipse on the 13th in your 9th house (definitely don't travel during the eclipse period). For students this shows major changes in their educational plans and strategy. Often schools and courses are changed and there are shake-ups in the school hierarchy. The rules change.

All Pisceans, students and non-students, will experience crises of faith or events that contradict their personal philosophy or belief system. The upper mental body (where we formulate these things) gets a shock. Thus false beliefs, or beliefs that are only partially correct, are cleansed from the system. There are shake-ups in your place of worship and in the lives of the people at your place of worship.

Your health is basically good this month, but there can be health scares, or changes in your health regime and diet. Job changes, changes in the conditions of work, are also happening.

The lunar eclipse of the 28th seems to affect you more strongly. You need to rest and relax more from the 22nd onwards, and especially around the eclipse period. As always, avoid risky, stressful activities. Do what needs to be done, but elective things (surgeries, trips, sky diving, bungee jumping, stressful meetings) are best rescheduled. This eclipse occurs in your 4th house and creates a family crisis or some crisis in the home. Be more patient with family members this period. Everyone is more temperamental. The dream life will be hyperactive during this period, but don't give too much credence to the dreams. Many people report 'nightmarish' kinds of dreams with a lunar eclipse in the 4th house but these things are just the roilings of the inner planes caused by the eclipse. They are not necessarily prophetic.

## December

Best Days Overall: 1, 2, 10, 11, 18, 19, 30, 31
Most Stressful Days Overall: 5, 6, 7, 12, 13, 25, 26, 27
Best Days for Love: 1, 2, 5, 6, 7, 10, 11, 20, 21, 31
Best Days for Money: 6, 8, 15, 16, 20, 21, 22, 24, 25
Best Days for Career: 8, 12, 13, 16, 25

Last month on the 22nd you entered a yearly career peak, and this continues in the month ahead until the 21st. Your focus on the career is good but your career planet is still retrograde. So there is a need to be more cautious. Progress by all means, but slowly, methodically and perfectly. Be more patient with the various delays that happen (seems to me it is indecision by superiors – they can't make up their mind or deliver on what they promise.) Jupiter's retrograde won't stop your success, but it might happen a bit later than you expected.

Though the lunar eclipse happened last month, you are still feeling the effects of it this month. Venus and Mercury – the two love planets in your chart – re-activate this point. Mercury re-activates it from the 15th to the 17th and Venus from the 20th to the 23rd. This can make the beloved more temperamental and bring dramas in his or her life. He or she should relax more during this period and avoid risk taking or undue stress. These two planets are also very involved in communication. So take more care here. Communication equipment and cars can be more temperamental than usual. (Problems in the love life are probably coming from miscommunication now.)

Continue to rest and relax more until the 21st. Enhance the health in the ways mentioned in the yearly report, but also give more attention to the liver and thighs (until the 21st) and to the spine, knees, teeth, bones, skin and overall skeletal alignment afterwards. Thigh massage is powerful until the 21st (and this strengthens the whole lower back as well); back massage is powerful afterwards.

The two love planets are in your 10th house of career from the 11th onwards. This gives many messages. You are being helped career-wise by your social circle. You advance your career by social means, by attending or hosting the right parties. You have an ability to meet (on a social level) the exact people who can help you. Your personal abilities are important, but your 'people skills' are more important career-wise these days.

Though there are challenges in love (when Mercury and Venus re-activate the eclipse point), basically love seems successful and happy this month. Your spouse, partner or current love is elevated and you appreciate him or her more. Love is important to you, high on your priorities, and thus you are able to meet and overcome the various challenges that arise.

With the two love planets in the 10th house you are attracted to power and status. You feel 'Oh, I can learn to love anyone, so I might as well choose the good provider and the high status person.' There are opportunities for office romances this period with bosses or superiors.

There are job changes, instability in the workforce (if you employ others) and changes in the conditions of the workplace from the 25th to the 31st. Be more patient with co-workers and employees then.